Oxford
Word Skills

UPPER-INTERMEDIATE – ADVANCED VOCABULARY

Ruth Gairns and **Stuart Redman**

*Learn to use the most important
words and phrases in English
topic by topic*

OXFORD

OXFORD

UNIVERSITY PRESS

Great Clarendon Street, Oxford, OX2 6DP, United Kingdom

Oxford University Press is a department of the University of Oxford. It furthers the University's objective of excellence in research, scholarship, and education by publishing worldwide. Oxford is a registered trade mark of Oxford University Press in the UK and in certain other countries

ISBN: 978 0 19 460574 8   Pack
ISBN: 978 0 19 460575 5   Student's Book
ISBN: 978 0 19 479862 4   Oxford Advanced Learner's Dictionary
                            10th edition app

Printed in China

This book is printed on paper from certified and well-managed sources

ACKNOWLEDGEMENTS

Back cover photograph: Oxford University Press building/David Fisher.

Front cover images: Alamy Stock Photo (woman with laptop/Mariusz Szczawinski); Oxford University Press (shark/Shane Gross), (hiker/Olga Danylenko); Shutterstock (man on scooter/OPOLJA), (CT scanner/zlikovec), (apple/Gunnar Pippel), (drilling platform/Oil and Gas Photographer), (protest poster/nicostock), (man with saxophone/Africa Studio), (dining/Pressmaster), (graffiti/Mehaniq).

Although every effort has been made to trace and contact copyright holders before publication, this has not been possible in some cases. We apologise for any apparent infringement of copyright and, if notified, the publisher will be pleased to rectify any errors or omissions at the earliest possible opportunity.

Disclaimer: This book includes some words which have or are asserted to have proprietary status as trademarks or otherwise. Their inclusion does not imply that they have acquired for legal purposes a non-proprietary or general significance nor any other judgement concerning their legal status. In cases where editorial staff have some evidence that a word has proprietary status this is indicated in the listing of that word in the Word list but no judgement concerning the legal status of such words is made or implied thereby.

The authors and publisher are grateful to those who have given permission to reproduce the following extracts and adaptations of copyright material:

p.20 Entries from *Oxford Advanced Learner's Dictionary*, 10th edition © Oxford University Press, reprinted by permission. p.104 Adapted from 'A Revolutionary Era in Medicine' from http://fiftyyears.healthcare.ucla.edu/, 1955-2005, UCLA Health, reprinted by permission. p.125 Extract from 'What's so wrong with coalition governments?' by Martin Kettle, Courtesy of Guardian News & Media Ltd. p.133 Extract from 'Media watchdog to investigate broadcasting of Christchurch livestream' by Jennifer Duke, 18 March, 2019, *The Sydney Morning Herald*, reproduced by permission. p.148 Extracts adapted from 'Here's how I exploited a gap in the market', an interview with Jeff Sacree', from www.businesslink.gov.uk, © Crown Copyright 2012, used under the terms of the Open Government Licence v1.0 and reprinted by permission of Jeff Sacree'/Gecko Head Gear Limited.

Sources: www.holisticonline.com, www.bbc.co.uk/news

Some of the ABOUT YOU answers were kindly supplied by the following people: Elżbieta Rudniak (Poland), Eva Paulerová (Czech Republic), Florence Waeni (Kenya), Franky Lau (China), Katalin Elekes (Hungary), Mallika Ghosh (India), Susana Dichiera (Argentina).

Alamy Stock Photo pp.22 (woman/Tetra Images), (tattoo/Scott Dumas), (old lady/David Grossman), 26 (diving/Wavebreakmedia Ltd), 34 (pinching/Hugh Threfall), 59 Clynt Garnham Lifestyle, 128 Maggie Sully, 132 dpa picture alliance, 156 (barn/Linda Kennedy),157 (guide book/Jeff Greenberg), 166 Incamerstock, 194 (shade/Paul Biggins); Getty Images pp.26 (split coffee/Lew Robertson), 34 (tapping/PhotoObjects.net), (punching/Rubberball Productions); Oxford University Press pp.56 (mango), (broccoli), 57(grater), 80 (Algarve), 85, 104, 137; Shutterstock pp.18 (drawing pin/Garsya), (paper clip/Gunchanit Thanompong), (nail polish/suravid), 22 (baby/Monkey Business Images), (grungy girl/Jetrel), (bing man/Discovod), 23 (woman in stripes/Daniella Danilejko), (woman in blue/Alena Ozerova), 24 Koldonov, 25 (clenched fist/Vidl Studio), (folded arms/Kopytin Georgy), (two people/fizkes), (young girl/Haley Alex), 26 (baby/New Africa), (praying/ildintoriak), (man/fizkes), (sweeping/Syda Productions), (shrugging/The Faces), (lipstick/Makistock), (leaning/baranq), (dragging/Elnur), (tearing paper/Obprod), (plugging in/Tang Wai Chung/Truphotos.com), (combing/Dirima), (folding/Cultura Creative RF), (sewing/Lightfield Studios Inc), (drilling/ALPHA PROD), (screw/Praful P Patil), 28 (hiker/seirceil), 29 (stretch/WeStudio), (press-ups/slonme), 31 FLPA, 32 Wavebreakmedia Ltd, 34 (squeeze/FREEPIK2), (grabbing/Photographee.eu), (cat/Tamonwan apaikawee), (hugging/Twinster Photo0, (slapping/Anton –Dios), (sun tan lotion/Maridav), 35 Prostock-studio, 36 (rash/Sanapth Chindathong), (lungs/Explode), white t shirt/Freeman Studio), 38 (skull/Baimeng), (black eye/rdgraphe), (sprained wrist/Chanintorn.v), (blister/Cherries), (bruise/BERNATSKAIA OKSANA), 39 (plaster/oatawa), (gauze/Todor Rusinov), (bandage/Pixel-Shot), 40 javi_indy, 42 (Joel/kikovic), (Makito/wong sze yeun), (marek/Olena Simko), (Jacinta/Zurijeta), 46 Stokkete, 47 michaeljung), 52 (mother and daughter/milatas), (daughter/comzeal images), 54 DONOT6_STUDIO, 56 (avocado), (grapefruit/Robert Zp), (apricot/Vitaly Korovin), (raspberry, aubergine/Nattika), (raisins/Diana Taliun), (celery/Kaiskynet Studio), (asparagus/zcw), (courgette/Superhenag168), (beetroot/Valentina Razumov), (spinach/Jiri Hera), (almonds/sinelev), (basil/Hortimages), (lentils/mtphoto19), (ginger/MRAORAOR), 57 (deep fat fryer/gowithstock), (casserole/Alekseykolotivin), (food processor/PERLA BERANT WILDER), (whisk/Jiri Hera), (colanderindigolotos), (peeler/M.Schuppich), (lemon squeezer/ViktoriyaFivko), (corkscrew/ajt), (scales/showcake), (knife/masik0553), (frying pan/Tatiana Popova), 62 (ambulance/Joerg Huettenhoelscher), (helicopter/ChiccoDodiFC), (radio/PunkerBarbyO), 64 PongMoji, 66 (suede/photocell), (silk/sindii), 68 (socket/Lazy Bear), (plug/K-U Haessler), (stool/JoEimaGe), (doormat/Stephen Lavery), (hoover/tale), (ironing board/socrates471), (smoke alarm/Zerbor0, (dustbin/Natalis Boroda0, (radiator/VH-Studio), (broom/akf ffm), (chest of drawers/ANTHONY PAZ), (doorbell/ArtWell), (bunk bed/Scott-lee), (bookcase/New Africa), (letter box/Happy Stock Photo), 69 (tap/banu sevim), (blind/SOLOTU), (porch step/Hannahmariah), 70 (yawning/Luis Molinaro), (pyjamas/Art Directors & Trip), (nightdress/WendyTDavis), (alarm/nito), 77 (man/mimagephotography), 79 Speedkinz, 80 (Prague/Jasmine_K), (China/Hung Chung Chih), 82 4H4 Photography, 83 Alan Curtis, 84 (terraced house/andersphoto), (semi-detached/DrimaFilm), 86 (tree/Potapov Alexander), (pond/Kwangmoozaa), (frog/Nancy Hixon), (greenhouse), 87 (bush/Volodymyr_Shutun), (digging/Syda Productions), (mowing/fotosparrow), (relaxing/Inigogutierrez), 92 (Bowie/Fabio Diana), (Queen/Muhammad suyanto), (cinema/Dean Drobot) (audience/aergondo2), 100 (phone charging/Remitski Ivan), (batteries/art_photo_sib), (solar panels/Smileus), 103 Scott Ward, 104 (kidney/Peyker), 107 Kay fochtmann, 111 Simon Ling, 114 AnMenshikova, 118 (tank/viper-zero), (helicopter/Thor Jorgen Udvang), (parachute/Phuong D Nguyen), (missile/aapsky), 138 (plumber/Andrey_Popov), (electrician/Lightfield Studios Inc), (carpenter/Dusan Petkovic), 150 (helmet/Ajintai), (lifeboat/Paul Brewer), (surfer/EpicStockMedia), 156 (old barn/Andrew Roland), 157 (anti snore device/Manju Mandavya), (clock/Photohedgehog), (cat/David Asch), (bike/Sergiy1975), 170 (skyscraper/Vladmir Zhuk), (cranes/Yakiv Korol), 181 (gold/Galina Tiun), (feather/Stargazer0, (bat/Rosa Jay), (post/Sulae), (rake/Oleksandr Kostiuchenko), (bedsheet/bane.em), (beetroot/Kyselov Inna), (bone/Leo Fernandes), (cake/space_heater), (log/josefauer), (asleep/fizkes), (sieve/Vadarshop), 194 (football/Lazlo Szirtesi).

All illustrations by: CCS Digital Education.

Contents

Acknowledgements 2

Introduction 6

EXPAND YOUR VOCABULARY

01 Meaning and style 10

02 Familiar words, new meanings 12

03 Word families 14

04 Collocation 16

05 Compounds 18

06 Using a dictionary 20

THE BODY

07 Describing appearance 22

08 Body language 24

09 Physical actions 26

10 Physical movement 28

11 Sight 30

12 Sounds and hearing 32

13 Touch 34

14 Illness 36

15 Injuries 38

PEOPLE

16 Character 40

17 Assessing character 42

18 Feelings 44

19 Relationships 46

20 Heroes and villains 48

21 Behaviour 50

22 Families 52

23 Manners 54

EVERYDAY LIFE

24 Food 56

25 Opinions about food 58

26 Cars and driving 60

27 Accidents 62

28 Weather 64

29 Clothes 66

30 At home 68

31 Sleep 70

32 Personal finance 72

33 Crime 74

34 Urban living 76

35 Rural life 78

LEISURE AND LIFESTYLE

36 Holidays 80

37 Holiday accommodation 82

38 Buying and renting 84

39 Gardens and gardening 86

40 Personal technology 88

41 Competitive football 90

42 Music 92

43 Plays and films 94

44 Socializing 96

A CHANGING WORLD

45 Describing change 98

46 Energy conservation 100

47 Wildlife under threat 102

48 Medical advances 104

49 Migration 106

50 Politics: ideology 108

INSTITUTIONS

51 Local government 110

52 Health care services 112

53 The police 114

54 Prisons 116

55 The armed forces 118

NEWS AND CURRENT AFFAIRS

56 News headlines 120

57 Writing for a newspaper 122

58 Politics in practice 124

59 Protest movements 126

60 Disasters 128

61 Investigations 130

62 Celebrity 132

63 Human interest stories 134

WORK AND BUSINESS

64 Jobs 136

65 Careers 138

66 Ways of working 140

67 The workplace 142

68 Time management 144

69 The business world 146

70 A successful business 148

CONCEPTS

71 Success and failure 150

72 Problems and solutions 152

73 Old and new 154

74 Time 156

WRITTEN ENGLISH

75 Link words and phrases 158

76 Academic English 160

77 Literature 162

78 Art 164

79 Scientific English 166

80 Technical English 168

SPOKEN ENGLISH

81 Everyday language 170

82 Phrasal verbs 172

83 Idioms (1) 174

84 Idioms (2) 176

85 Two-part expressions 178

86 Similes 179

87 Connecting speech 180

88 Sayings 182

89 Vague language 184

ASPECTS OF LANGUAGE

90 The passive 185

91 Prefixes 186

92 Suffixes that form nouns 188

93 Suffixes that form adjectives and verbs 190

94 Verbs and nouns with the same form 192

95 Verbs with prepositions 194

96 Nouns with prepositions 196

97 Adjectives with prepositions 197

98 Prepositional phrases 198

99 Adjectives 200

100 Adverbs 202

Answer key 204

Word list 236

Abbreviations 256

Introduction

What is *Oxford Word Skills*?

Oxford Word Skills is a series of three books for students
to learn and practise new vocabulary.

Level 1:
Elementary (CEFR levels A1 and A2)

Level 2:
Intermediate (CEFR level B1)

Level 3:
Upper-Intermediate – Advanced
(CEFR levels B2 and C1)

There are over 2,000 new words or phrases in each level, and all of the material can be used in the classroom or
for self-study.

How are the books organized?

Each level contains 100 units of vocabulary presentation and practice, with a unit being 1–2 pages, depending on the
size of the topic. New vocabulary is presented in manageable chunks, then immediately followed up with practice
exercises, often on the same page.

The units are grouped within modules containing 4–12 units. A majority of the modules are topic-based, e.g. People,
Leisure and lifestyle, News and current affairs, but some modules have a language focus, e.g. Expand your vocabulary,
Aspects of language.

The Upper-Intermediate – Advanced level also contains:

• an Answer key for all the exercises

• a Word list of all the vocabulary taught with a reference to the units where each item appears and the CEFR level
  for words/phrases in the Oxford 3000™/5000™ or Oxford Phrase List™.

Oxford Word Skills comes with the *Oxford Advanced Learner's Dictionary* app, which allows learners to find the meaning
of new words in English and provides a pronunciation model for the words. You will find pronunciation exercises
throughout the book which refer you to the ⓐⓟⓟ to check the correct pronunciation.

What vocabulary is included?

At Upper-Intermediate – Advanced level, the vocabulary includes:

- a wide range of topic areas, e.g. behaviour, competitive sport, medical advances

- a range of concepts, e.g. problems and solutions, time, old and new

- different fields of written English, e.g. literature, science, technical English

- a wide range of phrasal verbs and idioms

- various aspects of language, e.g. compounds, prefixes and suffixes, prepositional phrases

Throughout the three levels the main focus is on high-frequency vocabulary in everyday spoken English, although the higher levels increasingly add more language from different styles of English as well as more figurative use of language.

The selection of vocabulary at each level is based on frequency and usefulness, with the foundation being the Oxford 3000 or Oxford 5000. These are lists of 3,000 and 5,000 words, respectively, identified by the Oxford University Press ELT Dictionaries team as the   most important words for learners of English. These items have been divided in the Oxford 3000 into four levels in accordance with the CEFR (A1, A2, B1 and B2), and the Oxford 5000 contains additional words at CEFR levels B2 and C1.

- The Elementary level includes many items from A1, but with the majority of items at A2 level.

- The Intermediate level has a focus on B1 items from the Oxford 3000, as well as recycling items from the A2 level.

- The Upper-Intermediate – Advanced level concentrates on B2 items from the Oxford 3000, but also includes additional B2 items and C1 words from the Oxford 5000.

The Oxford 3000/5000 lists are supplemented by the Oxford Phrase List, which contains just under 1,000 phrases considered important for students at each level. The Upper-Intermediate – Advanced word list also draws on topic lists from OUP's learner's dictionaries, which identify key vocabulary items across a range of 60 topics. By using the Oxford 3000/5000 alongside the topic lists, we are able to focus on high-frequency vocabulary, but also to include vocabulary that may not have a high frequency overall, but will have great value in particular contexts, e.g. *overtake* when talking about driving, *extinct/extinction* when talking about climate change and the danger to wildlife, or *self-catering* when talking about holidays. By using the Oxford Phrase List, we are also able to ensure the best coverage of both words and phrases at each level.

We have taken great care to ensure that learners will be able to understand the meaning of all the new words and phrases by supplying a clear illustration, a simple definition, or an example of each word or phrase. Learners should be aware that many English words have more than one meaning. They should refer to the *Oxford Advanced Learner's Dictionary* APP for information on other meanings.

To the teacher

How can I use the material in the classroom?

New vocabulary is presented through:

- **visuals**

| 1 avocado | 2 mango | 3 watermelon | 4 grapefruit | 5 apricots | 6 raspberries |

- **sentences and short dialogues**

Time Management tips

- Do you **note down** jobs you have to do **on a daily basis**?
- Do you put up **reminders** in the office about these aims?
- Do you **prioritize** the tasks you have to **accomplish** by the end of the day?
- Do you **stick to** your **priorities, no matter what** happens?
- Do you focus on **one thing at a time**?

	note of sth
basis	a particular way in which sth is organized or done: **on a day-to-day/daily/weekly/regular basis**
reminder	sth that makes you remember sth **remind sb (of/about sth)** v
prioritize	put tasks, problems, etc. in order of importance so that you can do the most important first **priority** n: **a high/ low/ top priority**

Idiom	Meaning
I'm going to do the essay again. ~ ***What for?***	for what purpose or reason
Are you going to the party? ~ ***You bet!***	used to emphasize that you are keen to do sth
I've got my exam today. ~ OK. ***(The) best of luck.***	used to wish sb success in what they are going to do

- **different types of extended written text**

The Glasgow School of Art has been **devastated** yet again by a huge fire. More than 120 **firefighters tackled** the **blaze**, which began on Friday night and spread to a concert hall next door. There were no reported **casualties**, but police evacuated 27 people from nearby properties as a **precaution**. At the moment, there is no **suspicion** the fire was started **deliberately**, but the **intense** heat is preventing fire officers from getting in to **assess** the damage. First Minister, Nicola Sturgeon, **praised** the **courage** of the firefighters who fought to save the building.

GLOSSARY

devastate	destroy or damage sth badly **devastation** n
firefighter	a person whose job is to stop fires, working for the **fire brigade**
tackle	make an effort to deal with a difficult problem or situation
blaze	a large and often dangerous fire
casualty	a person who is killed or injured in a war or accident
precaution	sth you do in order to avoid danger or problems
suspicion	a feeling or belief that sth is wrong or that sb has done sth wrong **suspicious (of sb)** adj **suspect** v
deliberately	in a way that was planned **deliberate** adj SYN **intentional**
intense	very great, strong or serious: *intense heat/cold/pressure* **intensity** n
assess	judge or form an opinion about sth **assessment** n
praise	say that sb is good and should be admired for sth **praise** n
courage	the ability to do sth dangerous without showing fear SYN **bravery**; **courageous** adj

- Visuals provide a clear guide to meaning; sentences, dialogues and extended text show words being used naturally, with the meaning explained in a glossary (or within a table). The input varies from approximately 15 items in a single A or B section, to 25–30 items on a full page of input. Here is a procedure you could follow:

- Students study the visuals or written text in the presentation for five–ten minutes for an A or B section, or ten–fifteen minutes for a full page. This allows time for them to reinforce the connection between the visual input and the meanings, or to read through the glossary carefully to check the meaning of new items in the presentation sentences, dialogues or extended text. With the information from the glossary, students should then go back to the presentation text and check that they fully understand the meaning of the new words in those contexts.

Tell students to look at the extra words in the **glossary** (opposites, synonyms, derivatives, collocations and further examples) as this will help them to expand their vocabulary with minimal effort in many cases. It is also important to look at the **spotlight** boxes. The spotlight box is an additional feature which picks out an item or items of particular value. For example:

SPOTLIGHT *accept*	**SPOTLIGHT** expressing family similarities
Accept means 'say yes to an offer', but has some other meanings, too. **1** allow sb to be part of a group: *They **accepted me** as one of the family.* (as in the text) **2** agree to sth: *The council has **accepted** the latest proposal.* **3** admit you did sth wrong: *I **accept responsibility for** the mistakes.*	If you **resemble someone/something**, you look like or are similar to another person/thing. The emphasis is more on looks than character. **resemblance** *n* If you **take after someone**, you look or behave like an older member of your family. If you **follow in someone's footsteps**, you do the same job or have the same lifestyle as someone else, usually a member of your family.

- While students are working through the presentation, you can answer any questions they may have about the items. This is also an opportunity to provide a pronunciation model for your students to repeat; otherwise, the presentation stage is going to be a long silent phase. You might want to read a text aloud, or get students to read sections of it, etc.

- Students can move on to the first exercise, which they can check for themselves using the Answer key, or you can go over the answers with the whole class. This is probably a better approach, as you can also discuss why they might have arrived at a wrong answer and focus on practising the pronunciation if necessary. It is sensible to work through the exercises chronologically, as they tend to progress from pronunciation practice to receptive practice to controlled productive practice, and then quite often to freer productive practice in the ABOUT YOU or ABOUT YOUR COUNTRY activities.

- When you are satisfied with their answers to the first exercise, you can ask students to go on to further exercises, while you monitor them as they work individually or in pairs, and assist where necessary. When they have finished an exercise, you will find that many of the exercises – sentence completion and particularly dialogue completion – lend themselves to controlled speaking practice. Students can practise dialogues in pairs, or take it in turns to read out complete sentences to each other.

- TEST YOURSELF When they have completed written exercises, students can test themselves on the new vocabulary. The material has been designed so that students can cover the new words beneath a picture (using a book, notebook or piece of paper) while they look at the visuals and test themselves. They can do the same with some of the tables and glossaries: cover the new vocabulary and look at the meaning, or vice versa. This is a simple, quick and easy way for learners to test themselves over and over again, so there is no pressure on you to keep searching for different exercises. It is also useful to demonstrate this so that students can revise vocabulary in their own time using this 'cover and check' approach.

- You will often notice ABOUT YOU or ABOUT YOUR COUNTRY . These are personalized exercises which give learners an opportunity to use the new vocabulary in a freer way and within the context of their own lives. Students can write answers to these, but they make ideal pairwork activities for students to practise their spoken English while using the new vocabulary. If you use these as speaking activities, students could then write their answers (or their partner's answers) as follow-up. In the Answer key, possible answers for these exercises are provided by both native speakers and proficient non-native speakers from different parts of the world. This may be of particular value to a self-study learner, as a way of comparing answers.

How can students use the material on their own?

The material has been designed so that it can be used effectively both in the classroom or by learners working alone. If you want your learners to use the material for self-study, you can recommend that they use the book alongside the (APP), as it gives them a pronunciation model for items of vocabulary, as well as further practice exercises. For self-study learners in particular, it is a good idea to start with the first module on expanding your vocabulary. Self-study learners can check their answers to exercises using the Answer key, and test themselves using the 'cover and check' procedure explained above. They can also select the topics that interest them, or the topics where they most need to expand their vocabulary.

A Asking about meaning

A Would it be **accurate** to say that *student* and *pupil* are **synonymous**?

B No, not exactly. A *student* is a person who studies in a school, college or university. *Pupil* has a more **restricted** use. A *pupil* is someone who only studies in a school, especially a primary school.

A It's a bit **ambiguous** to say *she's a good student*, isn't it?

B Yes, you can **interpret** it in different ways. *Good* can mean 'well-behaved' or 'hard-working'.

A The meaning of *wrapping paper* is fairly obvious, isn't it?

B Yes, it's **self-explanatory**: just paper for wrapping presents and stuff.

A Can you give me a **precise** definition of *soul*?

B Well, it's **virtually** the same as *spirit*: the part of you that is believed to exist after you die. But *spirit* has several other meanings too.

GLOSSARY	
accurate	exact and correct; without mistakes OPP **inaccurate; accuracy** n
synonymous	having the same, or nearly the same meaning **synonym** n
restricted	controlled or limited
ambiguous	not clear; able to be explained in different ways **ambiguity** n
interpret	explain the meaning of sth **interpretation** n
self-explanatory	easy to understand and not needing more explanation
precise	clear and accurate SYN **exact; precision** n
virtually	almost, very nearly: **virtually the same virtual** adj

1 **Mark the stress on these words. Use the APP to help you.**

1	accurate	3	synonymous	5	ambiguity	7	interpretation
2	synonym	4	ambiguous	6	interpret	8	self-explanatory

2 **Is the meaning the same or different? Write S or D.**

1 The meaning is virtually the same. / The meaning is exactly the same. ....
2 They are both students in my school. / They are both pupils in my school. ....
3 The meaning is quite precise. / The meaning is quite restricted. ....
4 The sentence is ambiguous. / The sentence can be interpreted in two ways. ....
5 I don't know the exact meaning. / I don't know the precise meaning. ....
6 Tom is fairly inaccurate. / Tom makes very few mistakes. ....
7 His soul will live on. / His spirit will live on. ....
8 What she said was fairly ambiguous. / What she said was fairly accurate. ....

3 **Complete the sentences with the correct form of the word in capitals at the end.**

1 If you want to make something clear, it's better to avoid .... AMBIGUOUS
2 She always expresses herself with .... PRECISE
3 *Hide* and *conceal* are very similar, but not completely .... SYNONYM
4 Elsie is quite fluent but she lacks .... ACCURATE
5 I think this sentence is open to .... INTERPRET
6 The instructions were .... ; a child could understand them. EXPLAIN
7 They are .... opposites. VIRTUAL

4 **Answer the questions.**

1 What's the exact meaning of *huge*? ....
2 Which word is more restricted: *get* or *acquire*? Why? ....
3 Is the meaning of *waiting room* fairly self-explanatory? Why? / Why not? ....
4 Are *slim* and *thin* synonyms? Why? / Why not? ....
5 Is it accurate to say that a pupil studies in a secondary school? Why? / Why not? ....
6 *I picked up my bag.* Why could this sentence be ambiguous? ....

TEST YOURSELF

B Explaining style

Example	Meaning
'Thanks for your help, Sam,' she said **ironically**. *Sam hadn't helped at all.*	**ironically** using words to say the opposite of what you mean, often humorously **ironic** *adj*; **irony** *n*
The **literal** sense of *gold* is 'a valuable yellow metal used to make coins, jewellery, etc.'.	**literal** (of words and phrases) being the basic or usual meaning **literally** *adv*
Golden is used **figuratively** in the sentence *Working in this company is a golden opportunity for him.*	**figuratively** (of words and phrases) not used in the basic or usual way, but in a way that makes a description more interesting (**Golden** here means 'wonderful' or 'special'.) **figurative** *adj*
*She has **a heart of gold** is an example of a **metaphor**. It means 'she is a very kind person'.*	**metaphor** a word or phrase used to describe sb/sth else in a way that is different from its normal use **metaphorical** *adj* = **figurative**
The dictionary marks *stupid* as **disapproving**.	**disapproving** (often used in dictionaries) showing that sth is bad or wrong
In **slang**, a *shrink* is a psychiatrist or a psychologist.	**slang** very informal words and phrases, used by particular groups of people in spoken language
Swear words are **offensive** to many people and not **appropriate** in most everyday conversations.	**offensive** rude in a way that causes you to be upset or angry OPP **inoffensive** **appropriate** suitable or correct OPP **inappropriate**
*He called Tom 'an old woman'. How **insulting**!*	**insulting** rude or offensive **insult** *n, v*

> **SPOTLIGHT** *swear*
>
> **Swearing** is the use of **swear words** (= rude or offensive language). If you **swear at** somebody, you might make them angry.
> **Swear** can also mean to make a serious promise to do something.
> - *He **swore** that he would kill anyone who touched me.*

5 **Underline the words which usually suggest something negative.**

disapproving	figurative	inappropriate	insulting	irony
literal	metaphor	offensive	slang	swearing

6 **Circle the correct word(s). Sometimes both words are correct.**
1   The *literal / figurative* meaning of *curtain* is a piece of cloth which covers a window.
2   *The curtain fell on her career* is *figurative / metaphorical*. It means 'her career ended'.
3   *Irony / Slang* is commonly used to say the opposite of what you mean.
4   Ana is so kind; she has a heart of *silver / gold*.
5   It may be *appropriate / inappropriate* to ask someone how much they earn or how old they are.
6   He was being *ironic / offensive* – he didn't mean to be rude.
7   I think it was *a metaphor / an insult* to say you were stupid.
8   Swearing is *offensive / inoffensive* to many people.

7 **Complete the sentences with a suitable word.**
1   *Naïve* often has a negative meaning and is marked '.............................' in the dictionary.
2   *Flood* is one of those words that can be used literally or ....
3   He said my food was tasteless, which I found incredibly ....
4   *Knackered* is very informal, means 'extremely tired', and is an example of British English ....
5   The offer is a .... opportunity for my brother to work abroad for a year.
6   *Pull your socks up* is often used as a .... meaning 'you must work harder and do better'.
7   A man .... at me in the street because I got in his way. I was very upset.
8   They live .... just round the corner, so I see them every day.

TEST YOURSELF

A Using words and phrases figuratively

Familiar words may appear with an unfamiliar meaning (often a figurative meaning), or surrounded by other words that together form an idiom or common phrase.

As I **crawled** along the motorway, I was **having second thoughts about** staying with Marcus. I'd **been in two minds about** going in the first place, but it was **sweet of** him to invite me, and I **wasn't tied up**, so I said 'yes'. But now it **struck me that** perhaps he wanted to go out with me! How could I be so **thick**? Marcus was very nice, but a romantic relationship **was the last thing on my mind**. How can I **get out of** this, I wondered? Just then, the traffic suddenly started to speed up, and something went into the back of me. I pulled my mobile out of my bag. 'Is that you Marcus? Listen, **you're not gonna believe this**, but ...'

GLOSSARY	
crawl	(of a vehicle) move very slowly
have second thoughts (about sth)	start having doubts about a decision you have made
be in two minds about sth	be unable to decide what to do about sth
sweet (of sb)	kind (of sb): *It was **sweet of** you to come.*
be tied up	be busy and unable to do other things
strike sb (that) ...	(of a thought or idea) suddenly come into sb's mind
thick *inf*	stupid
be the last thing on sb's mind	be the thing that sb is least likely to be thinking about
get out of sth	avoid doing sth
you're not gonna believe this	used to introduce surprising and often unwelcome news (**gonna** *inf* = going to)

1 **Make sentences from the jumbled words.**

1 gonna / not / lost / this / I / but / you're / believe. ....

2 homework / out / I / this / get / doing / of / how / can ? ....

3 going / two / about / I'm / minds / to / in / Greece. ....

4 thing / on / university / mind / is / the / last / my. ....

5 it / take / of / sweet / to / us / was / him. ....

2 **Complete the dialogues with a word or phrase.**

1 Do you still want to go? ~ Actually, I'm having ....

2 Are you thinking of getting married? ~ No, that's the last thing .... !

3 Do you want to go to the wedding? ~ Not really, but I can't .... it.

4 You're not gonna .... , but ... ~ You've lost my keys, again! How could you?

5 Did he invite all of you? ~ Yes, it was very .... of him. He's a lovely man.

6 Are you going or not? ~ I'm still in .... about it, actually.

7 Did you think she looked like her sister? ~ Yes, I was .... by how similar they are.

8 Could we talk about it this morning? ~ I'm afraid I'm .... this morning.

9 Why are you so late? ~ Half the road was closed. We were .... along for ages.

10 He may not have understood the instructions. ~ Yeah, he's a bit ....

3 **Complete the sentences using words from above with their more usual literal meanings.**

1 Leyla is only eight months, so she's still .... across the living room floor.

2 It's a very .... book – almost 1,000 pages.

3 These oranges are lovely. They're very ....

4 The men were .... , with both hands behind their backs.

5 I saw him .... the dog with a large stick. I was really angry.

6 The policeman stopped me and asked me to .... the car.

7 I've just had a .... , Carrie. Do you think we could hire a car for the weekend?

8 I think his .... was disturbed when he had that accident.

📖 TEST YOURSELF

B Common verbs with less familiar meanings

The words in **bold** in the examples are very common when the verbs are used with the meanings in the table.

Verb	Examples	Meaning
get sb/sth to do sth	*I couldn't **get** him to leave the house.* *I finally **got** the car to start.*	make or persuade sb/sth to do sth
see what/how, etc. …	*We may be able to help. I'll **see** what Rob says.* *It may be ok. **Let's see** what happens.*	find out sth by looking, asking or waiting
keep	*We must eat the grapes – they won't **keep**.*	remain fresh
put	*I think he **put** it very well in his essay.*	say or write sth in a particular way ALSO **put sth into words**
push sb/yourself	*Some parents **push** their kids really hard.*	make sb work harder
leave sth to/with sb	*We need to book a table. I'll **leave that to you**.*	allow sb to take care of sth
make sth sth	*My watch says 10.20. What time do you **make** it?* *He bought ten more; I **make that** 25 now.*	think or calculate sth to be a particular time or number
bring sb/sth + **adverb/preposition**	*It was the war that **brought** him to power.* *What **brings** you here? ~ I've got a meeting.*	cause sb/sth to reach a particular condition or place
come with/in sth	*I'm sure the radio **comes with** batteries.* *The chairs **come in** four different colours.*	be sold or produced with a particular feature
do (for sb/sth)	*I peeled six potatoes. Will that **do**?* *Will these shoes **do for** the wedding?*	be enough/ acceptable in a particular situation

4 One word is missing in each sentence. What is it, and where does it go?

1 How did you him to do it? ~ I offered him money. ....
2 These batteries in all sorts of different sizes. ....
3 If both brothers come, that will it 20 altogether. ....
4 It's the fishing that most people to this part of the coast. ....
5 When I speak to the staff tomorrow, I'll what they think. ....
6 We'd better finish the cream: it won't after today. ....
7 He has great ideas but finds it difficult to them into words. ....
8 I've got a packet of noodles. Do you think that will for six people? ....

5 Complete the dialogues with suitable verbs.

A Hello. What **(1)** .... you to this part of the building?
B I can't **(2)** .... this new clock to work, and it didn't **(3)** .... with instructions.
A OK, **(4)** .... it with me. I'll **(5)** .... what I can do.
B Thanks. Oh, one other thing, we've run out of paper for the photocopier.
A Er, there's some over there. Will that **(6)** .... ?
B Yeah, that's plenty.

A What are the bookings like for this evening?
B We had two more this morning, so I **(7)** .... that 36 now.
A Ok, but we'll need more tables. Can I **(8)** .... that with you?
B Well, I'll **(9)** .... how things go, but I may have to **(10)** .... Mario to do it.
A OK, but don't **(11)** .... him too hard; he's had a very tough week.

6 ABOUT YOUR LANGUAGE Translate the verbs in the table into your own language. What verbs are used?

 TEST YOURSELF

By learning words that are part of the same word family, you can often increase your vocabulary quickly and easily. For example, you will probably know the words in the left-hand column below, but do you know the related words?

Word	Related word and its meaning	Example
mistake n	**mistake sb/sth for sb/sth** v wrongly think that sb/sth is sb/sth else	I **mistook** the woman in the café **for** a friend of mine.
certain adj	**certainty** n the state of being completely sure about sth OPP **uncertainty**	Is there any **certainty** things will improve?
problem n	**problematic** adj difficult to deal with; full of problems	Some places can be **problematic** for journalists.
possession n	**possess** v formal have or own sth	Some players just **possess** natural ability.
benefit n, v	**beneficial** adj having a good or useful effect	The extra money has been very **beneficial**.
require v	**requirement** n sth that you need or that you must have or do	A university degree is a minimum **requirement**.
house n	**housing** n buildings for people to live in **household** all the people who live in one house	We need more family **housing**. Most **households** have at least one car.
likely adv	**likelihood** n the chance of sth happening	There's not much **likelihood** of success.
handle v	**handling** n the way sb deals with sth/sb	The situation needs careful **handling**.
guide n,v	**guidelines** n (usually pl) official rules **guidance** n help or advice	There are **guidelines** on repairing old buildings. Our teacher gave us some **guidance**.
apologize v	**apologetic** adj showing you are sorry	It's his fault and he's very **apologetic**.
notice v	**noticeable** adj easily seen/noticed	The scar on his face is quite **noticeable**.
include v	**inclusive** adj (of the cost of sth) including everything **inclusion** n the fact of including sb/sth; the fact of being included	Bed and breakfast is £80, **fully inclusive**. The **inclusion** of dancing as part of the entertainment was unnnecessary.
compare v	**comparable** adj similar; able to be compared	This year looks good. Are there **comparable** figures for last year?
replace v	**replacement** n a thing that replaces sth that is old, broken, etc. **irreplaceable** cannot be replaced	The coffee machine isn't working, so can we get a **replacement**? My wedding ring is **irreplaceable**.
human n, adj	**humanity** n all the people in the world SYN **the human race** **humanitarian** concerned with trying to make people's lives better	War crimes are crimes against **humanity**. The war has caused a **humanitarian** crisis.
race n (of people)	**racism** n the unfair treatment of people who belong to a different race. The person who does this is a **racist**. **racist** adj	We must take action to stop **racism** in the workplace. He was attacked by a group of **racists**. The newspaper was **racist** and was closed down.
recognize v	**recognition** n the fact that you can identify sb/sth that you see	She'd seen me several times but showed no sign of **recognition**.

SPOTLIGHT related words with different meanings

Words in the same word family do not always have similar meanings. For example, the adjective **worth** can mean:
1 having a particular value;
2 used as a way of recommending: The castle is **worth seeing**.

It also has these related forms and meanings:
- The necklace is **worthless**. (= without value)
- He's a **worthy** champion. (= one who deserved to win)
- The meeting was **worthwhile**. (= important, interesting, etc.)

1 Mark the stress on these words. Use the 🔊 to help you.

problematic	likelihood	requirement	benefit	beneficial
worthwhile	recognition	comparable	apologize	irreplaceable
apologetic	household	humanity	humanitarian	possess

2 Circle the correct answer.

1 This painting is unique; it's *unreplaceable / irreplaceable*.
2 You get flights, accommodation, and food; the holiday is fully *included / inclusive*.
3 There is a *noticeable / noticed* difference between the two performances.
4 We're amateurs and they're professionals, so we're not *comparable / comparative*.
5 People are dying. It's a *humanitarian / humanity* crisis.
6 I enjoyed the trip: it was very *worthy / worthwhile*.
7 The delay was his fault, but he wasn't *apologizing / apologetic* about it.
8 People are homeless because there's a shortage of cheap *households / housing*.

3 Rewrite the sentences using a related word of the word in capitals. Keep the same meaning.

▶ Are you sure it will happen?   CERTAIN   Is there any certainty it will happen?
1 He deserved to win.   WORTH
2 Is there a chance we'll win?   LIKELY
3 Most families earn more than in the past.   HOUSE
4 Can you see that he's lost a lot of weight?   NOTICE
5 It's an unusual vase but has no value.   WORTH
6 People don't realize the importance of these measures.   RECOGNIZE
7 It was a very interesting conference.   WORTH
8 The tablets had a positive effect.   BENEFIT

4 Complete the dialogues with a suitable word.

1 Are there enough homes in the area?   ~ No, we need more ....
2 What can people do about the danger of infection?   ~ The government has issued ....
3 Was she sorry?   ~ Yes, very ....
4 Is that £65 for everything?   ~ Yes, it's fully ....
5 It's a difficult class to teach.   ~ Yes, they're very ....
6 Climate change affects everyone.   ~ Yes, it's a problem for ....
7 This lamp doesn't work   ~ Yes, I've already ordered a ....
8 It's a difficult situation.   ~ Yes, and it needs careful ....

5 Complete the sentences with a suitable word.

1 Some young parents would benefit from more .... on how to bring up children.
2 Several charities have warned that we are facing a .... crisis in parts of Africa.
3 The post office said the parcel would be delivered tomorrow, but there's no .... of that.
4 The .... of meals makes the total price very expensive.
5 Do you think Ivan .... the right qualities for the job?
6 I walked off with someone else's coat: I .... it for my own.
7 Flats in big cities are expensive in England. A .... flat in Spain would cost a lot less.
8 Some say we will win, others say we'll lose. There is a lot of .... about the result.

6 ABOUT YOUR COUNTRY Write answers to the questions, or talk to another student.

1 Do hotels usually give a fully inclusive price for a room and breakfast? ....
2 Is housing a particular problem in any part of the country? ....
3 Are prices generally comparable with other countries nearby, or are they very different? ....
4 Is there a minimum requirement for going to university? ....
5 Do you feel there are any problems with racism in your country? ....
6 Do you feel a degree of certainty about your future career? ....

 TEST YOURSELF

A Verb + noun

Collocation is the common combination of particular words with each other, and particular **collocations** may be different in your language. In English, certain verbs **collocate with** certain nouns. You will need to learn many of these **collocations**.

In any school, the headteacher obviously has to **make an effort** to **set an example** to their staff and students, and that starts by **treating** everyone **with respect**. It is also their job to **take responsibility** for important decisions that the school makes. If things go well, the headteacher **gets the credit**; if they don't, he or she has to be prepared to **take the blame**.

Carrie had been **spreading** a **rumour** that Sean and Sophie were going to have a baby, although she told everyone else to **keep it a secret**. It was, therefore, quite a shock when Sean finally **broke the news** to everyone that they were going to get a cat. We all **roared with laughter** – everyone except Carrie.

GLOSSARY	
make an effort (to do sth)	attempt to do sth, especially when it is difficult
set an example (to sb)	do sth good or well that people can try to copy or achieve: *set a good example*
treat sb with respect	behave towards sb in a polite and caring way OPP **treat sb like dirt**
take responsibility (for sth/sb)	accept a duty to deal with sth/sb, so that it is your fault if sth goes wrong OPP **pass the buck** make sb else responsible for a difficult situation
get the credit (for sth)	be admired and given the praise for doing sth successfully
take the blame (for sth)	accept responsibility for sth that goes wrong
spread a rumour	tell a lot of people about a piece of news or information that may not be true
keep (sth) a secret	not tell anyone about sth that others must not know ALSO **keep a promise / an appointment / a record**
break the news	be the first person to tell others about sth important
roar with laughter	laugh loudly or a lot

1 *Yes* or *No*?

1 If you keep a promise, is that a good thing? ....

2 If you get the credit for something, are you pleased? ....

3 If you pass the buck, are others happy? ....

4 If you take the blame, is that positive? ....

5 If you treat somebody like dirt, is that good? ....

6 If you spread a rumour, is that a good thing to do? ....

7 If you treat someone with respect, will they be pleased? ....

8 If you take responsibility, is that a bad thing to do? ....

2 Complete the sentences with a suitable *verb + noun* combination.

1 Teenagers respond well to her because she .... them with ....

2 I didn't tell anyone because Emma told me to .... it a ....

3 My sister has been .... a .... that I'm getting engaged. It's not true.

4 Tanya does a fantastic job, but doesn't always .... the .... she deserves.

5 It was a very funny joke, and everyone .... with ....

6 My parents .... a good .... to me, and now I always .... an .... to do the same with my children.

7 I can't remember who .... the .... about the wedding, but we were all delighted.

8 My boss never accepts responsibility for things. He always .... the .... and makes someone else .... the .... He's awful.

9 Young people must learn to .... for their actions; it's part of growing up.

3 There are many combinations with *take, make* and *set*. Do you know which verbs combine with each of these nouns?

control of sth	a limit	an impression	pleasure in doing sth	sth on fire
a profit	tablets	an offer	a look at sth	the standard	a noise

take: ....   *make*: ....   *set*: ....

🗋 TEST YOURSELF

B Adjective + noun

There are also many common *adjective + noun* collocations that you may need to learn. For example, a person you know well and like is a **close friend** (NOT a ~~near friend~~ OR an ~~intimate friend~~).

EXAMPLE	MEANING
I gave them a **detailed description** of the burglary.	a description full of information OPP **brief description**
He speaks with a **strong accent**.	a very noticeable accent OPP **slight accent**
Our **main concern** for the party is the weather.	most important worry SYN **principal concern**
It was a **typical example** of his stupidity.	very good example SYN **perfect example**
The house was **utter chaos** when I got home.	complete confusion ALSO **utter nonsense** ideas that you think are stupid or not true
The children had a **narrow escape**.	= they were lucky to escape safely
Nice to see a **familiar face** at the party.	a person you recognize and know
The **vast majority** of students passed.	a very large majority
My sister's ring is **pure gold**.	not mixed with anyting else ALSO **pure silk/cotton**
I thought he'd be tall but he was **the complete opposite**.	a person or thing that is as different as possible from sb/sth else SYN **the exact opposite**

4 Cover the text above and match 1–8 with a–h.

1	a familiar	....	a	escape
2	a typical	....	b	chaos
3	a vast	....	c	face
4	a slight	....	d	opposite
5	utter	....	e	accent
6	a detailed	....	f	majority
7	the exact	....	g	description
8	a narrow	....	h	example

5 Answer the questions. What's ...

1 a synonym for a **typical example**? ....
2 the opposite of a **slight accent**? ....
3 a synonym for the **main concern**? ....
4 the opposite of a **detailed description**? ....
5 a synonym for **the complete opposite**? ....
6 a noun that combines with **utter**? ....

6 Complete the dialogues with a suitable *adjective + noun* combination.

1 Was it true what your dad said? ~ No, it was .... Don't believe anything he says.
2 Did they all understand? ~ No, the .... I had to explain it.
3 You managed to avoid the accident? ~ Yes, but it was a ....
4 Are you worried about the exam? ~ Yes, my .... is that I get nervous.
5 Did the top feel nice when you tried it on? ~ Yes, lovely. It was ....
6 Do you know what she looks like? ~ Yes, my uncle gave me a ....
7 Did you see your old friends in Cardiff? ~ Yes, and it was great to see so many ....
8 Ingrid's English is good. ~ Yes, but she speaks with a ....
9 Do you get on well? ~ Yes, we're ....
10 Was everything tidy when you got there? ~ No, the place was in ....

7 ABOUT YOUR LANGUAGE **How would you translate the phrases above? Would you use similar adjective and noun combinations, or would they be different?**

....
....

TEST YOURSELF

5) Compounds

A Nouns

English has a large number of compound nouns formed from a *noun + noun*. Cover the compounds below and read the meanings. Do you know these compounds, or can you guess them?

drawing pin

paper clip

barbed wire

nail polish/varnish

Meaning	Compound noun
an official document that shows you are qualified to drive	driving licence
an official document showing when and where someone was born	birth certificate
a card given to customers by a shop to encourage them to shop there regularly. Each time they shop, they get money off goods they buy in the future.	loyalty card
a part for a car or machine to replace an old or broken part	spare part
confidence in yourself and your abilities	self-confidence
the number of years that a person is likely to live	life expectancy
a path or route that is quicker than the normal way	shortcut
the language that you first learn to speak as a child	mother tongue
food that is quick and easy to prepare and eat but not good for your health	junk food
a person that you admire and try to copy	role model

1 **Replace the crossed-out word with a word that forms a compound noun.**

1 Do you know a short ~~way~~ to the school from here? ....
2 Have you got any nail ~~paint~~? ....
3 Does she have enough ~~personal~~ confidence? ....
4 I ripped my shirt on the ~~twisted~~ wire around the field. ....
5 What's the average life ~~length~~ for men in your country? ....
6 I stepped on a drawing ~~nail~~ – it really hurt. ....
7 I need some paper ~~staples~~ to put these notes together. ....
8 Is it easy to get ~~new~~ parts for your car? ....

2 **Complete the compound in each sentence.**

1 What is your mother ....? What other languages do you speak?
2 Have you got a driving ....? How long have you had it?
3 Do you know where your birth .... is? If so, where?
4 Do you have any .... cards for different shops? If so, which?
5 Are there any short .... you often take? If so, where to?
6 Who has been the most important role .... in your life?
7 Do you ever wear .... polish? If so, what colour?
8 Do you often eat .... food? If so, what, and why?

3 ABOUT YOU **Write answers to the questions in Exercise 2, or ask another student.**

4 **Eight of the words below form compounds with *card*, one forms a compound with *pass*, and one forms a compound with *pass* and *card* (with the same meaning). Can you complete the compounds correctly?**

greetings   identity   bus   credit   rail   post   boarding   debit   SIM   gift

TEST YOURSELF

B Adjectives

Most compound adjectives have a hyphen (-).

> It was very much a **last-minute** decision to go, but the kids loved it and were very **well behaved**.

> My cousin is very **absent-minded**. We have a **long-standing** joke that whenever we meet, he pretends he doesn't know me.

> These boots are **worn out** now, but they've been incredibly **hard-wearing**.

> I have an uncle who is very **narrow-minded** and **self-righteous**. He thinks I'm **bad-tempered**, but it's only him who makes me angry; we argue all the time.

GLOSSARY	
last-minute	happening at the last possible moment
well behaved	(compounds with *well* are hyphenated before a noun but not after a noun) behaving in a way that people think is correct and polite: *a well-behaved child*
long-standing	that has existed or lasted for a long time
worn out	**1** (of a thing) no longer useful because it has been used so much **2** (of a person) exhausted from work or exercise
hard-wearing	(of a product) remaining in good condition for a long time
self-righteous	believing that what you say or do is right and other people are wrong
bad-tempered	often angry and easily annoyed

SPOTLIGHT adjectives with *-minded*

You can be **narrow-minded** (= not willing to listen to the ideas and opinions of others) OPP **broad-minded**, **open-minded**; **absent-minded** (= forgetful); or **single-minded** (= thinking in a concentrated way about sth and determined to achieve it).

5 **Answer the questions.**

1 If something is worn out, is it *no use* or *very comfortable*?
2 If something is last-minute, is it *very quick* or *at the last possible moment*?
3 If someone is single-minded, are they *determined* or *closed to new ideas*?
4 If something is hard-wearing, is it *uncomfortable* or does it *last a long time*?
5 If someone is worn out, are they *exhausted* or *unhealthy*?
6 If someone is absent-minded, are they *stupid* or *forgetful*?

6 **Form six compound adjectives using words from the box.**

long	worn	behaved	standing	minded	self
tempered	well	narrow	bad	righteous	out

7 **Complete the dialogues with a suitable compound adjective.**

1 He always thinks he's right, doesn't he? ~ Yes, he's very .... - ....
2 Had you planned to go? ~ No, it was a .... - .... decision.
3 Do you often meet up? ~ Yes, we have a .... - .... arrangement.
4 She's very determined, isn't she? ~ Yes, she's extremely .... - ....
5 He gets angry very easily. ~ I know, he's a very .... - .... man.
6 Your parents are always open to ideas. ~ Yes, they're very .... - ....

8 **Can you complete these compound adjectives using either *self* or *well*?**

.... known   .... confident   .... employed
.... behaved   .... dressed   .... conscious
.... service   .... informed

📑 TEST YOURSELF

A learner's dictionary includes a wide range of information that will help you to expand your vocabulary and use words more effectively when you speak and write. Look at these entries from the *Oxford Advanced Learner's Dictionary*.

The key (ⓘ) tells you that **reflect** is in the Oxford 3000 and is an important word.

The numbers tell you that **reflect** has different meanings.

re·flect ⓘ B1 ⊙ /rɪˈflekt/ *verb* **1** ⓘ B1 [T, usually passive] to show the image of sb/sth on the surface of sth such as a mirror, water or glass: **be reflected (in sth)** *His face was reflected in the mirror.* ◇ *She could see herself reflected in his eyes.* **2** ⓘ B1 [T, I] to throw back light, heat, sound,

... *work.* **4** ⓘ B2 [I, T] to think carefully and deeply about sth: *Before I decide, I need time to reflect.* ◇ **~on/upon sth** *She was left to reflect on the implications of her decision.*
...

Prepositions that follow **reflect** are shown in bold.

The words before the definition give a general idea of the different meanings of **count**.

count ⓘ A2 /kaʊnt/ *verb, noun*
■ *verb*
• SAY NUMBERS **1** ⓘ A2 [I] to say numbers in the correct order: *Billy can't count yet.* ◇ **~(up) to sth** *She can count up to 10 in Italian.* ◇ **~from sth (to/up to sth)** *to count from 1 to 10*
• FIND TOTAL **2** ⓘ A2 [T, I] to calculate the total number of
• INCLUDE **3** ⓘ B1 [T] **~sb/sth** to include sb/sth when you calculate a total: *We have invited 50 people, not counting the children.*

ab·sorb ⓘ+ B2 /əbˈzɔːb; NAmE -ˈzɔːrb/ *verb*
• LIQUID/GAS **1** ⓘ+ B2 to take in a liquid, gas or other sub-
...
• INFORMATION **4** ⓘ+ C1 **~sth** to take sth into the mind and learn or understand it SYN **take in**: *It's a lot of information to absorb all at once.*
...

Dictionaries often provide synonyms (**take sth in** is a synonym for one meaning of **absorb**) and opposites: these help you to expand your vocabulary.

The phrases in bold show common phrasal structures and/or collocations: they will help you to use **favour** naturally in typical contexts.

fa·vour ⓘ B1 ⓦ (*US* favor) /ˈfeɪvə(r)/ *noun, verb*
■ *noun*
• HELP **1** ⓘ B1 [C] a thing that you do to help sb: *Could you* **do me a favour** *and pick up Sam from school today?* ◇ *I'll ask Steve to take it. He* **owes me a favour**. ◇ *Thanks for helping me out. I'll* **return the favour** (= help you because you have helped me) *some time.* ◇ **as a ~ (to sb)** *I'm going as a favour to Ann, not because I want to.* ◇ **Do yourself a favour** (= help yourself) *and wear a helmet on the bike.* ⊃ EXPRESS YOURSELF at PERMISSION

Propose is a *formal* word and more common in written English.

pro·pose ⓘ B2 ⓦ /prəˈpəʊz/ *verb*
• SUGGEST PLAN **1** ⓘ B2 [T] (*formal*) to suggest a plan, an idea, etc. for people to think about and decide on: **~sth** *The*
...
~that... *She proposed that the book be banned.* ◇ (*BrE also*) *She proposed that the book should be banned.* ◇ **it is proposed that...** *It was proposed that the president be elected for a period of two years.* ◇ **~doing sth** *He proposed changing the name of the company.* ◇ **it is proposed to do sth** *It was proposed to pay the money from public funds.*

It is followed by a noun, a *that* clause, or an *-ing* form, so you cannot say: ~~He proposed us to go.~~

The grammar of each word is labelled, e.g. whether a noun is countable [C], uncountable [U], plural, or usually plural (as here), etc.

Idioms and phrasal verbs are listed at the end of the entry.

IDM ˌno ˈcomment (said in reply to a question, usually from a journalist) *I have nothing to say about that: 'Will you resign, sir?' 'No comment!'*

PHRV ˌcount aˈgainst sb | ˌcount sth aˈgainst sb to be considered or to consider sth to be a disadvantage in sb: *For that job her lack of experience may count against her.* ˌcount ˈdown (to sth) to think about a future event with
...

cir·cum·stance ⓘ B2 ⊙ /ˈsɜːkəmstəns, -staːns, -stæns; NAmE ˈsɜːrkəmstæns/ *noun* **1** ⓘ B2 [C, usually pl.] the conditions and facts that are connected with and affect a situation, an event or an action: *Police said there were no suspicious circumstances surrounding the boy's death.* ◇ **under... circumstances** *Under normal circumstances, your white blood cells are able to fight infections.* ◇ **in... circumstances** *The company reserves the right to cancel this agreement in certain circumstances.* ◇ *In exceptional circumstances, detainees could be denied access to a lawyer.*
...

1 Complete the sentences with the correct verb, and use the numbers opposite to say which meaning is being used.

1 There were about twelve on the bus, not _____ the teachers. ....
2 I think she'll have to go away and _____ on what we've said to her. ....
3 There's no liquid at the bottom because the sponge has _____ all the juice. ....
4 From the list, I have _____ fifteen who still haven't replied to the invitation. ....
5 There was too much information to _____ in one session; it was impossible. ....
6 In this game, one person closes their eyes and _____ up to 50, while the others hide. ....
7 He was standing behind me, but I could see his face _____ in the water. ....

2 Complete the sentences with a word from the opposite page.

1 Sam, could you _____ me a favour? ~ Sure. What is it?
2 How many people were there? ~ Lots, but I didn't actually _____ them.
3 There was so much information, I couldn't _____ it all in.
4 I only went to the party as a _____ to Anne.
5 Prime Minister, do you have anything to say? ~ No _____ .
6 You can change the date in certain _____ .
7 Could I ask a _____ ? ~ Yes, of course. What do you want?
8 I'm sure Bob will do it. He _____ me a favour.

3 Cross out the grammar mistake in each sentence and write the corrections at the end.

1 We could see our faces reflected on the water. ....
2 She proposed to leave the children behind. ....
3 You can take dogs into shops in certain circumstance. ....
4 There were ten people there, no counting the two of us. ....
5 I'll need to reflect in what he said. ....
6 He proposed us to take the car. ....

4 Use the ⒶⓅⓅ to complete these sentences. You will find the answers in the <u>full</u> dictionary entries for the words shown on the opposite page.

1 I _____ **myself lucky** to have a job that I really enjoy.
2 I'm _____ **favour** _____ equal pay.
3 **Under the** _____ , I would prefer not to say anything.
4 The whole incident _____ **badly on everyone** involved.
5 You can email us or **leave a** _____ on our website.
6 When you buy someone a present, **it's the thought that** _____ .

5 Look up these words in the ⒶⓅⓅ. What special information is given for each one? Write an example sentence for each.

inform ....
observe ....
finding ....
immune ....

6 ABOUT YOUR DICTIONARY Look in the ⒶⓅⓅ at the full entry for a very common word such as *face*, *head* or *take*. Note down five or six new collocations, phrases, or phrasal verbs that include the target word.

....
....
....

TEST YOURSELF

A Physical features

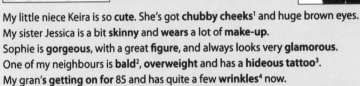
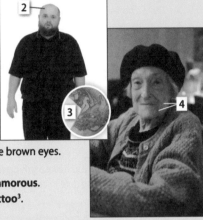

My little niece Keira is so **cute**. She's got **chubby cheeks**[1] and huge brown eyes.
My sister Jessica is a bit **skinny** and **wears** a lot of **make-up**.
Sophie is **gorgeous**, with a great **figure**, and always looks very **glamorous**.
One of my neighbours is **bald**[2], **overweight** and has a **hideous tattoo**[3].
My gran**'s getting on for** 85 and has quite a few **wrinkles**[4] now.

GLOSSARY

cute	pretty and attractive, often used to describe babies, puppies, etc.	**gorgeous** inf	very beautiful and attractive SYN **stunning**
		figure	the shape of a person's body
chubby	slightly fat, but in an attractive way	**glamorous**	appearing more exciting and attractive than ordinary people
skinny inf	too thin (**Slim** and **slender** are 'thin' in an attractive way.)	**overweight**	rather fat
make-up	cream, powder, etc. that you put on your face to make you look more attractive: **wear make-up**	**hideous**	very ugly
		be getting on for sth	be nearly a particular age, time or number: It's **getting on for** midnight.

1 Would <u>you</u> be *happy*, *unhappy* or *not sure* to be described in these ways?

bald chubby cute full of wrinkles glamorous gorgeous hideous overweight skinny slim stunning

HAPPY: .... UNHAPPY: .... NOT SURE: ....

2 Find six pairs of words in the box and explain the connection.

chubby	gorgeous	overweight	wrinkles	babies	wear
cute	skin	make-up	cheeks	stunning	fat

....
....
....

3 Complete the sentences.
1 My brother has now got a .... of a heart on his chest. I think it's horrible.
2 My mother's .... 50, but still has a great ....
3 Most babies seem to have a round face and chubby ....
4 I want people to think I'm .... , but not too skinny.
5 He's got a few .... now he's in his 70s, but I think they give his face character.
6 There's a picture of the two kittens asleep on a chair. They look very ....
7 My sister's boyfriends are usually quite ugly, but the new one is really ....
8 Film stars always look so .... , don't they? I'm sure they're different in real life.
9 My best friend Amelia is .... I wish I was that beautiful.
10 I don't .... much make-up these days.

TEST YOURSELF

B Clothes and appearance

DRESS FOR YOUR SHAPE

The **key to** dressing for your body shape is to **enhance** your best **features** and cleverly **conceal** the not so good ones. Here are a few **guidelines**:

* Wearing dark colours or **vertical stripes**[1] will **create the illusion** of being slimmer.
* For women, **high heels**[2] are **flattering** because they **exaggerate** the length of their legs.
* If you are pear-shaped (with narrow shoulders and **broad hips**[3]), jeans that sit below the **waist**[4] are flattering, as they **draw attention to** the waistline and make your bottom look smaller.

GLOSSARY

key to sth	the thing that makes you able to understand or achieve sth	**create an illusion (of sth)**	make sth appear true, which in fact is false
enhance	increase or improve the quality, value or status of sth	**flattering**	making sb look more attractive OPP **unflattering**
feature	a part of sb's face or body	**exaggerate**	make sth seem bigger, better, worse or more important than it really is **exaggeration** n
conceal formal	hide sth	**broad**	wide: **broad shoulders/hips** OPP **narrow** (We use **wide** more to talk about distance and geographical areas: The room was 4 metres **wide**.)
guidelines	information that can help you make a decision or form an opinion		
vertical	OPP **horizontal**	**draw (sb's) attention to sth**	make sb notice sth

4 Underline the main stress on each word. Use the 🔵 to help you.

conceal   create   enhance   exaggerate   exaggeration   guidelines   horizontal   illusion   vertical

5 Circle the correct answer.
1 If you create an illusion, you make something appear *true / false*.
2 Guidelines usually *stop you doing something / help you*.
3 Enhancing something is a *positive / negative* change.
4 Lines that go up and down are *horizontal / vertical*.
5 If you exaggerate something, you make it seem *more / less* important than it really is.
6 People came to the music festival from a *broad / wide* area.
7 If you wear something that is flattering, it makes you look *worse / better* than usual.
8 If you conceal something, others *can / can't* see it.

6 Complete the sentences.
1 The right clothes can show off your best .... , e.g. long legs or a slim waist.
2 I don't look good in jeans: my waist is quite small but I've got broad ....
3 Clothes with vertical .... make you look slimmer; high .... make you taller.
4 The .... to her success is talent, not good looks!
5 He wears a hat because he doesn't want to .... attention to the fact he's bald.
6 To say he's the best-looking man in the world is a bit of an ....
7 He's getting fat but he tries to .... it by wearing very loose jackets.
8 Those trousers are very .... : they make her look fat.
9 I've got .... shoulders, but quite a small .... I've never put on much weight.
10 I think it's useful when fashion experts give you .... on how to dress.

📖 TEST YOURSELF

A Reading the signs

BODY LANGUAGE can tell you a lot, but if you **jump to conclusions** when you are trying to **interpret** a particular **gesture**, you may **misinterpret** what it means. For example, people who look away to avoid **eye contact** may **not necessarily** be lying: they could just be very shy. To understand body language, therefore, we need to **observe** a **combination** of behaviour. With lying, for example, **look out for** any of these:

- avoiding eye contact
- **sweating** a lot
- **going red**
- **biting fingernails**[1]
- **constantly** moving about

GLOSSARY			
jump to conclusions	make a decision about sth too quickly, before you have thought about all the facts	**observe** *formal*	see or notice sth. An **observant** person is good at noticing things. **observation** *n*
interpret	decide that sth has a particular meaning **interpretation** *n* If you **misinterpret** sth, you give it an incorrect meaning.	**combination**	two or more things that exist or are put together
		look out for sth/sb	look and try to see or find sth/sb
gesture	a body movement you make to show a particular meaning	**sweat**	If you **sweat**, water appears on the surface of your skin because you are hot or nervous. **sweat** *n*
eye contact	looking into another person's eyes		
not necessarily	used to say that sth is possibly true but is not always true	**go red**	become red in the face, often when you're embarrassed SYN **blush**
		constantly	all the time or very frequently

1 Good or bad? Write G or B.

1 He sweats a great deal. ....
2 She goes red all the time. ....
3 She has strong powers of observation. ....
4 She never bites her fingernails. ....
5 He jumps to conclusions. ....
6 She's very observant. ....
7 He always makes eye contact. ....
8 He misinterprets what people say. ....

2 Complete the sentences with a suitable word.

1 You should stop and think before .... to conclusions.
2 The teacher said she'd .... out for more articles on body language.
3 In groups, I like to sit and listen, so I can .... how people react to each other.
4 I used to bite my .... a lot, but not any more.
5 Is it difficult to .... someone's body language if you don't know them well?
6 If you *go red*, does it mean you're angry? ~ No, not ....
7 I use hand .... a lot. Sometimes it annoys people.
8 The increase in the number of students is the result of a .... of different factors.
9 It was so hot in the room, I was starting to ....
10 I .... move my feet when I'm nervous – I can't stop it.

3 ABOUT YOU Write answers to the questions, or talk to another student.

1 Do you use lots of gestures? If so, what type? ....
2 Do you think you are good at making eye contact with people? ....
3 Do you think you are observant? For example, do you notice what people are wearing? ....
4 Do you ever bite your fingernails? If so, why? ....
5 Do you blush easily? If so, does it worry you? ....
6 Do you like sitting and observing people when you are in public places? If so, why? ....

🗒 TEST YOURSELF

B Interpreting gestures

Here are some common interpretations of gestures, but remember the danger of **making generalizations about body language**.

 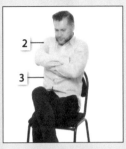  

1   A **clenched fist**[1] often shows **anger**.

2   People who **fold their arms**[2] and **cross their legs**[3] may be **defensive**, and may be **signalling** the fact that they disagree with you.

3   People who **lean towards**[4] each other are **displaying** an interest in one another.

4   Women who **fancy** someone often touch their hair. Women also lift their heads to show more of their neck when they're **flirting**.

GLOSSARY			
make generalizations (about sth)	make general statements about sth that may only be based on a few examples	**signal**	If you **signal** sth, you do sth that sends a particular message. **signal** n
anger	the state of being *angry*	**display**	show signs of sth **display** n
defensive	showing that you feel sb is criticizing you	**fancy** *inf*	be sexually attracted to sb
		flirt (with sb)	behave towards sb as if you find them sexually attractive, but not in a serious way

4 **Cross out the wrong word.**

1   flirt **with** / **by** someone
2   *make* / *do* generalizations
3   a clenched *hand* / *fist*
4   cross your **body** / **legs**
5   lean **by** / **towards** somebody
6   fold your **arms** / **legs**
7   send a **signal** / **display**
8   fancy *someone* / *with someone*

5 **Complete the sentences.**

1   Both girls like Conrad, and they're always .... with him.
2   She .... towards him and whispered something in his ear. I think she .... him.
3   If you say negative things about his work, he becomes a bit ....
4   I think I often .... my arms and .... my legs when I'm sitting.
5   A clenched .... sometimes indicates .... , but footballers also do it when they are happy because they've just scored a goal.
6   Certain gestures between couples clearly .... that they fancy each other.
7   Hand and body gestures can mean different things in different countries, so it can be dangerous to make .... about their meaning.
8   Even when he's angry, he doesn't really .... any signs of emotion.

6 **ABOUT YOU** **Write your answers, or talk to another student.**

1   Do you often fold your arms or cross your legs? If so, why? ....
2   Do you think you lean towards people to show you are interested? ....
3   Do you think you flirt much? ....
4   If you fancy someone, what gestures do you make? ....

 TEST YOURSELF

1 He's **crawling** along the floor.

2 She's **kneeling (down) and praying**.

3 She **spilt** the coffee.

4 He's **diving into** the water.

5 He's **sweeping** the floor.

6 She's **shrugging** her shoulders.

7 She's **putting on lipstick**.

8 He's **leaning against** a wall.

9 He's **dragging** the **cabinet** along the floor.

10 She's **tearing** a piece of paper **in half**.

socket

11 He's **plugging** it **in**.

12 She's **combing** her hair.

blanket

13 She's **folding** the **blanket** in half.

14 He's **begging for** money.

button

15 He's **sewing on** a **button**.

16 He's **nodding** his head.

screw

17 She's **screwing** it into the wall.

SPOTLIGHT *nod and shake your head*

In some countries, including Britain, you can **nod your head** (= move it up and down) to say 'yes', and **shake your head** (= move it from side to side) to say 'no'.

1 **Is the pronunciation of the underlined letters the same or different? Write S or D. Use the** APP **to help you.**

1 p<u>u</u>t / shr<u>u</u>g   ....
2 shr<u>u</u>g / b<u>u</u>tton   ....
3 c<u>o</u>mb / n<u>o</u>d   ....
4 l<u>ea</u>n / t<u>ea</u>r **v**   ....
5 sw<u>ee</u>p / kn<u>ee</u>l   ....

6 s<u>ew</u> / scr<u>ew</u>   ....
7 blan<u>ke</u>t / sp<u>i</u>ll   ....
8 s<u>ew</u> / c<u>o</u>mb   ....
9 l<u>ea</u>n / l<u>ea</u>nt   ....
10 <u>k</u>neel / com<u>b</u>   ....

2 **Write the past tense and the past participle of these verbs.**

1 beg   ....
2 sweep   ....
3 tear   ....
4 shake   ....
5 nod   ....

6 kneel   ....
7 sew   ....
8 put   ....
9 lean   ....
10 spill   ....

3 **Complete the phrases.**

1 fold something .... half
2 lean .... the wall
3 dive .... the lake
4 put .... lipstick

5 plug .... the kettle
6 kneel ....
7 sew .... a button
8 beg .... money

4 **Underline the correct answer.**

1 He was leaning against a *piece of paper / door*.
2 She folded the *towel / cabinet* in half.
3 He dragged the *body / wall* to the door.
4 I'm going to put on my *hair / lipstick*.
5 Could you plug in the *toaster / button*?

6 Kneel down on the *blanket / kettle*.
7 She dived into the *water / floor*.
8 He spilt the *drinks / blanket*.
9 She shrugged her *legs / shoulders*.
10 He crawled along the *water / carpet*.

5 **Complete the sentences.**

1 There are more and more homeless people .... for money in the streets.
2 People .... to God in a church.
3 I asked Dad if I could go, but he just .... his head.
4 She's only ten months, so she's still .... along the floor most of the time.
5 I tried to .... in the kettle, but there seems to be a problem with the ....
6 We all .... down on the floor to try and find my wife's lost contact lens.
7 Marta was so angry, she .... his letter in half and threw it in the bin.
8 Could you help me .... these sheets?
9 I tried to .... the chest of drawers but it damaged the floor.
10 He was .... his head, so I assumed it was OK to go in.

6 ABOUT YOU **Write your answers, or talk to another student.**

1 Do you ever (or often) spill things? ....
2 How often do you comb your hair? ....
3 Do you ever wear lipstick? ....
4 Are you good at sewing? ....
5 Do you pray? If so, what do you pray for? ....
6 Can you dive well? ....
7 In your country, if you nod your head, does it mean 'yes'? ....
8 In your country, are there a lot of people begging for money? ....
9 In your country do you use kettles to boil water for tea or coffee? ....

TEST YOURSELF

A Ways of moving

It was a nice day so we decided to **go for a stroll**.
I just spent the day **wandering** around town.
We were **hiking** in the countryside, and I **stumbled**[1] on
a rocky bit of path.
The soldiers **marched** along the street.
The police **charged** across the square towards
the protesters.
I **rushed** to catch my train.
Two policemen **chased** the robber across the park.
I **ran flat out** to get home before the others.

GLOSSARY

stroll	a slow, relaxed walk: *go for a stroll*; **stroll** *v*
wander (around/ about)	walk somewhere slowly, often without any particular aim or in any particular direction
hike	walk a long way in the country: *go hiking*
stumble (over/ on sth)	hit your foot against sth when you are walking or running and almost fall over **trip (over)**
march	walk fairly quickly with regular steps (like a soldier)
charge	run straight at sb/sth in a noisy or aggressive way
rush	move or do sth at great speed, usually for an important reason or because you are late for sth
chase	run after sb/sth in order to catch them **run after sb/sth**

SPOTLIGHT idioms and phrasal verbs with *run*

run flat out run as fast as you can
run off with sth take or steal sth:
- *The thief **ran off with** my handbag.*
run sb/sth over hit sb/sth with a vehicle:
- *I **ran over** the child's toy.*
run away escape from somewhere:
- *The boy threw a stone then **ran away**.*

1 Answer the questions.

1 Who often marches? ....
2 Who might run off with something? ....
3 Who might chase after people? ....
4 What animals sometimes charge at people? ....

5 Why do people rush? ....
6 Why do people trip over things? ....
7 Why do people wander around? ....
8 Where do people go hiking? ....

2 Correct any mistakes in the underlined verbs. Be careful: the answer may be correct.

1 We often go <u>chasing</u> in the countryside at the weekend.   ....
2 About 100 angry demonstrators <u>stumbled</u> down the street.   ....
3 The car appeared suddenly, so I had to <u>stroll</u> across the road.   ....
4 I <u>tripped over</u> and hurt my ankle.   ....
5 He was terribly upset when he <u>marched</u> over the cat.   ....
6 My dog loves to <u>charge</u> rabbits.   ....
7 It was a very hot humid day so we just <u>ran flat out</u> through the park.   ....
8 The teenager <u>ran away</u> because she was unhappy living at home.   ....

3 Complete the sentences.

1 When Jordan heard about his brother's accident, he .... to the hospital.
2 I .... and fell into some long wet grass.
3 We had lots of time so we decided to go for a ....
4 They broke into the shop then .... with the money across the park.
5 The police car was .... a black BMW through the streets at great speed.
6 My train was just leaving, and I had to run .... to catch it.
7 We had nothing to do so we just .... around for a couple of hours.

> TEST YOURSELF

B Physical exercise

My 20-minute **workout**

I'm not as **agile** as I used to be, and I was beginning to feel quite **stiff** early in the morning, so I asked a friend to **devise** a workout routine for me. First I **warm up** with some **stretching**[1] and **bending**, then I go on to more **demanding** activities, like **press-ups**[2] to **strengthen** my muscles. But the key for me is variety: I like a **constant** change of activity to stay **motivated**. It's also **vital** that you finish by **warming down** with fairly gentle activities.

1

2

GLOSSARY	
workout	a period of physical exercise you do to keep fit **work out** v
agile	able to move quickly and easily **agility** n
stiff	feeling some pain, and unable to move easily
devise	invent a method or plan of doing sth SYN **think sth up**
warm up	do physical activities to prepare the muscles for exercise OPP **warm down**
bend	move your body forwards and downwards **bent** adj
demanding	(used about a task) needing a lot of effort or skill
constant	happening or existing all the time or again and again
motivated	wanting to do sth badly, often for a reason **motivation** n
vital	extremely important SYN **essential, crucial**

SPOTLIGHT verbs with *-en*

You can add *-(e)n* to a few nouns and some adjectives to form verbs.
- *I want to **strengthen** my arms.* (= make them stronger)
- *They plan to **widen** the road.* (= make it wider)
- *The illness has **weakened** him.* (= made him weaker)

---

4 **Put these words in three groups according to the pronunciation of the letter 'i'. Use the ⒶⓅⓅ to help you.**

stiff   agile   agility   crucial   motivated   devise   demanding   widen   essential   vital

....

5 **Circle the correct answer(s). Sometimes both answers are correct.**
1   I worked in the garden yesterday, so I feel a bit *stiff / demanding* today.
2   It's easier to touch your toes if you *stretch / bend* your knees.
3   It's *vital / crucial* that you do exercises that are suitable for you.
4   You should warm *up / down* when you have finished your exercises.
5   My brother *thought up / devised* this new training method last year.
6   I can reach the ceiling if I *stretch / bend* my arms.
7   I do a short *workout / press-up* every morning.
8   I can't do certain activities because I'm not *demanding / agile* enough.

6 **Complete the sentences.**
1   I couldn't finish my exercises because of the .... phone calls I was getting.
2   I want to .... a way of doing more exercise during my working day.
3   If I .... forwards quickly, I get a bit of a pain in my back.
4   My brother does 30 .... - .... every day. He wants to stay fit so is very ....
5   You must do this exercise with your knees .... , not straight.
6   I've got a bad knee so I need to .... the muscles to give my knee more support.
7   My brother usually .... in the gym two or three times a week.
8   The problem is that a lot of people don't have the .... to exercise regularly.
9   I want to run a marathon next year, but I know it will be very ....
10   I had much more .... when I was younger. Now I feel stiff when I get up.

 TEST YOURSELF

A Are computers bad for your eyesight?

◉ eyeSIGHT

Many of us spend hours every day working at a computer. As a result, **eye strain** and **blurred vision** are common complaints. Most people also **blink** less frequently when they are **concentrating**, resulting in poor **tear** production, which can **irritate** the eyes. Here's how you can change your computer use and **ease** your **discomfort**:

▶ **adjust** your computer screen so that it is 50-65 cm from your eyes, just below eye level

▶ adjust the lighting to **eliminate** any very bright lights

▶ take frequent breaks, blink often to stop your eyes becoming dry, and let your eye muscles relax by looking into the distance every 15 minutes.

Remember: if a problem continues, see an **optician**.

GLOSSARY	
eyesight	the ability to see ALSO **sight** SYN **vision; good/ poor eyesight**
strain	an injury in part of your body often from using it too much: **eye strain, back strain**
blurred vision	If your **vision** is **blurred**, you cannot see clearly.
blink	shut and open your eyes quickly
concentrate	give all your attention or effort to sth **concentration** n
tear	a drop of liquid that comes out of your eye when you cry
irritate	cause a part of the body to be painful or sore **irritation** n
ease	make sth less unpleasant or painful
discomfort	a slight feeling of pain and being uncomfortable
adjust	change sth slightly to make it more suitable **adjustment** n
eliminate	remove or get rid of sth **elimination** n
optician	a person whose job is to test people's eyes, sell glasses, etc. An **optician's** is a shop where an optician works.

1 **The pronunciation of the letter 'i' is the same as in** *bit* **in eight of the cases underlined. Which four are different? Use the** 🔊 **to help you.**

irritate   vision   blink   optician   strain   eliminate   eyesight   discomfort

2 **Circle the correct word(s). Be careful: sometimes both words are possible.**

1   Did you know that pigs often have really poor *sight / vision*?
2   The optician can *eliminate / adjust* your glasses if they are too loose.
3   We are currently trying to *eliminate / ease* theft from our offices.
4   I can get eye strain if I *irritate / concentrate* for too long without taking a break.
5   These eye drops should *adjust / ease* the pain.
6   I could see a *strain / tear* in the corner of her eye.
7   If you get any *discomfort / irritation*, go and get your eyes checked.
8   She got a new pair of glasses from the *doctor's / optician's*.

3 **One word is missing in each line. What is it, and where does it go?**

1   Sore, tired or burning eyes are symptoms of eye.   ....
2   I went to the chemist's to get some stuff to the pain.   ....
3   I think these glasses will be fine with a small.   ....
4   Even with glasses, there are some problems you can't completely.   ....
5   The said I needed new glasses.   ....
6   Bright lights for a period of time can your eyes.   ....
7   People's vision can be a bit if they drink too much alcohol.   ....
8   There were in her eyes when she told me the sad news.   ....
9   The flash of a camera makes a lot of people.   ....
10   If you work too long, tiredness will affect your powers of.   ....

4 ABOUT YOU **Have you suffered from any of these problems? If so, what did you do about it? Write your answer, or talk to another student.**

 TEST YOURSELF

B A peaceful sight

We stood at the top of the hill for ages, **gazing** at the **spectacular** view below. In the distance, the port was **barely visible** through the early morning **mist**, but we could just **make out** the island. As we drove back down, I **caught a glimpse of** a waterfall and asked Marcello to stop. Then, all of a sudden, a young **deer** appeared with its mother. They **stood** completely **still**, looking at us **suspiciously**, then ran off and **vanished into thin air**.

GLOSSARY	
gaze at sb/sth	look at sb/sth for a long time because you are interested in them/it or are thinking about sth else **gaze** n
spectacular	very impressive to see
barely	only with great difficulty or effort SYN **only just**
visible	Sth that is **visible** can be seen. OPP **invisible**
mist	a thin cloud just above the ground making it difficult to see **misty** adj
make sth/sb out	see, hear or understand sth/sb with difficulty
stand still	stand without moving at all: *keep/stay/sit still*
suspiciously	carefully because you think there may be sth wrong or dishonest **suspicious** adj; **suspicion** n
vanish	disappear **vanish into thin air** disappear suddenly

SPOTLIGHT ways of seeing

If you **catch a glimpse of sth/sb**, you see it/them for a very short time and not clearly or completely. If you **glance at sb/sth**, you look at them/it for a moment. If you **spot sb/sth**, you see or notice sb/sth, especially suddenly or when it is not easy to do.
- We **caught a glimpse of** the actress as she left the theatre.
- I **glanced at** my watch to see if it was time to go.
- I **spotted** several mistakes in my work just before I handed it in.

5 Correct the spelling mistake(s) in each sentence.
1 The view was spectacular. ....
2 She looked at us suspisiously. ....
3 I could barily see them. ....
4 When the bird was stil, it was unvisible. ....
5 We just caught a glimse of the deer. ....
6 I granced at my friend. ....

6 Underline the words which are possible. More than one word is often possible.
1 The bottom of the valley was *invisible / misty / suspicious*.
2 The castle was *visible / standing still / spectacular*.
3 The man was badly dressed and looked *suspicious / spectacular / misty*.
4 After an hour, we finally *caught a glimpse of / spotted / glanced at* the rare bird.
5 Could you please *stand / wait / keep* still?
6 When Lia came in, I quickly *glanced at / gazed at / spotted* John next to me. He smiled.
7 We could *suspiciously / only just / barely* see the church in the distance.

7 Rewrite the sentences using the words in capitals. The meaning must stay the same.
1 He sat without moving while I drew him. STILL ....
2 I was only just able to see the boat on the horizon. MAKE ....
3 They were both watching me; I don't know why. GAZE ....
4 Those stars can't be seen without a telescope. INVISIBLE ....
5 We could barely see the trees through the mist. ONLY ....
6 After a while I could see Leo in the crowd. SPOT ....
7 The thief ran out of the building and disappeared. THIN AIR ....
8 I briefly saw Blanca as she left the shop. GLIMPSE ....
9 Please don't move. KEEP ....
10 I didn't believe he was telling the truth. SUSPICION ....

TEST YOURSELF

12) Sounds and hearing

A Things I don't want to hear

There are noises I love – when someone **bursts out laughing**, or people **cheer** at football matches, for example – but if I went **deaf**, there would also be noises I wouldn't miss:

- **background noise** of cars, machines, etc. that can be so **irritating**
- the sound of a child **in tears**
- the sound of someone **sneezing**[1] – that makes me worry I will be the next person to **catch their cold**.
- someone **whispering** behind me – I imagine they are talking about me!
- **overhearing** something unpleasant that I wasn't meant to hear
- someone **sighing**
- people **booing** at sports events or other occasions – it's very rude.
- my partner **snoring**!

GLOSSARY			
burst out laughing	suddenly start laughing, often loudly	**catch a cold**	get an illness: *catch a cold / (the) flu*
cheer	shout to show that you like sth or to encourage sb in a sporting event, etc. OPP **boo**	**whisper**	speak very quietly in sb's ear so others cannot hear **whisper** n: *He spoke in a whisper.*
deaf	unable to hear. **Blind** is unable to see.	**overhear**	hear what sb is saying, by accident, when they are speaking to sb else
background noise	sounds or noise that can be heard but aren't the centre of attention and are often unwanted	**sigh**	let out a long deep breath to show you are tired, sad, disappointed, etc.
irritating	annoying; making you angry	**snore**	breathe noisily through your nose and mouth when you are asleep
in tears	crying		

1 Correct the mistake in each sentence.
1 There was a lot of background noises. ....
2 We burst out laugh. ....
3 The poor boy was into tears. ....
4 Did you overhere what she said? ....
5 Please stop wispering like that. ....
6 My husband snorts in his sleep. ....

2 Find five phrases from the words in the box

background	in	catch	in a	burst out	whisper	tears	laughing	noise	a cold

....
....

3 Complete the sentences with a suitable word or phrase.
1 When you have a cold, you often .... a lot.
2 My next-door neighbour has been .... for several years, and now has a guide dog.
3 The poor man can't hear a thing: he's been .... for years.
4 If you spend time with someone with a cold, you might .... their cold.
5 If you don't want someone to hear what you are saying, you should ....
6 Most people stood up and .... when Liam won, but a couple .... It was a bit embarrassing.
7 One or two people have told me I .... in my sleep.
8 When my mother .... like that, I can tell she's disappointed.
9 I .... two people on the bus talking about unpleasant noises. It was quite funny.
10 A lot of young people talk very quickly and not very clearly. It's very ....

TEST YOURSELF

B A sound story

It was a dark and stormy night. I shut my eyes …

- I could hear a car **horn** in the distance.
- Several dogs were **barking**.
- I heard a **crash**.
- Someone **yelled**.
- A car door **slammed**.
- Something hit my window – it **cracked**.
- I heard **footsteps** in the hall.
- **Silence**. Then my door handle turned.
- I **screamed** and woke up.
- It was a **nightmare**. I breathed a sigh of relief.

GLOSSARY

horn	the thing in a car that makes a loud warning noise
bark	(of dogs) make a loud short noise or noises
crash	a sudden loud noise made by sth hitting sth, etc. **crash** v
yell	shout very loudly
slam	shut or make sth shut very loudly
crack	break or make sth break so that a line appears on the surface but doesn't break into pieces: *The glass has* **cracked**. *The stone* **cracked** *the windscreen.* **crack** n
footsteps	the sound or marks made when you walk or run
silence	no noise or sound at all
scream	make a loud, high, unpleasant sound **scream** n
(breathe) a sigh of relief	let out a long deep breath when sth unpleasant stops

SPOTLIGHT *nightmare*

A **nightmare** is a frightening or unpleasant dream. It is also used informally to describe a bad or unpleasant experience.

- *My trip to London was a* **nightmare**: *all the trains were delayed.*

4 **Put these words in three groups: 1** *no noise* **2** *a noise* **3** *a loud noise.*

crack   bark   sigh   yell   silence   scream   footsteps   slam   crash

1 ....   **2** ....   **3** ....

5 **Match 1–5 with a–e.**

1	The door	....	**a**	barked.
2	The car	....	**b**	cracked.
3	The dog	....	**c**	slammed.
4	The glass	....	**d**	screamed.
5	The woman	....	**e**	crashed.

6 **Replace the underlined words with a single word. Keep the same meaning.**
1 I walked into the classroom. There was <u>no noise at all</u>.
2 I opened the door and someone started <u>shouting really loudly</u>.
3 My partner has had <u>bad unpleasant dreams</u> for some time now.
4 I could hear <u>the sound of somebody walking</u> along the path towards the door.
5 He walked out angrily and <u>shut</u> the door <u>loudly</u>.
6 I heard the car's brakes and then a <u>loud noise of it hitting something</u>.
7 After I dropped the glass, it had <u>lines along the surface,</u> so I got rid of it.
8 A spider suddenly appeared, and Kasia <u>let out a high unpleasant sound</u>.

7 **Complete the text.**
Where I work is terrible. For a start, there's constant background noise from the traffic, with drivers sounding their car **(1)** .... all day long. Then there is a dog that's often tied to a tree outside, so of course it **(2)** .... all the time. And in my office I have several colleagues who are always **(3)** .... at each other – they can't talk in a normal voice – and can't seem to leave the office without **(4)** .... the door. It's an absolute **(5)** ...., and I breathe a **(6)** .... of **(7)** .... every day at 5.30 when it's time to go home.

 TEST YOURSELF

13 ⟩ Touch

A Ways of touching

1 She **squeezed** the bottle.

2 I **tapped** him on the shoulder.

3 He **grabbed** my bag.

4 She **pinched** my arm.

5 He **punched** him.

6 The cat **scratched** me.

7 They **hugged** each other.

8 She **slapped** his face.

9 She **rubbed** the suntan lotion on.

> **SPOTLIGHT** verbs and nouns
>
> Some of these verbs can be used as nouns with the same meaning.
> - She **gave** him **a punch/slap** on the arm.
> - He **gave** her hand **a squeeze**.
> - **Give** him **a tap** on the shoulder.
> - I **got** a **scratch** on the car.

1 Can you do this with one finger? Write *Yes* or *No*.

1 hug someone ....
2 rub someone/something ....
3 grab something ....
4 pinch someone ....
5 scratch someone ....
6 tap someone on the shoulder ....
7 slap someone ....
8 punch something ....

2 Answer the questions. Write *Yes* or *No*.

1 If you punch someone, do they usually laugh? ....
2 If you hug someone, are you trying to hurt them? ....
3 If you tap someone on the shoulder, are you trying to get their attention? ....
4 If you scratch your car, are you happy about it? ....
5 If you grab something, do you do it quickly? ....
6 If you pinch someone, is it nice? ....
7 If you slap someone, does it often hurt? ....
8 Can you squeeze a bottle of milk? ....

3 Complete the sentences.

1 He .... her hand until it started to hurt.
2 Someone .... me a .... on the shoulder, so I turned round.
3 The youth .... the woman's purse and ran off down the road.
4 When Sam left for his trip, he said goodbye to his wife and .... her a ....
5 People were horrified when the mother .... the child round the face.
6 Oliver .... his hands to keep warm.
7 The man .... Joe in the stomach, and he dropped to the floor.
8 Don't .... your mosquito bites – they'll start to bleed.

TEST YOURSELF

B Massage

A Simple Face **Massage**

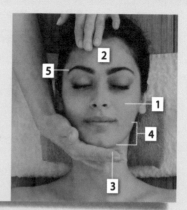

1 Start by **gently stroking** the whole face. With both hands, **slide** up the neck, across the **cheeks**[1], then up and over the **forehead**[2]. **Apply** gentle **pressure to** the sides of the head.
2 **Stimulate** the skin by gently **patting** the cheeks and neck.
3 Use your **fingertips**[3] to **lightly massage** the skin around the **jaw**[4].
4 To **release tension** around the eyes, **firmly** press down on the **eyebrows**[5] with your fingertips.
5 Massage the **scalp vigorously** as if shampooing your hair.

GLOSSARY	
massage	(see picture): *have a massage*; massage v
stroke	move your hand over sb's skin, hair, etc. gently and slowly
slide	move or make sth move smoothly along a surface
apply pressure (to sth)	press on sth hard with your hand, foot, etc.
stimulate	make a part of the body or skin more active
pat	touch sb/sth gently a number of times with a flat hand or both hands
tension	You have **tension** if your muscles are tight and not relaxed and you need to **release** (= free) the tension.
scalp	the skin that covers the part of the head where the hair grows

SPOTLIGHT adverbs of manner

Gently and **lightly** are soft, relaxed movements. **Firmly** is much stronger. If you move your hands **steadily**, you make regular movements. **Vigorously** means in a very energetic and active way. **energetically**.

---

4 **Are these actions usually gentle, or can they be quite vigorous?**

stroke   massage   slide   apply pressure   pat   stimulate

GENTLE: ....

USUALLY VIGOROUS: ....

5 **Cover the text and look at the face. What does each number identify?**

1 ....   3 ....   5 ....
2 ....   4 ....

6 **Complete the sentences.**

1 I often .... my forehead, cheeks and neck: it stimulates the skin.
2 I love going to have a .... – it's so relaxing.
3 She sat quietly, gently .... the cat.
4 The physio just used his fingertips to apply .... to the back of my neck.
5 When the hairdresser washes my hair, he massages my .... quite ....
6 The doctor .... pressure to the wound to stop the bleeding.
7 Don't use the whole of your fingers for massage, just the ....
8 I think a massage is one of the best ways to release .... in your body.
9 Massage and exercise help to .... blood circulation in the body.
10 The doors .... open automatically as you approach.
11 I tapped him .... on the shoulder to get his attention.
12 I pressed the button .... but still nothing happened.

TEST YOURSELF

A Types of illness

rash

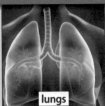
lungs

breast

MORE MINOR

hay fever:	an illness affecting the eyes, nose and throat, caused by breathing in **pollen**
a rash:	an area of red spots **commonly** caused by an illness or an allergy

MORE SERIOUS

an allergy:	a condition that makes you ill when you eat, touch or breathe certain things that don't normally make people ill, e.g. eating nuts. Allergies can be minor or very serious. **allergic (to sth)** *adj*
asthma:	a condition that gives people breathing difficulties
diabetes:	a disease caused by an **inability** to control the level of sugar in the blood

POTENTIALLY FATAL

cancer:	e.g. **lung** cancer, **breast** cancer: a very serious illness in which a **lump** grows in the body
a heart attack:	a sudden, serious illness when the heart stops working correctly

GLOSSARY

minor	not very big, serious or important
pollen	the powder produced by some plants
commonly	usually; very often; by most people
inability	the fact of not being able to do sth
potentially	that may possibly happen or become sth **potential** *adj*
fatal	causing or ending in death: *a fatal accident*
lump	a swelling under the skin which can be small or large

1 Is the pronunciation of the underlined letters the same or different? Write *S* or *D*. Use the 🔊 to help you.

1 h<u>ea</u>rt br<u>ea</u>st ....
2 all<u>e</u>rgy r<u>a</u>sh ....
3 diab<u>e</u>tes f<u>e</u>ver ....
4 aller<u>gy</u> lun<u>g</u> ....
5 d<u>i</u>abetes m<u>i</u>nor ....
6 h<u>ay</u> f<u>a</u>tal ....
7 <u>a</u>llergy <u>a</u>llergic ....
8 p<u>o</u>tential asthm<u>a</u> ....

2 Complete the sentences.

1 I'm .... to prawns. I get a .... on my face if I eat just one.
2 Drugs are a .... used treatment for many illnesses.
3 It's clear that smoking increases your risk of lung .... , which is .... fatal.
4 A friend of mine has a very serious .... If he eats peanuts, he has a bad reaction.
5 I get a bit of hay .... every summer, but it's only a .... problem. I don't worry about it.
6 If you are seriously overweight, it is a .... problem: you are more at risk from .... and, of course, heart ....
7 One of my friends died in a .... road accident.
8 The .... to control the level of sugar in the blood is .... very serious.

3 Combine words from the box to make sentences about the illnesses and their causes and symptoms.

hay fever	diabetes	asthma	breast cancer	rash
breathing difficulties	allergy	sugar	pollen	lump

....
....
....
....
....

TEST YOURSELF

B Medicine labels

These tablets must be **dissolved** in water.

For **short-term** use only.

DO NOT **EXCEED** THE STATED **DOSE**.

Please read the **enclosed leaflet** before taking these tablets.

Possible **side effects** may include stomach **disorders**.

Discard any remaining solution 60 days after opening the bottle.

If symptoms **persist**, **consult** your doctor.

Do not use after the **expiry date**.

SPOTLIGHT *exceed* and *excess*

1 do more of sth than is stated in an order or a law:
*Don't **exceed** the **stated dose**.*
*You shouldn't **exceed** the **speed limit**.*

2 be greater than a particular number, amount or quality:
*The cost won't **exceed** $5,000.* OR
*The cost won't be **in excess of** $5,000.*

---

4 True or false? Write *T* or *F*. Correct any false sentences.

1 Drugs can have *side effects*. ....
2 If something is *enclosed*, you can't open it. ....
3 You can read a *leaflet*. ....
4 A *disorder* means a machine isn't working. ....
5 If something *persists*, it stops. ....
6 '*In excess of* 50' is more than 50. ....
7 You can *dissolve* sugar in hot water. ....
8 If you *consult* someone, you disagree with them. ....

5 Add a word to complete an instruction or a common phrase.

1 Don't exceed the stated ....
2 a long-..................... solution
3 the expiry ....
4 in .... of 20 people
5 common side ....
6 Read the .... leaflet.

6 Use one word to complete the sentences on the right with the same meaning as those on the left.

1 It's all there in the information they provide. — It's all there in the ....
2 He's got something wrong with his stomach. — He's got a stomach ....
3 The information is included with this letter. — The information is ....
4 One teaspoon is the amount you should take. — One teaspoon is the ....
5 See a doctor if the symptoms don't go away. — See a doctor if the symptoms ....
6 Don't use after the end of July. — Don't use after the expiry ....

7 Complete the sentences.

1 You can buy aspirin, which .... in water; that avoids taking tablets.
2 I've had a .... cough for weeks now; the doctor thinks I should .... a specialist.
3 I ought to .... the contents of this bottle: it's been open for months.
4 The doctor gave me sleeping tablets, but it's only a ....-..................... solution.
5 This is a powerful drug so I mustn't .... the stated dose.
6 I've already had a .... with one doctor, but he wasn't very helpful.

TEST YOURSELF

A From head to toe

wrist

1

2

ankle

3

bruise

GLOSSARY	
fracture	break a bone or some other hard material
unconscious	in a state like sleep, often because of an injury or an illness OPP **conscious**
dislocate	put sth (usually a bone) out of its correct position
sprain	injure a part of your body, especially your wrist or ankle, by suddenly bending or turning it SYN **twist your ankle** (NOT USUALLY **twist your wrist**)
blister	a swelling on the surface of the skin that is filled with liquid and is often caused by rubbing or burning
bruise	get or make a blue, brown, etc. mark on the skin after sb has fallen, been hit by sth, etc. **bruise** n
hundreds (of sth) inf	a lot; a large amount: *hundreds of* things to do SYN **masses (of sth)**

My cousin **fractured** his **skull**¹ when he came off his motorbike. He was **unconscious** for several minutes.
I once got a **black eye**² in a fight at school.
I **dislocated** my shoulder playing rugby.
I **sprained** my **wrist** when I fell off my bike.
I **twisted** my **ankle** running for a bus.
I used to get lots of **blisters**³ on my feet from running.
I've **bruised** myself **hundreds** of times.

SPOTLIGHT verbs, nouns and adjectives

A number of the verbs above can also be used as nouns, and some of the past participles from these verbs can be used as adjectives.

- He's got several **fractures**.
- I've got a large **bruise** on my arm.

- a **sprained wrist**
- a **twisted ankle**
- a **dislocated arm**

1 Answer *Yes* or *No.*

1 Can you talk when you're conscious? ....
2 Can you twist your eye? ....
3 Can you sprain your ankle? ....
4 Can you fracture a fingernail? ....
5 Can you bruise your hair? ....
6 Can you dislocate a finger? ....
7 Can you get a blister on your hand? ....
8 Can you write when you're unconscious? ....

2 Put the following in order from most serious (1) to least serious (6). Give your reasons.

a twisted ankle ....
a fractured skull ....
a bruise on the arm ....
a dislocated elbow ....
a black eye ....
a blister ....

3 Complete the sentences.

1 He's injured himself .... of times playing rugby.
2 The man wasn't moving. I thought he was dead, but in fact he was ....
3 He told me he got a black .... when his dog jumped up and hit him in the face.
4 When I .... my finger, the doctor put it back into position – and it hurt!
5 His arm is black and blue from the .... he got from falling off the wall.
6 Do you often get .... on your feet from walking in new shoes?
7 Clara .... her leg skiing and hasn't been able to walk for weeks.
8 I sprained my .... , and then the next day I twisted my ....

4 ABOUT YOU Write your answers, or talk to another student.

1 How many of the injuries at the top of the page have you had?
2 Which of the injuries at the top of the page require a visit to the hospital? Which require a visit to the doctor?

....
....

TEST YOURSELF

B First Aid

FIRST AID: To clean a **wound**, you need to **bathe** it **thoroughly**. For a small cut, just put on a **plaster**. For a more serious wound, especially if it is **bleeding** quite a lot, cover it with a clean **dressing** to prevent **infection**, and then hold that **in place** with a **bandage**. Most cuts **heal** within seven days.

If a part of the body is **swollen**, apply a bag of frozen peas **wrapped** in a towel to reduce the **swelling**.

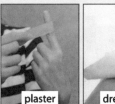
plaster
dressing
bandage

GLOSSARY

first aid	simple medical treatment that is given to sb, often before a doctor comes or before the person can be taken to a hospital	**bleed**	lose blood **bleeding** n
		in place	in the correct or usual position: **hold sth in place**
wound	an injury to a part of your body, especially a cut, and often from a weapon **wound** v (usually passive)	**heal**	(especially of a cut) become healthy again
		swollen	bigger than usual because of an injury or an illness. A **swollen** arm or leg from an injury may also be blue or purple. **swelling** n
bathe	wash part of the body, often for medical reasons		
thoroughly	in a careful and complete way	**wrap**	cover or tie sth around an object or part of the body

SPOTLIGHT *infection*

An **infection** is an illness caused by **bacteria** or a **virus**. (Both are small living things that can only be seen through a microscope.) An **infectious** illness or disease travels easily from one person to another.

---

5 Is the pronunciation of the underlined letters the same or different? Write *S* or *D*. Use the 🔵 to help you.

1. b**a**the b**a**ndage   ....
2. band**a**ge **i**nfection   ....
3. b**a**the pl**a**ster   ....
4. h**ea**l bl**ee**d   ....
5. v**i**rus **i**nfection   ....

6. w**ou**nd thor**ou**ghly   ....
7. thor**ou**ghly infecti**ou**s   ....
8. b**o**dy sw**o**llen   ....
9. w**ou**nd sw**o**llen   ....
10. bac**te**ria dr**e**ssing   ....

6 Complete the sentences.

1. We did a bit of first .... when I was at school.
2. My arm was quite .... after I fell and bruised it.
3. If I hit my nose hard, it often .... quite a bit.
4. It's not a bad cut, so I think it will .... quite quickly.
5. If you want to prevent infection, you need to clean the wound ....
6. Could you put your finger there to hold the dressing in .... ?
7. An infection can be caused by .... or a ....
8. He was .... in the leg when he was attacked by a man with a knife.
9. I put a large plaster on the cut to stop the ....
10. If you .... some packs of ice round the bruise, it will reduce the ....

7 Test your knowledge of first aid. Answer the questions.

1. What is the purpose of doing first aid? ....
2. What is the first thing you should do with a wound? ....
3. What can you put on a small cut? ....
4. Why do you need a clean dressing? ....
5. What is the purpose of a bandage? ....
6. How long does it take for most cuts to heal? ....
7. Why would you wrap frozen peas in a towel? ....
8. What is the main risk with an infectious disease or illness? ....

TEST YOURSELF

A Personal qualities

Online dating: find your dream partner

Galina's profile:

My friends describe me as a real **extrovert**. I'm an **enthusiastic**, **talkative** sort of person, but at the same time I love to hear other people's opinions. I'm also quite **decisive** and feel able to **assert myself** in different social situations. I have a very positive **attitude to** life, and I'm **truly passionate** about health and fitness. My sister describes me as a **lively** and **dynamic** person.

GLOSSARY

extrovert	a lively, confident person who enjoys being with other people OPP **introvert**; **extrovert** *adj*, **introverted**, **introvert** *adj*
enthusiastic	feeling or showing a lot of excitement or interest about sth/sb **enthusiasm** *n*
talkative	A **talkative** person likes to talk a lot.
decisive	able to make decisions quickly and with confidence
assert yourself	behave in a confident way and say clearly what you think or want **assertive** *adj*
attitude (to/towards/ about/on sth/sb)	the way you think or feel about sth/sb
truly	used to emphasize sth; very
passionate (about sth)	very enthusiastic or interested **passion (for sth)** *n*
lively	full of life and energy
dynamic	having a lot of energy and a strong personality

1 Is the pronunciation of the underlined letters the same or different? Write *S* or *D*. Use the ⒶⓅⓅ to help you.

1 d<u>y</u>namic   tr<u>u</u>ly   ....
2 pa<u>ss</u>ionate a<u>ss</u>ert   ....
3 pa<u>ss</u>ion   enthusi<u>a</u>stic ....
4 l<u>i</u>vely   d<u>y</u>namic   ....

5 talk<u>a</u>tive   intr<u>o</u>vert   ....
6 ass<u>er</u>tive   extro<u>ve</u>rt ....
7 enthu<u>si</u>asm deci<u>s</u>ive ....
8 <u>a</u>ssertive   <u>a</u>ttitude ....

2 Correct the mistake in each sentence.

1 My sister is absolutely passionate for skiing.   ....
2 She can't make up her mind about the holiday. She's not very deciding about things. ....
3 Maurice really needs to assert him in meetings. I never know what he thinks. ....
4 The professor talked with great enthusiastic about the new developments in chemistry. ....
5 Helene has a live personality and everyone likes her. ....
6 Her colleagues appreciate Anna's pleasant and dynamism manner. ....
7 My cousin has a passion of Scottish castles. He spends all his time visiting them. ....
8 I'm true passionate about the problem of global warming. ....

3 Complete the dialogues.

1 Su and Dan love climbing and they go all the time. ~ I know – they're .... about it.
2 Robina just concentrates on her own thoughts. ~ Yes, she's an ....
3 She's full of ideas and has lots of energy. ~ Yes, she's very ....
4 Oren is very confident and gets people to listen to what he thinks. ~ Yes, he's ....
5 Ryan is very interested and excited about the new school plans. ~Yes, he's very ....
6 Ruby loves to chat – she never stops. ~ Yes, she's very ....
7 Carly makes choices quickly and with confidence. ~ Yes she's very ....
8 The children are running about and having fun. ~ Yes, they're very .... today.
9 Adam's confident, open and enjoys being with people. ~ Yes, he's an ....

4 ABOUT YOU Write your answers, or talk to another student.

Who among your friends and family is …

an extrovert?   an introvert?   very talkative?   dynamic?
truly passionate about something? (What?)   assertive?   enthusiastic about cars?

▶ <u>My sister is an extrovert. She loves talking to people and is very confident.</u>

TEST YOURSELF

B Ideal match

Galina describes her ideal match:

I'm attracted to men who are **considerate** and **sensible**, and they should be happy to show **affection** too. I'm not looking for a **saint** – just a normal guy who is **sincere** and is looking for a **genuine** relationship. I don't like people who **show off** or **boast** about things. I'm interested in someone with **integrity** who is **decent** and has **ethical** values. And if they like the outdoor life, so much the better!

GLOSSARY	
considerate	thinking about other people's wishes and feelings SYN **thoughtful** OPP **inconsiderate; consideration** n
sensible	make good judgements based on reason and experience rather than emotion
affection	the feeling of liking or caring about sth/sb **affectionate** adj SYN **loving**
sincere	(of feelings or beliefs) showing what you really think SYN **genuine** OPP **insincere**
show off inf, disapproving	behave in a way that is intended to attract people's attention and make them admire you. A person who does this is a **show-off**.
boast	talk with too much pride about sth you have or can do
integrity	the quality of being honest and having strong moral principles
decent	honest, good and fair
ethical	connected with beliefs and principles about what is good and right **ethic** n: They're looking for people with a strong **work ethic**.

SPOTLIGHT *saint* and *holy*

1 A **saint** (abbreviations **S**, **St**) is a person that the Christian Church recognizes as being very **holy** (= good in a religious or moral way) because of the way they have lived or died.

2 In the text, a **saint** (inf) is a very good, kind person.

5 Positive or negative? Write *P* or *N*.

1 That woman is a real saint. ....
2 The decision is completely ethical. ....
3 He's a decent guy. ....
4 She shows off a lot. ....
5 He's very genuine. ....
6 I find him quite insincere. ....
7 She shows a lot of affection. ....
8 He's always boasting. ....
9 I think she's inconsiderate. ....
10 He has integrity. ....

6 Circle the correct word.

1 Angela arrived in an expensive outfit, covered in jewellery. I think she was *showing off / boasting*.
2 Mario adores his wife and is very *holy / affectionate* towards her.
3 I think you can trust Jamelia's judgement; she's very *affectionate / sensible*.
4 Do you think Mr Erickson is *ethical / sincere* about wanting to help us?
5 *Decent / Thoughtful* people don't go stealing from shopping malls.
6 We need people in this company who have a strong work *integrity / ethic*.
7 You have to be a *show-off / saint* to live with Duncan: he's a very difficult person.

7 Complete the sentences.

1 It's .... to give your seat to an elderly person on a bus or train.
2 Where I live, you should never show any .... to your husband or wife in the street.
3 A lot of people who .... off are unsure of themselves and are seeking attention.
4 Some people .... about their expensive holidays. It gets on my nerves.
5 .... people are kind and friendly towards strangers or foreigners.
6 People who keep you waiting for over fifteen minutes are really ....
7 In my country, shop assistants smile a lot and seem friendly, but I don't think that it's ....
8 In my country, most politicians have .... and can be trusted.

8 ABOUT YOUR COUNTRY Are the sentences in Exercise 7 true about your country? If not, what is the truth? Write your answers, or tell another student.

....
....
....

 TEST YOURSELF

Interviews were conducted on July 30th for the flight attendant training programme. We require a calm, confident and hard-working person.

	NAME	Interviewer's comments	?
	Joel Robbins	Joel seemed rather **arrogant** and **immature**. He started badly by saying some **idiotic** things about the company, showing that he wasn't at all **knowledgeable** about it. He **struggled** to answer the most basic questions.	no
	Makiko Yaguchi	I didn't know what to **make of** her at first, but as the interview progressed, I felt she was a very **capable** person, **mature** and **motivated**.	yes?
	Marek Novak	At first he **came across as** timid and **lacking in confidence**. However, as he relaxed, I could see he was actually quite **charming**. He seemed **conscientious** and **efficient**, and I think he would **take** the job **seriously**.	yes?
	Jacinta Ribeiro	I really took to Jacinta immediately. She **struck me as** a confident, **straightforward** candidate, and I feel she has great **potential**.	yes

GLOSSARY

arrogant	behaving in a proud, unpleasant way **arrogance** n
immature	behaving in a way that is typical of much younger people OPP **mature**
idiotic	very stupid SYN **ridiculous; idiot** n
knowledgeable	knowing a lot SYN **well informed**
struggle (to do sth)	try very hard to do sth when it is difficult or there are a lot of problems **struggle** n
capable	able to do things well
motivated	wanting to do sth, especially sth involving hard work **motivation** n
timid	shy and nervous
be lacking in sth	having none or not enough of sth ALSO **lack sth**

confidence	a belief in yourself and your abilities **confident** adj
charming	very pleasant **charm** n
conscientious	taking care to do things carefully and correctly
efficient	doing sth well without making mistakes or wasting time **efficiency** n
take sth/sb seriously	think that sth/sb is important and is worth your attention
take to sb/sth	start liking sb/sth
straightforward	honest and open about your feelings and opinions
potential	qualities in a person that exist and can be developed **potential** adj

SPOTLIGHT creating and forming an impression

make sth of sb understand the character of sb:
I didn't know what to **make of him. What do you make of** the new receptionist?
come across (as sth) make a particular impression SYN **come over (as sth)**:
- He **came over/across** very well in the discussion.
- He **comes over/across as** an efficient person.
  strike sb as sth give somebody a particular impression:
- She **struck me as** someone with potential. He **struck me as** odd.

1 Complete the table.

NOUN	ADJECTIVE
	arrogant
	confident
	efficient
	charming
motivation	
potential	
knowledge	
idiot	

2 Is the pronunciation of the underlined letters the same or different? Write *S* or *D*. Use the 🅰🅿🅿 to help you.

1 ma<u>t</u>ure   <u>ch</u>arm   ....
2 confid<u>e</u>nce   idi<u>o</u>t   ....
3 straightf<u>o</u>rward   well-inf<u>o</u>rmed   ....
4 p<u>o</u>tential   c<u>o</u>nfident   ....

5 ridicul<u>ou</u>s   seri<u>ou</u>sly   ....
6 c<u>a</u>pable   <u>a</u>rrogant   ....
7 ridic<u>u</u>lous   str<u>u</u>ggle   ....
8 con<u>sc</u>ientious   effi<u>c</u>ient   ....

3 Complete the dialogues in a suitable way.

1 Is Mr Morris knowledgeable about the business? ~ Yes, he's very ....
2 Does she say exactly what she wants?   ~ Yes, she's very ....
3 She seems like she's just out of school.   ~ I agree. She's too .... for our company.
4 Would he be organized and work quickly?   ~ I think so. His old boss said he was ....
5 Was it easy to fill in that long form?   ~ No, it was a real .... I didn't understand it.
6 That candidate's answers were idiotic!   ~ Yes, they were .... He'd be hopeless.
7 I liked him, but I'm worried that he's quite shy.   ~ Yes, he's rather ...., isn't he?
8 Would she have the right qualities for managing the office?   ~Yes, she seemed .... to me.

4 Rewrite the sentences using the word or a form of the word in capitals. Keep the same meaning.

1 What did you think of Aaron's character?   MAKE   .... ?
2 Josie found it hard to explain what she meant.   STRUGGLE   ....
3 Lawrence didn't seem that charming to me.   LACKING   ....
4 I didn't like Rollo at first.   TAKE   ....
5 Parminder made a very good impression in the interview.   COME   ....
6 Rupert gave me the impression of being capable.   STRIKE   ....
7 I think Ariana has qualities that can be developed.   POTENTIAL   ....
8 Vicky didn't seem to have much motivation.   MOTIVATED   ....

5 ABOUT YOU Complete the answers in a way that is true for you. If possible, talk to another student.

1 I am well informed about ....
2 I think people who are conscientious ....
3 If people are charming towards me, I ....
4 I feel confident when ....
5 It's sometimes a struggle for me to ....
6 If I meet someone who is arrogant, I ....
7 If someone doesn't take me seriously, I ....
8 I don't take to people who ....
9 In an interview situation, I think I probably come across as ....
10 If someone says something ridiculous in an interview, I think it could be because ....

📓 TEST YOURSELF

A Strong feelings

Word/Phrase	Example	Meaning
ecstatic	I was **ecstatic** about getting the new job.	very happy, excited and enthusiastic SYN **delighted, over the moon** inf
thrilled	Lou was **thrilled** to win the competition.	very excited and pleased
joy	It's always a **joy** to see the children.	sb/sth that gives you great pleasure **joyful** adj
astonished	I was **astonished** when they gave me the prize.	very surprised about sth you did not expect SYN **astounded**
shocked	I was **shocked** to hear she was so ill.	surprised and upset **shock** n, v
in tears	She was **in tears** by the time we got to the hospital.	crying; **tear** a drop of water coming from your eye
devastated	I was **devastated** when she left me.	very upset SYN **heartbroken**
desperate	Alone, without food or money, Janie was **desperate**.	having little hope and ready to do anything to change a terrible situation **desperation** n
ashamed	He stole the money, but felt very **ashamed** of himself afterwards.	guilty or embarrassed that you have done sth wrong **shame** n
disgusted	We were **disgusted** by the way the children were treated. It was awful.	very angry and upset about sth you do not like or agree with **disgust** n

1 Are these positive or negative? Write *P, N or P/N.*

1	ecstatic	5	shame	9	astonished
2	disgust	6	delighted	10	in tears
3	shock	7	desperation	11	thrilled
4	over the moon	8	joy	12	heartbroken

2 Circle the correct word(s) in italics. Sometimes both answers are correct.
1 I was *ashamed / astounded* when I heard that I'd come top in the exam.
2 Our daughter passed her driving test and we were *over the moon / devastated*.
3 My cat was killed in front of me by a driver; I was *heartbroken / joyful*.
4 There were cats on the table in the hotel kitchen. I was *thrilled / disgusted*.
5 Our team won the championship and we were all *desperate / ecstatic*.
6 The news about the flood was terribly sad: my sister was *in tears / delighted*.
7 My son was born on New Year's Day, and my family were *delighted / shocked*.
8 My brother has been missing for a week now and my dad and I are *ashamed / desperate*.

3 Complete the dialogues using vocabulary from the table.
1 I think she was very surprised at the news. ~ She was – absolutely ....
2 Mac's lost 20 kg because of his illness. ~ Yes, I was .... when I saw him.
3 Did he think he wouldn't be rescued? ~ Yes. He was ....
4 Was he terribly upset about the results? ~ Yes, he was absolutely ....
5 That boy cheated in his exams. ~ He should be very .... of himself.
6 I bet they were over the moon. ~ Yes, they were absolutely ....
7 She was really emotional about losing her job. ~ Yes, she was in ....
8 The hotel bedroom was really dirty. ~ Yes, I was .... when I saw it.

 TEST YOURSELF

B Expressing your emotions

ARE YOU the kind of person who **bottles up your emotions**? Do you find it difficult to **handle intense** feelings, or do you just **suppress** them? Do you feel that if you **reveal** too much about yourself, you could make yourself rather **vulnerable**. **Psychologists** say that suppressing your emotions over a long period of time is often ineffective and can **worsen** the situation. It can even lead to **severe anxiety** and **depression** at a later stage.

GLOSSARY

bottle sth up	stop yourself showing negative emotions or feelings especially over a long time: ***bottle up your emotions/feelings***
handle	deal with sth/sb: ***handle stress / your emotions***
intense	very strong, very great
suppress	stop yourself from having or expressing a feeling/emotion
reveal	make sth known to sb SYN **disclose** *formal*
vulnerable	weak and easily hurt, physically or emotionally
worsen	become or make sth worse than before
severe	extremely bad or serious
anxiety	the state of feeling nervous or worried that sth bad is going to happen **anxious** *adj*
depression	a medical condition in which sb feels very sad and anxious for a long time **depressed** *adj*

SPOTLIGHT *psychology* and related words

Psychology is the study of the mind and how it affects people's behaviour. A person who is trained in psychology is a **psychologist**. **Psychological** problems relate to the way somebody's mind works, e.g. some pain can be psychological rather than physical.

4 Underline the main stress on these words. Use the 🔊 to help you.

reveal	vulnerable	anxiety	worsen
severe	disclose	psychological	intense
anxious	psychology	psychologist	suppress

5 Replace the underlined word(s) with a word that has the same meaning.

1 I did a course in <u>the study of the mind and behaviour</u> at university. ....
2 He wouldn't <u>disclose</u> information if he thought it was secret. ....
3 It's a difficult time for him and he's <u>weak and easily hurt</u>. ....
4 Things have <u>got a lot worse</u> since the elections. ....
5 Donna has been suffering from <u>a very serious</u> depression. ....
6 I don't think Steven is <u>dealing with</u> the stress of school very well. ....
7 She has <u>very strong</u> feelings about Alastair; it's a love/hate relationship. ....
8 Last year I suffered from a period of <u>worry and nervousness</u>. ....

6 Complete the questions.

1 Do top sports people tend to .... stress well or badly?
2 Is it good for powerful people to show they are .... and have weaknesses?
3 Can you think of any problems that .... are currently studying?
4 Are there times when it's good to .... your emotions and stay silent?
5 How can people deal with .... feelings of loneliness?
6 Are there any professions where you think people suffer a lot from .... ?
7 What's the best thing to do if you're feeling very .... about something?
8 If you .... your emotions, do you think it affects your physical health?
9 Do you .... your anxieties or deeper emotions to a friend or a family member?
10 Have you ever studied .... at school or university? Would you like to?

7 ABOUT YOU **Write your answers to Exercise 6, or ask another student.**

....
....
....

 TEST YOURSELF

A Difficult relationships

When I married Vince, he already had two children from his first marriage, and they **took an instant dislike to** me. They **blamed** me for all their problems. I tried hard to get their **respect**, but they wouldn't **forgive** me for taking the place of their mother. They either **stared at** me without saying a thing, or were openly **aggressive**. It was a **tough** time, and it was **inevitable** that it finally **put a strain on** my relationship with Vince. I began to **regret** my decision to marry him. Fortunately, he **stuck up for me** when the kids were difficult, and over time, things **settled down** a bit.

SPOTLIGHT meanings of *tough*

Tough can mean:
1 difficult: *He had a **tough** childhood.* (as in the text)
2 strong and able to deal with difficult situations: *She'll be OK – she's **tough**.*
3 strict: *There are some **tough** new driving laws.*

GLOSSARY

take an instant/immediate dislike to sb	dislike sb as soon as you meet them	**aggressive**	angry and ready to attack sb
blame sb (for sth)	think or say that sb is responsible for sth bad	**inevitable**	that you cannot avoid or prevent **inevitably** *adv*
respect	polite behaviour towards sb/sth that you think is important	**put a strain on sb/sth**	create pressure and anxiety for sb/sth
		regret (sth / doing sth)	feel sorry about sth you have done
forgive sb (for sth/for doing sth)	stop feeling angry towards sb for sth that they have done wrong	**stick up for sb/yourself**	support and defend sb/yourself when they/you are criticized
stare (at sb/sth)	look at sb/sth for a long time	**settle down**	become calmer, more relaxed and less excited

1 **Positive or negative? Write *P* or *N*.**

1 The protests are putting a strain on the country. ....
2 I think he's forgiven me. ....
3 He's very aggressive. ....
4 She can stick up for herself. ....
5 She blames me for what happened. ....
6 Things are tough at work now. ....
7 Being poor has made him tough. ....
8 I really regret contacting him. ....
9 Things have settled down since the strike. ....
10 The war was inevitable. ....

2 **Complete the sentences.**

1 I don't .... leaving the job: it was the right decision.
2 As soon as I met him, I took an immediate .... to him.
3 The food was my responsibility, so I don't .... anyone else for the mistake in the order.
4 The lack of money put a terrible .... on our relationship.
5 Some children do what they like and have no .... for authority.
6 Please don't .... at those people; it's rude.
7 My brother accepted that he caused the accident, but I .... him; he's my brother.
8 Mum accused me of lying, but my sister .... up for me and said I was telling the truth.

3 **One word is missing in each line. Where does it go? Write it at the end of the line.**

I've been having a time at work recently. A young man joined the ... **1** ....
department and for some reason an instant dislike to me. His desk was close to mine, ... **2** ....
and he just sat and at me without speaking, which made me feel uncomfortable. ... **3** ....
Over time, he started to shout at me and became more and more until I felt ... **4** ....
quite nervous being near him. It put a big on me and my work began to suffer. ... **5** ....
One day, I decided it was time to stick for myself, so I told him his behaviour was ... **6** ....
terrible. I was shocked when he suddenly started crying and, of course, I what I ... **7** ....
had said to him. He thought that I him for the poor results in the department, when ... **8** ....
in fact, that wasn't the case. Eventually, things down, and we got on much better. ... **9** ....

📖 TEST YOURSELF

B Successful relationships

Now two years on, things are **looking up**. **Initially** the kids were really **nasty** to me and **reluctant** to **accept** me, but I gave up work to spend more time with them, and that helped to create a closer **bond**. I realized that I had been too **strict** with them and not **caring** enough; I just wasn't **sensitive to** their needs. To be honest, it was my own **fault** – I'm the adult and should have known better. It takes a lot of **patience**, but I'm feeling optimistic and I really enjoy being with them now.

GLOSSARY

look up *inf*	(of sb's situation or business) start to become better after a difficult period
initially	in the beginning **initial** *adj*
nasty	unkind; unpleasant SYN **mean**
reluctant (to do sth)	not wanting to do sth SYN **unwilling**; **reluctance** *n*
bond	a connection between people based on shared feelings or experiences
strict	If you are **strict**, you make people do what you want and do not allow them to behave badly.
caring	kind and showing that you care about people
sensitive (to sth)	understanding other people's feelings and being careful about them
fault	If sth bad is your **fault**, you made it happen.
patience	the ability to stay calm and not get angry when waiting for sth **patient** *adj*

SPOTLIGHT *accept*

Accept means 'say yes to an offer', but has some other meanings, too.

1 allow sb to be part of a group:
 They **accepted me** as one of the family. (as in the text)
2 agree to sth:
 The council has **accepted** the latest proposal.
3 admit you did sth wrong:
 I **accept responsibility for** the mistakes.

---

4 **Is the pronunciation of the underlined letters the same or different? Write *S* or *D*. Use the 📱 to help you.**

1 initi**a**lly reluct**a**nt ....
2 p**a**tience ini**t**ial ....
3 stri**c**t a**cc**ept ....

4 f**au**lt b**o**nd ....
5 loo**k** **c**aring ....
6 **s**ensitive reluctan**c**e ....

5 **Circle the correct word.**

1 She showed a *reluctance / unwilling* to speak about the event.
2 The *initial / initially* problem was money.
3 He's *sensible / sensitive* to the feelings of others.

4 She's a *caring / patience* nurse.
5 The mistake wasn't my *bond / fault*.
6 It can be a good thing if parents are *nasty / strict*.
7 My business is finally *accepting / looking up*.

6 **Replace the underlined word(s) with a word or phrase that keeps the same meaning.**

1 It's not my underlined responsibility if we're late. ....
2 They were very unwilling to leave. ....
3 She expects people to obey her all the time. ....
4 In the beginning it was a difficult relationship. ....
5 He admits responsibility for what happened. ....
6 I have no ability to wait for things for a long time. ....
7 It was strange moving to a different country, but I now feel welcome. ....
8 I had a tough time last year but things are improving now. ....
9 The children said some very unpleasant things about me. ....
10 There is a special connection between parents and their children. ....

📑 TEST YOURSELF

A Personal heroes

My **heroine** is my aunt Georgia, who worked with homeless teenagers. She was deeply **spiritual**, and I admire her **courage** and **dignity**. More than anyone, she has **inspired** me to **dedicate** my life to looking after people.

I really **looked up to** my grandfather. He was a lifeboat **captain** for 20 years, and showed remarkable **bravery** on many occasions – at times he was truly **heroic**.

GLOSSARY	
heroine	a woman who you admire for doing sth brave or good. A man is a **hero**. **heroic** *adj* showing extreme courage **heroism** *n*
spiritual	connected with your spirit, rather than the physical world
courage	the ability to do sth, even though it is dangerous, frightening or very difficult SYN **bravery**; **courageous**, **brave** *adj*
dignity	the ability to behave in a calm and serious manner in a difficult situation **dignified** *adj*
inspire	give sb the enthusiasm and desire to do sth **inspiration** *n*; **inspirational** *adj*
dedicate yourself/sth to (doing) sth	give a lot of time and effort to a particular activity or purpose because you think it is important
look up to sb	admire and respect sb, often sb older or in a higher position
captain	the person in charge of a ship or plane

1 Is the pronunciation of the underlined letters the same or different? Write *S* or *D*. Use the 🔊 to help you.

1 h<u>e</u>ro h<u>e</u>roism ....
2 cour<u>age</u> cour<u>age</u>ous ....
3 insp<u>i</u>re insp<u>i</u>ration ....
4 inspir<u>a</u>tion dedic<u>a</u>te ....
5 capt<u>ai</u>n sp<u>i</u>ritual ....
6 di<u>g</u>nity coura<u>g</u>e ....
7 dignif<u>ied</u> braver<u>y</u> ....
8 her<u>oi</u>ne her<u>oi</u>c ....

2 Complete the sentences with the correct form of the word in capitals.

1 He was so .... COURAGE
2 She's a personal .... of mine. HERO
3 She showed great .... BRAVE
4 He .... me in my work. INSPIRATION
5 I admired her .... DIGNIFIED
6 His behaviour was .... HERO
7 She was an .... leader. INSPIRE
8 He is a very .... person. SPIRIT

3 Complete the texts.

1 The person who has always been my .... is my mother. She looked after us all throughout the war. I was born during the war, and when the government tried to take us children away to another part of the country, she was very .... and fought to keep us with her.

2 I always .... up to my uncle. He was a .... in the navy and he .... me to join the navy myself when I grew up. On several occasions he rescued migrants who were lost at sea. To me he was a ....

3 Rosa Parks is a personal .... of mine. She refused to give up her seat on the bus in Alabama, a protest which eventually led to the end of 'white only' buses. She acted with great .... She said of herself, 'I was a person with .... and self-respect, and I should not set my sights* lower than anybody else just because I was black'.
* = decide that you want sth and try very hard to get it

4 ABOUT YOU Write your answers, or ask another student.
Do you have a personal hero or heroine? Who?
Who do you look up to? Why?
Do you know anyone who you would describe as courageous? Who?

....
....
....

TEST YOURSELF

B Personal villains

> Pop stars often start off as **rebels** with strong moral **principles**. But when they achieve **fame** and become rich, their **values** can change completely. I **loathe** that.

> I don't **approve of** drivers who **lose their temper** with other road users.

> A few boys **bullied** me at school, and since then I've always **despised bullies**.

> I **can't bear** all the rich, **greedy** people who seem to run the country. They are responsible for such **misery**.

SPOTLIGHT *principles and values*

Principles are strong beliefs that influence how you behave. **Values** (*pl*) are beliefs about what is right, wrong and important in life.
The words are very similar in meaning but are used in different expressions.
- *Eating meat is **against my principles**.*
- *I won't go there **on principle**.*
- *She has a different **set of values**.*

GLOSSARY

villain	a person who is morally bad or responsible for causing trouble or harm	bully	use your power to hurt or frighten a weaker person, or make them do sth. The person who does the **bullying** is a **bully**.
rebel	sb who opposes people in authority **rebel** *v*; **rebellious** *adj*	despise	hate and have no respect for sb/sth **despicable** *adj*
fame	the state of being famous	can't bear	*(usually in negatives and questions)* If you **can't bear** sth, you cannot accept or deal with sth because it is unpleasant. SYN **can't stand**
loathe	dislike sb/sth very much SYN **detest**		
approve (of sb/sth)	have a positive feeling towards sth/sb OPP **disapprove (of sb/sth)**; **approval** *n* OPP **disapproval**	greedy	wanting more food, power, etc. than you need **greed** *n*
lose your temper	become very angry	misery	great suffering of the mind or body SYN **distress**

5 Circle the words which are verbs.

rebelapprovaldetestfameprincipledespiseloseyourtemperdisapproveloathegreedbully

6 Complete the sentences.

1 The opposite of *approval* is ....
2 *Detest* means the same as ....
3 The related adjective for *despise* is ....
4 The related adjective for *rebel* is ....
5 *Distress* is another word for ....
6 The related adjective for *greed* is ....
7 *Can't stand* means the same as ....
8 *Approve* is followed by the preposition ....
9 The noun related to *famous* is ....
10 *Values* and .... have a similar meaning.

7 Complete the questions with words from the box in the correct form.

against	disapprove	rebellious	temper	villain	bear
greedy	rebel	values	bully	principle	despise

1 Do brothers sometimes .... their sisters, or can the opposite be true?
2 Is there anything you won't eat on .... ?
3 Do you often lose your .... ?
4 Are there any types of car drivers that you can't .... ?
5 As a teenager, were you a .... ? If so, what were you .... about?
6 Is it .... your principles to borrow money from friends?
7 Do you .... of any of your friends' partners? Why?
8 In your country, do young people and older people have different sets of .... ?
9 Do you think rich people are .... and just want more and more?
10 Is there anyone you .... and would consider a .... ?

8 ABOUT YOU Write your answers to the questions in Exercise 7, or ask another student.

....

....

 TEST YOURSELF

A Influences on behaviour

Why do we behave the way we do? Is it a case of **nature** or **nurture**?
According to behavioural psychologist Michael Woods, various factors
have an **impact on** our lives.

Parents **play a crucial part**; other **role models** are less **influential**.
Peer pressure is a significant factor.
People respond positively to **incentives**, but not the threat of punishments.
A **broken home** or **deprived** childhood needn't have a **damaging effect**.

ABOUT YOU

GLOSSARY

nature	the basic character of a person: *Violence isn't **in his nature**.*	**peer pressure**	the influence on your behaviour of people around you of the same age
nurture	the care and attention given to help sb develop **nurture** v	**incentive (to do sth)**	sth that encourages you to do sth, work harder, etc.
impact (on sth)	an effect or influence (on sth)	**broken home**	a family in which the parents are divorced or separated
play a part (in sth)	be involved and influential in developing sth	**deprived**	without sufficient food, education or money **deprive** v; **deprivation** n
crucial	extremely important because it will affect other things	**damaging**	having a bad effect on sb/sth: *a damaging effect* OPP **beneficial**
role model	a person you admire and learn from		
influential	able to influence the way other people think or behave		

1 **Find six compounds or phrases in the box.**

effect	nature or	pressure	a part	a deprived	a beneficial
a broken	peer	play	childhood	home	nurture?

....
....

2 **Are these positive or negative statements? Write *P* or *N*.**

1 She felt nurtured in the children's home.   ....
2 She's an influential role model.   ....
3 There is a lot of deprivation in this town.   ....
4 The amount of work had a damaging
  effect on me.   ....

5 More money proved to be a real incentive.   ....
6 A month's break was highly beneficial.   ....
7 He smoked because of peer pressure.   ....
8 Their broken home had an impact on
  the boys.   ....

3 **Complete the text.**

Danny's story is interesting. He came from a broken **(1)** ...., had a fairly **(2)** ....
childhood, and was stealing by the age of 13, largely because of peer **(3)** .... He also got into fights,
although it wasn't in his **(4)** .... to be violent. Then he started going to a local boxing club, which
had a real **(5)** .... on his life. The man who ran it was Danny's first positive role **(6)** .... ,
and he played a **(7)** .... part in changing Danny's attitude to life. His behaviour changed completely:
he gave up crime and became dedicated to his sport. He might even win a place in England's amateur boxing
team at the next Olympics, and that is a real **(8)** .... for him to train hard.

4 ABOUT YOU **Do you agree with the statements at the top of the page? Write your answers, or ask
another student.**

 TEST YOURSELF

B Teenage behaviour

COPING WITH ADOLESCENCE

When **adolescents** are making the **transition** to **adulthood**, their **conduct** can change a lot and can be difficult for parents. Teenagers need you to be **supportive** and **sympathetic** as they try to find their way towards independence. Encourage them to talk about their problems, but only **in their own time** and at their own **pace**. If you are **wise**, you will try to be **consistent** in the way you deal with them, and help them **cope with** the changes in their needs and emotions. And remember that it's just a **phase** they're going through.

GLOSSARY

cope (with sth)	deal successfully with sth difficult
transition (from sth to sth)	a change from one state or form to another
conduct	a person's behaviour in a particular place or situation
supportive	giving help or support to sb in a difficult situation
sympathetic (to/towards sb)	showing that you understand other people's feelings, especially their problems **sympathy** n
in your own time	when you are ready
pace	the speed at which sth happens: *at your own pace* (= as fast or as slowly as you like)
wise	able to make sensible decisions or give good advice because of your experience or knowledge **wisdom** n; **gain wisdom** become wiser
consistent	always having the same opinions, standards, etc. and not changing them
phase	a stage in the development of sth: *go through a phase*

5 **Circle the correct word.**

1 When you work with teenagers, you need to be *sympathetic / grown-up*.
2 My son has just become a *teenage / teenager*.
3 I think it's just a difficult phase she's going *through / to*.
4 What are the main problems for teenagers during *adolescents / adolescence*?
5 Just make your choices at your own *pace / time*.
6 Ariel's attitude changes all the time: she's not very *wise / consistent*.
7 Ollie's successfully made the transition from adolescence to *adult / adulthood*.
8 Cora is 17 now, so she isn't a *teenager / grown-up* yet.

6 **Complete the sentences using suitable words from the top of the page.**

1 It's always .... to think carefully before you speak.
2 The best way to .... with difficult situations is to laugh about them.
3 The most difficult .... of your life is in your twenties.
4 If you have problems, it helps to have a .... friend or partner.
5 The .... from childhood to adolescence is an easy one.
6 You need to be .... when creating rules for your children to live by.
7 You can only gain .... through years of life experience.
8 In order to get through your teenage years, you have to make decisions in your own .... and at your own ....
9 When your mother starts asking you for advice, you know you're an ....
10 I have great .... for families who are struggling with problem teenagers.
11 People accept bad .... from teenagers but not so easily from adults.

7 ABOUT YOU **Do you agree with the sentences in Exercise 6? Why? / Why not? Write your answers, or talk to another student.**

....
....
....

TEST YOURSELF

There is a **tendency** among some women to believe that **however hard** you try, you end up like your mother. Well, **it's hard to say** if that's **the case** with me because my mother **passed away** when I was only nine, and my father was left a **widower**. He did remarry several years later, and I was **brought up** by my father and **stepmother**. I know the **presence** of a new woman in the family can be difficult, but we have always had a really positive relationship. We are not **alike** in looks or character, but I think I've **picked up** one or two of her good habits. For example, I always remember to write **personally** to thank people for birthday or Christmas presents.

By my **teens**, my father told me that I was starting to **resemble** my mother a bit more, and it seems I have got one or two of her **characteristics**. (Like me, she didn't **take criticism** very well!) But I think it's now increasingly **apparent** that I **take after** my father more in character and behaviour. That's fine by me, although it seems to be the opposite with my two **siblings**, both sisters. My dad says that they **remind** him much more **of** my mother.

me with my mother when I was nine

me now at the age of 21

GLOSSARY			
tendency	If sb has a particular **tendency**, they are likely to behave or act in a particular way.	alike	very similar
however	used with an adjective or adverb to mean 'to whatever degree': *however hard, however much*	pick sth up	get a skill, habit, etc. by chance, without making an effort to get it
it's hard to say	= it's difficult to give an opinion	personally	by a particular person and not someone else
the case	the true situation	teens	the period between 13 and 19: *They're in their teens.*
pass away	die. We sometimes use **pass away** to avoid saying *die*. SYN **pass on**	characteristic	a typical feature or quality that sb has **characteristic (of sb/sth)** *adj*
widower	a man whose wife/husband has died. A **widow** is a woman whose husband/wife has died. We can use **late** in formal English to talk about sb's dead wife/husband: *the property of his late wife*	criticism	the act of expressing unhappiness and disapproval with sb/sth: *He can't take any criticism*; **criticize** *v*
bring sb up (*often passive*)	care for a child, teaching them how to behave, etc. SYN **raise**	apparent	easy to see or understand SYN **obvious**
		sibling *formal*	a brother or a sister
stepmother	the woman who is married to your father but is not your real mother ALSO **stepfather/daughter/son**, etc.	remind sb of sb/sth	If sb/sth **reminds** you of sb/sth else, they make you remember or think about the other person, place, thing, etc. because they are similar in some way.
presence	(of a person) the fact of being in a particular place		

SPOTLIGHT expressing family similarities

If you **resemble someone/something**, you look like or are similar to another person/thing. The emphasis is more on looks than character. **resemblance** *n*

If you **take after someone**, you look or behave like an older member of your family.

If you **follow in someone's footsteps**, you do the same job or have the same lifestyle as someone else, usually a member of your family.

1 **How many syllables are there in each of these words?**

tendency ....   widower ....   personally ....   resemblance ....
alike ....   characteristic ....   criticism ....   apparent ....

2 **Is the pronunciation of the underlined letters the same or different? Write S or D. Use the APP to help you.**

1 remi̱nd si̱bling   ....
2 si̱bling wi̱dower   ....
3 pre̱sence remi̱nd   ....
4 tende̱ncy obvio̱us   ....
5 apparent ali̱ke   ....
6 critici̱ze ali̱ke   ....

3 **Repace the underlined words with a word or phrase that keeps the same meaning.**

1 She is between 13 and 19.   ....
2 They aren't very similar.   ....
3 She looks like her mother.   ....
4 He has three brothers and sisters.   ....
5 It's difficult to give an opinion whether it will work.   ....
6 I'm not sure if that's the true situation with him.   ....
7 Her mother died last year.   ....
8 Constant optimism is just one of his typical features.   ....

4 **Complete the sentences**

1 Her husband died in the war so she's been a .... for many years.
2 If I speak to him .... , then I'm sure he'll understand.
3 There's a strong .... between the two sisters. People often say they are ....
4 .... hard I work, I still can't seem to understand this subject.
5 If you see them together, it's .... that they are twins.
6 Lea was upset because her mum .... her for wearing too much make-up.
7 I'm like Mum, but Martha .... after Dad much more in the way she behaves.
8 My mum wants to be there. She thinks the .... of a parent will make a difference.
9 My brother .... up playing guitar just from watching and listening to other guitarists.
10 I have a .... to talk too much when I'm nervous.

5 **Complete the dialogues with a word or phrase.**

1 Does Lucy .... you .... anyone? ~ Yes. She's just like Rachel, isn't she?
2 I had to tell Ben his work wasn't good enough. ~ I know, and he doesn't take .... very well, does he?
3 Will Joasia be a doctor like her dad? ~ Yes, I believe she's following ....
4 Have you always lived in London? ~ No, I was .... in the country, and moved here when I was 18.
5 Do you think your family will like your new girlfriend? ~ I don't know. It's ....
6 Is Don your real father? ~ No, he's my ....
7 Have you .... read the document? ~ Not yet, but I've heard what it contains.
8 Did his father run the company? ~ No, his .... mother did until her death.

6 ABOUT YOU **Write your answers, or talk to another student.**

1 Do you resemble either your mother or father?
2 Do you think you take after one of your parents more than the other?
3 If you have siblings, do you think you are alike in either looks and/or character?
4 Do you think there are any characteristics that are common to different members of your family?
5 Do you agree that daughters usually end up like their mothers? Do you think it might also be true that sons end up like their fathers?
6 Do you think you take criticism well?

....
....

TEST YOURSELF

A Table manners

chopsticks

In <u>Japan</u>, it is **considered** rude to cross your chopsticks, **lick** them, or **stick** them vertically into a bowl of rice and leave them pointing **upwards**.

In <u>France</u>, don't offer to **split** the bill: it is not **regarded as** very **sophisticated**. You either pay the bill, or someone else does.

In <u>the Philippines</u>, it is considered **good manners** to eat all the food on your plate.

In <u>Afghanistan</u>, wasting food is **unacceptable**. Eating or talking with your mouth full is **viewed as** being **discourteous**.

In <u>China</u>, it is **customary** to pass food to the elderly first. It can be **offensive** to remove rice from a bowl with a spoon.

GLOSSARY	
lick	move your tongue over the surface of sth in order to eat it, make it wet or clean it
stick	push sth, usually sth quite sharp, into sth else
upwards	moving or pointing towards a higher position OPP **downwards**
split	divide sth into two or more parts, and share it between different people
sophisticated	having experience of the world and knowing about fashion, culture, etc. OPP **unsophisticated**; **sophistication** n
manners pl	behaviour that is considered polite in a particular society or culture: *It's good/bad manners to …*
unacceptable	not agreed or approved of by most people in society OPP **acceptable**
discourteous	having bad manners and not showing respect for other people OPP **courteous**; **courtesy** n
customary	usually done in a particular place or situation
offensive	rude in a way that makes sb upset or annoyed OPP **inoffensive**; **offend** v

SPOTLIGHT *consider, regard, view*

These verbs all mean to think about something in a particular way. They are commonly used in passive constructions like this:
- *Apologizing is **considered (to be)** the correct thing to do.*
- *Apologizing is **regarded/viewed as** the correct thing to do.*

1 Write the opposites.

1	sophisticated	....	3	upwards	....	5 acceptable ....
2	offensive	....	4	courteous	....	6 good manners ....

2 Complete the sentences using the correct form of the word in capitals.

1 Their behaviour doesn't show much .... SOPHISTICATED
2 I'm sure it wasn't his intention to .... you. OFFENSIVE
3 Is it .... to arrive ten minutes late for a dinner? CUSTOM
4 His behaviour is occasionally rude and .... ACCEPT
5 The waiters are always very .... and polite. COURTESY
6 It was an .... remark, but for some reason it upset her. OFFENSIVE

3 Complete the words in the sentences.

1 It is quite c............................ to eat chicken legs or wings with your fingers.
2 Parents think it's important for children to have good table m............................ .
3 It is c............................ bad manners to eat everything you are given.
4 It is v............................ as polite to offer food to the elderly first.
5 It's d............................ to start eating your food before others have been served.
6 It's r............................ to criticize the host's food.
7 Talking with your mouth full might not be considered very s............................ .
8 It is customary among young people to s............................ the bill in restaurants.
9 It is viewed as rude to l............................ your knife, fork or spoon when you have finished eating, or
   s............................ your own knife, fork or spoon into dishes of food for the whole table.

4 ABOUT YOUR COUNTRY Are the sentences in Exercise 3 true or false, or does it depend on different factors? Write your answers, or ask another student.

 TEST YOURSELF

B Polite or impolite?

Dan Ella's behaviour is **exceptional** for a child of six.

Beth Yes, but that brother of hers is a bit **cheeky**.

....

Jo I don't think Giulio will **take offence** if you leave the party early.

Tom I just don't want to **put my foot in it**. I want to **impress** his family, and that wouldn't help.

Jo Well, you'd better **be on your best behaviour**, then!

....

Kaz I really **took exception** to Adam's **remarks**. He thought they were **humorous**, but actually, they were **deeply** offensive.

Ben Yes, I couldn't agree more. They showed a real lack of **judgement**. He has no **notion** of how to behave.

GLOSSARY	
exceptional	unusually good SYN **outstanding**
cheeky *inf*	(often used by adults about children) rude, often in an amusing way **cheek** *n*
take offence (at sth)	be upset or offended by sth that sb has said or done
put your foot in it (with sb) *inf*	accidentally say sth that offends or upsets sb
impress	If sth/sb **impresses** you, you admire it/them. **impressed** *adj*
be on your best behaviour	behave in the most polite way you can
take exception (to sth)	object strongly to sth and be angry about it
remark	a few words that give your opinion about sth SYN **comment**
humorous	funny and entertaining; showing a **sense of humour**
deeply	very; very much: ***deeply offensive/ upsetting/hurtful***
judgement	the ability to form opinions or make sensible decisions: ***show good/poor judgement***
notion (of sth)	an idea or an understanding of sth

5 **Is the speaker happy or unhappy? Write *H* or *U*.**

1 My wife has outstanding judgement. ....
2 I put my foot in it with Carla. ....
3 She took offence at my remark. ....
4 My boss has no sense of humour. ....
5 I made a really humorous comment. ....
6 I took exception to the criticism. ....
7 The hosts impressed me. ....
8 My little girl was on her best behaviour. ....

6 **Circle the words in italics which are possible. All three may be.**

1 He was *outstanding / put his foot in it / on his best behaviour*.
2 She made *a humorous / an upsetting / a cheeky* remark.
3 What she said showed *poor / impressed / good* judgement.
4 Unfortunately, she took *exception to / offence at / her foot in* what I said.
5 That little boy's behaviour is *exceptional / cheek / outstanding*.
6 I thought the comment deeply *offensive / poor / upsetting*.
7 He has *a sense of humour / no notion of politeness / poor judgement*.
8 He's not always well behaved but today he *impressed me / had no sense of humour / was exceptional*.

7 **Complete the texts.**

I have a very unusual friend called Erwin who likes to try and **(1)** .... people – he loves being admired. He's incredibly polite and has **(2)** .... table manners. I always feel rather uncomfortable with him, because I feel I have to be on my best **(3)** .... all the time. I'm very nervous about putting my **(4)** .... in it, especially if I go to his place for dinner. If I get there even five minutes late, he seems to take **(5)** ....

I've taken a strong dislike to one of the guys who works for me. He's very rude; in fact, I'd say he's **(6)** .... offensive. The other day he made a rude **(7)** .... about my appearance, which frankly is none of his business, and I really took **(8)** .... to it. Calling me 'carrot top' because of my red hair showed very poor **(9)** ...., I felt. He thought it was a **(10)** .... comment, but I didn't find it funny at all.

TEST YOURSELF

24) Food

A Fruit, vegetables, etc.

 1 **avocado**

 2 **mango**

 3 **watermelon**

 4 **grapefruit**

 5 **apricots**

 6 **raspberries**

 7 **raisins** (a type of **dried fruit**)

 8 **aubergines**

 9 **celery**

 10 **asparagus**

 11 **courgettes**

 12 **beetroot**

 13 **spinach**

 14 **broccoli**

 15 **almonds** (a type of **nut**)

 16 **basil** (a type of **herb**)

 17 **lentils** (a type of **pulse**)

 18 **ginger** (a type of **spice**)

---

1 **Is the pronunciation of the underlined letters the same or different? Write *S* or *D*. Use the 🔊 to help you.**

1   a̲vocado a̲pricot ....
2   gr**a**pefruit r**a**spberry ....
3   a̲ubergine avocad**o̲** ....
4   asparagus alm**o̲**nd ....

5   w**a̲**termelon c**o̲**urgette ....
6   aubergine gin**g**er ....
7   spin**a̲**ch g**i**nger ....
8   aub**e̲**rgine cel**e̲**ry ....

2 **Complete the foods.**

1   ma.................................
2   au.................................
3   bee.................................
4   av.................................
5   ra.................................
6   asp.................................

7   wat.................................
8   cou.................................
9   gra.................................
10   sp.................................
11   apr.................................
12   bro.................................

3 **Complete the sentences in a logical way.**

1   Celery is a type of ....
2   Basil is a type of ....
3   Almonds are a type of ....

4   Raisins are a type of .... fruit.
5   Ginger is a type of ....
6   Lentils are a ....

4 **Answer the questions.**

1   Which of the fruits at the top of the page have a stone in the middle?   ....
2   Which of the vegetables at the top of the page can you eat cooked or raw?   ....
3   Why do you normally add basil or ginger to food?   ....
4   Are nuts and lentils healthy or unhealthy?   ....

5 ABOUT YOU AND YOUR COUNTRY **Write your answers, or talk to another student.**

1   Tick (✔) the foods that you often grow in your country.
2   Put a cross (✗) by the ones you think you have never eaten.
3   Can you add to the list six more types of fruit, six vegetables, another nut, another herb, another dried fruit and another spice?

....

TEST YOURSELF

B Kitchen equipment

Equipment	used to ...	what?
deep-fat fryer	deep-fry	fish, potatoes, etc.
casserole	braise/stew (cook meat slowly in liquid in a closed container)	meat, vegetables
food processor	chop, slice, mix	meat, vegetables, etc.
whisk	beat SYN whisk	eggs, cream
colander	drain	vegetables, pasta, etc. that have been washed or cooked in water

Equipment	used to ...	what?
grater	grate	cheese, e.g. parmesan
peeler	peel	vegetables, fruit
lemon-squeezer	squeeze	lemons, oranges, limes
corkscrew	open	wine bottles
kitchen scales	weigh	all types of food
carving knife	carve	usually meat
frying pan	fry	meat, fish, vegetables

6 Find six compound words in the box.

frying	lemon-	kitchen	food	carving	deep-fat
processor	fryer	pan	knife	squeezer	scales

....

....

7 Write down the equipment you would need to ...

1 drain vegetables cooked in water ....
2 braise/stew meat ....
3 open a bottle of wine ....
4 chop and slice vegetables ....

5 beat eggs ....
6 weigh food ....
7 cut meat into slices ....
8 fry meat or vegetables ....

8 Write down a food or type of food you often ...

1 squeeze ....
2 grate ....
3 deep-fry ....
4 weigh ....

5 slice ....
6 braise ....
7 carve ....
8 peel ....

9 ABOUT YOU How much of the kitchen equipment above do you think you have in your kitchen? Are there any items of equipment you don't have that would be very useful?

....

 TEST YOURSELF

A Taste

☆☆☆☆☆   ★☆☆☆☆   ★★☆☆☆   ★★★☆☆   ★★★★☆   ★★★★★

☆☆☆☆☆

I thought the food looked quite **appetizing**, but I soon changed my mind. First of all, the bread was **stale**. I then started with very **salty** ham with melon, which wasn't **ripe**. My main course was a type of curry, which I thought would be really **spicy**, but was actually quite **bland**. My husband ordered a **rare** steak (hoping it would be **lean** and **juicy**), but instead got a piece of grey meat that was **well done** and **tough**. And the cooked vegetables were almost **raw**. The chocolate tart for dessert was far too **rich** – and very **fattening**. That was probably my mistake. Anyway, we finished with coffee that was very **bitter**. We won't be going back!

wendy
waytogo

> **SPOTLIGHT** adjectives ending in -y
>
> Adjectives ending in -y are often used to describe flavours and smells, e.g. **salty**, **spicy**, **creamy**, **fruity**, **juicy**, **greasy** (= full of oil from cooking), etc. They can mean 'full of something'.
> - *This soup's very **salty**.*
> Or they can mean 'having a similar flavour/smell'.
> - *chicken with a **spicy** sauce*
> - *a wine with a **fruity** smell*

GLOSSARY

appetizing	(of food) that looks or smells attractive, making you feel hungry. An **appetite** is a strong desire for sth, especially food.	**lean**	(of meat) having little or no fat
		tough	(of meat) difficult to cut and eat OPP **tender**
stale	(of food, especially bread; also of air) old and not fresh	**raw**	not cooked
ripe	(of fruit) ready to be picked and eaten	**rich**	(of food) containing a lot of fat, butter, eggs, sugar, cream, etc, which makes you feel full very quickly
bland	(of food) lacking in taste and flavour SYN **tasteless**	**fattening**	(of food) that makes people fat
rare	(of meat) only cooked a short time (still red inside). Other ways of cooking meat are **medium** or **well done**.	**bitter**	having a sharp unpleasant taste; not sweet. We use **sour** to describe the taste of a lemon.

1 Underline the possible answers. One, two or three may be possible.

1. The meat was very *lean / bitter / tender*.
2. The chocolate was *greasy / sweet / rich*.
3. The vegetables were *tasteless / bland / stale*.
4. The bread was *fresh / raw / stale*.
5. The soup was *salty / tender / ripe*.
6. My steak was *rare / well done / tough*.
7. The chips were *ripe / greasy / sour*.
8. The peaches were *tasteless / sweet / ripe*.

2 Complete the phrases in a suitable way.

1. You don't want bread that is ....
2. You don't want fruit that isn't ....
3. You don't want meat that is very ....
4. You don't want coffee that is too ....
5. If you're on a diet, you don't want food that is ....
6. And you always want food to look ....

3 Complete the words in the text.

We found a table by the window. I had quite an **(1)** a........................... after our long walk, and I started with the Thai soup which should be hot and **(2)** s........................... . It was, and the flavours were really good. Unfortunately, it was also a bit too **(3)** s..........................., so I needed to drink quite a lot of water with it. My steak was nice and **(4)** l........................... and cooked just as I like it, i.e. not completely **(5)** r........................... but very **(6)** r........................... . Unfortunately, the pepper sauce was quite **(7)** b........................... (I like it hot and very peppery), and the chips with it were a bit **(8)** g........................... . I finished with a chocolate pudding. It was quite **(9)** r........................... but still very nice.

 TEST YOURSELF

B Live to eat or eat to live

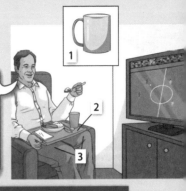

While some people live to eat, I **couldn't care less** about food. In the morning I have a **mug**[1] of **instant** coffee and **cereal** if I'm lucky. I then take a **packed lunch** (a sandwich and a banana) or **pop in** to the **self-service canteen** for something around 12.30. In the evening, I generally **heat something up** that I've bought in the supermarket, then eat it on a **tray**[2] on my **lap**[3] while watching TV. At the weekend, I **treat myself to a takeaway**. I think my most important piece of kitchen equipment is probably my **tin opener**.

GLOSSARY

I couldn't care less (about sth/sb) *inf*	= it does not matter to me at all (This can sound a bit rude.)	**self-service**	(of a restaurant, shop, etc.) where you serve yourself and then pay.
instant	(of food) that can be prepared quickly and easily, usually by adding hot water: *instant coffee*	**canteen**	the place in a school, office, factory, etc. where the people who work there can get meals
cereal	a food that is made of grain, often eaten for breakfast with milk	**heat (sth) (up)**	become or make sth hot or warm
		treat sb/yourself (to sth)	give sb/yourself sth special; pay for sth for sb else
packed lunch	food that you prepare at home and take with you to eat at work or school	**takeaway**	food that you buy in a restaurant but eat somewhere else
pop in (to somewhere)	make a quick visit somewhere, e.g. a shop or a person's home	**tin opener**	a tool that you use for opening a tin of food SYN **can opener**

4 Finish the words or phrases.

1 Where's the tin .... ?
2 This restaurant is self-............................... .
3 You just have to heat the meal ....
4 Have a chocolate. Go on, treat ....!
5 You decide. I couldn't care ....
6 Mum made me a packed ....

5 Complete the dialogues.

1 Are you going out tonight? ~ Yes, I'm .... Jess to an expensive meal.
2 I haven't got real coffee. ~ That's OK. .... is fine.
3 Could I have tea rather than coffee? ~ Sure. Cup or .... ?
4 Where shall I put the .... of drinks? ~ Oh, on the dining-room table, please.
5 Do you want to stay in or go out? ~ I couldn't .... less. You decide.
6 Shall we go out to eat? ~ No, let's get a .... and come back here.
7 Why were you late? ~ Oh, I just .... in to see Carmen on my way home.
8 Do they have waiters in the new café? ~ No, it's all ....

6 Complete the questions.

1 Do you drink real coffee or .... coffee?
2 Do you drink coffee out of a cup or a .... ?
3 Do you have .... with milk for breakfast, or do you prefer something hot?
4 Would you be happy with a .... lunch instead of a cooked meal?
5 Do you eat in a school or office .... ?
6 Do you always cook fresh food or are you happy to .... prepared or frozen food?
7 Do you often get a .... rather than cook at home?
8 How do you .... yourself if you want to eat something special?
9 Do you ever eat food on your .... while watching TV?

7 ABOUT YOU Write your answers to Exercise 6, or talk to another student.

....
....
....

TEST YOURSELF

A The car

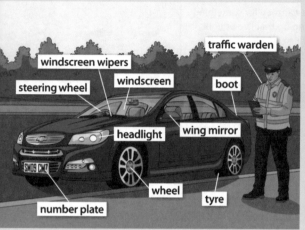

windscreen wipers
steering wheel
windscreen
traffic warden
boot
headlight
wing mirror
wheel
tyre
number plate

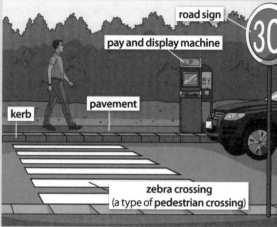

road sign
pay and display machine
pavement
kerb
zebra crossing
(a type of **pedestrian crossing**)

1 Combine words in the box to form eight compound nouns.

wing	steering	pedestrian	road	parking	traffic	windscreen	warden
number	crossing	wheel	wiper	mirror	plate	meter	sign

....

....

2 **What is it?**
1 It's on the outside of the wheel.   ....
2 You look through it when you're driving.   ....
3 It's where people walk.   ....
4 You park next to it.   ....
5 It identifies your car.   ....
6 It helps people to cross the road.   ....

3 **Complete the sentences.**
If you want to …
1 change direction, turn the ....
2 store luggage, open the ....
3 see in the rain, turn on the ....
4 see at night, turn on the ....
5 overtake, look in your ....
6 know the speed limit, look for a ....

4 ABOUT YOU AND YOUR COUNTRY **Write your answers, or talk to another student.**
1 Do you have zebra crossings in your country? Do motorists stop for pedestrians? ....
2 Do you have and use pay and display machines? What methods of payment are there? ....
3 Do you have traffic wardens? What is your attitude to them? ....
4 Do you fit special tyres on your car in the winter? ....
5 Do you have automatic headlights and/or windscreen wipers? If so, are they helpful? ....
6 Do people park on the pavement in your country? ....

 TEST YOURSELF

B Driving a car

- The first thing you have to do is start the car and **pull away** from the kerb.
- You **steer** the car to control its direction.
- If you want to go faster, you **accelerate**.
- If you want to **slow down**, you **put on the brakes**.
- If you want to go back, you **reverse**.
- If you change direction suddenly, e.g. to avoid hitting something, you **swerve**.
- If you drive fast on a wet road and **brake** too quickly, you may **skid**.
- If you pass another car going in the same direction, you **overtake**.
- With a **manual** car, you need to **change gear** all the time (from 1 to 5/6 and reverse).
- You need to be **alert** at all times and **on the lookout** for any **potential hazards**.

GLOSSARY	
pull away (from sth)	(of a vehicle) start moving
accelerate	(of a vehicle or person) start to go faster SYN **speed up**; OPP **slow down**; **accelerator** n the pedal in a car, etc. that you press to control the speed
skid	slide sideways or forwards in an uncontrolled way
manual	With a **manual** car, you operate the gears by hand. OPP **automatic**
alert	watching or listening with all your attention: *be on the alert (for sth/sb)*
be on the lookout (for sth/sb)	pay attention in order to see, find or avoid sth
potential	that may possibly happen SYN **possible**
hazard	a danger or risk **hazardous** *adj*

5 Cover the text and glossary, then complete the definitions.

1 **pull away** = start ....
2 **manual** = operated by ....
3 **be on the lookout** = pay ....
4 **swerve** = change direction ....

5 **steer** = control the .... of the vehicle
6 **skid** = slide because you have .... control of the vehicle

6 Replace the underlined words with words that keep the same meaning.

1 You need to speed up. ....
2 I can't go back any further. ....
3 Ice can be a real danger. ....
4 Birds are a possible problem. ....
5 You can't pass another car here. ....
6 You have to be on the alert. ....
7 I changed direction suddenly to avoid the child crossing the road. ....
8 OK, you can move forward now. ....

7 Complete the sentences in a suitable way.

1 You shouldn't .... on a bridge.
2 You shouldn't .... the car with one hand.
3 When you slow ...., you should .... gradually, not suddenly.
4 You should always be .... when you drive. If you feel tired, take a break.
5 People shouldn't drink and drive: otherwise, they are a .... danger to themselves and others.
6 If you skid, take your foot off the brake and change to a higher ....
7 I don't know why people drive manual cars. It's much better to drive an ....

8 ABOUT YOU Do you agree with the sentences in Exercise 7, and do you always follow the advice? Write your answers, or talk to another student.

....
....
....

TEST YOURSELF

ambulance

helicopter

We reported earlier this morning on a major **incident** on the M5 just before the Gloucester **Service Station**. **Eyewitness** reports say a large lorry **pulled out** from the **inside lane** and **collided with** a BMW that was overtaking. The lorry then **spilled** part of its **load** of wood, causing a **massive pile-up** as vehicles crashed into falling **logs**. The driver of the BMW was reported to be in a **critical condition** and has been taken by **helicopter** to Bristol Southmeads Hospital, while **ambulances** have taken a further six or seven **casualties** to a nearby Gloucester hospital. We understand a passenger in the BMW died **at the scene** of the accident.

Two **lanes** of the motorway are now completely **blocked** and will be for some time, according to accident investigators. 'Vehicles are **scattered** all over the motorway and the damage is **extensive**,' said one. 'It's just **chaos** at the moment.' The police are advising motorists to **exit via Junction** 12, or avoid the area completely, if at all possible.

GLOSSARY

incident	sth that happens, especially sth unusual or unpleasant	**log**	a thick piece of wood that has fallen or been cut from a tree
service station	a place at the side of a motorway where there is a restaurant, toilets, petrol, etc.	**critical**	dangerous or serious: *a patient in a **critical condition***
eyewitness	a person who has seen a crime, accident, etc. and can describe it afterwards SYN **witness**	**casualty**	a person who is killed or injured in an accident or a war
pull out	(of a car, etc.) move away from the side of a road	**scene**	the place where sth happens: *at the scene of the crash/crime*
lane	a section of a road that is marked by white lines to keep traffic separate: *inside lane*; *overtaking lane*	**block**	make it difficult or impossible for sth/sb to pass
		scatter	spread over a large area
collide (with sth/sb)	crash into sth; hit sth very hard while moving **collision** n	**extensive**	large in area or amount: ***extensive damage***
spill	go over the edge of a container by accident; make sth do this	**chaos**	a state of great confusion and a lack of order **chaotic** adj
load	sth that is being carried (usually in large amounts) by a person, vehicle, etc. **load** v put a large amount of sth into sth else	**exit**	a place where traffic can leave a road or motorway **exit** v
		via	through a place
massive	very big SYN **huge**	**junction**	a place where roads meet; here, the place where a road goes off a motorway
pile-up	a crash that involves several cars		

1 The pronunciation of the letter 'i' is the same as in *bit* in eleven of the cases underlined. Which four are different? Use the 🔵 to help you.

incident   service   witness   collide   spill   critical   collision   pile-up   massive   extensive   via   exit

....

2 How many syllables are there in each of these words? Use the 🔵 to help you.

blocked   casualty   via   exit   scattered   chaos   ambulance   helicopter

....

3 Divide these words into the four groups below. A word may go in more than one group.

lane   eyewitness   collide   ambulance   exit   junction   pile-up   helicopter   casualties

TRANSPORT	PEOPLE	ROADS	ACCIDENT

4 What can you remember from the text? Write *T* (True) or *F* (False). Correct any sentences that are wrong.

1   The incident happened in the morning. ....
2   Nobody saw what actually happened. ....
3   A lorry collided with a BMW. ....
4   The lorry spilled a load of bricks. ....
5   One person died on the way to hospital. ....
6   An ambulance took the driver of the BMW to hospital. ....
7   There were two or three other casualties. ....
8   Two lanes of the motorway are now open. ....
9   There is a lot of damage to vehicles. ....
10   Police are now advising motorists to enter via junction 12 of the motorway. ....

5 Right or wrong? Write *R* or *W*, and correct any definitions that are wrong.

1   If you *pull out* in a car, you get out while it is moving. ....
2   A *junction* is a place where you turn left or right. ....
3   *Massive* means very big. ....
4   A *lane* is the side of a road. ....
5   *Casualties* are people walking by when an accident happens. ....
6   *Scattered* means in lots of different places. ....
7   If you *collide with* something, you almost hit it. ....
8   *Chaos* is complete confusion. ....
9   An *ambulance* takes ill or injured people to hospital. ....
10   If you *block* somebody, you hit them. ....

6 Complete the sentences.

1   We stopped at a .... on the M4 for petrol and to get something to eat.
2   If the road is clear, you should stay in the inside .... of a motorway.
3   We passed one lorry carrying a .... of material to one of the building sites.
4   Lorry drivers, protesting against the rising cost of fuel, ... two lanes of the M32 today. The protest ended after an hour, and police described it as only a minor ....
5   I was going to go on the motorway, but then decided to go .... the smaller villages, which was a nicer route. Unfortunately, there was an accident, with vehicles everywhere. It was ....
6   Keep going until you get to a large .... with the A420. Turn right there.
7   It was a bad accident and several cars suffered .... damage.
8   The car crashed into a pile of .... at the side of the road. The wood went everywhere.
9   There was a huge .... on the M3 this morning involving half a dozen vehicles. One person died and several are in a .... condition.
10   If you're going to Bristol, take the M4 and .... at Junction 19 or 20.

📋 TEST YOURSELF

A Conditions

English weather is unreliable, **to say the least**. We can have winters that are **bitterly cold** or extremely **mild**, and summers with long **spells** of hot weather when it can get very **humid**, or ones that stay generally cloudy and **dull**. Almost any day outside of summer can be mild or **chilly**. Equally possible are **torrential rain**, **thick fog**, **flashes of lightning**, **scattered showers** and the **odd rainbow**.

rainbow

GLOSSARY			
to say the least	used to say that sth is much worse or more serious than you are saying	**chilly**	(of the weather) too cold to feel comfortable
bitterly cold	extremely cold	**torrential rain**	heavy rain SYN **a downpour**
mild	during cold weather, warmer than you expect	**thick fog**	= fog that is difficult to see through SYN **dense fog**
spell	a short period of time: *a spell of hot/cold weather*	**flash**	a sudden bright light that comes and goes quickly: *a flash of lightning*
humid	(of climate) warm and feeling slightly wet **humidity** n	**scattered showers**	rain spread over a large area or happening several times during a period of time
dull	(of the weather) not bright, with a lot of clouds	**odd**	not regular or fixed; happening occasionally

1 **Which is worse, or are they the same?**

1 cold OR bitterly cold ....
2 thick fog OR dense fog ....
3 hot OR hot and humid ....
4 a chilly day OR a mild day ....
5 torrential rain OR a downpour ....
6 a dull day OR a bright day ....
7 the odd shower OR scattered showers ....
8 quite wet OR quite wet, to say the least ....

2 **Replace the underlined word(s) with a single word that keeps the same meaning.**

1 We've had a number of showers today. ....
2 We had a short period of cold weather last week. ....
3 It's been really cold this winter. ....
4 We had very heavy rain this morning. ....
5 I drove through some very bad fog. ....
6 It was too cold to feel comfortable today. ....
7 I thought it would be cold, but actually it was warmer than I expected. ....
8 We get the occasional spell of hot weather. ....

3 **Complete the texts.**

While we were out, we had a sudden (1) .... of rain followed by several (2) .... of lightning. It was a bit frightening and we also got very wet, to say the (3) .... But then the rain stopped, the sun came out and there was a beautiful (4) .... By the end of the day I was sweating: it was hot and the (5) .... was unbearable.

It was (6) .... cold for May, and even by midday it still felt quite (7) .... Yesterday had been quite hot, but today was cloudy and (8) .... with (9) .... expected later, though not heavy or lasting for any period of time.

TEST YOURSELF

B Effects of weather

Many people in this country listen to the **weather forecast** very **closely**, as it can have a **significant** impact on people's lives. Farmers are obviously **dependent on** weather conditions for the success of their crops, but the weather affects everyone:

* A **heatwave** can eventually lead to water **shortages** and **drought**.

* When there is heavy snow and **blizzards**, traffic **comes to a standstill**, and this causes **widespread disruption** on the roads.

* **Gales** cause damage to people's property, and this may be widespread.

GLOSSARY	
weather forecast	a description of the weather that is expected in the coming days
closely	carefully and with interest
significant	important enough to be noticed and have an effect
dependent (on sth/sb)	needing sth/sb to support you
heatwave	a period of unusually hot weather
shortage	a situation where there is not enough of sth OPP **surplus**
drought	a long period without rain
blizzard	a bad storm with strong winds and a lot of snow
come to a standstill	reach a situation in which all activity or movement has stopped ALSO **bring sth to a standstill**
widespread	found or happening over a large area: *widespread damage*
disruption	a situation in which it is difficult for sth to continue in the normal way
gale	a very strong wind. A **breeze** is a light, usually pleasant, wind.

4 Is the pronunciation of the underlined letters the same or different? Write *S* or *D*. Use the 🔊 to help you.

1 widespr<u>ea</u>d h<u>ea</u>twave ....
2 short<u>age</u> dam<u>age</u> ....
3 surpl<u>u</u>s blizz<u>a</u>rd ....
4 g<u>a</u>le dam<u>a</u>ge ....
5 surpl<u>u</u>s disr<u>u</u>ption ....
6 dr<u>ough</u>t th<u>ough</u>t ....

5 Circle the correct answer.

1 A surplus is *too much / not enough* of something.
2 A breeze is a *strong / light* wind.
3 Disruption *causes / doesn't cause* problems.
4 If you are dependent on something, you *need / would like* it.
5 A blizzard usually has *strong winds / very low temperatures*.
6 A significant effect is quite *small / large*.
7 A forecast talks about the *future / past*.
8 A heatwave is a *day / period* of hot weather.

6 Complete the texts.

The weather **(1)** .... yesterday predicted heavy snow during the night, and they were right. Traffic came to a **(2)** .... on the A4 this morning, and there was widespread **(3)** .... on many of the minor roads as well. I will certainly listen **(4)** .... to the forecast tonight!

Farmers in this country are **(5)** .... on rain for their crops to grow and flourish, and if the current **(6)** .... continues with no further rain, it will be a second year of **(7)** .... , and that means serious water **(8)** ....

We had 65 mph **(9)** .... today, and this has caused **(10)** .... damage to a number of houses. If these conditions get worse, the damage will become more **(11)** ....

7 ABOUT YOUR COUNTRY **Write answers to the questions, or ask another student.**

1 Which of the weather conditions on pages 64 and 65 are common in your country? ....
2 What effect do they have on people's lives? ....
3 Which of the weather conditions are rare in your country? ....

📇 TEST YOURSELF

A Different styles

1 **plain top** (without a **pattern**)
2 **waistcoat**
3 **check/checked skirt**
4 **suede shoes**
5 **cap**
6 **strap**
7 **short-sleeved shirt**
8 **V-neck(ed) sleeveless jumper**
9 **sandals**
10 **silk top**
11 **tight-fitting skirt** (OPP **loose-fitting**)
12 **bracelet**
13 **high-heeled shoes**

1 **Who wears the following most often? Is it men, women, or both equally?**

1 caps ....
2 suede shoes ....
3 silk shirts ....
4 short-sleeved shirts ....
5 bracelets ....

6 V-neck jumpers ....
7 high-heeled shoes ....
8 sandals ....
9 waistcoats ....

2 **Complete the sentences with a suitable word.**

1 I really like men in three-piece suits, with trousers, jacket and ....
2 I've got one really tight-fitting dress, but usually I prefer .... clothes.
3 My sister wears flat shoes most of the time but .... shoes for special occasions.
4 I don't like bright patterns, so I usually wear .... shirts.
5 My sister has a very glamorous, tight-fitting black and white .... skirt.
6 I wear .... a lot in the summer because my feet get so hot.
7 Most men only wear short-................................. shirts in the summer.
8 Since my dad went bald, he has started wearing a .... to keep his head warm.
9 I've got a grey backpack with adjustable shoulder ....
10 Some men like wearing .... -fitting T-shirts to show off their muscular bodies.

3 ABOUT YOU **Write your answers, or talk to another student.**

1 Do you have any clothes in suede or silk? If so, what? ....
2 Do you often wear sandals in the summer? If not, what do you prefer? ....
3 Do you wear a lot of short-sleeved tops or shirts? If so, when? ....
4 Do any members of your family wear a cap? If so, why? ....
5 Do you tend to prefer plain tops and shirts, or something with a pattern? ....
6 Do you ever wear waistcoats or V-neck jumpers? ....

TEST YOURSELF

B Special occasions

For my brother's **stag party**, we all had to march round town wearing **kilts**[1], with large **badges**[2] on our chests saying: *If lost, return to Scotland.*

At a recent **fancy-dress** party, my husband went as a woman cleaner wearing a **wig** and **apron**[3], and carrying a **bucket**[4] of water and a **mop**[5]. He looked silly.

I like to **dress up** for weddings and wear something **elegant**. The only problem in Britain is the weather. You can be standing around in a **glamorous outfit**, **shivering** at the same time.

In my house, **barbecues** are very **casual affairs**: T-shirt, shorts and **flip-flops**[6].

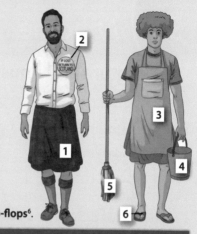

GLOSSARY			
stag party	(ALSO **stag night**) a party for men only given for a man shortly before his wedding. A **hen party** is the same for women.	**glamorous**	looking more exciting or attractive than ordinary people
fancy dress	special clothes you wear to a party where people dress up to look like a different person	**outfit**	a set of clothes that are worn together for a particular occasion
wig	a covering made of real or false hair that you wear on your head	**shiver**	shake slightly, especially because you are cold or frightened
dress up	put on more formal clothes, usually for a special occasion	**barbecue**	(*abbreviation* **BBQ**) an outdoor meal or party when food is cooked on a metal frame on an open fire
elegant	attractive and showing a good sense of style	**casual**	very relaxed and informal
		affair	an event or situation

4 Is the pronunciation of the underlined letters the same or different? Write *S* or *D*. Use the 🅐🅟🅟 to help you.

1 fan<u>c</u>y dre<u>ss</u> ....
2 <u>s</u>tag ca<u>s</u>ual ....
3 wi<u>g</u> sta<u>g</u> ....
4 <u>sh</u>iver ca<u>s</u>ual ....
5 glam<u>o</u>rous eleg<u>a</u>nt ....
6 <u>a</u>ffair <u>a</u>pron ....
7 glamor<u>ou</u>s b<u>u</u>cket ....
8 b<u>u</u>cket dress <u>u</u>p ....

5 What's the answer?

1 You might wear one if you haven't got any hair. ....
2 You might wear one to do the cooking. ....
3 You go to one of these pretending to be someone else. ....
4 You might need this to wash the kitchen floor. ....
5 People from Scotland sometimes wear these. ....
6 You might do this if you are very cold. ....
7 Men and women sometimes wear these on their feet on a beach. ....
8 People may wear one of these to show they belong to an organization or support something. ....
9 People often like to do this to look elegant for special occasions. ....
10 You have these outdoors and cook food on an open fire. ....
11 People like to look this to appear more attractive and exciting than ordinary people. ....
12 You might buy this to look elegant at a special occasion. ....

6 ABOUT YOU Write your answers, or talk to another student.

1 Have you ever been to a stag or hen party? If so, what was it like? ....
2 Have you been to any fancy-dress parties? If so, who did you pretend to be? ....
3 Do you like dressing up? If so, what occasions do you dress for? ....
4 When you buy clothes, do you often buy complete outfits? If so, why? ....
5 Do you prefer to wear casual clothes most of the time? If so, what do you usually wear? ....
6 Do you often go to barbecues? If so, are they fairly casual affairs, and what do you usually wear? ....

🗒 TEST YOURSELF

A Furniture and household objects

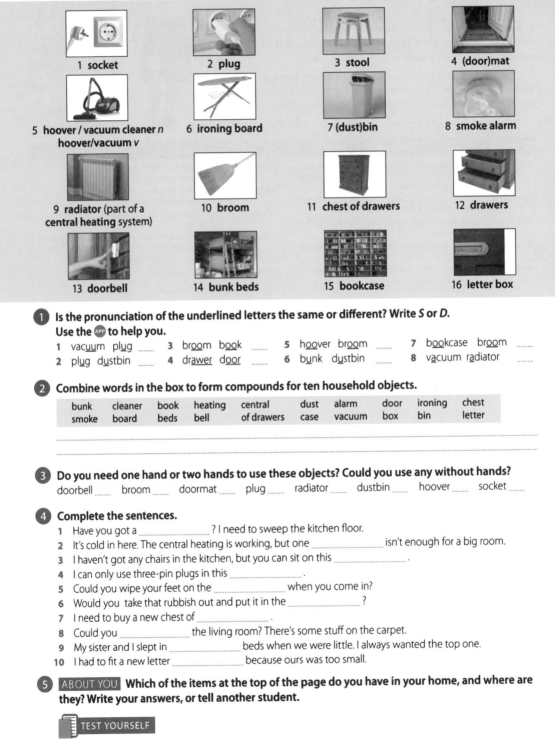

1 socket

2 plug

3 stool

4 (door)mat

5 hoover / vacuum cleaner *n*
hoover/vacuum *v*

6 ironing board

7 (dust)bin

8 smoke alarm

9 radiator (part of a central heating system)

10 broom

11 chest of drawers

12 drawers

13 doorbell

14 bunk beds

15 bookcase

16 letter box

1 Is the pronunciation of the underlined letters the same or different? Write *S* or *D*.
Use the **APP** to help you.

1 vac<u>uu</u>m pl<u>u</u>g ....
2 pl<u>u</u>g d<u>u</u>stbin ....
3 br<u>oo</u>m b<u>oo</u>k ....
4 dr<u>awer</u> d<u>oor</u> ....
5 h<u>oo</u>ver br<u>oo</u>m ....
6 b<u>u</u>nk d<u>u</u>stbin ....
7 b<u>oo</u>kcase br<u>oo</u>m ....
8 v<u>a</u>cuum r<u>a</u>diator ....

2 Combine words in the box to form compounds for ten household objects.

| bunk | cleaner | book | heating | central | dust | alarm | door | ironing | chest |
| smoke | board | beds | bell | of drawers | case | vacuum | box | bin | letter |

....
....

3 Do you need one hand or two hands to use these objects? Could you use any without hands?

doorbell .... broom .... doormat .... plug .... radiator .... dustbin .... hoover .... socket ....

4 Complete the sentences.

1 Have you got a .... ? I need to sweep the kitchen floor.
2 It's cold in here. The central heating is working, but one .... isn't enough for a big room.
3 I haven't got any chairs in the kitchen, but you can sit on this ....
4 I can only use three-pin plugs in this ....
5 Could you wipe your feet on the .... when you come in?
6 Would you take that rubbish out and put it in the .... ?
7 I need to buy a new chest of ....
8 Could you .... the living room? There's some stuff on the carpet.
9 My sister and I slept in .... beds when we were little. I always wanted the top one.
10 I had to fit a new letter .... because ours was too small.

5 ABOUT YOU Which of the items at the top of the page do you have in your home, and where are they? Write your answers, or tell another student.

TEST YOURSELF

B Household chores

MUST DO THIS WEEK!

- clean the inside of the oven – it's very **greasy**
- order a **dozen** bottles of wine for Jacinta's party
- **get hold of** a **plumber's** number to fix the **dripping**¹ tap in the **loo**
- get new **blinds**² for the **spare** bedroom
- paint **step**³ in front of the **porch**⁴
- get **rough estimate** for painting the **outside** of the house

GLOSSARY	
greasy	covered in fat and oil from cooking **grease** n
dozen	twelve **half a dozen** = six
get hold of sth	find sth that will be useful **get hold of sb** find or make contact with sb
plumber	a person whose job is to fix problems with water, pipes, radiators, etc.
loo inf	a toilet
spare	not used now but kept for possible future use: *a spare room/tyre*
estimate	a clear idea of the cost, size, etc. of sth: *a rough estimate* (= an approximate idea) **estimate** v
outside	the outer side or surface of sth SYN **exterior**

6 Is the pronunciation of the underlined letters the same or different? Write *S* or *D*. Use the 🔊 to help you.

1 estim<u>a</u>te n estim<u>a</u>te v ....
2 est<u>i</u>mate bl<u>i</u>nd ....
3 d<u>o</u>zen r<u>o</u>ugh ....
4 h<u>a</u>lf sp<u>a</u>re ....
5 r<u>ou</u>gh pl<u>u</u>mber ....
6 plum<u>b</u>er <u>b</u>linds ....

7 Replace the underlined words with words that have a similar meaning.

1 Could you get me <u>six</u> eggs? ....
2 Is anyone in the <u>toilet</u>? ....
3 Is the room at the end a <u>free</u> room? ....
4 I need to <u>contact</u> a builder. ....
5 Do you have the number of a <u>person who can fix leaking pipes</u>? ....
6 I need to get an <u>idea of the cost</u>? ....
7 The inside of the oven gets <u>covered in fat and oil</u>. ....

8 Complete the sentences.

1 I want to get .... of some wood to make a small gate for the front garden.
2 The .... of the house needs painting. We'll do it when the weather improves.
3 Be careful walking down the .... : they're a bit dangerous when it's been raining.
4 You always get some .... on the wall around the cooker – it's from all the fat.
5 We decided to build a .... to give the front door more protection from the rain.
6 The tap in the sink keeps .... I must ring the plumber.
7 Six won't be enough. Could you get me a .... bottles of fizzy water?
8 We used to have curtains in the bedroom, but now we've got ....

📓 TEST YOURSELF

A Before, during and after sleep

BEFORE: You might be **exhausted** after a busy day, perhaps feel **sleepy**, start **yawning**¹ and decide it's time for bed. You might wear **pyjamas**² or, if you're a woman, possibly a **nightdress/nightie**³ (*inf*). When you get into bed, you might **set the alarm**⁴. Soon, if you're lucky, you will **fall asleep**.

DURING: When you're asleep, you have dreams and possibly **nightmares**. Some people **snore**. At this point they're **fast asleep**.

AFTER: 7.00am.The alarm **goes off**. It might wake you up, or you might be **wide awake** already. People without an alarm might **oversleep**, others might decide to **have a lie-in**.

GLOSSARY	
exhausted	very tired, either physically or mentally SYN **worn out**
sleepy	tired and ready to go to sleep
fall asleep	start sleeping SYN **go to sleep/get to sleep**; **get back to sleep** sleep again after you have woken up
nightmare	a bad or frightening dream
snore	breathe noisily while you are asleep
fast asleep	sleeping deeply SYN **in a deep sleep** OPP **wide awake**
go off	(of an alarm) ring or make a noise
oversleep	sleep longer than you should or want
have a lie-in	stay in bed later than usual

SPOTLIGHT *sleep*

There are a number of words and phrases derived from *sleep*:
A **heavy sleeper** sleeps well. A **light sleeper** wakes easily.
A **sleeper** can also be a night train with beds for passengers.
A **sleeping bag** is a large bag you sleep in when you are camping.
A **sleeping pill/tablet** is a medicine you take to help you sleep.

1 Cover the glossary and spotlight. What words or phrases are being defined?

1 very tired, physically or mentally ....
2 clothes some women wear in bed ....
3 medicine to help you sleep ....
4 sleep longer than you want to ....
5 a bad dream ....

6 stay in bed later than usual ....
7 a night train with beds for passengers ....
8 open your mouth wide because you are tired ....
9 You sleep in this in a tent. ....
10 breathe noisily while asleep ....

2 Replace the underlined word(s) with words or phrases that keep the same meaning.

I was <u>really tired</u>, so I went to bed quite early last night. I <u>got to sleep</u> without a problem and very soon I was <u>in a deep sleep</u>. Unfortunately, in the middle of the night, I had a <u>bad dream</u>, which woke me up. After that, I was awake for ages and didn't <u>fall asleep again</u> until about half past four, so when the alarm <u>rang</u> just after seven, I didn't hear it and I <u>carried on sleeping</u>. When I finally woke up, I still felt a bit <u>tired</u>.

1 ....
2 ....
3 ....
4 ....
5 ....
6 ....
7 ....
8 ....

3 Complete the questions?

1 Are you a .... sleeper or a .... sleeper?
2 Do you normally wear .... in bed?
3 Do you normally set an .... when you go to bed?
4 Do you usually feel .... awake as soon as you wake up?
5 Do you often have a .... at the weekend?
6 Do other people ever tell you that you .... when you're asleep?
7 Have you ever taken sleeping .... ?
8 Do you own or ever use a sleeping .... ?

ABOUT YOU

....
....
....
....
....
....
....
....

4 ABOUT YOU Write your own answers to the questions in Exercise 3, or talk to another student.

TEST YOURSELF

B Sleep habits

Antonio
I **sleep like a log** wherever I am.

Ella
If I eat late, it **disturbs** my sleep and I often **have a restless night**.

Hiroko
I work late and get up early so that **restricts** my sleep to about five hours.

Raul
Lack of sleep makes me really **irritable**.

Suzanna
I sleep well **as long as** I **establish** a good routine and **stick to** it.

Carla
I'm **sensitive** to light and need to sleep **in total darkness**.

Nick
I **suffer from insomnia**, so I never get much sleep.

Agnieszka
During the day, I often **have a nap**.

Omar
When there are things **on my mind** – like exams – I sleep badly.

GLOSSARY

sleep like a log	sleep very well OPP **have a restless night**
disturb	stop sb doing sth, e.g. working, sleeping or thinking
restrict	put a limit on sb/sth
irritable	becoming angry easily
as long as	on condition that SYN **provided that**
establish	start or create sth such as a system, organization, etc.
stick to sth *inf*	continue with sth and not change to anything else
sensitive (to sth)	easily affected by sth which may cause pain or upset
darkness	the state of being dark: *in total darkness*
insomnia	If you suffer from **insomnia**, you are often unable to sleep.
have a nap	have a short sleep, e.g. for half an hour
on my mind	If sth is **on your mind**, you're thinking or worrying about it.

5 The pronunciation of the letter 'i' is the same as in *bit* in most of these examples. Which two are different? Use the **APP** to help you.

disturb   restrict   irritable   establish   stick   sensitive   provided   insomnia

6 The pronunciation of the letter 's' is the same as in *sit* in most of these examples. Which two are different? Use the **APP** to help you.

sleep   disturb   restless   establish   as long as   stick   darkness   insomnia

7 Combine words in the box to form six phrases.

have	sleep	insomnia	have a restless	a nap	in total
night	suffer from	like a log	my mind	darkness	have something on

....

....

8 Complete the sentences with a word or phrase.
1 I get very .... if I don't sleep well.
2 I sleep well .... I'm in my own bed. I don't sleep well in strange beds.
3 After a relaxing bath and a hot drink, I always sleep ....
4 Try to go to bed at the same time every night. Have a routine and .... to it.
5 I had too much to eat and drink last night, and I had a very .... night.
6 I didn't sleep well last night because I've got a lot of things on ....
7 Most experts say that you need to .... a bedtime routine to sleep well.
8 I've been staying up late to revise for exams and that has .... the amount of sleep I get.
9 If I'm .... during the night, I find it difficult to get back to sleep.

9 ABOUT YOU Read the statements at the top of the page again. Are they true for you? Write your answers under each statement, or ask another student.

TEST YOURSELF

A Spending and saving

Are you good at looking after your money? For example, do you:

- keep a clear record of **outgoings**, e.g. **debit card** payments, or do you find you are largely **unaware** of how much you are spending?

- keep your account **in credit** all the time, or are you sometimes **overdrawn**?

- pay your credit card bills **promptly**, or do you allow **debts** to **mount up**?

- check all the **transactions** in your **bank statements**, or do you just **ignore** them?

- think you're **cautious** with money, or do you waste large **sums** of money?

GLOSSARY	
outgoings (*pl*)	the amount of money a person or business has to spend regularly, SYN **expenditure** OPP **income** the money you earn from work or savings
debit card	a plastic card used for taking money directly from your bank account
unaware (of sth)	not knowing or realizing that sth is happening OPP **aware**; **awareness** *n*
be in credit	If you **are in credit**, there is money in your bank account. OPP **be overdrawn**
promptly	without delay **prompt** *adj*
debt	the amount of money you owe sb
mount up	increase gradually in size SYN **build up**, **accumulate**
transaction	a piece of business between people. In banking, you **put** money **into** an acount, or **take** it **out / withdraw** it.
bank statement	a printed record of activities in an account over a particular period
ignore	pay no attention to sth
cautious	careful about what you say or do, to avoid mistakes; not taking risks
sum (of sth)	an amount of money

1 **Is the pronunciation of the underlined letters the same or different? Write *S* or *D*. Use the** APP **to help you.**

1 expendi<u>t</u>ure transac<u>t</u>ion ....
2 c<u>au</u>tious withdr<u>aw</u> ....
3 de<u>b</u>t de<u>b</u>it ....
4 aw<u>are</u> overdr<u>aw</u>n ....
5 <u>a</u>ware c<u>au</u>tious ....
6 withdr<u>aw</u> ign<u>ore</u> ....

2 **Complete the sentences.**

1 I'm completely .... of how often I make .... card payments because I never write them down. I have to go online to look at my bank .... in order to see all the .... I've made.
2 I keep a reasonable .... of money in my bank account – enough to keep it in .... And I like to pay all my bills .... ; that way I don't forget.
3 I didn't keep a record of my .... this month. Now I'm .... and I've got various ....
4 My sister is very stupid: she even .... letters from her bank telling her she needs to .... money .... her account.

3 **Complete the dialogues with a single word.**

1 Did you take some money out? ~ Yes, I .... £100.
2 Is there money in your account? ~ No, I'm afraid I'm ....
3 Do you know what you spend? ~ Yes, I keep a record of all my ....
4 Do you always pay credit card bills? ~ Yes, otherwise debts can .... up.
5 Is he careful with money? ~ Yes, he's very ....
6 Does the company want the money now? ~ Yes, they have asked for .... payment.
7 She doesn't earn much, does she? ~ No, she's on quite a low ....
8 Does he waste a lot of money? ~ Yes, he has no .... of what things should cost.

4 ABOUT YOU **Write your answers to the questionnaire at the top of the page, or talk to another student.**

....
....
....

📓 TEST YOURSELF

B Looking after your money

Creating a personal budget

Few people bother to **budget**, which is why so many are in debt. You must **calculate** the total income coming in each month, and the total going out, both regular outgoings and all other expenses. Then, **subtract** the expenses from the income. If there's a **surplus**, don't spend it: **pay off** any money you **owe** (in other words, your debts), and keep the rest for emergencies. If there is a **shortfall**, then you must take action. Consider where you can **economize** and **make cutbacks**. And don't expect anyone else to **subsidize** you and pay your debts.

GLOSSARY

budget	plan how much to spend and what to spend it on. A **budget** is the amount of money available to spend with a plan for spending it.
calculate	use numbers to find a total number, amount or distance SYN **work (sth) out; calculation** n
subtract sth (from sth)	take one number from another to calculate the difference SYN **take sth away (from sth)**
pay sth off	finish paying money that you owe for sth
owe	have to pay sb for sth that you have received or borrowed
economize	reduce the amount of money, time, goods, etc. that you use SYN **make cutbacks**
subsidize	give money to sb to help them pay for sth **subsidy** n

SPOTLIGHT *surplus, deficit, shortage, shortfall*

A **surplus** is more of something than is necessary. If it is money, the opposite is a **deficit**; if it is food, petrol, etc, the opposite is a **shortage**.
A **shortfall** is the difference between what you have and what you need.

5 Underline the words connected with money, and tick the words connected with numbers.

budget   owe   calculate   economize   work something out

subsidize   subtract   pay sth off   deficit   take sth away

6 Is the pronunciation of the underlined letters the same or different? Write *S* or *D*. Use the 🅰🅿🅿 to help you.

1 s<u>u</u>btract s<u>u</u>bsidize   ....
2 sub<u>si</u>dize econom<u>i</u>ze   ....
3 defi<u>c</u>it sub<u>s</u>idy   ....
4 c<u>u</u>tback calc<u>u</u>late   ....
5 b<u>u</u>dget c<u>u</u>tback   ....
6 <u>o</u>we ec<u>o</u>nomize   ....

7 Circle the odd one out, then write what the other two words have in common.

1 a) shortfall   b) surplus   c) deficit   ....
2 a) shortage   b) calculation   c) shortfall   ....
3 a) economize   b) take away   c) subtract   ....
4 a) economize   b) make cutbacks   c) subsidize   ....
5 a) deficit   b) shortage   c) budget   ....
6 a) work out   b) calculate   c) pay off   ....

8 Complete the texts.

The floods in the spring are now causing severe food **(1)** .... throughout the country, and this will leave many farmers with a significant **(2)** .... in their income, and perhaps hoping for a government **(3)** .... to help them.

I'm not careful with money and don't often budget , but then I decided to keep a record of my regular outgoings. At first, it was difficult to **(4)** .... all my expenses, but I managed after a while. One month, I realised I had a **(5)** ...., and that I would have to **(6)** ....

I'm ashamed to say that when I went to university I was still unable to **(7)** .... So, I borrowed money and ended up **(8)** .... lots of money to different people. Eventually my parents came to the rescue and **(9)** .... me for much of the three years during my degree.

🗎 TEST YOURSELF

A Types of crime

Some of these crimes involve **threatening** people (= saying you will cause trouble for them, and possibly hurt them if they do not do what you want). Most of these crimes are also **deliberate** (= you intend to do them; SYN **intentional**), but not always.

GLOSSARY

manslaughter	(*slaughter* pronounced like *daughter*) killing sb illegally but not deliberately	**blackmail**	demanding money from a person by threatening to tell sb else a secret about them **blackmail** v. The person is a **blackmailer**.
arson	deliberately setting fire to sth, especially a building. The person is an **arsonist**.	**kidnapping**	taking sb away illegally and keeping them prisoner, especially in order to get money **kidnap** v. The person is a **kidnapper**.
rape	forcing sb to have sex, especially using violence **rape** v. The person is a **rapist**.	**shoplifting**	stealing goods from a shop by leaving without paying for them. The person is a **shoplifter**.
fraud	cheating sb in order to get money or goods illegally	**mugging**	attacking sb, or threatening to attack sb in order to steal their money, especially in a public place **mug** v. The person is a **mugger**.
bribery	giving money to sb to persuade them to help you, especially by doing sth dishonest **bribe** v		

1 Put the crimes in the three columns below.

shoplifting	mugging	manslaughter	bribery
arson	kidnapping	rape	fraud

involves violence

....
....
....

may involve violence

....
....
....

doesn't involve violence

....
....
....

2 Circle the crimes which usually involve money.

arson	fraud	mugging
manslaughter	bribery	blackmail
shoplifting	rape	kidnapping

3 Write down the person who commits these crimes.

1 shoplifting/ ....
2 blackmail/ ....
3 arson/ ....

4 kidnapping/ ....
5 rape/ ....
6 mugging/ ....

4 Complete the sentences.

1 I was .... outside my office by a man with a knife who demanded money from me.
2 He wasn't guilty of murder, but was found guilty of ....
3 The boy was .... outside his home and held prisoner for weeks.
4 There is often a notice in stores saying that '........................... will be prosecuted'.
5 He stopped the woman in the street, ... her with a knife, and took her money.
6 The man accused of .... the girl insists that she agreed to have sex with him.
7 He .... the policeman with both money and expensive holidays.
8 He said he did it, but claims it was not ....
9 She .... him by threatening to tell the police about the money he stole.
10 He went to prison for credit card ....

TEST YOURSELF

B Causes of crime

What do you think?

- Some people think that it is the people closest to us when we are growing up who have the greatest responsibility for shaping our **moral** standards.

- Crime rates tend to be higher in **slum** areas, and for children from these areas, crime can become an **attraction** because it offers a way of becoming richer. They join **gangs** and **drift into** crime.

- Another cause is the **abuse** of alcohol and drugs which can force people into crime.

- Some argue it is personal weakness or **parental neglect**, made worse by a lack of **discipline** at home or in school, that leads people into crime.

- Some believe that if **penalties** for **offenders** were **harsher**, crime would go down.

GLOSSARY	
moral	concerned with principles of right and wrong behaviour **morals** n pl
slum	an area of a city that is very poor and where the houses are in bad condition
attraction	a feature or quality that makes sth seem interesting and enjoyable
gang	a group of young people who often cause trouble
drift into sth	start doing sth without a particular plan or purpose
abuse	the use of sth in a way that is wrong or harmful: *suffer abuse* **abuse** v
parental	connected with parents
neglect	the fact of not giving enough care or attention to sb/sth **neglect** v
discipline	the practice of training people to obey rules and punishing them if they do not
penalty	a punishment for breaking a law, a rule or a contract
offender	a person who commits a crime
harsh	severe, strict or cruel

5 Circle the words which have a negative meaning.

slum   attraction   gang   abuse   discipline
neglect   penalty   parental   moral   harsh

6 Replace the underlined words with a single word that keeps the same meaning.

1 It's basically a <u>very poor area of the city with houses in bad condition</u>. ....
2 The parents have <u>not given enough care and attention to</u> these children. ....
3 Some of the children need better <u>training to obey rules</u>. ....
4 There's a <u>very unpleasant group of youths</u> waiting at the end of the street. ....
5 The children have suffered <u>from wrong and harmful treatment</u>. ....
6 Many <u>people who commit crimes</u> go on to commit further crimes. ....
7 It's all about <u>knowing the difference between right and wrong</u>. ....
8 If you see no future for yourself, crime is an <u>exciting idea</u> with possibilities of money. ....

7 Complete the sentences on the right. Keep the same meaning as the sentences on the left.

1 It's the responsibility of the parents.   It's a ....
2 They have abused the children.   The children have ....
3 The teenagers do what they like.   The teenagers lack ....
4 The issue is all about right and wrong.   It's a ....
5 The law is too soft.   We need ....
6 I committed crimes with no real plan or purpose.   I just ....
7 There hasn't been enough care and attention.   There has been a lot of ....
8 Young people like money.   For young people, money is a big ....

8 ABOUT YOU Look at the opinions about the causes of crime at the top of page. Do you agree? What about crimes committed by people who <u>aren't</u> poor?

....
....
....

📖 TEST YOURSELF

A The inner city

… the **inner** city streets became very narrow, so I parked the car and went the rest of the way on foot. I soon **regretted** that decision. The pavements were **filthy** with **litter**, and there was a gang of **youths hanging around** on one of the street corners. I started to feel **concerned for** my safety, so I turned into a long **passage** at the back of a factory. It was covered in **graffiti**, and two **homeless** young men were sleeping on the cold **damp** ground. It was a **depressing** place altogether.

GLOSSARY

inner	close to the centre of a place. The **inner city** is often associated with social and economic problems.
regret	(with an -*ing* form or noun) feel sorry that you did sth or that you did not do sth **regret** *n*
filthy	very dirty
litter	the paper that people don't want and leave on the ground
youth	a young man, usually one you do not have a good opinion of
hang around/ about *inf*	stay in or around a place not doing very much
concerned (about/for sth)	worried **concern** *n, v*
passage	a long narrow area with walls on either side that connects one room or place with another
graffiti *pl*	pictures or writing on a wall in a public place
homeless	having no home
damp	a little wet
depressing	making you feel very sad and without enthusiasm **depressed** very sad and without enthusiasm

1 Circle the words which usually suggest a negative idea.

regret   filthy   litter   abandon   damp
homeless   hang around   graffiti   depressing   concerned

2 Complete the definitions with a single word.

1 filthy = very ....
2 the inner city = ... parts of a city close to the centre
3 regret = feel .... you did or did not do something.
4 litter = paper left on the ....

5 damp = a little ....
6 concerned = ...
7 depressing = making you feel ....
8 graffiti = ... on a wall in a public place

3 Complete the sentences.

1 You sometimes see quite a lot of .... people in big cities; it's very sad.
2 We walked along a narrow .... from the park to the road.
3 There was a lot of .... in the family when the children didn't arrive.
4 It's not a nice area: you get a lot of .... hanging around.
5 Two workmen were cleaning the .... off the side of a bridge.
6 The street was filthy, and it was pouring with rain. It was very ....
7 You often see teenagers .... around in the centre of town with nothing to do.
8 It started to rain so I .... not taking an umbrella.

4 ABOUT YOUR COUNTRY **Do you often see these things in your country? Write your answers, or talk to another student.**

- litter on the ground ....
- graffitti ....
- homeless people sleeping in the street ....
- filthy pavements ....
- gangs of youths ....

TEST YOURSELF

B In the suburbs

I live in a block of flats that is **surrounded by** trees, which is rather nice. **On the whole**, it's considered a **desirable district** because it's a nice quiet **suburb**, near local shops and good schools, but also **handy** for town. The main **drawback** is that, although there is a pub **nearby**, it's not a particularly **lively** area – there's not much **going on** in the evenings, so you have to go into town for a **decent** nightlife. The other thing is that as time **goes on**, the area is getting more **built-up**, and **that's a shame**.

SPOTLIGHT *go on*

This phrasal verb has several meanings:
1 **be going on** be happening or taking place (as in the text)
2 (of time) pass SYN **go by**: *As time went on/by, things improved.*
3 (of a situation) continue: *It could go on like this for a long time.*

GLOSSARY

surround	be or go all around sth: **be surrounded by sth**; **surrounding** *adj*	**drawback**	sth that is not good or causes problems SYN **disadvantage**
on the whole	generally, but not true in every case SYN **in general, generally**	**nearby** *adv, adj*	not far away in distance: *We went to a **nearby** restaurant.* (NOT *We went to a near restaurant.*)
desirable	wanted, often by many people	**lively**	full of interest, with things to do
district	an area of a town or country that has particular features	**decent**	of a high enough standard: *They have **decent** food there.*
suburb	an area where a lot of people live, outside the centre of a town	**built-up**	(of an area of land) with a lot of buildings
handy (for sth) *inf*	located near to things you need SYN **convenient (for sth)**	**shame**	a fact or situation that makes you feel disappointed SYN **pity**: *That's a shame/pity.* *What a shame/pity.*

5 Do the words and phrases in italics have the same meaning? Write *S* or *D*.

1 *In general / On the whole* it's a nice place. ....
2 They live *nearby / next door*. ....
3 It's *convenient / decent*. ....
4 What a *pity / shame*. ....

5 A *handy / lively* area. ....
6 What's *going on / happening* here? ....
7 The school is very *handy / built-up*. ....
8 It's quite a poor *suburb / district*. ....

6 Complete the sentences with a word or phrase.

1 There used to be lots of open spaces, but now it's a really .... area.
2 I live in a pleasant ...., about two kilometres from the centre.
3 Unfortunately, the whole area is .... by factories, which is a big ....
4 It's very .... because it's close to my children's school and the place where I work. The .... area is also nice, with a park, children's playground and open spaces.
5 It's close to the centre and quite a poor .... There are good shops .... but in the evening it can be dangerous. The council say the area will improve, but I expect it to .... like this for ages.
6 For young people it's not that .... in the evenings, which is a .... However, it does have a few .... restaurants, which is good.
7 There are one or two drawbacks, but .... it's a nice place to be.
8 For many families, the most .... aspect of the area is that it has good schools.

7 ABOUT YOU Write your answers, or ask another student.

1 Is the area where you live built-up, or is there a feeling of space? ....
2 What is your home surrounded by? ....
3 What shops do you have nearby? ....
4 Is your home handy for most things? ....
5 What are the drawbacks? ....
6 As time goes on, do you think the area will improve or get worse? Why? ....

 TEST YOURSELF

A Living in the country

I live **on the outskirts of** a village. There's a **shallow stream** that runs along the bottom of my garden, and **beyond** that, a lovely **meadow**. So, it's a very **quiet spot**. Of course, not everything is perfect. Public transport in the country is very **infrequent**, and in the winter you can **occasionally** feel a bit **isolated**. **Nevertheless**, I wouldn't **swap rural** life for life in a town or city.

GLOSSARY	
outskirts	the part of a town furthest from the centre: *on the outskirts of a town/city/village*
shallow	not having much distance between the top and the bottom OPP **deep**
stream	a very small river
beyond	on or to the further side of sth
meadow	a field covered in grass, often used for hay
spot	a particular area or place: *a quiet spot*
infrequent	not happening often OPP **frequent; frequency** n
occasionally	sometimes but not often
isolated	without much contact with other people **isolation** n
nevertheless	despite sth you have just mentioned
swap	exchange one thing for another
rural	connected with the country and country life

1 Correct the spelling mistakes.

1 medow ....
2 freqwent ....
3 outskirt ....
4 shalow ....
5 ocassionally ....
6 nevertheles ....
7 swop ....
8 streem ....

2 Replace the underlined word(s) with a single word that keeps the same meaning.

1 I wouldn't <u>exchange</u> my old cottage for a modern house. ....
2 There's a <u>very small river</u> running through the village. ....
3 The bottom of the garden is a very quiet <u>area</u>. ....
4 We feel <u>we lack contact with other people</u>. ....
5 We do get snow in winter but it's <u>not often</u>. ....
6 I walked through a lovely <u>field covered in grass</u>. ....
7 <u>On the further side of</u> the river there is a church. ....
8 We go there <u>sometimes but not often</u>. ....
9 It's very quiet in the evenings. <u>Despite that</u>, I still like it. ....
10 I used to live on the <u>edge</u> of the village. ....

3 Complete the sentences.

1 You can walk across if you take your shoes off – the stream is very ....
2 There isn't much contact with the neighbours, so they do suffer from ....
3 Rain isn't .... in the east of the country. The climate is surprisingly dry.
4 There isn't much to do in the evening in a village. ...., I still love it.
5 A feeling of peace and calm is one of the joys of .... life.
6 My cousin lives on the .... of the town, quite close to the countryside.
7 What about the .... of the bus service? How often do buses run?
8 Just .... the post office, you can see the bridge on your right.
9 We walked across the meadow and found a quiet .... for our picnic.
10 The river is very .... here, so don't let the children go in.

TEST YOURSELF

B Farming

Martin Dobbs runs a **mixed** animal and **arable** farm. He **keeps** a **herd** of 75 **dairy** cows, which supplies milk and cream to local suppliers in the area, but that is in **combination** with a range of **crops**, including both **cereals** and fruit.

Although farming is becoming an **increasingly** difficult way to **earn a living**, Martin has never considered doing anything other than working in agriculture, which both his father and grandfather did before him. His son and one full-time **labourer** help him. When he dies, he will **pass on** the farm to his son.

SPOTLIGHT *mixed*

Mixed can refer to:
1 different types of thing: *mixed farming* (as above)
2 good and bad qualities: *I have **mixed feelings** about the farm.*
3 consisting of different kinds of people: *People of **mixed race**.*

---

4 **Combine words in the box to form six phrases.**

arable	cereal	mixed	physical	earn	herd
labour	crop	a living	feelings	of cows	farm

....

....

5 **Complete the sentences on the right. Keep the same meaning.**

1 We are an <u>arable farm</u>.   We mostly ....
2 We have <u>over 100</u> cows.   We have a ....
3 We <u>grow cereals and keep animals</u>.   We are a ....
4 We <u>grow cereals and vegetables</u>.   We are an ....
5 We only have <u>milking cows</u>.   We are a ....
6 <u>How does he earn a living</u>?   What .... ?
7 My son will get the farm <u>after I die</u>.   I will ....
8 We grow many <u>types of grass for food</u>.   We grow various ....

6 **Complete the questions.**

1 Do most farms in the area grow a .... of cereals and fruit/vegetables?
2 Do they now rely .... on machines to do the work?
3 What kinds of animals do farmers .... ?
4 What kinds of .... do farmers grow?
5 Do many people .... a living from farming?
6 Is it common for farmers to .... on a farm to their children?
7 Is there a shortage of .... , or is it easy to employ farm .... ?
8 Do people have .... feelings about machines replacing human labour?

7 ABOUT YOUR COUNTRY **Write answers to the questions in Exercise 6, or talk to another student.**

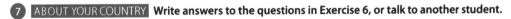

....

....

 TEST YOURSELF

CITY BREAKS IN PRAGUE

Prague is a **stunning** city, and this **thriving** capital of the Czech Republic makes a romantic and **vibrant** city-break destination. A stroll through Prague's streets is a **delight**: its architecture is **remarkably diverse**. Charles Bridge and the Astronomical Clock have both **undergone restoration**, but the city was amazingly untouched by the Second World War.

UNWIND ON THE ALGARVE

The **resorts** on the Algarve, with their golden sandy beaches, are a great place to relax. **Laze around** on the golden sandy beaches, enjoy the atmosphere of traditional fishing villages like Alvor, or just **wander round** Albufeira's old town, which still **retains** its wonderful **charm**.

OFF THE BEATEN TRACK ON THE GREAT WALL OF CHINA

Our China **trek** offers a **unique** experience for the **adventurous** traveller who wants to **get away from it all**. Apart from the spectacular scenery, you will have the rare opportunity to camp in a **remote** part of rural China and experience local life in its most **unspoilt** state.

GLOSSARY

stunning	extremely attractive or impressive	**laze around/about**	relax and do very little
thriving	growing and developing, and very successful SYN **flourishing**	**wander around/ round**	walk slowly without a real purpose or direction
vibrant	full of life and energy; exciting	**retain** *formal*	keep sth
delight	sth that gives sb great pleasure **delightful** *adj*	**charm**	a pleasant or attractive quality or feature **charming** *adj*
remarkably	in an unusual or surprising way **remarkable** *adj*	**off the beaten track**	far away from other people and houses SYN **remote**
diverse	very different from each other, and of various kinds	**trek**	a long hard walk, often in the mountains
undergo	experience a process of change	**unique**	being the only one of its kind
restoration	the work of repairing old buildings, paintings, etc. **restore** *v*	**adventurous**	liking to try new things **adventure** *n*
unwind *inf*	relax, especially after working hard SYN **take it easy**	**get away from it all**	go somewhere different to have a rest or holiday
resort	a place which is known as a holiday destination: *a beach/ski resort*	**unspoiled** (ALSO **unspoilt**)	(of a place) beautiful because it has not been changed or built on

1 Complete the dialogues.

1 Is the town centre quite different now?   ~ Yes, it has .... major changes.
2 Is it still a thriving place?   ~ Yes, it's ....
3 Is the restaurant quite cheap?   ~ Yes, it's .... good value.
4 There's nowhere like Cuenca.   ~ That's true. It's ....
5 The village hasn't changed at all.   ~ No, it's completely ....
6 I've heard the villa is miles from anywhere.   ~ Yes, it's very ....
7 Have you been there before?   ~ Yes, it's a very popular beach ....
8 Is it a really enjoyable place?   ~ Yes, an absolute ....

2 Replace the underlined word(s) with a single word that keeps the same meaning.

1 He's running a <u>flourishing</u> clothes business.   ....
2 Just look at that <u>beautiful</u> view of the mountains.   ....
3 My son's interests are very <u>varied</u>.   ....
4 That particular building is <u>the only one in existence</u>.   ....
5 The villa was really <u>off the beaten track</u>.   ....
6 The old town is a <u>surprising and unusual</u> place.   ....
7 We just want to <u>relax and do very little</u>.   ....
8 The old buildings in the centre need to be <u>repaired</u>.   ....

3 Complete the text.

Great Expectations ...

After a hard time at work, I was looking forward to taking it (1) .... for a couple of weeks on a Greek island. The villa was by the sea and off the (2) .... At least, that's what I had understood from the holiday brochure, but the reality was somewhat different. The villa was undergoing (3) .... , so I had to stay in a nearby beach (4) .... , where most people were trying to do the same as me: (5) .... around on the beach during the day, and then (6) .... round the streets in the evening. Sadly, the place turned out to be (7) .... noisy and unpleasant, so my idea of getting (8) .... all just didn't happen.

4 Replace words in the text with words from the box so that the meaning stays the same.

| unwind | thriving | diverse | vibrant | stunning | restore | remarkable | wander | retain |

Lisbon is surrounded by seven hills, and from most of them you have beautiful views of this unusual and surprising city, which has managed to keep so much of its varied architecture and cultural heritage. But it is also a modern, flourishing European capital, and in recent years the city has managed to repair many of the old buildings. For tourists, one of the most popular parts is the *Alfama* where you can casually walk around and enjoy the charms of the old town. The *Chiado* district is famous for shops and restaurants, but for really exciting nightlife, head for the *Bairro Alto*. Then, after all that, you can relax on the nearby beaches of *Cascais* and *Estoril*: wonderful places to visit.

....
....
....

5 ABOUT YOU Write your answers, or ask another student.

What do you want from a holiday?
Do you want to go somewhere vibrant and exciting? ....
Do you want to laze around on a beach and unwind? ....
Do you want to go somewhere off the beaten track and get away from it all? ....
Do you want a holiday with adventure? ....
Do you like to wander around interesting towns and villages? ....

TEST YOURSELF

A Luxury accommodation

When we go away, the last thing we want is to find that everywhere is **fully-booked**, no **vacancies** anywhere, ending up in a **miserable B and B** (or **Airbnb**), possibly **in the middle of nowhere**. Therefore, we always **book well in advance** and go for something fairly **exclusive, preferably** in a town. It doesn't have to be a **grand** or **impressive** building, but we do expect **luxury** and first-class service in order to **justify** the high prices these places charge. **Having said that**, high prices are no **guarantee** of high quality.

SPOTLIGHT accommodation

A **B and B** (ALSO **B & B** – *abbreviations of* **bed and breakfast**; ALSO **guest house**) is like a fairly cheap hotel but it does not serve evening meals.

Airbnb is a private company in which members offer accommodation in a room, flat or house they own. This is all arranged online.

GLOSSARY

fully-booked	(of a hotel, restaurant, theatre, etc.) full; no places available	**preferably**	used to show which person or thing would be better or preferred
vacancy	a room in a hotel that is available: *no vacancies*	**luxury**	beautiful and expensive things **luxurious** adj
miserable	unpleasant, making you feel unhappy	**impressive**	causing a feeling of admiration because of its size, quality, importance, etc. SYN **grand**; **impress** v
in the middle of nowhere	far away from other people and houses	**justify**	give or be a good reason for sth
in advance	before a particular time or event: ***book well in advance*** (= book a long time before you go)	**having said that**	used to introduce an opinion that makes what you have just said seem less strong
exclusive	expensive and reserved for special people	**guarantee**	a promise that sth will be done or that sth will happen **guarantee** v

1 **Underline the main stress on these words.**

justify   vacancy   luxury   in advance   miserable   guarantee   luxurious   exclusive   preferably   fully-booked

2 **Good news, bad news, or could it be either? Write *G*, *B* or *either*.**

1 The meal was impressive. ....
2 The hotel was fully booked. ....
3 They gave us a guarantee a taxi would be there. ....
4 There were still vacancies at the hotel. ....
5 The B&B was in the middle of nowhere. ....
6 The weather was miserable. ....
7 This area is rather exclusive. ....
8 The room wasn't luxurious. ....

3 **Complete the dialogues with a suitable word or phrase.**

1 Was the breakfast good?   ~ Yes, very good. ...., there wasn't a lot of choice.
2 Which floor do you want?   ~ I don't mind, but .... overlooking the garden.
3 Have you reserved a room?   ~ Yes, we booked well ....
4 Will they refund your money?   ~ Yes, they .... that when I rang and cancelled.
5 It's very expensive.   ~ I know, but they .... that by the high quality of the rooms.
6 Are there still rooms available?   ~ No, we got the last ...., so they're .... now.
7 Was the building very grand?   ~ Yes, we were ....
8 It's a very expensive place, isn't it?   ~ Yes, but I like a bit of .... on my holidays.

4 **ABOUT YOU** **Write your answers, or talk to another student.**

1 Do you book your holidays well in advance? ....
2 Do you often stay in fairly luxurious hotels? ....
3 Do you ever stay in a B&B or use Airbnb? ....
4 Do you like being in the middle of nowhere for your holiday? ....
5 Do you think high prices usually guarantee high quality in your country? ....
6 What do you look for most in holiday accommodation? ....

📖 TEST YOURSELF

B Budget accommodation

We're not **mean**, but we've generally **opted for** holidays which only require a fairly limited **budget**: occasionally in a **caravan**[1], but more often we go camping or stay in a **youth hostel**. The thing that **appeals to** me about camping is not just **expense** – it's cheap - but it also **enables** us to move around more freely, and we like that **flexibility**. And **given that** we generally **live in comfort**, I think it's good for the children to experience a type of holiday which is a bit different. When we **go away** we are quite **strict** about them not using their phones.

GLOSSARY

mean	wanting to keep money and not spend it on others OPP **generous**	**enable sb/sth to do sth**	make it possible for sb/sth to do sth
opt for sth	choose sth	**flexibility**	the ability to be changed easily **flexible** adj OPP **inflexible**
budget	an amount of money you are able to spend on sth	**given (that)**	when you consider sth
youth hostel	a cheap and simple place to stay, especially for young people	**comfort**	the state of having a life with everything you need, or being physically relaxed: **live in comfort**
appeal (to sb)	be attractive or interesting to sb **appealing** adj	**go away**	leave home for a period of time, especially for a holiday
expense	the money that you spend on sth: **an extra expense**	**strict**	not allowing people to break rules or behave badly

5 **Complete the dialogues with a word or phrase.**

1 Can you choose when you travel? ~ Yes, there's lot of .... with dates and times.
2 It's a very expensive holiday. ~ Yes, especially .... that he doesn't earn much.
3 My uncle is paying for my holiday. ~ Wow, that's very .... of him.
4 Are you here this weekend? ~ No, we're .... for a few days.
5 Are you hiring a car as well? ~ No, that's an extra .... We'll take buses.
6 We need to stay somewhere really cheap. ~ OK, how about a .... or a
   .... ?
7 Some people love camping but it doesn't .... to me personally.
8 Do you always eat together, even on holiday? ~ Yes, my parents are very .... about that.

6 **Rewrite the sentences using words from the box. Keep the meaning the same.**

flexible	budget	opt for	mean	enable	appealing	expense	comfort

1 He never wants to spend money.
2 If it's a cheap place, we can stay a bit longer.
3 We have a limited amount of money to spend.
4 The date can be changed easily.
5 We chose something quite simple.
6 I want to have a pleasant life and everything I need.
7 A room with a balcony costs more money.
8 A caravan doesn't interest me.

7 **ABOUT YOU** **Write your answers, or talk to another student.**

1 Have you ever stayed in a caravan or youth hostel? If so, what were they like? ....
2 Do budget holidays appeal to you, or do you prefer to stay somewhere in comfort? ....
3 Do you have a limited budget when you go on holiday? ....
4 Do you restrict using your phone (for work) when you're on holiday? ....
5 Do you like staying in one place or the flexibility of being able to move around? ....
6 Do you remember your parents being strict with you about anything on holiday? ....

TEST YOURSELF

A Buying

Hi Matt

Just wanted to let you know we've sold our **terraced**[1] house, and moved in to a larger **semi-detached**[2] property further out of town. It doesn't look that big from the outside, but the **interior** is really **spacious**: large **entrance hall**, with a wide **staircase**, and **open-plan** kitchen, dining room and living room. The bedrooms are also a good size, which is great. We need to do some **decorating** and probably **put in** a new kitchen, but **basically** the **overall** condition is quite good. The other **bonus** is that it was actually cheaper than our other house, **largely** because of the location, so we don't need such a big **mortgage**. …

Send

GLOSSARY	
interior	the inside part of sth OPP **exterior**
spacious	having a lot of space; large in size
entrance hall	the area directly inside the front door of a building
staircase	a set of stairs
open-plan	(of the inside of a building) not divided into separate rooms
decorating	the act of putting paint, etc. on a wall or ceiling of a room or house: *do (some / a bit of) decorating*
put sth in	fix equipment or furniture into position so it can be used SYN **install**
basically	used to say what the most important or most basic aspect of sth is SYN **essentially**
overall	generally; when you consider most things
bonus	sth good that you get in addition to what you expect
largely	mostly
mortgage	money you borrow in order to buy a house or flat: *take out a mortgage* (= organize a mortgage)

1 Find an underlined letter in the right-hand box with the same pronunciation as the underlined letter(s) in the left-hand box. Use the ⒶⓅⓅ to help you.

spacious	staircase	mortgage		camera	late	saw
detached	entrance	overall		flat	care	damage

....

....

2 Complete the sentences.
1. There are one or two small differences, but .... the flats are the same.
2. We've got a narrow .... up to the second floor.
3. The .... of the house needs money spent on it, but the .... is fine.
4. The price is .... to do with location.
5. We didn't need a ....
6. There's also a garage at the back. That's a ....
7. There are a few things wrong with it, but .... it's fine.
8. We are going to do some .... in the bedrooms.
9. The living room is really ....
10. We plan to .... a new shower.

3 Complete the questions.
1. Are .... and semi-........................... houses common?
2. Is it common in flats to have a large entrance .... ?
3. Do people often prefer an open-........................... design?
4. Do most people .... a mortgage to buy a flat or house?
5. Do people usually do the .... themselves, or employ someone to do it for them?
6. When people buy a new home, do they often .... new bathrooms or kitchens?

4 ABOUT YOUR COUNTRY Write your answers to Exercise 3, or talk to another student.

 TEST YOURSELF

B Renting

I've finally found somewhere to rent. It's been difficult as there aren't many **rental** properties **on the market** at the moment. It's on the top floor of a three-**storey** house – I guess it was originally the **attic** – and I've taken out a one-year **lease**, but the **landlord** is happy for me to **extend** that if I want to. It's **unfurnished**, so I will have to buy a lot of new stuff, but it has recently been redecorated, and there's quite a lot of **storage** space. It's a two-bedroom flat, and I've already got a **flatmate** to share the rent with me, so it's not too expensive. I've just got to sign the **contract** now and pay the **deposit** along with one month's rent. I move in next week.

GLOSSARY

rental	A **rental property** is a property that you rent rather than buy.	**extend**	make sth longer or larger, in space or time: *extend a building*; *extend a lease*; **extension** n
on the market	available for sb to buy or rent	**unfurnished**	without furniture OPP **furnished**
storey	one floor or level of a building: *a multi-storey car park*	**storage**	the process of keeping sth in a particular place until it is needed; space where things can be kept
attic	the space or room under the roof of a house ALSO **loft**		
lease	a legal agreement that lets you use a building for a fixed period of time in return for rent	**flatmate**	a person who shares a flat with one or more people
landlord	a person who rents out a house/flat or room to people for money. A **landlord** can be a man or a woman; a **landlady** is a woman only.	**contract**	a written legal agreement: *sign a contract*
		deposit	money that you pay when you rent sth and that you get back when you return it without damage

5 Underline the main stress on these words. Use the ⒜ to help you.

rental   attic   landlord   extend   unfurnished   flatmate   contract   deposit

6 Underline the correct answer. Both answers may be possible.

1 Is the flat a *rent / rental* property?
2 Who is the *landlord / landlady*?
3 I'm storing stuff in the *attic / loft*.
4 I need to find a *flatguy / flatmate*.
5 There's lots of *storey / storage* space.
6 It's a six-month *rent / lease*.
7 I'll move in after I *write / sign* the contract.
8 I hope I can *intend / extend* the lease.

7 Complete the dialogues in a suitable way.

1 Are you moving in soon? ~ Yes, I just have to sign the .... tomorrow.
2 Are you living there on your own? ~ No, I've got a couple of ....
3 Is there plenty of space to put things? ~ Yes, there's loads of .... space.
4 Do you have to pay anything before move in? ~ Yeah. You pay a .... – usually about a month's rent.
5 What if you want to stay more than a year? ~ I've already asked about an .... to the lease.
6 Do you need to buy much furniture? ~ No, the flat is fully ....
7 Have you bought the flat? ~ No, it's a ....
8 You're on the first floor? ~ Yes, that's right, but it's a four-.. building.

8 ABOUT YOUR COUNTRY Write your answers, or talk to another student.

1 Is it common to rent flats? ....
2 Are they usually furnished or unfurnished? ....
3 Is a one-year lease the normal length of a contract? ....
4 Are landlords/landladies usually happy to extend a rental contract? ....

 TEST YOURSELF

A A natural garden

I've always wanted a garden that copies the best of **nature**. So, having **acquired** a country cottage with land around it, I'm now creating my own **wildlife** garden. I will need to remove a few old tree **roots**[1] that make planting difficult, but generally the project is going well. A gentle **slope** drops down from the cottage to a **pond**[2], where I've discovered quite a rare **species** of **frog**[3], which I obviously want to protect.

Near the pond is a **greenhouse**[4]. I will grow tomatoes, but it's largely **intended** for more **tropical** fruits that you can't normally grow in England, such as melon and guava. There's already a variety of **mature** plants in the garden, and a **shed** where I can keep all my tools. Finally, I'm hoping to attract birds to build their **nests** in an old **hollow** tree in the small **wood** I have along one side of the garden.

GLOSSARY

acquire *formal*	get sth by buying it or being given it
wildlife	animals, birds, and insects that live in a natural state
slope	a piece of land that is higher at one end than the other **slope** v
species	a group of plants or animals that are all similar and can breed together
intended (for sth)	planned or designed for sth
tropical	coming from or found in very hot parts of the world
mature	fully grown or fully developed
shed	a small simple building, usually built of wood, and often found in gardens
nest	a place where birds lay their eggs and live with their young **nest** v
hollow	with a hole or empty space inside
wood (ALSO **woods**)	an area of trees, smaller than a forest

SPOTLIGHT *nature*

We can say someone is interested in **nature** ([U] = the physical world and everything that lives in it). We don't talk about being ~~in the nature~~. We can say:

- *I like being* **in the countryside** OR *looking at* **beautiful scenery**.

1 Circle the correct answer(s). Sometimes both answers are possible.

1 The *lake / pond* is about 30 cm deep.
2 The trees are *fully grown / mature*.
3 There's a great view of the *scenery / nature*.
4 We have a lot of *tropic / tropical* fruit.
5 How did you *get / acquire* the land?
6 I'm very interested in *nature / the nature*.
7 We need to protect *wildlife / wildliving*.
8 I like being in the *scenery / countryside*.

2 Find five pairs of words in the box. Write a sentence to explain the connection each pair has.

frog	tools	birds	wildlife	trees	nature	nest	pond	shed	roots

....

3 Complete the sentences.

1 The .... is spectacular: beautiful lakes surrounded by mountains.
2 For the plants to grow, water has to get down to the ....
3 I often go for a walk in the .... It's a great place to see birds.
4 The garden isn't big, but there may be a chance to .... more land next to it.
5 The lights are .... for the garden when we sit out on warm summer evenings.
6 I read that there are 369,000 .... of flowering plants in the world.
7 From one end of the garden, there is a gentle .... which goes down to the river.
8 I love pineapple, but growing .... fruit in this country is not easy.
9 It gets very hot in the .... , so it's great for growing tomatoes and cucumber.
10 The tree was .... , so birds could go in and out very easily.

TEST YOURSELF

B Gardening through the seasons

SPRING: Add **compost** to improve the **soil**.
Cut back any **bushes** that have got too big.
Dig the ground if it's not too **muddy**.

SUMMER: Mow the lawn once a week.
Weed the garden, little and often.
Find a nice **bench, put your feet up**[1] and enjoy the garden.

AUTUMN: Tidy **hedges** and fallen leaves.
Routine **maintenance**, e.g. clean tools and clean the shed.

bush · digging · spade

lawnmower · lawn

bench · 1

mow
pt **mowed** *pp* **mowed / mown**

GLOSSARY

compost	a mixture of decaying plants and food that is added to soil to help things grow. **Compost** makes soil more **fertile**.	**weed**	remove **weeds** (wild plants growing where they are not wanted, especially in a formal garden) **weeding** *n: do some weeding*
soil	the top part of the earth in which trees and plants grow	**put your feet up**	sit down and relax , especially with your feet raised and supported
cut sth back	remove some of a plant's stems or branches to improve future growth	**hedge**	a line of bushes growing close together around a garden or field
muddy	(of the earth) wet from too much rain **mud** *n*	**maintenance**	keeping sth in good condition by checking or repairing it regularly **maintain** *v*

4 Good news or bad news? Write *G* or *B*.

1 The ground is muddy. ....
2 We've got lots of compost for the garden. ....
3 I've just mowed the lawn. ....
4 The lawn is full of weeds. ....
5 There's loads of digging to do. ....
6 I'll be able to put my feet up. ....
7 The soil is fertile. ....
8 The hedges need cutting back. ....

5 Replace the underlined words with a word or phrase that keeps the same meaning.

1 Have you got <u>something I can use for digging</u>? Have you got a .... ?
2 I'm going to <u>sit down and relax</u>. I'm going to ....
3 He's going to <u>cut</u> the <u>grass</u>. He's going to ....
4 You'll need to <u>reduce the size of</u> this bush. You'll need to ....
5 I'm going to <u>improve the soil</u>. I'm going to add ....
6 Where's the <u>machine to cut the grass</u>? Where's the .... ?
7 There's a <u>line of bushes</u> round the field. There's a ....
8 I need to <u>take out the weeds</u>. I need to do ....

6 What do you know about gardening? Answer the questions.

1 Why add compost? ....
2 Why is mud a problem? ....
3 Do you need to weed the garden? ....
4 How frequently might you mow the lawn? ....
5 What do you do with plants and bushes that are getting too big? ....
6 What's the purpose of a garden bench? ....
7 Do you ever need to tidy a hedge? ....
8 Give examples of routine maintenance. ....

TEST YOURSELF

A Downloading an app on your phone

- **Launch** the chosen app store on your device.
- **Scroll down** to **browse** the available apps.
- **Tap** the app you want.
- **Tap** 'get' if it is free, or the price if it is to be paid.
- Select **install** if it is free, or 'buy' when the **icon switches**.
- **Key in** your password or use touch ID when **prompted**.

If you have a problem downloading an app, you may not have enough available **storage** on your device. You can manage your storage in **Settings**.

GLOSSARY	
scroll up/down	move text up or down on the screen so that you can read the different parts
browse	look through different websites without reading everything **browsing** n A **browser** is a program that lets you see documents on the internet.
tap (on) sth	hit sth/sb quickly and lightly: *tap the icon to open the app*
install	put a new program onto a computer or device **installation** n
icon	a small symbol on a computer or smartphone screen that represents a program or a file
switch	change or make sth change from one thing to another
key sth (in)	put information into a computer using a keyboard
prompt	encourage or tell sb to do sth on a computer
storage	the process of keeping information on a computer and the way that it is kept
settings *pl*	the place on a computer or device where you can choose the way it looks or works

SPOTLIGHT *launch*

In computing, **launch** means 'start a program'. **Launch** is also used with the meaning 'start an activity' with a range of nouns in other contexts.

- *launch a campaign / an investigation / an appeal / an enquiry / an attack*

1 **Correct the errors.**

1 stroll up a document ....
2 tap the ikon ....
3 lanch the programme ....
4 brouse the website for help ....
5 instal the program ....
6 The computer will promt you to act. ....
7 Go to setting to change sounds. ....
8 How much data storige have you got? ....

2 **Cover the glossary. Which words are being defined?**

1 put information into a device using a keyboard ....
2 touch something, e.g. an icon, quickly ....
3 change from one thing to another ....
4 start a program, an app, etc. ....
5 a program that lets you read documents on the internet ....
6 the process of keeping information and the way it is kept ....
7 move text on a screen up so that you can read it ....

3 **Complete the dialogues.**

1 Did you manage to put the program on your computer? ~ Yes, I .... it successfully.
2 Where did you find out about that new restaurant app? ~ I was just .... on a food website.
3 How will I know what to do next? ~ The program will .... you to continue or cancel.
4 How do I open the app? ~ You just .... the icon on the screen.
5 Where are the answers to the quiz questions? ~ They're at the bottom of the document. Just .... down a bit.
6 How do I check the battery on my phone? ~ Go into .... and click on 'battery'.
7 What are the police doing about computer crime? ~ They've .... various investigations.
8 How do I send a message? ~ Tap on this ....

TEST YOURSELF

B Routine maintenance

1. Don't leave your device charging all the time. When fully charged, **unplug** the power **cable**.

2. Use an **antivirus** program, and keep it **updated**.

3. Remember to do regular **backups** of your data. If you use your computer a lot, **back** your work **up** every day.

4. Don't turn the computer off every time it **freezes**. Wait a while before you decide whether or not to **reboot**.

5. Clean your computer screen by **wiping downwards** with a **damp** cloth. Don't let any water drops get into the computer: they could **ruin** the **internal components**.

GLOSSARY	
unplug	remove the plug of a piece of electrical equipment from the power supply OPP **plug (sth) in**
cable	a set of wires covered in plastic or rubber that carries electricity, etc.
antivirus	designed to find and destroy computer viruses
update	make sth more modern by adding new parts or information **update** n
backup	a copy of the information on your computer that you keep in case you lose the information **back sth up**
freeze	When your computer **freezes**, you cannot move any images because of a system problem.
reboot	switch off a computer then start it again immediately
wipe	remove dirt, liquid, etc. from sth using a cloth or your hand
downwards	towards the ground or towards a lower level OPP **upwards**
damp	a little bit wet
ruin	damage sth so badly that it loses its value, pleasure, etc.
internal	connected with the inside of sth OPP **external**
component	one of several parts of which sth is made

4 Is the pronunciation of the underlined letters the same or different? Write *S* or *D*. Use the **APP** to help you.

1 r<u>ui</u>n   antiv<u>i</u>rus   ....
2 antiv<u>i</u>rus   w<u>i</u>pe   ....
3 <u>u</u>pwards   pl<u>u</u>g in   ....
4 c<u>a</u>ble   upd<u>a</u>te   ....
5 d<u>a</u>mp   extern<u>a</u>l   ....
6 downw<u>a</u>rds   antivir<u>u</u>s   ....

5 Answer the questions.

1 If you *ruin* something, can you still use it?
2 If you *reboot* your computer, do you turn it on or off?
3 When you *wipe* something, are you cleaning it?
4 Does a computer have one *component* or many?
5 Is a computer mouse an *internal* or *external* component?
6 If you don't have a *backup* of your data, is that sensible?
7 Does a *cable* connect something to a power supply?

6 Complete the questions with a suitable word.

1 Does your computer screen often .... ?
2 Have you got .... software to protect the data on your device?
3 How do you clean your screen? With a .... cloth or some other way?
4 And do you wipe the screen upwards or .... ?
5 How often do you .... your software?
6 What time of day do you usually .... in your phone to charge it?
7 Do you .... your data once a day/week/month or never?
8 If you use a desktop computer, do you ever .... it after you've shut down?

7 ABOUT YOU Write your answers to the questions in Exercise 6, or tell a partner.

 TEST YOURSELF

A The championship

THE PREMIER LEAGUE

As the championship **reaches** its **climax**, Manchester City and Liverpool are still challenging for the **title**. Man City's next **opponents** are Fulham, **at home**, which looks to be a **relatively** easy game. Liverpool, however, face much **tougher opposition**, **away** at Arsenal. The manager is not **underestimating** the difficulty of the task. 'Arsenal are a quality side and still **contenders** for a place in the top four, so our **priority** is just that one game, and not to think about the championship title.'

GLOSSARY	
league	a group of sports clubs that compete with each other for a prize
climax	the most important and exciting part of a book, film, game, etc.: *reach a climax*
title	the position of being the winner in a competition, especially in sport: *She has three world titles in cycling.*
opponent	(in sports or competitions) a person/ team who plays against sb
at home	If a team plays **at home**, they play in their own stadium. OPP **away (at** Arsenal, etc.); **home** *adj*, **away** *adj*: *an away/home game*
relatively	to quite a large degree, especially when compared with others
tough	difficult
(the) opposition	the person or team you compete against in sport
underestimate	think that sb/sth is not as strong, good, etc. as they really are OPP **overestimate**
contender	a person or team with a chance of winning a competition
priority	sth that is more important or you must do before anything else: *a top priority*

1. **Underline the main stress on these words. Use the ⒜ to help you.**

| climax | underestimate | opponent | contender |
| relatively | priority | opposition | overestimate |

2. **Answer the questions.**
   1. If something is *relatively* easy, is it quite easy or extremely easy?
   2. If it's a *tough* game, is it a very physical game, or a difficult game?
   3. Is the *opposition*, a team you are playing against or a team you don't like ?
   4. In a competition, is a *contender* the team who is going to win it?
   5. If something is a *priority*, is it quite important or very important?
   6. If you've observed the opposition carefully, are you likely to *underestimate* them, *overestimate* them, or judge them well?
   7. Does a *climax* come at the beginning or the end?
   8. Does a *league* involve one team or many teams?

3. **Complete the sentences.**
   1. Our .... in the next game are a team that have won two championships, so it will be a very .... match.
   2. After his injury, Brown's top .... now is to get back to full fitness.
   3. There are no weak teams in the League, so you should never .... the opposition.
   4. There are 20 teams in the Premier ....
   5. Last week's game was .... easy, but the next match will be much tougher.
   6. Inter Milan are playing well, so they will be .... again for the championship.
   7. We are at .... this week to Spurs, and .... at Liverpool the following week.
   8. With just one round of games to go, the championship is now .... a climax.
   9. Chelsea have now won three premiership .... in recent years.

▤ TEST YOURSELF

B What do football supporters think?

The new manager has **transformed** our season, and getting players back from injury has been a real **boost**. We had **no chance** of qualifying for Europe at Christmas, but now it's a possibility.

CHELSEA

We lack a bit of **consistency** and the manager is **under pressure**. However, I still think we have **a real chance** of being in the top four and **qualifying** for The Champions League.

SPURS

We have a habit of **dominating** the opposition, then we **throw** it **away** at the end. Last week's **defeat** was a bad one, but I still think we **stand a chance of getting** into the top four.

ARSENAL

We've **sorted out** one or two problems off the **pitch**, but after three defeats **in a row**, there may only be **an outside chance** of making the top four.

GLOSSARY

consistency	the quality of always behaving in the same way or having the same standard, etc. **consistent** adj OPP **inconsistent**
under pressure	in an anxious situation, often because sb is forcing you to do sth in a certain way
qualify (for sth)	win the right to enter a competition or continue to the next stage of it **qualification** n
transform	change sth completely, usually in a positive way **transformation** n
boost	sth that helps or encourages sb/sth

dominate	be more powerful, important or noticeable than others **domination** n; **dominant** adj
throw sth away	waste or not use an opportunity
defeat	an occasion when sb fails to win or be successful against sb else OPP **victory**
sort sth out	find a solution to a problem
pitch	an area of ground where you play certain sports: **a football/rugby pitch**
in a row	one after another, without a break

SPOTLIGHT *chance*

Chance is used in many phrases.
- There's **no chance** that we will reach Sydney before night.
- We've only got an **outside chance** of promotion to the Premier League. (= a very small chance) OPP a **real/ good chance**
- Do you think we **stand a chance of** winning? (= have a possibility of winning)
- This season could be my **big chance**. (= opportunity for success) He's retiring soon, so this is his **last chance** to lead the team. (= final opportunity)

4 Complete the sentences.

1 The noun from qualify is ....
2 The opposite of defeat is ....
3 The opposite of consistent is ....
4 The noun from dominate is ....
5 The noun from transform is ....
6 The noun from consistent is ....

5 Positive or negative? Write *P* or *N*.

1 It's been a real boost. ....
2 We've sorted it out. ....
3 Another defeat. ....
4 He transformed the team. ....
5 We're inconsistent. ....
6 Three victories in a row. ....
7 I threw it away. ....
8 I've been under pressure. ....
9 We've got a real chance. ....
10 We were dominant. ....

6 Complete the sentences.

1 Next season could be my last .... of winning the championship.
2 The .... is in bad condition because of the heavy rain.
3 If we win the next two games, it will be a .... for the players and supporters.
4 One more victory and it will be three wins in a ....
5 We just .... away games that we really should win easily.
6 One week we play well, the next we're rubbish; we lack ....
7 If we win on Saturday, we will .... for the next round in the competition.
8 I know the team is under ...., but they have to .... out their problems.
9 Unfortunately, in our last four games, we've had one victory and three ....
10 I don't think we .... a .... of winning the title.

7 ABOUT YOU Do you support a team? If so, how have they been playing recently? Write sentences using vocabulary from above, or tell a partner.

TEST YOURSELF

Will a song **stand the test of time?**

What is it about a pop song that makes it **compelling** not only as **a hit single** when it's released, but for future generations as well? Take, for example, *Bohemian Rhapsody* by Queen. Is it the interesting **lyrics**, the **melodies** or the fascinating changes of **rhythm** that make it so popular? Much less **complicated**, on the **surface** at least, but no less successful is: *All You Need is Love* by the Beatles. The **sentiment** in its **catchy chorus** couldn't be simpler, and it is such an easy song to **sing along to**. Or is it the personality and quality of the singer or the band that **determine** whether the song will **engage** the listener or not? David Bowie's music is certainly **memorable** for those reasons; the colourful characters he created, such as Ziggy Stardust, only add to that.

Are great songs ones that you recognize as great the first time you **encounter** them, or are there some that you need to listen to several times before they have an effect? *Eleanor Rigby* by The Beatles is perhaps an example of one which you need to listen to carefully because of its complex lyrics (e.g. 'wearing the face that she keeps in a jar by the door'), but also because it was such an original and different type of pop song at the time.

But whatever **criteria** you use to measure the greatness of a pop song (or any **genre** of music), one thing seems true for all of them: they have the ability to stand the test of time because people can **relate to** them and still see them as **relevant** decades after they were first written.

GLOSSARY

stand the test of time	If sth **stands the test of time**, it is remembered positively for a long time, or functions successfully for a long time.
compelling	that makes you pay attention to it because it is so interesting and exciting
hit	a popular and successful song, often called **a hit single**
lyrics	the words of a song
melody	a tune, especially the main tune in a piece of music written for several instruments or voices SYN **tune**
rhythm	a regular repeated pattern of sounds or movements
complicated	difficult to understand SYN **complex**; **complicate** v
surface	the outer appearance of a person, thing or situation; the qualities you see or notice that are not hidden
sentiment	a feeling or an opinion, especially one based on emotions
catchy	(of a tune or the words of a song) easy to remember
chorus	the part of a song that is repeated
sing along (to sth)	sing a song at the same time as listening to it
determine	discover the facts about sth or calculate sth exactly SYN **establish**; **determination** n
engage formal	succeed in attracting and keeping sb's attention and interest
memorable	worth remembering or easy to remember SYN **unforgettable**
encounter formal	meet sb unexpectedly **encounter** n
criteria pl (sing **criterion**)	the standards that you use when you make a decision or form an opinion about sb/sth
genre formal	a particular type or style of literature, art, film or music
relate to sth	feel able to understand sth
relevant	important and useful OPP **irrelevant**; **relevance** n

1 Is the pronunciation of the underlined letters the same or different? Write *S* or *D*. Use the 🔵APP to help you.

1 cat<u>ch</u>y <u>ch</u>orus ....   6 <u>rhy</u>thm <u>ly</u>rics ....
2 rel<u>a</u>te eng<u>a</u>ge ....   7 <u>g</u>enre en<u>g</u>age ....
3 memor<u>a</u>ble relev<u>a</u>nt ....   8 cr<u>i</u>teria s<u>i</u>ngle ....
4 rel<u>a</u>te surf<u>a</u>ce ....   9 <u>ge</u>nre <u>en</u>gage ....
5 c<u>o</u>mpelling mel<u>o</u>dy ....   10 sentim<u>e</u>nt memor<u>a</u>ble ....

2 Circle the words in the box which we usually associate with music.

rhythm	compelling	tune	encounter	catchy	sing along
melody	chorus	criteria	hit single	lyrics	genre

3 Answer the questions.

1 What's the noun formed from *determine*? ....
2 What's a synonym for *complicated*? ....
3 What's the opposite of *relevant*? ....
4 What's the singular form of *criteria*? ....
5 What is the related noun for the verb *encounter*? ....
6 What's a synonym for *memorable*? ....

4 Replace the underlined words with a word or phrase that keeps the same meaning.

1 The song is <u>very easy to remember</u>. ....
2 He played a <u>series of musical notes</u> on the piano. ....
3 *One Direction* had a number of <u>very successful songs</u> in the 2010s. ....
4 I really like the <u>bit of the song that gets repeated</u>. ....
5 The <u>words of the song</u> are interesting. ....
6 This type of music is <u>difficult to understand</u>. ....
7 The band thinks it's important that young people <u>are able to feel and understand</u> the music.
   ....
8 I just love that <u>regular repeated pattern of sound</u>. ....

5 Complete the sentences.

1 Websites often choose the 'best' pop songs, but what are the .... for selection?
2 I like the song because of the lyrics and the catchy ....
3 Marie likes pop, but classical is still her favourite music ....
4 I first .... Hungarian folk music on a visit to Budapest five years ago.
5 Many protest songs were written about the Vietnam war, but they still seem just as .... today, and many young people can still .... to them.
6 Great performers have a natural ability to .... their audiences.
7 The most .... concert I've ever been to was in Edinburgh last year. It was amazing!
8 Many young people seem to see the .... of music to their lives more than art or literature.
9 Music journalists often try to .... what makes a great singer. Is it the qualities in their voice or their ability to convey a range of emotions?
10 On the .... , a song may seem quite positive, but when you listen to the lyrics a few more times, it can sometimes reveal a deeper and more pessimistic meaning.

6 ABOUT YOU Write answers to the questions, or talk to another student.

1 Do you agree with the text about the features of a great song? ....
2 Is there anything else you think is important in a great pop song? ....
3 What attracts you the most? Is it: the melody? the rhythm? the lyrics? ....
4 Do you often sing along to pop songs in English? ....
5 Is the sentiment expressed in a song important? Why? ....
6 Can you think of several more pop songs that have stood the test of time? ....

📋 TEST YOURSELF

A A fabulous play

> ★★★★★
> *The Woman in Black* is a **fabulous ghost story**. With just a minimal **set** and few **sound effects**, this drama will **scare you to death!**

> ★★★★★
> A **superb adaptation** of Susan Hill's **classic** novel. The **tension** is maintained throughout the production, and the **cast** of two are **sensational!** The **applause** went on and on.

> ★★★★★ The critics have been **unanimous** in their **praise**. A must-see thriller!

GLOSSARY

fabulous	extremely good, excellent SYN **sensational, superb**	**classic**	(of a book, play, etc.) one of the best and most important, and having lasting value
ghost story	a story about the spirit of a dead person that sb hears or sees	**tension**	a feeling of anxiety or stress because you are nervous **tense** *adj*
set	the scenery and furniture used in a play, film, etc.	**cast** (+ *sing* OR *pl verb*)	all the people who act in a play or film
sound effects	sounds that are made artificially in a play, film, etc. to make it more realistic, e.g. wind, thunder	**applause**	the sound of an audience showing approval by hitting their hands together **applaud** *v* SYN **clapping; clap** *v*
scare sb to death	make sb very frightened **Scared stiff** means very scared'.	**unanimous**	agreed by everyone
adaptation	a book or play that has been made into a film, TV programme, etc.	**praise**	words that show approval of or admiration for sb/sth **praise** *v*

1 Put the words in the correct column below based on the pronunciation of the underlined letters. Use the 🅰🅿🅿 to help you.

f<u>a</u>bulous   sens<u>a</u>tional   sc<u>are</u>   <u>a</u>dapt   cl<u>a</u>ssic
c<u>a</u>st   appl<u>au</u>se   <u>au</u>dience   un<u>a</u>nimous   pr<u>ai</u>se

ACTOR	**PLAY**	**FAR**	**HAIR**	**CAUGHT**	**THEATRE**

2 Circle the correct word. Both answers may be possible.

1 I didn't like the acting, but I thought the *set / cast* was good.
2 The play was frightening. It scared me to *die / death*.
3 There were great sound *affects / effects*.
4 I thought the play was absolutely *superb / sensational*.
5 The book is a *classic / classical*.
6 The play is an *adaption / adaptation* from a book.
7 Are you keen on *ghost / spirit* stories?
8 Did they *applause / applaud* at the end?
9 These scary stories can create a lot of *praise / tension*.

3 Complete the dialogues.

1 Were you frightened?   ~ Yes, I was scared ....
2 Is it based on an original story?   ~ No, it's an .... of a novel.
3 Was the acting good?   ~ Yes, the whole .... was excellent.
4 Did everyone agree?   ~ Yes, the decision was ....
5 Have people liked the play?   ~ Yes, it's had .... from almost everyone .
6 The audience just kept clapping.   ~ I know. The .... was incredible.
7 Will we still be reading it in 50 years?   ~ Definitely. It's a ....
8 Were people nervous?   ~ Yes, I felt a bit ....

 TEST YOURSELF

B A disappointing film

A I went to see the latest **blockbuster** at the local cinema last night. I wasn't **convinced** by it.

B Me neither. I had quite **high expectations** because the critics seem to like it, but I thought the action **sequences** were **somewhat predictable**, and it just lacked any **originality**.

A Yes, they were **poor**. I think the worst **aspect**, though, was the **screenplay**, which was not **convincing** at all. And I couldn't hear some of it either – **subtitles** might've helped.

SPOTLIGHT *subtitles and dubbing*

Subtitles translate what is said in a film into a different language; they appear at the bottom of the screen. They are also used to help deaf people. If a film is **dubbed**, the spoken words of the film are replaced by words in another language.

GLOSSARY

blockbuster *inf*	a very popular and successful film or book
convinced	completely sure about things **convincing** making sb believe that sth is true
expectation	a hope that sth good will happen: *have high/low expectations (of sth)*; *live up to expectations*; *exceed expectations*
sequence	a set of events, actions, etc. which have a particular order and lead to a particular result
somewhat	to some degree SYN **rather**
predictable	If sth is **predictable**, we know in advance that it will happen or what it will be like. OPP **unpredictable**
originality	the quality of being new and interesting and not seen before
poor	not good; lower in quality than was expected
aspect	a particular part or feature of sth
screenplay	the words that are written for a film and how they are to be acted

4 Underline the stress on these words. Use the 🔵APP to help you.

aspect	expectation	somewhat
blockbuster	screenplay	subtitles
convinced	sequence	unpredictable

5 *Yes or No?*

1 If a film is predictable, do you know what will happen? ....
2 If a film is somewhat long, is it very long? ....
3 Does a sequence always involve more than one? ....
4 If the plot of a film is convincing, is that positive? ....
5 If something exceeds your expectations, is it what you expected? ....
6 Can you go to a screenplay? ....

6 Complete the sentences.

1 I knew what was going to happen at the end. ~ Yes, it was very ....
2 My sister thought the ending was good, but I didn't think it was very ....
3 Did the film live up to your .... ?
4 There's a great action .... in the film involving a car chase.
5 The film was OK, but overall I came away feeling .... disappointed.
6 The actors were good, but they were helped by a fabulous ....
7 Some people don't like foreign films with subtitles and prefer it when they are ....
8 In the summer they often show these big .... at the cinema, largely for kids.

7 Complete the responses, agreeing with the first speaker but without repeating the underlined words.

1 The screenplay <u>wasn't good</u>, was it?   ~ No, it was ....
2 Was it <u>better than you thought it would be</u>?   ~ Yes, it ....
3 I wasn't <u>completely sure about the story</u>.   ~ No, I wasn't ....
4 I didn't like that <u>particular feature</u> of the film. ~ No, I didn't like that ....
5 Is the film <u>in the original language</u>?   ~ Yes, but it has ....
6 I didn't know <u>what was going to happen</u>.   ~ I agree, the ending was very ....
7 The film needed <u>some new and interesting ideas</u>. ~ Yeah, there was no ....
8 I thought the plot was <u>rather</u> confusing.   ~ I agree. I found it ....

📖 TEST YOURSELF

44) Socializing

A Organizing a party

- The **host** is expected to do most of the **preparation**, such as providing food and drink. This can be expensive and **time-consuming**, so consider asking others to **make a contribution** and bring something.
- You don't want the **prospect** of too much to **clear up**, so consider **disposable** plates and cutlery, which can be recycled after use.
- Don't advertise it on the internet **beforehand**. You don't want **gatecrashers**.
- Parties take a while to **get going**. Music or party games will **liven** things **up**.
- Finally, don't **get carried away**. You're planning a party, not a theme park.

GLOSSARY

host	a person who invites guests to a meal, a party, etc. **Hostess** can be used for a woman.
preparation	the act or process of getting ready for sth or making sth ready
time-consuming	needing a lot of time: *a time-consuming process*
contribution	sth that you give or do to help sth be successful: *make a contribution (to sth)*; **contribute** v
prospect	the possibility that sth will happen
clear (sth) up	make sth clean and neat, often by putting things back where they belong
disposable	made to be thrown away after single use
beforehand	before sth else happens or is done
gatecrasher	sb who tries to get into a party without an invitation
get going	(of a party or event) start to become enjoyable
liven (sth) up	become or make sth more exciting
get carried away	become too excited or lose control of your feelings

1 Underline the stress on these words. Use the ⓐ to help you.

time-consuming   contribution   beforehand   get going
contribute   disposable   gatecrasher   liven up

2 Complete the dialogues with a suitable word.

1 Whose party is it? ~ Paula and Stefano are the ....
2 Can we throw these plates away? ~ Yes, they're ....
3 Can we spend what we like on the party? ~ Yes, but don't get carried ....!
4 Did this take long? ~ Yes, it was very .... - ....
5 Why didn't you tell me Will was going to be there? ~ I didn't know ....
6 Why did you turn up the music? ~ To .... things up a bit.
7 Did people help out at the party with the food? ~ Yes, everyone made a ....
8 I wouldn't like the .... of organizing a wedding ~ Oh, it's ok as long as there are other people to help.

3 Complete the words in the text.

... and the party was great! There was lots of food, but I think Lia did most of the **(1)** ....
(2) ...., so she still had time to enjoy herself. And most of the guests **(3)** ....
something, either by bringing a bottle of something, or some food. She also put a couple of big guys near the door to stop **(4)** ...., which was sensible. It was quiet to start with, but it soon got
(5) ...., and when the disco started, things really **(6)** .... I imagine there was a lot to **(7)** .... the next day, but I hope Lia thought it was worth it.

Send

4 ABOUT YOU **What do you think of the advice in the text? Is there anything that would be unusual or unacceptable in your country? Write your answers, or ask another student.**

....
....
....

TEST YOURSELF

B In other people's company

Shall we **pop round** and see Gina?

Yes, she may **fancy** a bit of **company**.

It's been lovely, Ela, but we'd **better be off**.

That's ok. It was really **good of you** to come.

Is Aaron a bit **awkward in company**?

Mm. I don't think he enjoys **socializing**.

You always get a **warm welcome** at Laura's.

Yes, we **have a good laugh** whenever we go there.

> **SPOTLIGHT** company [U]
>
> - *I enjoy* **company**. (= being with other people)
> - *She's* **good company**. (= enjoyable to be with)
> - *They enjoy* **their own company**. (= being by themselves)
> - *He's not very good* **in company**. (= with other people)
> - *I'll* **accompany** *you*. (formal = go with you)

GLOSSARY

pop round/over/in *inf*	make a short visit to a person or place SYN **call round, call on sb**	**be off**	leave a place: *I must be off. / I'd better be off.*
fancy sth / doing sth *inf*	want sth or want to do sth	**good of sb (to do sth)**	willing to help; showing kindness to other people
awkward	embarrassed or not relaxed with other people	**warm welcome**	If sb gives you a **warm welcome** or **welcomes you with open arms**, you feel relaxed in their home: **welcome** *v, adj*: **make sb feel welcome**
socialize (with sb)	meet and spend time with people in a friendly way	**have a (good) laugh**	enjoy the occasion SYN **have a good/ great time**
you, etc. had better do sth	you should do sth		

5 Rewrite the sentences without using the underlined words. Keep the same meaning.

1 She's not very good <u>with other people</u>.   She's not very good ....
2 What <u>would you like to do</u>?   What do .... ?
3 We always <u>enjoy the occasion</u>.   We always have ....
4 I think I <u>should leave now</u>.   I think I'd ....
5 He's very <u>uncomfortable with people</u>.   He's very ....
6 She <u>made me feel relaxed in her home</u>.   She gave me a very ....
7 I think he likes <u>being by himself</u>.   I think he likes his ....
8 Someone will <u>go with</u> you.   Someone will ....
9 Did you <u>feel relaxed at her place</u>?   Did she make you .... ?
10 We'll <u>make a short visit</u> a bit later.   ~ We'll .... a bit later.

6 Complete the dialogues with a suitable word or phrase.

1 She is always nice to be with. ~ Yes, she is. She's very ....
2 Where have you been? ~ We just .... round to see Charlotte.
3 Was your dad there? ~ Of course. He was at the door to .... us.
4 He doesn't like being with people much, does he? ~ No, he prefers his ....
5 Max stays in a lot these days. ~ I know. He doesn't .... as much as he used to.
6 Did Miles move your stuff? ~ Yes, it was very .... to help.
7 Do you prefer being on your own? ~ Not at all. I enjoy .... , you know that.
8 Were the locals friendly when you moved in? ~ Oh yes, they welcomed us with ....
9 Do you want to .... round tonight on your way home? ~ Yes, that would be great.
10 We must .... now, but it was great seeing you. ~ You too. Have a good trip.

 TEST YOURSELF

45 Describing change

A Types of change

Example	Meaning
I find it difficult to **adapt to** so much new technology.	change your behaviour because the situation has changed SYN **adjust (to sth)**
We've **altered** our plans: we're now arriving at 6.00, not 7.00.	make sth different but without changing it completely **alteration** n
Civil servants are now **amending** the document.	change sth slightly, usually to correct a mistake in a statement, document, etc. **amendment** n
Democracy has **evolved** over hundreds of years.	change gradually, often from sth simple to sth more complicated **evolution** n
There are new proposals to **reform** the prison system.	change a law, system, organization, etc. to make it better **reform** n
Some people want to **restore** the monarchy in certain countries.	return sth to its former state or condition, e.g. a building, a painting **restoration** n
They were going to let him go, but they **reversed** their decision.	change sth so it is the opposite of what it was before: **reverse a decision/policy**; **reversal** n
Computers have **transformed** our lives.	completely change the appearance or character of sth, often to make it better **transformation** n
It's a big **transition** from school to full-time work.	a period of change from one state or condition to another: **in transition**

1 **Write the nouns related to these verbs.**

1 restore ....
2 amend ....
3 transform ....
4 reverse ....
5 evolve ....

2 **Organize these words into the categories below.**

| evolve | restore | amend | adapt | alter | reform | reverse | transform | adjust |

1 a verb that describes complete change: ....
2 two verbs that describe changing something back: ....
3 a verb that describes gradual change: ....
4 two verbs that describe a change to improve something: ....
5 two verbs that involve a change in behaviour: ....
6 a verb that describes changing only a part of something: ....

3 **Complete the sentences with a suitable word.**

1 The new furniture has completely .... their living room.
2 Part of the 18th century tower was damaged, but they are planning to .... it.
3 As a company we believe in .... , not revolution.
4 They've changed their minds completely: this is a .... of the previous policy.
5 Solicitors want to .... some of our outdated divorce laws.
6 I've lost so much weight that I'll need to .... some of my clothes.
7 Now he has children, he will have to .... to a very different lifestyle.
8 I had to .... one of the documents as there were several errors in it.
9 We've had to make one or two .... to the timetable because of the extra course.
10 He will remain in charge during the period of ....

TEST YOURSELF

B Change management

Managing change

Most employees **resist** change that is **enforced** and **imposed upon** them. So, if a company wants to **pursue** a policy that aims to **bring about sweeping**, or even **subtle** changes, managers need to remember that their role is to **facilitate** change and not impose it. This requires an **ongoing consultation** process with the staff, so that any changes have their support before they are **implemented**.

GLOSSARY	
resist	refuse to accept sth and try to stop it happening **resistance** n
enforce	make people obey sth; **enforce the law**; **enforcement** n
impose sth (on/upon sb)	make sb accept sth against their wishes
pursue	follow or try to achieve sth over a period of time: **pursue a policy/goal**
bring sth about	make sth happen
subtle	not easy to notice or understand: **a subtle difference**; OPP **obvious**
facilitate	make an act or process easier to achieve
ongoing	continuing to develop: **an ongoing process/ investigation**
consultation	the act of discussing sth with sb before making a decision **consult sb** v; **consultative** adj: **a consultative process/committee**
implement	make sth that has been decided start to happen SYN **put sth into practice**; **implementation** n

SPOTLIGHT adjective + *change*

A number of adjectives are commonly used with the noun *change*.
- *sweeping/radical/major/wholesale* changes (= big changes)
- *a refreshing/welcome* change (= pleasantly new or different)

---

4 Good or bad management, according to the text? Write G or B.

1 They've enforced the change. ....
2 They've resisted any change. ....
3 There has been a consultative process. ....
4 They've imposed change. ....
5 They've introduced refreshing changes. ....
6 They want to facilitate change. ....

5 Replace the underlined words with different words that keep the same meaning.

1 It's only a small difference but we believe it will have an effect. ....
2 He wants to introduce radical changes. ....
3 The new furniture is a welcome change. ....
4 They have the power to make people obey the law. ....
5 They plan to implement a number of changes. ....
6 The new measures will create further changes. ....
7 Staff have refused to accept any changes. ....
8 Suggesting change is one thing but putting it into practice is more difficult. ....
9 I believe there is a continuing investigation into the disappearance of the funds. ....
10 She has tried to make discussions easier between staff and management. ....

6 Complete the text.

When the new headteacher arrived, it was rumoured that she planned to **(1)** .... a policy of **(2)** .... changes to the way the school was organized, and that she wouldn't be very sympathetic to staff who showed any real **(3)** .... However, unlike the former head who tried to **(4)** .... change without discussing it with anyone first, Mrs Palmer has **(5)** .... members of staff, and that has been a **(6)** .... change. She set up a staff committee, and we have been involved in an **(7)** .... process of **(8)** .... for about two months. And we have already **(9)** .... a few changes, which have made an **(10)** .... difference.

TEST YOURSELF

Easy ways to **conserve** energy in the home

- **Switch to energy-saving eco** light bulbs. They are better for the environment and they last much longer. They are more expensive to buy, but they greatly reduce your energy **consumption** and **in the long run** are a significant financial **saving**.

- Never leave electrical **appliances on standby**, or leave your mobile phone **charging**[1] unnecessarily. Get rid of your **tumble dryer**: it **consumes** masses of energy.

- Every year we throw away thousands of batteries. If these are not **disposed of** safely **landfill** sites will become even more **toxic**. Use **rechargeable batteries**[2] or, **better still**, solar **chargers**.

- With a 'smart' meter, you can **monitor** the amount of energy you use, and even control your consumption when you are away from home.

- If you are not planning to move in the near future, **solar panels**[3] are a good **long-term investment**. You will make a saving on your electricity bills as well as receiving money for the electicity you **generate** and sell back to National Grid*.

* The National Grid is the network in the United Kingdom connecting power stations and ensuring that electricity generated anywhere can be used to satisfy demand anywhere.

GLOSSARY			
conserve	avoid wasting sth **conservation** n	**charge sth (up)**	pass electricity through sth to store it there **charger**[2] n
switch (to sth)	change or make sth change from using one thing to using another	**tumble dryer**	a machine that uses hot air to dry clothes
-saving	not wasting anything: *energy-saving*, *a labour-saving device*	**dispose of sth**	get rid of sth that you do not want or cannot keep **disposal** n
eco-	(short for **ecology/ecological**) relating to the environment: *an eco-disaster*	**landfill (site)**	an area of land where large amounts of rubbish are buried
consumption	the act of using energy, food or materials. A person is a **consumer**. **consume** v	**toxic**	poisonous: *toxic chemicals/gases/substances*
saving	an amount of sth, such as money or time, that you do not need to spend or use	**better still**	even better. **Still** is used here and with other comparative adjectives to make a comparison stronger: *longer still*
appliance	a machine you use at home, e.g. a fridge, a washing machine	**monitor**	watch and check sth over a period of time to see how it develops or changes
on standby	If a TV is **on standby**, it is connected to the power supply but is not in use.	**investment**	a thing that is worth buying because it will be useful and helpful
		generate	produce or create sth: *generate electricity*

SPOTLIGHT *in the short/medium/long term*

These expressions are used to describe what will happen a short, medium or long time in the future.

- *The reforms won't happen **in the short term**.*
- *We plan to move **in the long term** (SYN **in the long run**).*

Short-/medium-/long-term can also be used as adjectives.

- *Hiring unqualified staff is only a **short-term** solution.*

1 Mark the stress on these words and phrases. Use the APP to help you.

appliance	disposal	on standby
better still	energy-saving	tumble dryer
conserve	in the long run	conservation

2 Good or bad, in terms of energy-saving? Write G or B.

1 I left the TV on standby overnight. ....

2 We don't use eco-light bulbs. ....

3 I switched to rechargeable batteries. ....

4 Our energy consumption didn't increase over the winter. ....

5 The machine gives out toxic substances. ....

6 The company has introduced energy conservation measures. ....

7 He left the phone charger on all day. ....

8 We've reduced what we send to the landfill. ....

9 I've removed the water-saving device from our taps. ....

10 We have fitted solar panels. ....

3 Complete the phrases in these sentences.

1 We spend too much time just looking at ....-............ solutions.

2 I think dishwashers are one of the best ....-............ devices.

3 We've just had 12 .... fitted on the roof.

4 I'm afraid I often leave the TV ....

5 I've got a washing machine, but there isn't room for a .... dryer.

6 The oil spill off the coast was an ....-............................ .

7 Wind turbines will provide us with a lot of our energy needs in the ....

8 A lot of rubbish still gets buried in ....

9 It's more eco-friendly and economical to use rechargeable ....

10 I have decided to .... to a different energy supplier.

11 We need to get rid of any .... chemicals.

12 Where can we .... of these batteries in the most ecological way?

4 Complete the questions.

1 Have you got a tumble .... ? If so, could you manage without it?

2 When you .... your mobile phone, do you leave it plugged in overnight?

3 Do you .... the amount of electricity you use every day/week?

4 Do you know how much electricity you .... in an average week?

5 How many electrical .... in your kitchen do you use regularly?

6 Do you always turn off lights in rooms you aren't using to .... energy?

7 Do you use rechargeable .... , or better .... , a solar .... ?

8 Which energy-............................ steps in the article on the opposite page do you actually take?

9 Are you an above-average or below-average .... of electricity?

10 Do you think solar panels are a waste of money or a good .... ?

11 Do you know how much electricity (%) in your country is .... by solar energy?

12 Do you think you have made financial .... in recent years by using public transport more?

5 ABOUT YOU Answer the questions in Exercise 4, or ask another student.

....

....

....

 TEST YOURSELF

A Conservation

With the ongoing **clearing** of forests (also called **deforestation**), many animals are losing their **natural habitat** and starting to **decline** in numbers. In some **regions, conservation** groups **point out** that some animals are already **dying out** and are **in danger of extinction**. One **instance** of this is the African elephant, which is now **considered to be** an **endangered species**.

GLOSSARY	
clear	remove sth that may not be wanted
habitat	the place where a plant or animal is usually found: *the elephant's natural habitat*
decline	become smaller, weaker, or less good **decline** *n*: *be in decline*
region	a part of a country or the world **regional** *adj*
conservation	the protection of the natural world **conserve** *v*
point sth out	mention sth in order to give people information about it and make them notice it
die out	disappear
instance (of sth)	an example or case (of sth): *for instance*
consider sb/sth to be sth	think of sth/sb in a particular way ALSO **consider sb/sth as sth**
endangered	in danger of becoming extinct (see spotlight)
species	a group of plants or animals that are all similar and can breed together

SPOTLIGHT *extinction* n and *extinct* adj

If a plant or animal is **extinct**, it no longer exists.
- *Some sharks are **becoming extinct**.*
- *Some sharks are **in danger of extinction**.*
- *This species is **on the verge of extinction**.*
  (= very close to extinction)

1 Is the meaning of the sentences the same or different? Write *S* or *D*.
1 The tiger population is in decline. / There are fewer tigers than there were. ....
2 We are destroying their natural habitat. / We are destroying their natural habits. ....
3 Tigers are on the verge of extinction. / Tigers are almost extinct. ....
4 There are laws to conserve their habitat. / There are laws to clear their habitat. ....
5 Flooding is a regional problem. / Flooding is a problem everywhere. ....
6 This species of butterfly is endangered. / This species of butterfly has died out. ....
7 I've seen widespread deforestation. / I've seen many forests cleared. ....
8 Large numbers are declining. / Large numbers are dying out. ....

2 Complete the phrases with suitable words.
1 in .... of extinction
2 point something ....
3 .... habitat
4 .... decline
5 on the .... of extinction
6 endangered ....

3 Complete the dialogues with a single word in each space.
1 Has the dodo died .... ? ~ Yes, it's ....
2 Are forests still being .... ? ~ Yes, it's all part of the process of ....
3 25% of birds are in danger of .... ~ Yes, and many more are in ....
4 Are there water shortages everywhere? ~ Yes, but they're a lot worse in some ....
5 You can see animals in a zoo. ~ Yes, but it's better to see them in their natural ....
6 Which animals in particular are .... ? ~ Well, the snow leopard, for ....
7 What can people do to help with .... ? ~ It's mostly about education and being aware of your surroundings.
8 Many birds are also .... in numbers. ~ Yes, and if we're not careful some of our birds could .... out altogether.
9 We can't go on consuming as much energy as we do. ~ I know. I keep .... this out to my family.
10 Your aunt knows all about this. ~ Oh yes, she is .... an expert on conservation.

📇 TEST YOURSELF

B The rhino

Under **threat**: the rhino[1]

- **Poaching poses** the greatest threat to this species, despite the ban on trade in **rhino horn**, which is **sought after** for **decorative** purposes and used in some forms of medicine.

- **Civil war**: War **diverts funds** from conservation, and the high levels of poverty in affected areas increase the **likelihood** that people will **end up** poaching. In some African countries, civil war has led to a serious decline in rhino populations.

- **Habitat loss**: Deforestation has **wiped out** a great deal of rhino **territory**, with a serious drop in the numbers of rhinos that are **breeding**.

horn

1

GLOSSARY			
threat (to sb/sth)	the possibility of trouble or danger: *be under threat*	divert sth/sb (from sth, to sth)	change the direction of sth, especially away from its original purpose
poaching	hunting animals, birds, etc. illegally. The person is a **poacher**.	likelihood	SYN **probability**
pose	create or give sb sth that they must deal with: *pose a threat/risk/problem*	end up (doing sth)	find yourself in a place/situation that you did not plan/expect to be in
sought after	wanted by many people because it is of high quality or rare	wipe sth out	destroy sth completely
decorative	(of an object or a building) intended to look attractive or pretty	territory	an area that an animal considers as its own **territorial** *adj*: Wolves are *territorial* animals.
civil war	war between groups from the same country	breed	(of animals) have sex and produce young animals

4 **Cross out the error in each sentence. Write the correct word at the end.**

1 Cash will need to be divested from one project to another. ....
2 They want to increase numbers but some animals won't feed in zoos. ....
3 The factory puts a real danger to wildlife in the area. ....
4 Opposing groups have been fighting a civic war for years. ....
5 This disease could kill out the whole breed. ....
6 The horn of the animal is sought over by poachers. ....
7 Rhino horn and elephant tusk have a decorational use. ....
8 This poses a threaten to both humans and wildlife. ....

5 **Complete the sentences.**

1 The disagreement could result in .... war.
2 Poachers want rhino ....
3 Can we .... the money from there to here?
4 Crocodile skin is highly sought ....
5 We could end .... in a difficult situation.
6 Poaching .... a real danger to the species.
7 This breed of penguin could be wiped ....
8 Poachers are a real .... to the rhinos' survival.

6 **Replace the underlined word(s) with a word or phrase that has the same meaning.**

1 There is little <u>probability</u> of things improving soon. ....
2 You should avoid going into the lions' <u>land</u>. ....
3 He was sent to prison for <u>illegal hunting</u>. ....
4 These animals are <u>in real danger</u>. ....
5 The animal is extremely <u>protective of its land</u>. ....
6 He is a <u>person who kills tigers illegally</u>. ....
7 Some species find it difficult to <u>produce young animals</u>. ....
8 We <u>finally found ourselves</u> in the middle of the forest. ....

⊟ TEST YOURSELF

A **revolutionary era** in medical **advances**

In recent decades, we have seen **radical** changes in **conventional** medicine:

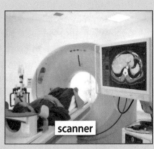

scanner

- 60 years ago, **scanners** did not exist. **Diagnostic** tools were **restricted** to basic X-ray machines.

- Children suffered from **infectious** diseases, for which there was no effective **cure**. Now **vaccines** have **eradicated** some of these illnesses and diseases.

- In the past, if you had a major **operation**, you would be **confined to bed** for weeks. Today, many operations use **procedures** requiring day **surgery** only.

- In the past, the **mortality rate** for patients with **organ** failure, such as heart, lung or **kidney** failure, could be 100%. Today, **transplants enable** many patients to **resume** a normal life.

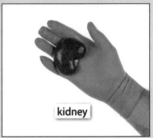

kidney

- The **survival** rate for many cancers has improved considerably over the last forty years.

- **Vitamins** and **minerals** are necessary for good health. There are more **supplements** on the market now for people who do not get enough of certain vitamins or minerals from their normal diet.

GLOSSARY

revolutionary	producing great changes **revolution** n	**be confined to bed / a wheelchair**	have to stay in bed / a wheelchair
era	a period of time that has a particular quality or character	**procedure**	a medical operation that may or may not require your body to be cut open
advance (in sth)	progress made in science, medicine, technology, etc.	**rate**	the number of times sth happens within a particular period: *survival rate*, *birth rate*, *mortality rate*
radical	new, different and likely to have a great effect	**organ**	a part of the body that has a particular function e.g. the heart, the brain
conventional	usual or traditional; not new or different **convention** n	**transplant**	an operation in which a damaged organ is replaced with one from a **donor** (= sb who gives part of their body, blood, etc.) **transplant** v
diagnostic	used for finding out what physical or mental problem sb has **diagnose** v; **diagnosis** n		
restrict	limit the size, number or amount of sth **restriction** n	**enable sb/sth to do sth**	make it possible for sb/sth to do sth
infectious	(of a disease / an illness) can easily be passed on to another person **infection** n; **infect** v	**resume** *formal*	begin sth again after an interruption
		vitamin	one of several substances in certain foods that help us grow and be healthy, e.g. *vitamin C*, *vitamin D*
cure	a medical treatment that makes a sick person well again **cure** v	**mineral**	a natural substance, such as coal, salt, etc. Some **minerals** are present in food and drink and important for good health.
vaccine	a substance which is put into the blood and protects the body from disease. The process of giving **vaccine** is **vaccination**. **vaccinate** v	**supplement**	sth that is added to sth else. **Vitamin supplements**, usually taken in the form of tablets, add vitamins to your diet.
eradicate *formal*	destroy or get rid of sth completely SYN **wipe (sth) out**		

SPOTLIGHT *surgery*

Surgery is medical treatment in which your body is cut open so that a part can be removed or repaired. SYN **an operation**, **operate** v. The place where this happens is an **operating theatre**, and the person who does it is a **surgeon**. **surgical** *adj*

1 Is the pronunciation of the underlined letters the same or different? Write *S* or *D*.
Use the 🔊 to help you.

1 r<u>e</u>volutionary <u>e</u>ra ....
2 v<u>i</u>tamin m<u>i</u>neral ....
3 rad<u>i</u>cal d<u>i</u>agnose ....
4 vacc<u>i</u>ne vacc<u>i</u>nate ....
5 con<u>f</u>ined vac<u>c</u>ine ....
6 <u>c</u>onfined <u>c</u>onventional ....
7 <u>e</u>ra <u>e</u>nable ....
8 revolution<u>a</u>ry adv<u>a</u>nces ....
9 res<u>u</u>me infecti<u>ou</u>s ....

2 Complete the table.

NOUN	VERB	ADJECTIVE
revolution	-	....
....	restrict	-
surgery	-	....
vaccine, ...	....	-
diagnosis	....	....
....	transplant	-
infection	....	....

3 *Yes* or *No?*

1 If a disease is eradicated, does it mean it has been restricted? ....
2 Does an organ donor receive an organ from someone else? ....
3 Does a radical change mean a very big change? ....
4 If you have a disease which is diagnosed, does it mean you are better? ....
5 Does it matter if your diet doesn't contain any vitamins? ....
6 Is conventional medicine new and different? ....
7 If a disease is infectious, can you catch it? ....
8 Does surgery involve an operation? ....

4 Complete the sentences.

1 Her injuries were serious, so they took her straight to the operating ....
2 There are prizes for the most important technological ....
3 Most people get the vitamins and minerals they need, but doctors recommend .... for some people if they lack certain things in their diet.
4 Many changes have taken place since the Victorian ....
5 I wanted to know the current survival .... for breast cancer.
6 The .... involves inserting a tube into the ear to reduce infection.
7 His life was saved thanks to an organ ....
8 Some foods contain a lot of vitamins and ....
9 There are some treatments available, but sadly no effective ....
10 Alongside conventional .... , other forms of treatment have become popular in recent years.

5 Complete the dialogues.

1 Polio has been .... , I believe. ~ Yes, it's been almost completely ....
2 In some areas, lung cancer treatment is .... to non-smoking patients only. ~ Yes, I think that may be true for patients needing an organ .... as well.
3 The government has a policy to .... the elderly against flu. ~ I know, but there's often a shortage of the appropriate .... when it's needed.
4 I don't like all these drugs some doctors give you. I don't trust .... medicine. ~ Really? But there have been some fantastic .... in drugs in recent decades.
5 Are hospitals much cleaner places than they were many years ago? ~ Yes. Better hygiene has greatly reduced the spread of ....
6 The surgeons had to .... on Jason; it was a difficult .... ~ Yes, he was .... to bed for ages. Fortunately he's now recovering.
7 My aunt is having a .... new procedure for her damaged hip. ~ I know. If it succeeds, she'll be able to walk again and .... a normal life.
8 Why did doctors fit the tube in Malcolm's throat? ~ I think it .... him to breath more easily.

📖 TEST YOURSELF

A People on the move

Word	Meaning	Example
flee (from) sth/sb pt/pp fled	escape from a dangerous situation, place or person very quickly	Thousands of people are **fleeing** the bombing in the city.
refugee	sb who is forced to leave their country for political, religious or environmental reasons	Many **refugees** have crossed the border to escape the war.
refuge	shelter or protection from trouble or danger	The men had to **take/seek refuge** in the French embassy.
asylum	the protection a country gives to a refugee	The numbers **seeking / applying for asylum** have increased recently.
ethnic	connected with or belonging to a nation or race that shares a cultural tradition	**an ethnic community**
minority	a small group within a community or country that is different because of race, religion, etc.	**Ethnic minorities** make up 10% of the town's population.
racial	existing between people of different races	**racial tension/violence**
discrimination	the practice of treating sb or a group in society less fairly than others	a victim of **racial/sex discrimination**
prejudice (against sb/sth)	a strong dislike of sb, especially based on race, religion or sex, and not on reason or experience	Their decision was based on **prejudice** and a complete lack of understanding.

SPOTLIGHT *migration*

Migration is the movement of people or animals from one place to another. People are **migrants**.
Immigration is the process of coming to live in a country that is not your own. People are **immigrants**. **migrate** v
Emigration is the process of going to live in another country that is not your own. **emigrate** v

1 Is the pronunciation of the underlined letters the same or different? Write *S* or *D*. Use the 🔊 to help you.

1 fl<u>ee</u> refug<u>ee</u> .... 3 pr<u>e</u>judice r<u>e</u>fuge .... 5 <u>e</u>thnic m<u>i</u>nority .... 7 r<u>a</u>cial <u>e</u>migration ....
2 ref<u>u</u>ge asyl<u>u</u>m .... 4 m<u>i</u>gration m<u>i</u>nority .... 6 prej<u>u</u>dice ref<u>u</u>ge .... 8 as<u>y</u>lum m<u>i</u>grant ....

2 Circle the correct word(s). Sometimes both words are possible.

1 In 2017–2018, *immigration / emigration* from the UK to other parts of the world increased.
2 Most refugees who *seek / apply* asylum do so in a country neighbouring their own.
3 Representatives of the city's *ethnic / racial* communities are involved in the discussions.
4 The villagers took *refugee / refuge* in nearby towns.
5 In the past, there was more racial *prejudice / discrimination*.
6 People *fled / flew* in terror to escape the flood.
7 Ignorance is often behind the prejudice against *migrants / immigrants*.
8 Women and children were forced to *seek / take* refuge in the local church.

3 One word is missing in each line. What is it, and where does it go?

1 There's no limit on the number of people given political in this country. ....
2 Racial and sexual is against the law in matters of employment. ....
3 Economic to richer countries has existed for centuries. ....
4 There are over 2,000 seeking political asylum in this country. ....
5 Nearly half a million people were forced to their homes during the civil war, and many of them refuge in the mountains, away from the fighting. ....
6 My neighbour has always had a against people whose skin is a different colour. ....
7 Asians only form a small within the population. ....
8 There has been a lot of tension between different ethnic groups. ....

📓 TEST YOURSELF

B Migration: a personal experience

Moving from my **native** country was a huge **culture shock**. There was a lot to get used to – not least of all the food! But I didn't suffer the prejudice or **hostility** that some migrants experience. **For the most part**, people have accepted me for what I am, including my religious **faith**. They've seen beyond the **stereotype**. And **for my part**, I recognize the need for **integration** in order to be able to **live in peace with** my neighbours. I still have feelings of **nostalgia** for my **country of origin**, and I suppose I will always be a foreigner in some respects; but this is home now, and I have no **desire** to go back.

GLOSSARY

native	connected with the place where you were born and lived for the first few years of your life: *your native country/land/city*
shock	the feeling you get when sth unpleasant happens. **Culture shock** is the confusion and anxiety that sb may feel when they visit or first live in another country.
hostility (to/ towards sb)	very strong aggressive feelings against sb/sth **hostile** *adj*
faith	a strong belief in sth, often a **religious faith**
stereotype	a fixed idea of what a particular type of person or thing is like, but which is often not true **stereotypical** *adj*
integration	the process of becoming a full member of a group or society **integrate (into sth)** *v*
live in peace (with sb)	live without arguing with other people
nostalgia	a feeling of sadness mixed with pleasure when you think of happy times in the past **nostalgic** *adj*
origin	a person's social and family background: *a person's country of origin* (= where they were born)
desire	a strong wish: *have a desire / no desire to do sth*

SPOTLIGHT idioms with *part*

for the most part mostly; usually
for my part speaking for myself ALSO **for his/her, etc. part**
in part partly; to some extent: *His success was due in part to luck.*
have a part to play (in sth) be able to help sth
- *We all have a part to play in the fight against racial discrimination.*

4 Combine words/phrases in the box to form six phrases.

culture	live	faith	have no	to play	country
desire to do sth	have a part	of origin	in peace	shock	religious

....

....

5 Cross out the word which is wrong. Write the correct word at the end.

1 Why is there so much hostility for politicians in this town? ....
2 The problems are due in partly to overcrowding. ....
3 Do you have feelings of nostalgic for your childhood? ....
4 He doesn't fit the stereoscope of a typical 30-year-old businessman. ....
5 The government policy is to aid newcomers' integrity into society. ....
6 I'm a natural New Yorker: in fact, I've never lived anywhere else. ....

6 Complete the dialogue.

Beth When you first emigrated, what things did you have to get used to?

Amy Well, obviously the climate! But seriously, in my **(1)** .... country, many people no longer have a strong religious **(2)** .... , whereas here, religion is at the heart of people's lives, so that added to my sense of culture **(3)** .... I discovered that for the most **(4)** .... people had a **(5)** .... view of how western women behave, as they seemed surprised when they got to know me. I dressed appropriately and behaved sensitively, as I had no **(6)** .... to upset people. Basically, **(7)** .... my part, I just wanted to **(8)** .... into society as best I could.

Beth And do you feel that's happened?

Amy To be honest, people have never been **(9)** .... towards me – quite the opposite. People here just want to live in **(10)** .... with each other, as I do. Having said that, I will always be something of a foreigner here, and I still feel **(11)** .... sometimes when I think of home.

TEST YOURSELF

Capitalism: the economy is owned and run by companies and individuals, not the state. In Britain, capitalism is **associated with** the **Conservative Party** (called **Conservatives** or **Tories**), which tends to **favour the status quo** and is **opposed to radical** change.

Socialism: the economy of a country is **partly** controlled by the state, and there is a belief that **wealth** should be **distributed** equally. In Britain, **socialists** are usually **left-wing**, but not **extremists**. Socialism is usually associated with the **Labour Party**, although the party has generally favoured a **moderate** form of socialism.

Liberalism: this is a belief in personal and economic freedom, supporting gradual social and political change. In Britain, many **liberals** vote for **centre parties**, the most **prominent** being the **Liberal Democratic Party**.

Communism: a **communist** system is based on common **ownership** of the **means** of production, and everyone is supposed to share the wealth it creates.

GLOSSARY

ideology a set of ideas that an economic or political system is based on **ideological** adj

associated with sth/sb connected with sth/sb **associate** v, **association** n

favour support and agree with sth/sb **favour** n: **be in favour (of sth/sb)**

status quo the existing situation: **maintain the status quo**

opposed to sth/sb disagreeing strongly with sth/sb **oppose** v; **opposition** n. **The Opposition** is the main political party that is opposed to the government.

radical in favour of complete political or social change

partly in part but not completely SYN **to some extent**

wealth a large amount of money that a person or country owns **wealthy** adj

distribute share sth among a number of people **distribution** n

left-wing strongly supporting the ideas of socialism OPP **right-wing** strongly supporting the ideas of capitalism ALSO **on the left / on the right**

extremist a person whose political views are generally not considered to be normal or reasonable **extreme** adj OPP **moderate** n, adj

centre party a political party that is neither left-wing nor right-wing: **in the centre**

prominent important or famous

ownership the state of owning something: **public/private ownership**

means (of sth / doing sth) an action, object or system by which a result is achieved; a way of doing sth: **the means of production** (= the materials and equipment needed to produce things); **a means of transport; a means of identification / of contacting sb**

SPOTLIGHT suffixes -ism and -ist

The suffix **-ism** is often associated with beliefs and ideologies, and the suffix **-ist** is often used for both the person and adjective derived from these beliefs.

- *capitalism*   *capitalist*
- *socialism*   *socialist*
- *communism*   *communist*
- *extremism*   *extremist* (BUT the adjective is **extreme**.)
- *conservatism*   *conservative*

There are exceptions.

- *liberalism*   *liberal*

1 **Mark the stress on these words. Use the APP to help you.**

ideology   ideological   capitalism   conservative   status quo   oppose
opposition   extremism   associate   association   distribute   distribution

2 **Complete the table.**

NOUN	PERSON	VERB	ADJECTIVE
ideology	-	-	
conservativism		-	
socialism		-	
		-	liberal
	-	associate	
	extremist	-	
	-	distribute	-

3 **True or false? Write *T* or *F*, then change one word to make the false sentences true.**

1 A capitalist economy is owned by the people and run by the state. ....
2 People associate liberals with personal freedom. ....
3 Socialists believe that wealth should be shared equally. ....
4 A liberal believes in economic freedom and radical political change. ....
5 The Conservative Party in Britain believes in socialism. ....
6 Socialists believe that everyone should own the means of production. ....
7 Extremists tend to have moderate beliefs. ....
8 Capitalism and communism are ideologies with different beliefs. ....

4 **Complete the sentences with the opposite meaning to the first half of the sentence.**

1 He's left-wing, but she's ....
2 I'm poor, but he's ....
3 He's in favour of it, but she's ....
4 He wants change, but she prefers to maintain the ....

5 She has extreme views, but his are quite ....
6 They're on the left and right, but I'm ....
7 They were in government, but now they're ....
8 He's a capitalist, but I'm a ....

5 **Complete the sentences.**

1 I believe in the equal .... of wealth.
3 I'm in .... of reducing the age at which young people can vote.
5 Do you believe that water should be in public or private .... ?
4 I don't .... the Conservative Party with radical change.
5 Is it important to .... the status quo?
6 The US is an extremely .... country, and yet many people there are very poor.
7 I agree with their policies to some ....
8 Angela Merkel was the most .... politician in Western Europe from 2000 to 2020.
9 It may not be completely the government's fault, but they are .... responsible.
10 He may not be an actual member of the Labour Party, but does he have any .... with it?

6 **ABOUT YOU AND YOUR COUNTRY** **Write answers to the questions, or ask another student.**

1 What are the main political parties in your country? Are they right-wing, left-wing or centre parties? ....
2 Would you describe yourself as quite radical or fairly moderate in your views? ....
3 Do you generally favour the status quo? ....
4 Are you often opposed to the policies of the government? ....
5 Would you describe yourself as quite liberal in many of your views? ....
6 Do you usually carry any means of identification with you? ....
7 What means of transport operate in your town? ....

TEST YOURSELF

51) Local government

A Local election manifesto

Independent party **manifesto** for the local **council** elections. We will:

- **stand up for** the community and speak **on behalf of residents** on **green** issues.
- **take** complaints **seriously** and **give** neighbourhoods **a say** in local decisions.
- **allocate** better funding for youth projects and **ensure** they are properly managed.
- provide **grants** for **voluntary** organizations that help with the elderly and disabled.

GLOSSARY

manifesto	a written statement by a political party saying what they believe in and what they intend to do	**take sth/sb seriously**	think that sth/sb is important and deserves respect
council	the organization that provides local government in a city or area. A **councillor** is an elected member of the council.	**say**	the right to give your opinion before a decision is made: *give sb a say*; *have a say in sth*
stand up for sth/sb	support or defend sth/sb SYN **stick up for sb** inf	**allocate sth (to sb/sth) (for sth)**	give sth officially to sb/sth for a particular purpose
on behalf of sb / on sb's behalf	as the representative of sb; in order to help sb	**ensure**	make sure that sth happens or is definite
resident	a person who lives in a particular place. A **citizen** also means a person with the legal right to belong to a particular country.	**grant**	a sum of money given, often by the government, for a particular purpose
green	connected with protecting the environment	**voluntary**	(of work) done by people (called **volunteers**) who choose to do it without being paid. The **voluntary sector** refers to charity organizations.

1 Complete the words.

1 r ___ s ___ d ___ nt
2 ___ ns ___ r ___
3 v ___ l ___ nt ___ ry
4 co ___ nc ___ l
5 ___ ll ___ c ___ te
6 m ___ n ___ f ___ ___ t ___
7 c ___ ___ n ___ ___ ll ___ r
8 v ___ l ___ ___ t ___ ___ r

2 One word is incorrect in each sentence. Cross it out and write the correct word at the end.

1 I've read the manifest and didn't agree with any of it.
2 They should have a say to what happens in our city.
3 Do you think the councillors will make our ideas seriously?
4 My sister's done a lot of work for the volunteer sector.
5 She spoke on behalf for all of us.
6 They should stand out for people who don't have a say.
7 We must assure that the councillors keep their promise.
8 The council are giving us a grand to help with the work.

3 Complete the sentences.

1 There are no local .... in my town willing to speak on my ....
2 We don't have paid staff. We rely solely on .... and the voluntary ....
3 I don't really feel I .... a say in local politics.
4 Local politicians should .... up for people and .... their ideas seriously.
5 Do you think you can get a .... from the council to make your home greener?
6 Christian has been a .... in the UK for ten years, but he remains a Danish .... with a Danish passport.
7 We need to take .... issues more seriously if we are really concerned about the planet.
8 We can't touch the money: it has already been .... to social services.
9 Local government has to .... that accurate records are kept of all expenditure.
10 The .... takes all complaints very seriously.

TEST YOURSELF

B The role of the mayor

THE **MAYOR** OF LONDON is elected by any Londoners **eligible** to vote, and has quite a **high profile**. The mayor is the capital's **spokesperson** with a range of powers and duties. He or she **sets** the annual **budget** for the Greater London **Authority**, and plays a key role in the running and **funding** of various projects. The mayor **heads** the Mayor's Office for Policing and Crime who provide **policing** in the capital. The mayor also **chairs** Transport for London, and sits on various **committees**.

GLOSSARY	
mayor	the most important chosen or elected official in a town or city
eligible	allowed by rules or laws to do or receive sth OPP **ineligible**
high profile	Sb/sth with a **high profile** gets attention and is easily noticed.
spokesperson	sb who speaks on behalf of a group or an organization
budget	the amount of money a person or an organization has to spend on sth: **set the budget** (= decide what the budget should be)
authority	the people or an organization who have the power to make decision or who have a particular area of responsibility
funding	money for a particular purpose
head	lead or be in charge of sth, e.g. a department or and organization **head** n
policing	the activity of keeping order in a place with police **police** v
chair	be in charge of a meeting: **chair a meeting** (see spotlight)
committee	a group of people who are chosen to make decisions or deal with a particular subject: **a committee meeting**; **sit on a committee**

SPOTLIGHT gender and people nouns

These titles can be used about a man or a woman.
- **chair/chairperson/chairman**
- **spokesperson/spokesman**
- **mayor**

The titles of **chairwoman, spokeswoman** and **mayoress** are also used but only refer to a woman.

4 **Circle the words which are possible. One, two or three words may be possible.**

1 The *budget / mayor / funding* is not sufficient.
2 The *committee / authorities / policing* have the power to change the rules.
3 My uncle is the *spokesperson / mayoress / chairman*.
4 The town has a high *profit / policing / profile*.
5 David Tomkins is the *chairman / chairperson / chair* of the transport committee.
6 We heard the *spokesperson / spokesman / mayoress* making a statement to the press.
7 He's the new *mayor / budget / head*.
8 She *chairs / sits on / sets* the committee.

5 **Complete the sentences with a suitable word.**

1 We need a large force to .... the city.
2 People under 21 are .... to vote.
3 Mrs Bryant will .... the meeting.
4 He was reported to the immigration ....
5 She sets the annual ....

6 I sit on a number of ....
7 He was elected .... last year.
8 She .... the department.
9 It's a very high- .... job.
10 We need more .... for medical research.

6 ABOUT YOUR TOWN/CITY **Write your answers, or ask another student.**

Do you have a mayor? If so, are they elected or appointed? ....
Is it a high-profile job? ....
Do you know what their duties are? ....

 TEST YOURSELF

A What is available?

HEALTH CARE: FREQUENTLY ASKED QUESTIONS

▸ Do I need to **register with** a GP?
▸ How do I get **referred to** a **specialist**?
▸ Can I get free **prescriptions**?
▸ **What if** I **suspect** a doctor has made a mistake?

▸ How do I become a **participant in** a **clinical** trial?
▸ Can I get **cosmetic surgery free of charge**?
▸ Are all medical records **confidential**?

GLOSSARY

health care	the service of providing medical care	**suspect**	have an idea that sb is guilty of sth, but without definite proof
register (with/for sth)	put your name on an official list. You can also **enrol on a course** or **enrol at a school**.	**participant (in sth)**	sb who is taking part in an activity or event
refer sb (to sth)	send sb to sb/sth for help, advice, etc.	**clinical**	related to the examination and treatment of patients and their illnesses: *a clinical trial*;
specialist	a person who is an expert in a particular area of work or study **specialist** *adj*		*clinical research*
prescription	an official piece of paper given to you by a doctor that enables you to get a particular medicine from a pharmacy **prescribe** *v*	**cosmetic surgery**	medical treatment intended to improve sb's appearance
What if …?	What would happen if …?	**free of charge**	If sth is **free of charge**, it costs you nothing.
		confidential	meant to be kept secret: *strictly confidential*

1 **Form five phrases from words in the box.**

> of charge   free   care   clinical   strictly   surgery   trial   cosmetic   confidential   health

....

....

2 **Complete the sentences.**

1 The patient has a rare illness, so she will need .... treatment.
2 All medical treatment has to be strictly .... between the doctor and patient.
3 Some cosmetic .... is available on the National Health Service.
4 Go and see if the doctor will .... something for that terrible cough.
5 What .... I need urgent health .... ? Where should I go?
6 When I moved to Brighton, I had to .... with a doctor near my home, and at the same time,
I .... on a free first-aid course.
7 I asked the doctor to .... me to a .... because of my long-term problem with my skin.
8 How many .... are taking part in the clinical .... for the new cancer drug?

3 **Complete the text.**

When you move to a new area, in order to get free health **(1)** .... , you need to
(2) .... with a doctor. For many common illnesses, the doctor will give you a
(3) .... , which you collect from a pharmacy. They are free **(4)** ....
if you are under 16, over 60, or pregnant. If you have a serious problem which involves seeing a
(5) .... , you can get **(6)** .... to one by your doctor. Your medical
records are **(7)** .... , but you can see your own records by asking at your surgery. If you
(8) .... that somebody has made a mistake with your treatment, you should speak to the
medical staff first about your case before taking any further action.

4 ABOUT YOUR COUNTRY **Can you answer the questions at the top of the page about your health service? Write your answers, or ask another learner.**

....

....

 TEST YOURSELF

B In hospital: patients' experiences

> The doctors and nurses were very **dedicated** and **kept me informed** at all times.

> I know the staff were **rushed off their feet**, but nobody **took any notice of** my calls for help.

> I felt **miserable** when I was admitted, but I had **absolute** confidence in the nursing staff and soon felt **my old self** again.

> I was **admitted** to the **ward**, seen by a **junior** doctor, then nothing happened for two days.

> I felt the whole time that my **well-being** was the staff's **prime concern**.

GLOSSARY

dedicated	working hard at sth because it is important to you	absolute	total and complete
		self	the type of person you are: *my old self*; *my real self*
inform	tell sb about sth: *keep sb informed (about sth)*	ward	a room or an area in a hospital for patients with the same type of condition
be rushed off your feet	be extremely busy with too many things to do	junior	having a low rank in an organization or profession OPP **senior**
take (no) notice of sb/sth	pay (no) attention to sb/sth	well-being	general health and happiness
miserable	very unhappy or uncomfortable	prime	main; most important: *a prime concern*

5 Circle the correct answer(s). Both answers may be possible.

1 I was rushed off my *foot / feet*.
2 She took *no / any* notice of me.
3 I was *admitted / discharged* to the cancer ward.
4 He's back to his *old self / self*.
5 I need to *convalesce / recuperate*.
6 They *kept / made* me informed.
7 They were *junior / senior* doctors.
8 His health was my *main / prime* concern.
9 Patients need rest and *recuperation / well-being*.
10 The staff are *admitted / dedicated* to patient care.

6 Replace the underlined words with a word or phrase that keeps the same meaning.

1 They didn't pay any attention to me. They took ....
2 They told me what was happening. They kept ....
3 I was incredibly busy. I was rushed ....
4 That's part of his true character. That's part of his ....
5 She needs to spend time getting better. She needs to ....
6 I felt really unhappy and uncomfortable. I felt ....
7 I'm worried about his general health and happiness. I'm worried about his ....
8 The staff work hard and care a lot. The staff are ....

7 Complete the sentences with a suitable word.

1 When you are .... to hospital, you are taken to a .... for your stay.
2 In hospital, patients are always .... informed about their treatment.
3 Staff in hospitals are .... off their feet all the time.
4 For the doctors and nurses, the patient's .... is their .... concern.
5 There are more senior doctors than .... doctors.
6 Most patients have .... confidence in the staff.
7 Recuperation (or ....) usually takes place at home.
8 When you have recovered sufficiently, you will be .... from hospital with all the medicines you need for the first week.

8 ABOUT YOUR COUNTRY Do you know if the sentences in Exercise 7 are true for your country?

....
....

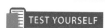 TEST YOURSELF

Police **procedures**

An arrest is when a police **constable detains** someone **suspected** of an **offence**. In the UK, the police can arrest you if they have a **valid** arrest **warrant (issued** by a **magistrate)**, or if they have reasonable **grounds** for suspecting you have committed or **are about to** commit an offence. You are **cautioned** and then taken to a police station as soon as possible. Once you are **in custody**, you have the right to legal advice from a **solicitor**. If there is sufficient evidence, the police will **charge** you, and you will then appear in court where a magistrate will decide whether you should be **remanded in custody** or **released on bail**.

If your case goes to trial, you will either be **convicted of** the crime, or found innocent and **acquitted**. If you are found guilty, you will be **sentenced** by a judge.

SPOTLIGHT *the police*

A **police officer** is any member of the **police force**. In the UK, a **(police) constable** (abbreviated as **PC**) is an officer of the lowest **rank** (= position in an organization). Above the rank of constable is the **sergeant**, the **inspector**, and so on. The **chief constable** is the head of each regional police force.

GLOSSARY

procedure	the usual or correct way for doing sth
detain	keep sb in an official place, e.g. a police station, and prevent them from leaving: *be detained in custody*
suspect sb of (doing) sth	believe that sb is guilty of sth, though you do not have proof. A person is a **suspect**.
offence *formal*	a crime: *commit an offence*
valid	legally or officially acceptable OPP **invalid**
warrant	a legal document signed by a judge that allows the police to do sth. A **search warrant** is a warrant to search sb's property.
issue	give or say sth to sb officially: *issue a warrant/ visa*
magistrate	an official who acts as a judge in the lowest courts of law
grounds (for sth/ doing sth) *(usually pl)*	a reason for sth
be about to (do sth)	be going to do sth very soon
caution sb *formal*	warn sb officially that anything they say may be used against them as evidence in court

custody	the state of being in prison while waiting for trial: *in custody*
solicitor	a lawyer who gives legal advice and prepares legal documents
charge sb (with sth)	say officially you believe sb has committed a crime
remand sb	send sb away from court until their trial: *be remanded in custody*
bail	money left with a court of law to ensure that a prisoner will return for their trial. A judge can either **grant bail** or **refuse bail**.
convict sb (of sth)	say officially in court that sb is guilty of a crime
acquit sb (of sth)	state formally that a person is not guilty of a crime
sentence sb (to sth)	(of a judge) tell sb who has been found guilty of a crime what their punishment will be: *He sentenced him to two years in prison.*

1 Underline the stress on these words. Use the 🔊 to help you.

detain	suspect *v*	suspect *n*	offence	invalid	magistrate
custody	solicitor	remand	convict	acquit	constable

2 Write the missing preposition.

1   be detained .... police custody
2   have grounds .... doing something
3   charge someone .... an offence

4   convict someone .... an offence
5   acquit someone .... a crime
6   sentence someone .... five years

3 Complete the phrases with suitable words.

1   a police ....
2   commit an ....
3   .... a search warrant

4   remand someone in ....
5   .... bail OR refuse bail
6   convict OR .... someone

4 Write your answers.

1   Who issues an arrest warrant?
2   Who detains someone?
3   Who offers legal advice?
4   Who is able to grant bail?
5   Who is remanded in custody?
6   Who cautions someone?
7   Who has a lower rank than a sergeant?
8   Who is above a sergeant?
9   Who is the head of a regional force?
10   Who sentences someone?

5 Complete the sentences.

1   A PC is the lowest .... in the police force.
2   A search .... allows the police to search someone's property.
3   After someone has appeared before a magistrate and is awaiting trial, they will often be ....
    in custody.
4   Police have to follow very strict .... when they arrest someone, otherwise solicitors may argue
    that an arrest is not ....
5   The police can detain someone if they .... that this person has committed an ....
6   When police arrest someone, the first thing they do is .... them.

6 Complete the text with words from the opposite page.

ARRESTED IN ROAD RAGE INCIDENT

An 82-year old man is facing prison after an angry incident at a road junction in which he pointed a gun at another driver and was, possibly, (1) .... to use it. A young police (2) .... arrested the man, before taking him to the police station, where he was (3) .... Once he was in (4) .... , the (5) .... refused to say anything, and also refused his right to speak to a (6) .... The police later (7) .... him with several (8) .... , including the illegal possession of a weapon. The man will now appear before a (9) .... tomorrow morning, where he hopes to be (10) .... bail. However, his case will almost certainly go to trial, and if he is (11) .... , he could be (12) .... to a lengthy period in prison.

TEST YOURSELF

A The prison system

An important element of the criminal justice[1] system is punishment for breaking the law. Since the **abolition** of **capital punishment** in the UK, **imprisonment** has been the most serious punishment. It satisfies our need for **justice**[2] and longer prison sentences are meant to be a **deterrent**. Furthermore, criminals who are **locked up** are no threat to society, and **rehabilitation** programmes in prison give criminals a chance to change their behaviour. However, the current system is **in crisis**. More people are being **imprisoned**, a significant percentage **reoffend**, and for some criminals, prison is simply **regarded** as an **occupational hazard**. Is it just our way of taking **revenge**? If so, can we **justify** its continued existence?

GLOSSARY	
abolition	the official ending of a law, system or institution **abolish** v
capital punishment	punishment by death
imprisonment	the act of putting sb in prison **imprison** v SYN **lock sb up** inf
justice	1 the legal system that punishes people who have committed crimes 2 the fair treatment of people
deterrent	a thing that makes sb less likely to do sth **deter** v
rehabilitation	the process of helping people to live a normal life after they have been ill or in prison **rehabilitate** v
crisis	a period of great difficulty and uncertainty: **be in crisis**
reoffend formal	commit a crime again. A person is a **reoffender**.
regard sth/sb as sth	think about sth/sb in a particular way
hazard	a risk or a danger. An **occupational hazard** is a risk that is part of a particular job.
revenge	action you take to punish sb because they made you suffer: **take revenge (on sb) (for sth)**
justify	show that sth is right or fair **justification** n; **justifiable** adj

1 Underline the stress on these words. Use the [APP] to help you.

abolish	abolition	capital punishment	deterrent
rehabilitate	rehabilitation	reoffender	occupational
hazard	justify	justification	justifiable

2 Rewrite the sentences on the left, using the sentence beginnings on the right. Keep the same meaning.

1 He's been imprisoned. He's been locked ....
2 She thinks of me as a friend. She regards ....
3 They hang people for some crimes. They have ....
4 Can we justify the prison system? Is the prison system .... ?
5 He was imprisoned for life. He got life ....
6 It changed after they abolished the law. It changed after the ....
7 It's one of the risks of the job. It's an ....
8 Do many people commit a crime again? Are there many .... ?
9 She wants him to suffer for what he did to her. She wants to take ....
10 It's a period of great difficulty. At the moment we are in ....

3 Complete the words in the questions.

1 Do you believe you can r............................... most criminals?
2 Why do so many people r............................... and go back to prison?
3 Do you think prison is an effective d............................... ?
4 Do you believe in c............................... punishment?
5 Would you like to a............................... anything in your criminal justice system?
6 Is there ever any j............................... for taking r............................... on someone who has harmed you?
7 Is the prison system in c............................... in your country?
8 Do you believe in the criminal j............................... system? In your view, does it represent true j............................... ?

4 [ABOUT YOU] **Write your answers to Exercise 3, or ask another student.**

[TEST YOURSELF]

B A different system

GRENDON is not a typical **institution** within the prison system. It is constructed **exclusively** on the **principles** of **group therapy**, and operates more as a community than a prison for offenders. The **inmates** are all serving long sentences, and a high **proportion** are guilty of violent crime. Yet the prison is different from the normal system in almost every way, with an absence of physical force and **segregation**. The prison is divided into five **self-contained** communities, the prisoners are not **confined in cells**, and decisions are only taken with their **consent**.

SPOTLIGHT *self*

Before nouns and adjectives, **self-** means 'of, to or by yourself'.

- **Self-contained** communities are able to exist without outside help.
- On a **self-catering** holiday, you do the cooking yourself.
- **Self-assessment** is judging your own progress.

GLOSSARY

institution	a large important organization with a particular purpose. An **institute** is similar but usually for education or a particular profession.	**segregation**	the policy of separating people of different sex, race, religion, etc, and in prison, by the type of crime committed **segregate** v
exclusively	completely; with nothing else: We rely **exclusively** on aid.	**confine sb/sth in sth**	keep sb/sth within an enclosed area **confinement** n: **solitary confinement** (= a punishment in which a prisoner is kept alone in a separate cell)
principle	a law, rule or theory that sth is based on		
group therapy	the use of group discussion for the treatment of a physical or mental problem or illness	**cell**	a lockable room for prisoners in a prison or police station
inmate	one of the people living in an institution such as a prison	**consent**	agreement about sth **by common consent** with everyone's agreement; **by mutual consent** with the agreement of both of the sides involved
proportion	a part or share of the whole amount or number		

5 Circle the correct answer(s). Sometimes both answers are possible.
1 Solitary *confinement / consent* is part of the punishment.
2 The *prisons / cells* are quite small.
3 The management course is based on self-*catering / assessment*.
4 I think the trip requires the parents' *agreement / consent*.
5 The prison had to *segregate / confine* the men and women in separate cells.
6 It is based *exclusively / partly* on the original model.
7 Most of the *inmates/ prisoners* are female.
8 Prisons have similarities with many other *institutions/institutes*.

6 Complete the dialogues with a single word.
1 Do they discuss each other's problems? ~ Yes, it's a type of group ....
2 Do they separate men from women? ~ Yes, there's a policy of ....
3 Do you do the cooking yourselves? ~ Yes, it's all self-................................. .
4 Are they locked up every night? ~ Yes, and the .... are very small.
5 Did everyone agree with the change? ~ Yes, it was made by common ....
6 Are many of the men violent? ~ Yes, quite a high ....
7 Did you both agree to the deal? ~ Yes, it was by .... consent.
8 They want prisoners to work together. ~ Yes, The system is based on the .... of teamwork.
9 Was he kept in a cell on his own? ~ Yes, he was in solitary ....
10 Do they rely on charities? ~ No, not .... They get some money from the government.

7 ABOUT YOU What do you think of this prison? Is it likely to be more successful than a normal prison? Write your answers, or ask another student.

....
....
....

 TEST YOURSELF

The US Military

comprises five **branches** in its field of **operations**: the army, the navy, the air force, the marine corps and the coast **guard**, all under **civilian** authority. More than 1.35 million people **serve** in the professional

tank

full-time military, with a further 800,000 in **the reserve** army. (There is no longer **compulsory military service**, though men aged 18-25 must register for it if the need arises.) The US military **distinguishes between enlisted** personnel, who **make up** about 85% of the **armed** forces and carry out **fundamental** operations such as **combat** and administration; and officers, who manage and supervise operations. The range of jobs is **vast**, but **encompasses** such **diverse** activities as running a hospital, **commanding** a **tank**, flying military **aircraft**, programming computers, maintaining **weapon** systems, etc.

helicopter

parachute

missile

GLOSSARY			
the military	a country's army, navy and air force SYN **the armed forces**; **military** *adj*	**enlisted**	(especially US English) relating to members of the permanent armed forces below officer rank. **Enlist** is to join the armed forces.
branch	a part of a large organization: *a branch of a bank*	**armed**	carrying a gun or other weapon **arms** *n (pl)*
operation	an organized activity, often involving the military or police	**fundamental**	central and forming the necessary basis of sth
guard	a person or group of people who protect sth/sb **guard** *v*	**combat**	fighting between forces: *armed/unarmed combat* (= fighting with/without guns, bombs, etc.)
civilian	not belonging to the armed forces. A person is a **civilian**.	**vast**	extremely large: *the vast majority*; *vast numbers*; *a vast amount*
serve	do useful work: *serve your country / in the army*, etc.	**encompass** *formal*	include sth within an area or area of activity
the reserve(s)	an extra force that performs part-time duties and is available if needed	**diverse**	different from each other and of various kinds **diversity** *n*
compulsory	If sth is **compulsory**, you have to do it. SYN **obligatory**; OPP **optional**	**command**	be in charge of sb. A person can also **be in command (of sth/sb)**.
military service	time spent serving in the military, especially as a compulsory period for young people	**aircraft**	any vehicle that can fly and carry goods or passengers
distinguish between A and B	recognize a difference between two people or things SYN **differentiate (between) A and B, make a distinction (between A and B)**	**weapon**	an object such as a knife, gun or bomb that is used for fighting: *nuclear/chemical weapons*; *a deadly/lethal weapon* (= that can kill sb)

SPOTLIGHT *comprise, consist of, make up*

These verbs describe the way in which something is formed.
- *The group **comprises / consists of / is made up of** 30 people.*
When you mention some of the parts first, use **make up** or **comprise**.
- *Men **make up / comprise** the majority of the group.*

1 **Answer the questions. Use the 🔵 to help you.**

1 The pronunciation of the letter 'a' is the same as in **p*a*rk** in five of the cases underlined. Which one is different?

_a_rmed   br_a_nch   comm_a_nd   encomp_a_ss   gu_a_rd   v_a_st   ....

2 Which three underlined letters are pronounced the same as in **b*i*t**, and which three are pronounced the same as in **b*e*t**?

c_i_vilian   d_ea_dly   differ_e_ntiate   _e_ncompass   enl_i_sted   w_ea_pon

....

....

3 The pronunciation of the letter 'i' is the same as in **b*i*t** in nine of the cases underlined. Which three are different?

c_i_vilian   compr_i_se   d_i_stingu_i_sh   d_i_verse   enl_i_sted   m_i_litary   m_i_ss_i_le   obl_i_gatory

....

2 **Use word(s) from the box to form nine compound words or phrases.**

unarmed	majority	the armed	lethal	service	your country
forces	combat	be in	a distinction	make	serve
military (x 2)	weapon	command	aircraft	the vast	

....

....

3 **Replace the underlined word(s) with a <u>single</u> word that has a similar meaning.**

1 To run an army requires a <u>very large</u> amount of money.   ....

2 The decision will be taken by the <u>armed forces</u>.   ....

3 A brigade <u>is made up</u> of approximately 5,500 men and women.   ....

4 The right to self-defence is one of their <u>central</u> beliefs.   ....

5 There was very little armed <u>fighting</u>.   ....

6 The men are from very <u>different</u> backgrounds.   ....

7 Six soldiers were on duty to <u>protect</u> the camp.   ....

8 I wanted to serve my country, so I <u>joined</u> as a soldier.   ....

9 This knife is a <u>lethal</u> weapon.   ....

10 They don't <u>recognize a difference</u> between men and women.   ....

11 The work <u>includes</u> many different tasks and responsibilities.   ....

12 Is military service <u>obligatory</u>?   ....

13 A brigadier is a high-ranking officer, and <u>is in charge of</u> a large group of soldiers.   ....

14 Ensuring the safety of the ships will be a large <u>organized</u> military <u>activity</u>.   ....

4 **Complete the text with suitable words.**

The British **(1)** .... forces is **(2)** .... of the army, the navy and the air force. As head of state, the Queen is theoretically in **(3)** .... of the armed forces, but in practice that is the job of the British Prime Minister. Approximately 146,000 men and women **(4)** .... in the professional armed forces (often referred to as the 'regulars'), with a further 36,500 in the **(5)** .... The armed forces are also supported by a number of **(6)** .... agencies owned by the Ministry of Defence. The navy is the **(7)** .... of the armed forces which is responsible for Britain's nuclear **(8)** .... , which **(9)** .... four Trident nuclear missile submarines.

5 ABOUT YOU AND YOUR COUNTRY **Write your answers, or ask another student.**

1 Has your country got a professional military? ....

2 Do you have a reserve army? ....

3 Do you have military service? ....

4 Are the police usually armed in your country? ....

5 Have you ever:

stood next to a tank? ....   flown in a helicopter? ....

owned or used a deadly weapon? ....   dropped from a parachute? ....

been in a professional army? ....   done military service? ....

📖 TEST YOURSELF

Headlines	Meaning
Arms deal probe	**arms** *formal* weapons, especially used by the armed forces **deal** an agreement, especially in business **probe** an investigation into sth **probe** v
Mother's **plea** to **kidnappers**	**a plea (for sth)** *formal* an important and emotional request **kidnapper** sb who takes a person away illegally and keeps them as a prisoner, usually in order to get money (called a **ransom**) **kidnap** v
Government **pledges** more **aid**	**pledge** formally promise to give or do sth **pledge** n **aid** money, food, etc, that is sent to a country to help them
Senate **urges** caution	**urge** advise or try hard to persuade sb to do sth
Bid to **axe** rail **chief**	**bid** an effort to do sth or get sth **bid** v **axe** remove sb from their job; get rid of a service, system, etc: *Bus company plans to **axe** part of rural service.* **chief** the most important or one of the most important people in a company, often used in job titles: *a **police chief***
Minister vows to quit	**minister** a senior member of a government who is in charge of a government department or a branch of one **vow** make a formal and serious promise to do sth **vow** n
Bomb **blast wrecks** factory	**(bomb) blast** an explosion **wreck** destroy sth **wreck** n
Boost for voters	**boost** sth that helps or encourages people **boost** v
Go-ahead for road **scheme**	**go-ahead** formal permission to do sth **scheme** an official plan or system for doing sth
IMG **cease** trading	**cease** *formal* stop (sth) happening or existing. A **ceasefire** is an agreement between two sides to stop fighting.
Doctor **cleared of** negligence	**clear sb (of sth)** prove that sb is innocent of doing sth wrong
Injury **blow for United**	**blow** shock or disappointment
New flood **alert**	**alert** a warning
Police **foil** bomb **plot**	**foil** prevent a plan from succeeding **plot** a secret plan by people to do sth wrong or illegal SYN **conspiracy**; **plot** v
PM **rules out** referendum	**rule sth out** reject the possibility of sth
Lords back **hunting** ban	**the Lords** (OR **the House of Lords**) in Britain, the second and higher part of Parliament, after *the House of Commons*, whose members are not elected by the people of the country **back** give help or support to sb/sth **backing** n **hunting** the act of killing wild animals for food or sport

> **SPOTLIGHT** headline words
>
> Certain words often appear in newspaper headlines because they are very short, e.g. *bid, plea, quit*. Other words give stories a more dramatic effect, e.g. *blast, boost*.

1 Is the pronunciation of the underlined letters the same or different? Write *S* or *D*. Use the 🅰 to help you.

1 pl<u>ea</u> pl<u>e</u>dge ....
2 b<u>oo</u>st bl<u>ow</u> ....
3 pl<u>e</u>dge ah<u>ea</u>d ....
4 pr<u>o</u>be v<u>ow</u> ....

5 <u>a</u>xe <u>a</u>lert ....
6 wre<u>ck</u> <u>sc</u>heme ....
7 s<u>ch</u>eme <u>ce</u>ase ....
8 m<u>i</u>nister consp<u>i</u>racy ....

2 Good news or bad news for the people in the headlines? Write *G* or *B*.

1 Further blow for house buyers ....
2 Company axes chairman ....
3 Doctors given go-ahead for new drug ....
4 Company ceases operations ....
5 PM gets backing from parliament for new rail system ....
6 New deal for manager ....
7 Boost for farmers ....
8 Army foils criminal plot ....

3 Match 1–10 with a–j.

1 vow ....
2 plea ....
3 bid ....
4 conspiracy ....
5 blow ....
6 alert ....
7 probe ....
8 scheme ....
9 blast ....
10 deal ....

a secret plan
b official plan
c request
d explosion
e investigation
f promise
g warning
h disappointment
i agreement
j attempt

4 Replace the underlined words to create typical headlines.

1 New <u>weapons agreement</u> ....
2 Government <u>promises</u> to <u>support</u> new hospital ....
3 <u>Permission</u> for rail <u>plan</u> ....
4 Company <u>managing director forced from his job</u> ....
5 <u>Help and encouragement</u> for big banks ....
6 Latest statistics a <u>shock and disappointment</u> for the economy ....
7 <u>Men who took child</u> demand <u>money for her return</u> ....
8 <u>Senior members of the government strongly advise</u> delay ....
9 Motorcyclist <u>found innocent</u> of child's death ....
10 PM <u>rejects the possibility of</u> further tax cuts. ....

5 Write your own headlines for these news stories. Keep to a maximum of six words for each headline and use the present tense for verbs.

1 An explosion has destroyed a new shopping centre

2 Senators reject the possibility of more money and help for poor countries

3 Shareholders attempt to force the chairman to resign

4 Officers prevent a secret plan to escape from prison

5 Attempt to change law on killing wild animals for sport

6 There are new warnings about the dangers of certain food

 TEST YOURSELF

WRITING A NEWS STORY

The first thing to consider is the type of story you are writing and the type of **publication** you are writing for: this will determine the style of writing.

Here are a few guidelines:

1   When you look at your **blank** screen, imagine your reader and what will interest them most.

2   If it is a **specialist** publication, you can **assume** a greater knowledge **on the part of** the reader. If it is a serious newspaper, you can also use longer sentences. But remember that space is the most **precious commodity** in a print newspaper; long sentences **take up** space. Avoid difficult words and long sentences, especially in **mass-market** publications, but don't **talk down to** your readers.

3   Your **opening** has to engage the reader **instantly** and summarize what the story is about. A good introduction will state why the story is being written and **grab** the reader's **attention**. This **sets the tone** for the rest of the piece.

4   **Quotes** are good – they add colour and personal experience – but if you are **citing** from specific sources, keep it short, **otherwise** the story will lose **pace** and direction. Sometimes the quote has to be there to provide **precision** – when the actual words are crucial to the message.

GLOSSARY

publication	a book, magazine, etc. that is available to the public; the act of printing a book, etc. or sth in a newspaper	**talk down to sb**	speak to sb as if they were less important or intelligent than you
blank	empty, with nothing written on it	**instantly**	immediately **instant** adj
specialist	having or involving knowledge in a particular area of work or study	**grab sb's attention**	get sb's attention or interest
		tone	(of a piece of writing) the general character and attitude of sth: **set the tone**
assume	think or accept that sth is true but without proof **assumption** n	**quote** inf	(abbreviation of **quotation**) the exact words that sb uses. If you **quote** sb, you repeat the exact words that sb uses. **cite** v formal
on the part of sb / on sb's part	experienced or done by sb		
precious	valuable or important	**otherwise**	used to state what the result would be if sth didn't happen or sth weren't true
commodity formal	a thing that is useful or has a useful quality		
take up sth	fill or use an amount of space or time	**pace**	the speed at which sth happens
mass	affecting or involving a large number of people: **mass-market books**, **mass unemployment**. A **mass** is a large amount or quantity of sth.	**precision**	the quality of being exact, accurate and careful SYN **accuracy**

SPOTLIGHT *opening*

Opening (n) has three meanings:
1 the beginning or first part of sth (as above):
   *The story has a strange **opening**.*
2 an act of making sth open:
   *I went to the **opening** of the Picasso exhibition.*
3 a small hole that sb/sth can pass though:
   *There's a small **opening** in the wall where you can see the castle.*
Opening can also be used as an adjective.
   *My **opening** sentence was a bit too long.*

1 Underline the adjectives.

massprintblankpreciousquoteinstantlyotherwisepacespecialistopening

2 Is the pronunciation of the underlined letters the same or different? Write *S* or *D*. Use the  to help you.

1 c̲ite c̲ommodity   ....
2 t̲one qu̲ote   ....
3 inst̲antly c̲ommodity   ....
4 ass̲ume ass̲umption   ....

5 spec̲ialist prec̲ious   ....
6 o̲therwise p̲ublication   ....
7 o̲pening t̲one   ....
8 p̲ace m̲ass   ....

3 Complete the sentences.

1 Every time I write a story, I start with a .... piece of paper.
2 I started with a fairly gentle .... paragraph.
3 He started with a joke and that set the .... for the rest of the story.
4 Don't .... you know what people are thinking: that's dangerous.
5 Certain journalists are always .... various authors and sources.
6 One of the first rules of journalism: never .... down to your audience.
7 I think I put in too much detail, and that slows down the .... of my writing.
8 It's a specialist paper, so it's my .... that readers will already know the background to the story.
9 It was a mistake on the .... of the readers to believe I was totally objective.

4 Replace the underlined words with a word or phrase that keeps the same meaning.

1 I went to the <u>first night</u> of the exhibition.   I went to ....
2 You must <u>get</u> the reader's <u>interest</u>.   You must ....
3 I can recognize his style <u>immediately</u>.   I can recognize his style ....
4 It was <u>my</u> mistake.   It was a ....
5 We'll be late <u>if</u> we <u>don't</u> leave now.   We must leave now, ...
6 There are <u>thousands unemployed</u>.   There is ....
7 Did you <u>use</u> her <u>exact words</u>?   Did you .... ?
8 Freedom is <u>valuable and important</u>.   Freedom is ....

5 Complete the questions.

1 Why is it important to consider the type of .... you are writing for?
2 What can you assume if you are writing for a .... magazine or newspaper?
3 What must you never do if you are writing for a .... market?
4 What is the most precious .... in a newspaper?
5 What are two or three things your .... has to achieve?
6 .... are good, but why is it important to keep them short?

6 Now answer the questions in Exercise 5 without looking back at the text.

....
....

7 ABOUT YOUR COUNTRY Write your answers to the questions below, or talk to another student.
Can you think of:
any specialist publications written for very knowlegeable readers?
any mass-market newspapers?
any famous people who are often quoted in newspapers or on TV?

....
....
....

TEST YOURSELF

A A referendum

In 2016 there was a **referendum** in the UK **concerning** membership of the EU: to remain in the EU, or to leave the EU. The **debate divided** the nation and created a huge amount of **conflict**, even within families. Eventually, in a very **closely-fought contest**, there was a **narrow majority** for 'leave' (51.9% versus 48.1%). The **turnout** was high (just over 72% of the **electorate** voted), but that still meant that the outcome was decided by only 37% of the total electorate, and some have questioned, therefore, to what extent the result really represents the democratic **will** of the people. The British government then spent three years trying to **negotiate** an agreement that the British parliament could support.

GLOSSARY	
referendum	an occasion when all the people of a country can vote on an important issue
concerning	about sth; involving sb/sth SYN **regarding**
debate	an argument or a discussion expressing different opinions
divide	cause disagreement **division** n
conflict	a situation in which people, groups or countries are involved in a serious disagreement
closely	used to indicate that two or more things differ by only a small amount: *a closely-fought contest* (= a contest won or likely to be won by a small amount)
contest	a struggle to gain control of sth
majority	the number of votes by which one party wins an election, a discussion, etc: *a narrow majority*, e.g. 52% OPP *a clear majority*, e.g. 66%
turnout	the number of people who vote in a particular election
electorate	the people in a country or an area who have the right to vote
will	what sb wants to happen in a particular situation: *the will of the people*
negotiate	try to reach an agreement by formal discussion **negotiation** n

1 Underline the stress on the following words. Use the 🔊 to help you.

concerning	debate	conflict	divide	contest
turnout	negotiate	referendum	electorate	

2 Replace the underlined words with a word or phrase that keeps the same meaning.
1 The politician refused to answer questions <u>on the subject of</u> his private life. ....
2 They managed to get <u>just over 50% of the votes</u>. ....
3 The issue has <u>caused disagreement across</u> the country. ....
4 The result represented about 70% of the <u>people who have a right to vote</u>. ....
5 The <u>number of people who vote</u> is often low in local elections. ....
6 Both sides will have to <u>discuss this to reach an agreement</u>. ....

3 Complete the sentences.
1 There was a .... in the UK in 1973 on membership of the Common Market.
2 If banning cars is the .... of the people, politicians may have to go along with it.
3 The two countries have been in .... for months now, but nothing has been decided.
4 There has also been a long .... in the media in Scotland about Scottish independence.
5 The two parties are very .... matched, so it will be an interesting .... between them.
6 There has been serious .... in England for decades over membership of the EU. People have very strong and different opinions.

4 What can you remember? Cover the text and answer the questions.
1 What took place in June 2016 in the UK? ....
2 What was it about? ....
3 How did the people react to this event? ....
4 What was the result? ....
5 How many people voted? ....
6 What happened after that? ....

📇 TEST YOURSELF

B Coalition government

In a parliamentary system, a **coalition** government is one in which two or even **multiple** political parties **cooperate**, thus reducing the **dominance** of any one party. Broadly speaking, there are two models. The first is to form a coalition before the election. The second is to form a coalition after the election, retaining a party's **core philosophy** and ideals, but then negotiating with other parties to form an administration that can **govern** the country. **Advocates** say that coalition government leads to **consensus**-based politics, which produces **compromise**, while opponents say that no-one gets what they voted for.

GLOSSARY	
coalition	a government formed by two or more parties working together
multiple	involving many different people or things
cooperate (with sb)	work together with sb else in order to achieve sth
dominance	the fact of being more powerful or important than sb else **dominant** *adj*
core	the most important or central part of sth
philosophy	a set of beliefs or an attitude to life that guides sb's behaviour
govern	legally control a country or its people and be responsible for laws, etc.
advocate	a person who supports or speaks in favour of sb/sth, especially a public plan of action **advocate** *v*
consensus	an opinion that all members of a group agree with
compromise	[C] an agreement made between two people or groups in which each side gives up some of the things they want so that both sides are happy at the end; [U] the act of reaching a **compromise**; **compromise** *v*

5 **Is the pronunciation of the underlined letters the same or different? Write *S* or *D*. Use the 🔊 to help you.**

1 c<u>oa</u>lition   c<u>oa</u>l   ....
2 g<u>o</u>vern   d<u>o</u>minance   ....
3 advoc<u>a</u>te *n* advoc<u>a</u>te *v*   ....
4 advo<u>c</u>ate   philos<u>o</u>phy   ....

5 philos<u>o</u>phy   consens<u>u</u>s   ....
6 c<u>oo</u>perate   s<u>oo</u>n   ....
7 compr<u>o</u>mise   c<u>o</u>nsensus   ....
8 comprom<u>i</u>se   dom<u>i</u>nant   ....

6 **Complete these words.**

1 gov..................................
2 coop................................
3 advo................................

4 comp................................
5 phi..................................
6 mul..................................

7 coal................................
8 dom................................
9 cons................................

7 **Answer the questions.**

1 What is required for a *coalition*? ....
2 If you you reach a *consensus*, how many people agree with you?..
3 If you *govern* a country, how much control do you have?..
4 If you advocate something, are you *for it* or *against it*?..
5 Is dominance a fact of being *richer* or *more powerful* than others?...
6 If you reach a *compromise*, what are you prepared to do?...

8 **Complete the sentences.**

1 It's a complicated government policy and will involve .... governmental agencies.
2 It's not easy to give up certain things you want and accept certain things you don't, but in the end we all have to .... sometimes.
3 Whoever gets a majority will have the opportunity to .... the country.
4 The CDU (Christian Democratic Union) have been the .... political party in Germany in recent years.
5 If we don't .... with other groups, we'll never achieve anything.
6 The belief in democracy is at the .... of their political and moral ....
7 The prime minister has always been a strong .... of personal choice and freedom.
8 If no single party gets a majority, there will have to be some type of .... to form a government.

📖 TEST YOURSELF

Extinction **Rebellion protest** blocks the Strand

During the *Extinction Rebellion** **demonstrations** in April, the police arrested over 1,000 people and charged 53 **in connection with** the climate change protests across five UK cities. In response to these arrests, the group **staged** another demonstration yesterday outside the Royal Courts of Justice. They **occupied** much of the Strand, and by **erecting barriers** and sitting in the road, they effectively blocked the **entire** area for almost eight hours. No arrests were made and the police have recognised their right to protest. Nevertheless, the Chief Constable has made it clear that the police do have a duty to **uphold** the rule of law, and cannot **tolerate** significant **disruption** to communities across the capital.

Meanwhile, the group has **called on activists** to participate in a summer of 'creative acts of civil **disobedience**', which they hope will force government into taking action.

Extinction Rebellion* is a political **movement with a **mission** to **avert** climate catastrophe and **minimise** the risk of ecological collapse, and with it the extinction of **human beings** altogether. They aim to do this through non-violent **resistance**.

GLOSSARY

rebellion [U, C]	opposition to authority by an organized group
protest [U, C]	the expression of strong disagreement with or opposition to sth. A person is a **protester**. **protest** *v*
demonstration	a public meeting or march at which people show they are protesting against sth or supporting sth. A person is a **demonstrator**. **demonstrate** *v*
in connection with sth/sb	for reasons connected with sth/sb
stage	organize and take part in action that needs careful planning
erect	put sth in position and make it stand *upright* (= in a vertical position)
barrier	an object like a fence that stops people moving forward
entire	including everything, everyone or every part
uphold	support sth that you think is right and make sure it continues to exist
tolerate	allow sb to do sth that you do not agree with SYN **put up with sth**
disruption	a situation in which it is difficult for sth to continue in the normal way
call on sb to do sth	ask or demand that sb do sth
activist	a person who works to achieve political or social change
disobedience	refusal or failure to obey
movement	a group of people who share the same ideas or aims
mission	particular work that you feel it is your duty to do
avert	prevent sth bad or dangerous from happening
minimize	reduce sth, especially sth bad, to the lowest possible level
being	a living creature: *a human being*
resistance [U, *sing*]	opposition to or dislike of an idea, plan, etc; refusal to obey

SPOTLIGHT *occupy*

Occupy has several meanings:
1 enter a place in a large group and take control of it (as above)
2 fill or use a space, an area or an amount of time: *The bed occupies half the room.*
3 live or work in a room, building, etc: *We occupy the 12ᵗʰ floor of the building.*

1 **Underline the stress on these words. Use the** 🔊 **to help you.**

rebellion   minimise   protester   uphold   demonstrators   avert
erect   occupy   demonstration   meanwhile   protest *n*   disobedience

2 **Circle the words which suggest public protest.**

demonstration   mission   disruption   rebellion
uphold   disobedience   tolerate   resistance   occupy

3 **True or false? Write *T* or *F*. If false, explain why.**

1 If you erect something, you make it stand upright.
2 If someone upholds the law, they are trying to break it.
3 If you avert an accident, you see it.
4 If you tolerate something, you stop it happening.
5 A building which is occupied is empty.
6 A barrier is put somewhere to prevent someone from going somewhere.
7 If you minimize something, you reduce it slightly.
8 A rebellion is a person who is demonstrating against something.

4 **Replace the underlined word(s) with a word or phrase that keeps the same meaning.**

1 The protesters pulled down the <u>metal fences</u> that the police had put across the road.
2 There was even greater <u>refusal to obey</u> today at the march.
3 The <u>people who are working to get political change</u> are meeting in the square.
4 The demonstration caused considerable <u>problems and interruptions</u>.
5 There could be a lot of <u>opposition</u> to this plan.
6 A new <u>political group</u> has formed around concerns about hate crimes.
7 The government has <u>asked</u> people to cooperate with them at this time of crisis.
8 We're <u>organizing</u> a march through the city to protest about cuts to public spending.
9 The <u>whole</u> village is opposed to the council plan for more new homes.
10 The local community won't <u>put up with</u> any more disruption.

5 **One word is missing in each sentence. What is it, and where does it go?**

1 We weren't treated like human at the demonstration – more like animals. It was disgusting.
2 The organizers of the march have called activists to avoid any forms of violence.
3 Although the demonstration will cause problems, the police are keen to the disruption.
4 Reporters want to interview the protesters in with the events of last night.
5 The offices have been by an employment agency for over forty years.
6 They were careful to any potential danger to the neighbourhood.
7 We joined a group of who were carrying banners protesting about climate change.
8 The airline has attempted to avert during the pilots' strike.
9 We should no longer up with our politicians continually ignoring global warming.
10 It was the protesters who the barriers in order to keep themselves safe.

6 **Complete the texts.**

Economic instability in the country has led to the emergence of a new protest **(1)** .... called 'Fight to Survive'. Their **(2)** .... is to bring about political change through civil **(3)** .... : acts such as marching, sitting in the road or strikes. At the same time, they wish to **(4)** .... any disruption to the general public, and they are aware that actions such as **(5)** .... government buildings are rarely **(6)** .... by the authorities.

A group of **(7)** .... have been protesting in front of Parliament about animal rights. The **(8)** .... started at 8.00 a.m. in Hyde Park, and led to a march towards Parliament Square with **(9)** .... carrying signs saying 'Meat is Murder' and 'Think with your heart, not your stomach'. They are **(10)** .... on Members of Parliament to pass laws ensuring that animals have equal rights with human **(11)** .... , and they are planning to **(12)** .... further demonstrations in the coming weeks.

 TEST YOURSELF

60) Disasters

A An earthquake

Earthquake **hits** Pakistan

Last night a sudden earthquake **struck** a region in Kashmir, and reports suggest that hundreds lost their lives as buildings **collapsed** while they slept. Thousands are now being **evacuated**, but there are fears that many are still **trapped** inside their homes, so the **death toll** could rise **significantly**. The exact **scale** of the damage will not be known for several days or even weeks, but it has already been **considerable**, and reports are coming in of **numerous tremors** in the surrounding area. The next 48 hours will be crucial, not only to **rescue** more people but also to **maintain** supplies of water and electricity.

GLOSSARY	
hit	happen suddenly and have a harmful or damaging effect on sth/sb SYN **strike**
collapse	(of a building) fall down or fall in suddenly
evacuate	move sb away from a dangerous place **evacuation** n
trap	If sb is **trapped**, they are inside sth and cannot get out.
death toll	the number of people killed in a disaster, accident, etc.
significantly	to a degree that is important or easily noticed **significant** adj: **a significant effect/ improvement**
scale	the size of sth, especially when compared with other things
considerable	very large in size or amount
numerous formal	existing in large numbers
tremor	An **earth tremor** is a small earthquake.
rescue	take sb from a dangerous place to safety SYN **save; rescue** n
maintain	make sth continue at a certain level or standard

1 The pronunciation of the underlined letters is the same in all but one example. Which one? Use the 🅰🅿🅿 to help you.

c<u>o</u>llapse   signific<u>a</u>nt   numer<u>ou</u>s   evac<u>ua</u>te   c<u>o</u>nsider<u>a</u>ble   trem<u>o</u>r   ....

2 Replace the underlined words with a word or phrase that keeps the same meaning.

1 Many buildings <u>fell to the ground</u> during the earthquake.   ....
2 We've had <u>many</u> reports of possible earth tremors.   ....
3 The villagers have all been <u>moved from the village</u>.   ....
4 There are people who are <u>inside their homes and cannot get out</u>.   ....
5 Scientists believe the hurricane will <u>reach and attack</u> Florida within 24 hours.   ....
6 The <u>number of people killed</u> could be as high as 2,000.   ....
7 The storm has caused <u>a great deal of</u> damage.   ....
8 Many of those trapped were <u>taken to safety</u> by the helicopter.   ....
9 Experts will try to assess the <u>relative size</u> of the problem when all the facts are known.   ....
10 The situation has become <u>quite a lot</u> worse with the continuing bad weather.   ....

3 Complete the text.

When an earthquake **(1)** .... a city, there is always a danger that buildings will **(2)** .... and people will be **(3)** .... inside. As soon as the immediate danger has passed, the first job will be the **(4)** .... of people from the area, and to **(5)** .... anyone still in danger. While the government will send in supplies of food, it is very difficult to **(6)** .... a supply of clean drinking water. There is also the risk of further earth **(7)** ...., which can have a **(8)** .... effect on the level of damage. It may be weeks later before anyone can really judge the **(9)** .... of the disaster, and what the final death **(10)** .... might be.

 TEST YOURSELF

B Fire

The Glasgow School of Art has been **devastated** yet again by a huge fire. More than 120 **firefighters tackled** the **blaze**, which began on Friday night and spread to a concert hall next door. There were no reported **casualties**, but police evacuated 27 people from nearby properties as a **precaution**. At the moment, there is no **suspicion** the fire was started **deliberately**, but the **intense** heat is preventing fire officers from getting in to **assess** the damage. First Minister, Nicola Sturgeon, **praised** the **courage** of the firefighters who fought to save the building.

GLOSSARY	
devastate	destroy or damage sth badly **devastation** n
firefighter	a person whose job is to stop fires, working for the **fire brigade**
tackle	make an effort to deal with a difficult problem or situation
blaze	a large and often dangerous fire
casualty	a person who is killed or injured in a war or accident
precaution	sth you do in order to avoid danger or problems
suspicion	a feeling or belief that sth is wrong or that sb has done sth wrong **suspicious (of sb)** adj **suspect** v
deliberately	in a way that was planned **deliberate** adj SYN **intentional**
intense	very great, strong or serious: **intense heat/cold/pressure intensity** n
assess	judge or form an opinion about sth **assessment** n
praise	say that sb is good and should be admired for sth **praise** n
courage	the ability to do sth dangerous without showing fear SYN **bravery; courageous** adj

4 Underline the main stress on these words. Use the APP to help you.

devastate   firefighter   casualty   precaution   deliberate   suspect
assessment   courage   courageous   intensity   intentional   suspicion

5 Complete the sentences on the right with a single word. Keep the same meaning.

1 There is a suspicion it was deliberate.   The police .... it was deliberate.
2 The intense heat caused problems.   The .... of the heat caused problems.
3 Fire chiefs are assessing the damage.   Fire chiefs are making an .... of the damage.
4 The firefighters showed great courage.   The firefighters were very ....
5 The area was devastated.   The area suffered huge ....
6 They evacuated people to avoid danger.   They evacuated people as a ....
7 One died and four were injured.   There were five ....
8 They're making an effort to deal with the problem.   They're .... the problem.

6 Agree with the first speaker, without using the underlined word(s) they use.

1 Was it a big <u>fire</u>?   ~ Yes, a huge ....
2 Was it <u>intentional</u>?   ~ Yes, they think it was started ....
3 I imagine they needed fire<u>fighters</u>.   ~ Yes, they called the fire ....
4 They were very <u>courageous</u>.   ~ Yes, they showed great ....
5 Do the officers <u>judge</u> the outcome?   ~ Yes, they make the final ....
6 I hope people <u>admire them for what they did</u>.   ~ Yes, they received a lot of ....
7 Do the police <u>think the shopkeper has done something wrong</u>?   ~ Yes, they are ....
8 Was <u>strong</u> pressure really put on her to make a decision?   ~ Yes, very ....

7 Complete the sentences with a suitable word.

1 Most of the .... went to hospital.
2 Somebody call the fire ....
3 There is .... pressure on the fire service.
4 The PM .... everyone for their bravery.
5 Investigators have to .... the damage.
6 There is a .... that the fire was deliberate.

TEST YOURSELF

A A police investigation

Somerset police were last night called to the 200-**acre estate** of **Lord** and Lady Appleby, where a body was found in a fishing lake on the property. A dog walker **notified** the police after spotting a hat and **fragments** of clothing **floating** on the lake, and we received **confirmation** early this morning that they had discovered the body of a young man who had **drowned**. He has not yet been **formally** identified, and police from the neighbouring **county** of Devon are providing **assistance** with the investigation.

GLOSSARY

acre	a unit for measuring an area of land (approx. 4,000 square metres)	**float**	stay on or near the surface of sth and not sink
estate	a large area of land, usually in the country, that is owned by one person or one family	**confirmation**	a statement, letter, etc. that shows that sth is true or definite
lord	a man of high rank in the *nobility* (= people of high social class) or sb who has been given the title 'lord' as an honour and is entitled to sit in the House of Lords	**drown**	die because you have been underwater too long and cannot breathe; kill sb in this way
		formally	officially; in a way that follows an agreed way of doing things
notify	officially tell sb about sth	**county**	an area of Britain that has its own local government
fragment	a small part of sth that has broken off or come from sth larger	**assistance**	help or support

1 Is the pronunciation of the underlined letters the same or different? Write *S* or *D*. Use the 🅰🅿🅿 to help you.

1 <u>lo</u>rd <u>fo</u>rmally ....
2 <u>a</u>cre <u>a</u>ssistance ....
3 <u>a</u>cre <u>fra</u>gment ....
4 fl<u>oa</u>t n<u>o</u>tify ....
5 c<u>o</u>nfirmation n<u>o</u>bility ....
6 c<u>ou</u>nty dr<u>ow</u>n ....

2 Replace the underlined word(s) with other words that keep the same meaning.

1 They announced it <u>officially</u>. ....
2 They want some kind of written <u>statement</u>. ....
3 He <u>died underwater</u>. ....
4 The paper boat <u>stayed on the surface of</u> the water. ....
5 There were <u>small pieces</u> of metal everywhere. ....
6 They owned a large <u>area of land</u>. ....
7 We will provide them with more <u>help</u>. ....
8 I will <u>inform</u> the police. ....

3 Complete the sentences.

1 I have a very large garden; it's about half an ....
2 I broke a bottle, and there were .... of glass all over the floor.
3 A person who has died will need to be .... identified by their next-of-kin.
4 I could see a plastic bag .... in the water.
5 If you change your personal details in any way, you should .... your bank.
6 If you are offered a job and accept it, the company will require written ....
7 He wasn't born into the nobility, but was later given the title of ....
8 The girl .... because she fell into deep water and couldn't swim.

4 ABOUT YOUR COUNTRY **Write answers to the questions, or ask another student.**

1 Do you have a word in your language for an area of land that is approximately an acre? ....
2 Do you have many large estates in your country? ....
3 Do you have an equivalent of a *lord* in your country/language? ....
4 Is your country divided into areas equivalent to British counties? ....
5 If someone dies at home of natural causes, who should you notify? ....

📓 TEST YOURSELF

B A media investigation

The media **regulator** has launched a formal investigation into Australia's biggest news television **networks** after complaints about the live **broadcast** of a shooting in Christchurch, New Zealand. Some **broadcasters** put **edited** versions of the **live stream** on their channels, but **commentators** have argued that none of the content should have been **broadcast**.

A spokeswoman for one network said they always took reasonable steps to avoid offence, **distress** or **prejudice**, unless doing so was regarded as being in **the public interest**. It's a **delicate balancing act** said another station, which had shown brief **clips** of the shooting.

GLOSSARY

regulator	a person or an organization that controls an area of business or industry and makes sure it operates fairly **regulation** *n*
network	a group of radio or TV stations that are connected and that broadcast the same programmes at the same time
broadcast	a radio or TV programme **broadcast** *v*; **Broadcasters** are companies that send out radio or TV programmes.
edit	take what has been filmed or recorded and decide which parts to show
live stream	a live broadcast of an event over the internet **live-stream** *v*
commentator	a person who is an expert on a subject and talks or writes about it on radio, TV or in a newspaper
distress	a feeling of great worry or unhappiness
prejudice	an unreasonable dislike of or preference for a person, custom, etc, especially when based on race, religion, sex, etc.
delicate	needing skill and sensitive treatment
interest	a good result or an advantage for sb: *be in the public interest*
balancing act	a process in which sb tries to please two or more groups who want different things
clip	a short part of a film that is shown separately

5 Underline the stress. Use the APP to help you with the words, and see where the main stress is in the phrases in the Answer Key.

regulator   network   edit   distress   in the public interest
live stream   commentator   prejudice   delicate   balancing act

6 Circle the words which are directly connected with the media (i.e. TV, radio or the internet).

network   regulator   broadcaster   clip
prejudice   balancing act   edit   live stream

7 Form six phrases using words in the box.

a public library	a balancing interest	a media prejudice	in the public act	a film clip	racial regulator

....

....

8 Complete the sentences.

1   Advertisements for a new film often show .... from the film.
2   The event is being .... live on TV, but you can also watch recorded highlights later.
3   News bulletins are not allowed to show violent acts because they cause .... to many viewers.
4   The film has been .... and most of the violence removed.
5   You can watch a .... of the concert on the day.
6   Sometimes TV networks report on difficult things because they are in the .... interest; other times you don't show certain events. It's a .... balancing act.
7   Some TV programmes are accused of .... against certain groups of people.
8   There were complaints that the sports .... has made racist remarks about some players, so the media .... has launched an investigation.

 TEST YOURSELF

A Celebrity and the media

Celebrities **deserve privacy**

A survey **conducted** on privacy and the media has **revealed** that most people think there should be little or no **coverage** of the private lives of celebrities. This **contrasts** strongly with the huge success of celebrity magazines, which go into great detail about the lives of people **in the public eye**. It also **emerged** from the **findings** that people did not want politicians to have their private lives **exposed** in the same way. Certain **tabloids** were thought to be particularly guilty of **prying into** the lives of famous people.

SPOTLIGHT *emerge*

Emerge has several different but closely related meanings.
1 become known (as above)
2 come out of a hidden place: *She **emerged** from the lake.*
3 start to exist or appear: *After the election, new groups started to **emerge**.*

GLOSSARY	
deserve	If you **deserve** sth, it is right that you should have it because of what you have done or the way you have behaved.
privacy	the state of being alone and not watched or disturbed by others
conduct *formal*	organize and/or do a particular activity: *conduct a survey / an experiment*; SYN **carry sth out**
reveal	make sth known to sb **revelation** *n*
coverage	the reporting of news in newspapers, on TV, etc.
contrast (with sth)	show a clear difference when close together or when compared
in the public eye	well known to many people through TV or newspapers
findings (*usually pl*)	information learned as the result of research
expose	show sth that is usually hidden
tabloid	a newspaper full of pictures and/or stories about famous people, often thought of as less serious than other papers
pry (into sth)	try to find information about people's private lives

1 **Circle the word(s) that are correct. More than one word may be possible.**
  1 Papers are often good at *conducting / revealing / exposing* the truth.
  2 They have *carried out / deserved / conducted* a survey on people's hobbies.
  3 I don't like the way the papers *deserve / pry into / conduct* people's private lives.
  4 Have you read the *coverage / tabloids / findings* today?
  5 This new information *exposes / contrasts with / reveals* what we already know.
  6 New celebrities *emerge / pry into / deserve* all the time.
  7 I'm sure the facts will *be revealed / be conducted / emerge* soon.
  8 *Findings / Coverage / Privacy* of the news on TV is pretty good.
  9 They will publish further *findings / revelations / tabloids* in tomorrow's paper.
  10 The refugees *pry into / deserve / expose* our help.

2 **Complete the text with suitable words from the top of the page.**
The New Yorker **(1)** .... out a survey among 650 young people in NY, and it **(2)** .... some interesting and quite disturbing **(3)** .... on how some teenagers view celebrity. Many believe that because they work hard, celebrities **(4)** .... to be famous. It also **(5)** .... from the survey that lonely teenagers are more likely to follow the lives of people in the public **(6)** .... These findings **(7)** .... with the views of most older people, who have less respect for celebrities and also think they don't deserve **(8)** ....

3 **Complete the questions with suitable words.**
  Then write your answers, or ask another student.

ABOUT YOU AND YOUR COUNTRY

  1 In your country, do you have .... newspapers? ....
  2 Are they often guilty of .... into the private lives of people in the .... eye? ....
  3 Are you happy about this, or do you think celebrities deserve some .... ? ....
  4 What are the advantages and disadvantages of being a TV .... ? ....

📖 TEST YOURSELF

B Celebrity headlines

Rocky **allegedly** back in **rehab**

Football club **rocked** by **scandal**

Shamona speaks of her marriage **hell**!

Rumours of **custody** battle over baby Sahara

Fellow celebs* **rally to** Tom's **defence**

Famous celeb loses a **fortune**!

*abbreviation of **celebrities**

SPOTLIGHT *hell*

Hell can be used in very different ways.
1 In some religions, it is believed to be the place where bad people go after death. OPP **heaven**
2 a very unpleasant experience or situation in which people suffer (as above): *He went **through hell** during the trial.*
3 a swear word that some people use when they are annoyed or surprised. Some people may find it offensive: *Oh **hell**, I've burnt the toast!*

4 Is the pronunciation of the underlined letters the same or different? Write *S* or *D*. Use the APP to help you.

1 all**e**gedly all**e**gation ....
2 alle**g**edly alle**g**ation ....
3 sc**a**ndal r**a**lly ....
4 fort**u**ne st**u**dent ....
5 reh**a**b reh**a**bilitation ....
6 r**u**mour c**u**stody ....
7 rum**ou**r cust**o**dy ....
8 f**e**llow d**e**fence ....

5 Rewrite the sentence using the word in capitals. Keep the same meaning.

1 He is said to have lost all his money. ALLEGEDLY ....
2 They acted to protect her. DEFENCE ....
3 They say she has a lot of money. FORTUNE ....
4 Jason has the legal right to look after his son. CUSTODY ....
5 He's had a terrible time recently. HELL ....
6 She's had support from people who work with her. FELLOW ....

6 Complete each dialogue.

A I heard a **(1)** .... that the health minister is about to resign. Do you think it's true?
~ Well, there has been an **(2)** .... that he's involved in a financial **(3)** ....
Really? If that's true, it would really **(4)** .... the government, wouldn't it?
~ Yes, and his life would be **(5)** .... for a while.

B One of the tabloids is **(6)** .... that the star of the new Mad Max is in **(7)** .... again.
~ I'm not surprised. He has already lost a **(8)** .... from gambling.
That's right. And he lost **(9)** .... of his young son because of that.
~ Poor guy. Still, I expect his **(10)** .... celebs will **(11)** .... round and
(12) .... him.

TEST YOURSELF

A Amazing but true!

OPERATED ON AFTER 55 YEARS!

A German woman who spent 55 years with a pencil **stuck** in her brain has finally had most of it removed. She had fallen over holding the pencil when she was four. It went **directly** through her cheek and then into her brain. **Ever since**, she had had to **endure severe** pain because doctors **dared** not operate. The three-**inch** long pencil was finally removed on Friday in a very **delicate** operation, all except the **tip** of the pencil. The woman is said to be **making a speedy recovery**, and **mysteriously** the **remaining** tip seems to be causing her no problems at all.

GLOSSARY

stuck (in sth)	unable to move or be moved
directly	in a direct line or manner
ever since	continuously since the time mentioned
endure *formal*	experience or deal with sth that is painful or unpleasant, especially without complaining SYN **bear, put up with sth**
severe	very bad or serious
inch	a unit of measurement equal to 2.54 centimetres
delicate	showing or needing very skilful and careful treatment
tip (of sth)	the thin pointed end (of sth)
make a speedy/ rapid recovery	get well again quickly after an illness
mysteriously	in a way that is difficult to understand or explain **mysterious** *adj*
remaining	still existing or needing to be dealt with

SPOTLIGHT *dare*

Dare means 'be brave enough to do something'.
- *I **dare** you to ask him.* (= Are you brave enough to ask him?)
It is usually used in questions and negative forms.
- ***How dare you** say that!* (= I am very angry that you said that.)
- ***Don't you dare** come near me!* (used to give someone a strong warning)

1 Circle all the adjectives you can find in the word snake.

dareseveredirectlyremaininginchmysteriouslytipstuckrapidsincedelicate

2 Circle the correct answer(s). Both answers may be possible.

1 The *tip / edge* of the cat's tail is white.
2 I made a *speedy / rapid* recovery.
3 The pain can be quite *severe / mysterious*.
4 She's got a *delicate / mysterious* virus.
5 He had to *endure / put up with* a lot of pain.
6 How dare you *do / to do* that!
7 It's about *two inches / five centimetres* long.
8 There were seven and I've had six, so where's the *left / remaining* one?
9 I bought it in 2012 and have lived there *ever / ever since*.

3 Complete the dialogues with a suitable word or phrase.

1 Was the pain bad? ~ Yes, I didn't think I could .... it much longer.
2 It must be so difficult operating on the brain. ~ Yes, it's a very .... procedure.
3 You've put on weight. ~ How .... you say that!
4 How's Tania? ~ No idea. I haven't seen her .... her accident last year.
5 I .... you to ask that girl out. ~ Mmm. What do you think she'll say?
6 Where has he gone? ~ They have no idea. It's a very .... disappearance.
7 Is Tina getting better? ~ Yeah, apparently she's making a ....
8 I'm going to tell the teacher you copied my answers. ~ Oh, don't you .... do that!
9 Was Karen hurt? ~ No. She was on the same bus, but not .... involved in the accident.
10 What did you say about a nail? ~ It got .... in his foot. It was quite difficult to get out.

TEST YOURSELF

B A survival tale

A DRAMATIC TALE

An Australian farmer has described how he spent SEVEN days sitting on the **upper** branches of a tree above a **swamp** full of **deadly** crocodiles. The 53-year-old man said he was forced to take the action after his horse **accidentally stumbled** and he fell off. The horse **panicked** and **galloped** off, leaving David **stranded**. He managed to climb a nearby tree and realized he could either **stay put** and hope to be found by a rescue team, or try to climb down, **taking a chance on** being eaten by a crocodile. After a week, and nearly **starving**, he was **spotted** by helicopters and rescued.

crocodile

GLOSSARY

tale	an exciting description of an event	**gallop**	When a horse or similar animal **gallops**, it moves across the ground very fast.
upper	at or near the top of sth OPP **lower**		
swamp	an area of ground that is very wet or covered in water and in which plants, trees, etc. are growing	**be stranded**	be in a place from which you have no way of leaving
		stay put *inf*	stay where you are rather than moving away
deadly	causing or likely to cause death	**take a chance (on sth)**	decide to do sth, knowing it is a risk
accidentally	by chance; in a way that was not planned		
stumble	hit your foot against sth while walking or running and nearly fall	**starve**	suffer or die because you do not have enough food to eat
panic (panicked; panicking)	suddenly feel frightened so that you cannot think clearly **panic** *n*	**spot**	see or notice sb/sth, especially suddenly or when it is not easy to do so

4 Is the meaning similar or different? Write S or D.

1 We had to stay put for an hour.	We couldn't move for an hour.	
2 The snake was deadly.	The snakes was nearly dead.	
3 Don't look for an opportunity.	Don't take any chances.	
4 We were attacked.	We were stranded.	
5 He stumbled and fell.	He tripped and fell.	
6 I was on an upper slope of the mountain.	I was near the top of the mountain.	
7 The horse galloped towards the lake.	The horse walked towards the lake.	
8 The area was covered in water.	It was like a swamp.	

5 Complete the definitions.

1 If it's deadly, it can ....
2 If you starve, you can ....
3 If you spot something, you .... it.
4 If it happens accidentally, it's by ....
5 If you stumble, you nearly ....
6 If you panic, you don't think ....

6 Complete the dialogues with a suitable word or phrase.

1 Did you stay fairly calm?   ~ No, I'm afraid I was in a ....
2 Was the land very wet?   ~ Yes, they found me in a ....
3 How did they see you?   ~ Fortunately, they .... my white hat.
4 Is that a true story?   ~ I don't know, but it's an interesting ....
5 Was it safe to move around?   ~ No, too risky, so I decided to ....
6 Could you get out of the village?   ~ No, we were ....
7 Is that the upper limit of money we can spend?   ~ No, the complete opposite. It's the ....
8 You stayed where you were during the flood?   ~ Yes, I didn't want to take ....

 TEST YOURSELF

plumber

electrician

carpenter

D.H. Electronics are **seeking** a new **Chief Executive**

Rising complaints about the number of **civil servants** in this country

Manual workers in short supply

Government wants to create thousands of new **apprentices**

I've been a **jeweller** and **librarian**. Now, I'm a **housewife**.

Senior posts in Health Service still left **vacant**

I do **casual work** as a **barman** in the evenings.

It's very hard to find good **plumbers**, **electricians** and **carpenters nowadays**.

Being an **accountant** not as **lucrative** as it used to be!

I used to be a **butcher**, but now I'm a **handyman**.

New tax **incentives** for the **self-employed**

More people unwilling to accept low-**status** jobs

You need to be pretty **tough** to be a **bodyguard**.

We need more **entrepreneurs**, says Industry Minister

GLOSSARY

seek *formal* — try to find or get sth

executive — a person who has an important position as a manager in a business, organization, etc. A **chief executive** is the person with the highest rank in a company or organization.

apprentice — a young person who works for a fixed period of time in order to learn the skills needed in a particular job. An **apprenticeship** is the state of being an apprentice.

casual — (of work) not permanent or regular: *casual work/labour*

barman — (female **barmaid**) a person who serves drinks from behind a bar in a pub

butcher — a person who sells meat

handyman — a man who is good at doing practical jobs inside or outside the house, as a hobby or as a job

tough — strong enough to deal with difficult conditions or situations

bodyguard — a person whose job is to protect sb

civil servant — a person who works for the **civil service**, which is all the government departments

jeweller — a person whose job is to buy, sell, make or repair **jewellery** such as *necklaces* and *watches*

librarian — a person who works in or is in charge of a library

housewife — (male **househusband**) a person who doesn't have a job outside the home and spends their time cleaning the home, looking after the family, etc.

nowadays — at the present time, in contrast with the past

incentive — sth that encourages you (to do sth)

self-employed — working for yourself and making money from your own business

entrepreneur — a person who makes money by starting or running a business, especially one involving financial risk

manual — using your hands

senior — having a high position in a company or organization

post *formal* — a job, especially an important one SYN **position**

vacant — (of a job in a company) available for sb to take **vacancy** *n*

accountant — a person whose job is to manage or examine the financial accounts of a company. **Accountancy** is the name of the profession.

lucrative *formal* — allowing sb to earn a lot of money

status — the social or professional position of sb/sth in relation to others: *low/high status*

1 **Is the pronunciation of the underlined letters the same or different? Write *S* or *D*. Use the 🔊 to help you.**

1 b<u>u</u>tcher pl<u>u</u>mber ....
2 plum<u>b</u>er li<u>b</u>rarian ....
3 <u>c</u>arpenter <u>b</u>arman ....
4 bar<u>man</u> handy<u>man</u> ....
5 apprenti<u>ce</u> serv<u>a</u>nt ....

6 st<u>a</u>tus <u>ca</u>sual ....
7 l<u>i</u>brarian appren<u>ti</u>ce ....
8 v<u>a</u>cant m<u>a</u>nual ....
9 lucr<u>a</u>tive <u>a</u>ccountant ....
10 appr<u>en</u>tice <u>en</u>trepreneur ....

2 **Mark the main stress on these words.**

apprentice	handyman	executive	entrepreneur
lucrative	librarian	electrician	nowadays
civil servant	vacancy	bodyguard	self-employed

3 **What's my job?**

1 I sell rings and necklaces. ....
2 I do lots of different small jobs. ....
3 I work for a government department. ....
4 I serve drinks in a pub. ....
5 I'm training to be a plumber. ....
6 I protect famous people. ....

7 I make things with wood. ....
8 I fix sinks and toilets. ....
9 I lend books. ....
10 I sell meat. ....
11 I look after the financial side of the business. ....
12 I do just about everything in the home. ....

4 **Which of these jobs are quite well-paid?**

1 apprentice ....
2 electrician ....
3 barman/barmaid ....

4 civil servant ....
5 housewife ....
6 casual work ....

7 accountant ....
8 manual worker ....
9 librarian ....

5 **Complete the sentences with a suitable word.**

1 The health service is always .... more nurses; they are in such short supply.
2 They're not looking for junior staff; they want .... staff.
3 You can earn a lot of money as an entrepreneur. It can be very ....
4 In the past there were many opportunities, but .... it's more difficult to find a job.
5 I've always enjoyed .... work. That's why I became a carpenter.
6 Max used to work for a company, but he's been self-........................... now for five years.
7 If you're looking for work, try the post office: they've got lots of ....
8 My dad has just become the new chief .... of a big advertising company.
9 You have to be .... if you want to join the armed forces as a marine.
10 There's no .... to work for that company because the pay and conditions are so bad.
11 The chief executive had been in the .... for nearly ten years, but when he retired and the job became ...., it was offered to a much younger man.
12 Though I've worked in different government departments, I've spent my whole career in the ....

6 ABOUT YOU **Write your answers, or talk to another student.**

1 Do you have experience of any of the jobs in this unit? ....
2 Are you attracted to any of them? ....
3 Would you prefer to be self-employed? ....
4 Do you think you need incentives to work hard? ....
5 Are you good at manual work? ....
6 If you were looking for casual work in the evenings, would you be happy to be a barman/barmaid? ....
7 Do you think apprenticeships are a good idea? ....
8 Would you be happy as a housewife or househusband? ....
9 Would it matter to you if your job had low status? ....

TEST YOURSELF

A Market sectors

We advertise jobs across a range of market **sectors. Register** by email now, and you can be first in line to apply for jobs as they appear.

Just select any two sectors in which you have experience and/or **qualifications.**

☐ retail
☐ administration
☐ manufacturing
☐ market research

☐ **human resources**
☐ **finance**
☐ **recruitment**
☐ **insurance**

GLOSSARY

sector	a part of the business activity of a country **public sector** the sector controlled by the government **private sector** the sector controlled by private companies	**market research**	the study of what people want to buy and why
register (with sth)	put a name on an official list **register** n	**human resources**	(often abbreviated **HR**) the department in a company that deals with employing and training people
qualifications	the exams you have passed or courses you have finished	**finance**	the activity of managing money **financial** adj
retail	selling goods to people directly in shops, on the internet, etc.	**recruitment**	the business of finding people for job vacancies **recruit** v
administration	(often abbreviated as **admin**) the process or act of managing sth such as an organization or a business	**insurance**	an arrangement with a company in which you pay them money and they agree to pay the costs if, for example, you die or are ill, or if you lose or damage sth
manufacturing	the business of producing goods in factories, etc.		

1 **Underline the main stress on these words. Use the** APP **to help you.**

qualifications   administration   manufacturing   market research
human resources   finance   recruitment   insurance

2 **What sector do these people work in?**

1   I try to discover what customers want.   ....
2   I have to look for the best way to use people in the company.   ....
3   I sell clothes.   ....
4   I sell policies to people as protection against illness.   ....
5   I work in car production.   ....
6   I work in an office, in charge of a small group.   ....
7   I control the money in our firm.   ....
8   I help to find jobs for people.   ....

3 **Complete the text.**

I'm still doing my accountancy exams, but I've already **(1)** .... with a recruitment company that helps young people to find work. And when I finally get my accountancy **(2)** .... , it should help me find a career in **(3)** .... , preferably in the private **(4)** .... , and eventually run my own business, like my dad. He started in **(5)** .... , where he worked on the production of motorbikes, but ended up with his own business.

4 ABOUT YOU **Look at the website again. Which sectors do you have experience or qualifications in? If you're still studying, would you like to work in any of these market sectors in the future?**

....
....
....

📔 TEST YOURSELF

B Job prospects

Two years ago, I got a **challenging** job with good **prospects** in local radio. I worked hard, and as a **reward**, I was **promoted** and **transferred** to a different **department**. Then, all of a sudden, things started going wrong: one colleague **got the sack**, and another **handed in his notice**. Two months later, ten people were **made redundant**. I didn't want to be **out of work**, so I decided to look **elsewhere**. I applied for a job in TV and was **appointed** assistant director. Amazing!

GLOSSARY

prospects *pl*	the chances of being successful in the future	**department**	a section of a business, university, etc.
challenging	difficult to do, but interesting and enjoyable **challenge** *n*	**hand in your notice**	give your employer a formal letter saying that you will leave your job SYN **resign**; **Quit** (*inf*) means 'leave your job'.
reward	sth you get because you have done sth helpful, worked hard, etc. **reward** *v*	**make sb redundant** (*often passive*)	make sb leave their job because they are not needed any more
promote (*usually passive*)	give sb a better job at a higher level in a company **promotion** *n*	**out of work**	not working and unable to find a job SYN **unemployed**
transfer sb/sth (from …to …)	move sb/sth from one place to another	**elsewhere**	in or to another place
		appoint	choose sb for a job

5 **Is the meaning the same or different? Write S or D.**

1 a challenge / a reward   ....
2 fire someone / dismiss someone   ....
3 be promoted / be appointed   ....
4 promotion / prospects   ....
5 reward someone / promote someone   ....
6 hand in your notice / resign   ....

7 be sacked / be rewarded   ....
8 transfer someone / move someone to another office   ....
9 quit / hand in your notice   ....
10 make someone redundant / fire someone   ....
11 get the sack / sack someone   ....
12 out of work / unemployed   ....

6 **Complete the sentences with a single word, with the meaning of the words in brackets.**

1 My job's very ....   (difficult but interesting)
2 I want to transfer to another ....   (section of the business)
3 I have good .... in my job.   (chances of success)
4 I'd really love to be ....   (given a higher-level job in the company)
5 I'm bored at work, so I'm going to look ....   (in another place)
6 I've never been ....   (out of work)
7 I'd hate to have to .... someone.   (dismiss)
8 If I hated my job, I would definitely ....   (hand in my notice)
9 I was very happy to be .... to the job I currently have.   (chosen for the job)
10 I think .... is usually a reward for hard work.   (a higher level job)
11 With less work available, I was made ....   (not needed)
12 I didn't like it, so I decided to ....   (leave my job)

7 ABOUT YOU **Have you got a job? If so, are the sentences in Exercise 6 true for you? Write *True* or *Not true*, or talk to another student who has a job.**

....
....
....

 TEST YOURSELF

A Freelance work: the pros and cons

You **are** not **accountable to** anyone but yourself.

Working for a number of employers gives you an **insight into** different companies.

You may **be better off**, and you don't have to rely **solely** on one company.

Working from home makes it easier to **balance** work **and** family responsibilities.

You don't have a **guaranteed** income or **additional** financial benefits, e.g. a company pension.

You will **encounter** quiet periods, a **degree of** isolation, and perhaps loneliness.

Work can **get in the way of** your home life and your free time.

GLOSSARY	
freelance	earning money by selling your work or services to different organizations rather than being employed by just one **freelance** *adv*
the pros and cons (of sth)	the advantages and disadvantages of sth
accountable to sb	responsible for your decision or actions and expected to explain them if asked. If you are **not accountable to anyone**, you are **your own boss**.
insight into sth	a clear understanding of what sth is like: *have / give sb insight into sth*
be better off	have more money OPP **be worse off**
solely	only, not involving sb/sth else: *be solely responsible for sth*
balance A and/ with B	give equal importance to two contrasting things
guarantee	promise that sth will happen **guaranteed** *adj*; **guarantee** *n*
additional	more than is usual, or mentioned before SYN **extra**
encounter	experience sth, especially sth unpleasant or difficult
get in the way (of sth)	prevent sb from doing sth, or prevent sth happening

SPOTLIGHT *degree*

A **degree of sth** is a certain level or amount of sth, and it is commonly used in these ways:

- *Cooking **requires a degree of** skill.*
- *I have **a (greater) degree of** freedom in my new job.*
- *I can do what I like, **to a degree**.* SYN **to an extent**

1 Underline the main stress on these words and phrases. Use the 🔊 to help you.

freelance   accountable   insight   guarantee   additional   encounter

2 Replace the underlined words with a word or phrase that has a similar meaning.

1 We <u>experienced</u> a few problems during the project. ....
2 There is a certain <u>amount</u> of stress working freelance. ....
3 I enjoy being <u>my own boss</u>. ....
4 The project gave me an <u>understanding of</u> how the company works. ....
5 She tried to <u>give equal importance to</u> her career and her family. ....
6 There are various <u>advantages and disadvantages</u> with regular employment. ....
7 I could do what I liked in the job, to <u>a degree</u>. ....
8 Looking after the children sometimes <u>prevents me from</u> doing my work. ....

3 Complete the text with suitable words or phrases.

I was a **(1)** .... designer for 10 years. I liked being my own **(2)** ....
and the fact that I was **(3)** .... responsible for everything I did. Naturally, I
(4) .... a certain **(5)** .... of isolation, but I didn't mind that, and I was
generally **(6)** .... off, so I was able to buy a nice house. However, when I had children,
the work did get **(7)** .... of my family life, so I went back to a regular job with a
(8) .... income, plus the **(9)** .... benefits of a company car and pension.

4 ABOUT YOU **Have you ever worked freelance? If so, did you enjoy the same advantages and encounter similar problems? Write your answers, or talk to another student.**

....
....
....

TEST YOURSELF

B Working in a team: the pros and cons

✓ Working as **part of a team** with a common goal **fosters team spirit**.

✓ **Collaboration** and **mutual** feedback are **fulfilling** and make people feel **valued**.

✓ Bringing together **diverse** skills is generally more productive.

✗ If someone doesn't **fit in**, that can be **disruptive** for the whole team.

✗ Teams can **suppress** individual **enterprise** and **initiative**.

✗ Individuals can sometimes **get away with** being lazy.

GLOSSARY			
part	a person or thing that, working together with others, forms part of a single unit: ***part of a team***	**value**	think that sb/sth is important
		diverse	different from each other and of various kinds
foster	help sth to develop SYN **encourage, promote**	**fit in (with sb/sth)**	be accepted by the others in a group
team spirit	loyal feelings towards a group, team, or society	**disruptive**	causing problems, and making it hard to continue with sth
collaboration (with sb)	the act of working with others to produce sth	**suppress**	prevent sth from growing, developing or continuing
mutual	used to describe a feeling that two people have for each other equally: ***mutual respect/trust***	**enterprise**	the ability to think of new ideas and make them successful
		initiative	the ability to take decisions and act alone: ***use your initiative***
fulfilling	giving personal satisfaction SYN **rewarding; fulfil** v	**get away with sth**	avoid doing sth, or manage to do less than expected

5 Positive or negative? Write *P* or *N*.
1 He showed enterprise during the project. ....
2 She can be disruptive in the office. ....
3 I don't feel valued. ....
4 The work was fulfilling . ...
5 The team members have diverse skills. ....
6 He doesn't use his initiative. ....
7 She gets away with poor-quality work. ....
8 There is mutual trust between the members. ....

6 Rewrite the sentences without using the underlined words. Keep the same meaning.
1 He <u>wasn't accepted by the others</u>. He didn't ....
2 She can <u>act on her own</u>. She can ....
3 They <u>did most of it together</u>. There was a lot ....
4 He <u>escaped without punishment</u>. He got ....
5 I need someone <u>to think up new ideas</u>. I need someone with ....
6 They have a lot of respect <u>for each other</u>. They have a lot of ....

7 Complete the sentences with suitable words from the top of the page.
1 My boss appreciates what I do, and that helps me to feel ....
2 To feel .... of a team, it helps to have a manager who works to build team ....
3 You need people who will .... a good atmosphere in the team.
4 The people in my office are all different and all from very .... backgrounds.
5 One colleague has a lot of loud phone calls, and that is .... for others in the group.
6 I used to work for a boss who tried to .... any individual enterprise, which was very frustrating. With my new boss, however, I enjoy the work and find it very ....

8 ABOUT YOU **Do you agree with the pros and cons above? Can you think of any others? Write your answers, or talk to another student.**

....
....
....

 TEST YOURSELF

A An industrial dispute

Talks to **settle the dispute** between Royal Mail bosses and the CWU union have **broken down** again, so the union has decided, following the support of its members in a **ballot**, to set a date for strikes as early as next month. They claim it is not just a pay dispute, but an attempt to **halt** the **closure** of 2,500 post offices around the country. For the government, though, there is a great deal **at stake**. If the management **gives in** to the demands, it could **set a precedent** for other groups, who may feel more **inclined** to **step up** their own claims for higher **wage** settlements.

GLOSSARY	
settle	put an end to an argument or a disagreement
dispute	a disagreement, often official, between people or groups: *a pay/industrial dispute; settle a dispute*
break down	(of talks/negotiations, etc.) fail
ballot	a system of voting in which votes are made in secret **ballot** v
halt	prevent sth from continuing
closure	a situation in which a school, factory, etc. is permanently shut
at stake	If sth is **at stake**, you will lose it if a plan or action is not successful.
give in	agree to do sth that you do not want to do
precedent	sth that happened in the past which is seen as a rule or example for others in a similar situation to follow
inclined to do sth	likely to do sth or tending to do sth
step sth up	increase the amount of an activity in order to achieve sth
wage (ALSO **wages** *pl*)	a regular amount of money you earn, often paid weekly: *a high/low wage*

SPOTLIGHT *set + noun*

Set is used with many nouns and often means 'fix something for others to copy', e.g. **set a standard / a precedent / an example**. It can also mean 'decide on something', e.g. **set a date/limit**.

1 Circle the words which suggest that something is stopping, failing or going wrong.

dispute	give in	step up	break down
halt	precedent	closure	inclined to

2 Complete the sentences with a suitable verb.

1 The manager .... the standard for others to follow.
2 We must act now in order to .... the dispute.
3 The union must .... their members before they can go ahead with strike action.
4 The 5% wage settlement has .... a precedent for other unions.
5 The government has failed to .... the economic decline, so things look bad.
6 If their demands aren't met, some workers will .... their call for strike action.
7 We mustn't .... to their demands. We will fight to the end.
8 The negotiations started well but they've just .... for some reason.

3 Complete the dialogues.

1 Is it the only factory to close? ~ No, there have been lots of other ....
2 Are they taking a risk with the new IT company? ~ Yes, there's a lot at ....
3 Why are they going on strike? ~ It's a .... over pay, I believe.
4 Has this happened before? ~ No, it would set a ....
5 Have they reached an agreement? ~ No, the talks ....
6 What will happen if you leave? ~ I think others may be .... to follow.
7 Is the dispute about pay? ~ Yes, basically they want higher ....
8 Will they go on strike? ~ Maybe, but they must have a .... of members first.

 TEST YOURSELF

B Working conditions

What **fringe benefits** can you expect from your job?

* a company **pension**?
* an annual **bonus**?
* health or **dental** insurance?
* paid **sick leave**?
* **maternity/paternity** leave?
* a **commission** (on certain jobs)

What **rights** do you have?

* the right to join a **trade union**?
* Are you **entitled to strike**?
* the right to a **minimum** level of paid holiday?

GLOSSARY

(fringe) benefit (*usually pl*)	an advantage you get from a company in addition to the money you earn SYN **perk**
pension	money paid regularly by a government or company to sb when they retire: *a state/company pension*
bonus	an extra amount of money, often added to a wage or salary, as a reward: *an annual bonus*
dental	connected with teeth: *dental treatment*
leave	a period of time when you are allowed to be away from work for a holiday or a special reason: *annual/unpaid/sick leave*
maternity	the state of being or becoming a mother: *maternity leave*, ALSO *paternity leave* (for fathers)
commission	an amount of money paid to sb for selling goods which increases with the amount sold
right	a moral or legal claim to have or get sth or to behave in a particular way
trade union	an organization of workers that exists to protect its workers
entitle (sb to sth) (*often passive*)	give sb the right to have or do sth
strike	a period of time when an organized group of employees refuse to work because of a disagreement over pay or conditions: *be/go on strike*
minimum	the smallest that is possible or allowed: *the minimum wage/charge*

---

4 **Form seven compound words or phrases from words in the box.**

minimum	fringe	maternity	state	dental	go on	trade
pension	strike	wage	leave	union	benefit	treatment

....

....

5 **Complete the sentences.**

1 Most countries have .... leave, but not always paternity leave.
2 I've always belonged to a trade ....
3 We only get an annual .... if the company is doing well.
4 The workers are planning to .... strike next week.
5 The company pays sick .... up to a certain number of weeks.
6 When you retire, will you be .... to a state and company .... ?
7 I think most workers in the UK have a .... to join a .... union, but I don't think members of the emergency services can go on ....
8 I get 10% .... on everything I sell.
9 I believe everyone has the .... to refuse overtime over a certain number of hours.
10 Most people have a .... of 20 days' paid .... every year.

6 ABOUT YOU **Write your answers, or talk to another student.**

1 Have you got a job? If so, which of the perks above do you get? What other perks do you get? Which are the most important to you? ....
2 Are you entitled to all the rights above? ....
3 If you haven't got a job, which of the perks above sound the most important, and why? ....

 TEST YOURSELF

A Some important reminders

Time Management tips

- Do you **note down** jobs you have to do **on a daily basis**?
- Do you put up **reminders** in the office about these aims?
- Do you **prioritize** the tasks you have to **accomplish** by the end of the day?
- Do you **stick to** your **priorities, no matter what** happens?
- Do you focus on **one thing at a time**?
- Do you try to **anticipate** so you can organize tasks better?
- Do you **delegate** tasks and responsibilities as far as possible?
- Do you set **deadlines** for tasks and stick to them?

SPOTLIGHT *no matter what/how, etc.*

No matter what/how, etc. means 'it doesn't matter what/how, etc.' or 'it isn't important what/how, etc.'. It is similar to **whatever**, etc.

- *No matter what happens, don't panic.* = *Whatever happens, don't panic.*
- *You'll find work no matter where you are.* = *Wherever you are, you'll find work.*

GLOSSARY	
note sth down	write sth quickly SYN **make a note of sth**
basis	a particular way in which sth is organized or done: *on a day-to-day/daily/weekly/regular basis*
reminder	sth that makes you remember sth **remind sb (of/about sth)** v
prioritize	put tasks, problems, etc. in order of importance so that you can do the most important first **priority** n: *a high/low/top priority*
accomplish	succeed in doing or completing sth SYN **achieve**
stick to sth	continue doing sth despite difficulties
one (thing) at a time	separately; individually
anticipate	expect sth will happen and prepare for it
delegate sth (to sb)	give part of your work or power to sb in a lower position
deadline	a time or date before which sth must be finished

1 Underline the stress on these words. Use the 🔊 to help you.

reminder   prioritize   accomplish   anticipate   deadline   delegate

2 Circle the correct word(s). More than one word may be possible.

1 Once you have *prioritized / accomplished* your daily goals make sure you do them all.
2 I had to *remind / delegate* him about the conference next month: he'd forgotten.
3 You need to set a time limit, *no matter what / whatever* happens.
4 I tend to check emails on a daily *basis / base* – *wherever / whatever* I am in the world.
5 The organizers hadn't *prioritized / anticipated* how many people would attend.
6 There's nothing worse than a manager who can't *delegate / stick to* the priorities.
7 We've *accomplished / achieved* a lot this month.
8 Employing a new manager is now my top *reminder / priority*.

3 Complete the dialogues.

1 How often do you review the figures?   ~ Usually on a monthly ....
2 He won't give up, even if it's hard.   ~ I know, he always .... to the task.
3 Were you surprised Jack was angry?   ~ Yes. I didn't .... that at all.
4 Do you remember the dates of meetings? ~ No, I often need a ....
5 You should get your assistant to do it.   ~ I know, I should .... work more often.
6 Have you got my email address?   ~ No, let me just .... of it.
7 Will you finish the project this week?   ~ Yes, I'll do it no .... what happens.
8 It's been a real achievement.   ~ Yes, we've .... a great deal.
9 Will the work be done by a certain date?   ~ Yes, I always set .... for tasks.
10 Is the time of the meeting in your diary?   ~ No, I need to .... it ....
11 Do you try to do everything at once?   ~ No, one thing ....

4 ABOUT YOU Do you think any of the time management tips are more important than others? Write your answers, or ask another student.

....

 TEST YOURSELF

B Email stress

The new office workers' plague

If you are constantly **interrupted by** the need to read your emails, your **nerves are on edge.** Over a third of workers say that they are increasingly **overwhelmed** by the **endless stream** of emails they receive, and are **stressed out** by the pressure to respond to them **promptly.** Research has found that some employees check their emails every few minutes, leaving them both **frustrated** and not very **productive.** Women seem particularly **badly-hit** by this **flood** of correspondence. One of the researchers said that email is 'an amazing tool' but agreed that it is **getting out of control.** The advice is to **set aside** two or three specific email reading times each day.

GLOSSARY

interrupt	stop sth/sb from doing sth **interruption** n
nerves pl	feelings of worry and anxiety. If your **nerves are on edge,** you feel very nervous or excited.
be overwhelmed (by sth)	have so many things that you cannot deal with them **overwhelming** adj (of things to do) so many that you feel stressed
endless	seeming to last for ever
stressed out inf	too anxious and tired to be able to relax **stress sb out** phrasal v
promptly	quickly; without delay **prompt** adj
frustrated	feeling annoyed or impatient because you cannot do or achieve what you want. Sth that makes you **frustrated** is **frustrating.**
productive	producing good results. A person's **productivity** is how much they produce in a given period.
badly-hit	badly affected by sth ALSO **severely/hard hit**
be/get out of control	be/become impossible to deal with OPP **be under control**
set sth aside	keep sth, especially money or time, to use later SYN **put sth aside**

SPOTLIGHT metaphorical use of words

A **plague** is a serious fast-spreading disease which often results in death. In the title, though, it is used metaphorically and describes something that causes a lot of trouble. A **stream** is a small river, but here it means 'a continuous flow of things'. A **flood** is a large amount of water from a river or rain, but in the text it means 'a large quantity of something arriving at the same time'.

---

5 Circle the correct answer(s). Both answers may be possible.

1 I always send a *prompt / promptly* reply to emails.
2 The amount of work was *overwhelmed / overwhelming.*
3 We've been *badly / severely* hit by a computer virus.
4 I've had a *stream / plague* of enquiries about the vacant job.
5 We always *put / set* aside some money each month for a party at work.
6 We've had a *plague / flood* of letters this week expressing support.
7 I got very *frustrated / frustrating* by the constant interruptions.
8 People were *streaming / flooding* out of the building.

6 One word is missing in each sentence. What is it, and where does it go?

1 Our spending has got of control. ....
2 He still hasn't called. My are on edge. ....
3 Fortunately, the situation is control. ....
4 I was overwhelmed the response. ....
5 There's so much work. I'm out. ....
6 He keeps me when I'm working; it's annoying. ....

7 Complete the questions with a suitable word from the top of the page.

1 Do you have a constant stream of .... when you're working/studying?
2 When you work/study, do often waste time, or are you usually quite .... ?
3 If you don't think you're achieving much, what might improve your .... ?
4 Do you think it's important to reply to emails ...., or can they sometimes wait?
5 Do you often feel .... out because of work or studies?
6 Do you ever feel you have an .... amount of work and you'll never finish it?

8 ABOUT YOU Write your answers to Exercise 7, or ask another student. Give reasons or examples.

....
....
....

📋 TEST YOURSELF

A Business takeovers

Warburg **takeover imminent**

The battle for Warburg Glass may soon be over. Under the **leadership** of the **former** chairman Matthew Cavendish and with the **backing** of **corporate finance**, a new group is now **mounting** a fresh takeover **bid**. An initial bid has already been rejected, but an improved offer is on the **agenda** for the next meeting of **shareholders**, and this time the **outcome** could be different. City analysts believe Cavendish could **strike a deal** within weeks, **setting off** a new round of **mergers** and **acquisitions**.

SPOTLIGHT *takeover, acquisition, merger*

In a **takeover**, one company takes control of another company by buying most of its shares. In an **acquisition**, one company buys another company which cannot offer its shares for sale to the public. In a **merger**, two companies agree to join and form a single company.

GLOSSARY	
imminent	likely to happen soon
leadership	the state or position of being a leader: *under sb's leadership*
former	having a particular position in the past: *the former president/boss*
backing	help SYN **support**; **back** v
corporate	connected with a corporation: *corporate finance/strategy*
mount	organize and begin sth: *mount a challenge/campaign*
bid	an offer to pay a particular price for sth *bid* v
agenda	a list of items to be discussed at a meeting
shareholder	sb who owns shares in a business or company
outcome	the result or effect of an action or event
deal	an agreement, especially in business, for the conditions of buying or doing sth: *strike/make/conclude a deal*
set sth off	start a process or series of events

1 Complete the definitions with a single word.
1 *Imminent* means something will happen ....
2 The *outcome* of something is the ....
3 If you *set something off*, you .... it.
4 A *shareholder* .... shares in a company.
5 In a *takeover*, you take .... of another company.
6 A *former* boss was the boss in the ....
7 If you have *backing*, you have ....
8 If you *make a deal*, you have an ....

2 Complete the sentences.
1 If we're lucky, we could .... a deal next week.
2 He wants to buy the company and has already made one ....
3 If there is more uncertainty, it could .... off another wave of selling.
4 John Emery is preparing to .... a challenge for the leadership.
5 The takeover hasn't happened yet, but it's ....
6 Wainwrights have already bought one company; this could be their second ....
7 The sale price is the main item on the .... for the next meeting.
8 It is likely to be a very large business deal which relies on .... finance.

3 Rewrite the sentences without using the underlined words. Keep the same meaning.
1 She <u>used to be</u> my boss.   She's my ....
2 <u>He will be leader of</u> the group.   The group will be under ....
3 I need <u>them to support me</u>.   I need their ....
4 We could <u>reach an agreement</u>.   We could strike ....
5 Will the <u>people who hold shares</u> be happy?   Will the .... be happy?
6 Are you expecting a different <u>result</u>?   Are you expecting a different .... ?
7 Will they <u>offer more money</u>?   Will they make .... ?
8 The two companies have agreed <u>to join</u>.   The two companies have agreed a ....

📖 TEST YOURSELF

B Describing business activity

Shares have **climbed** in recent weeks

JPS still **pursuing hostile** takeover despite opposition

Denham's **issues fresh** profit warning

Prices have **soared** this year

Shares **reach** a new **peak**

Ibisco **floats** possible store closures

Markets **collapse** in the wake of coup

Sales **plunge** by 40%

GLOSSARY			
climb	(of prices, temperature, etc.) increase in value or amount	**hostile**	(of a takeover) not wanted by the company that is to be bought
soar	rise very quickly SYN **rocket**	**peak**	the point when sth/sb is at its highest, its best, etc: **reach a peak**
collapse	decrease suddenly in value or amount		
in the wake of sth/sb	coming after or following sth/sb	**plunge**	(of prices, temperature, etc.) decrease suddenly in value and amount SYN **plummet**
coup	a sudden change of government that is illegal and often violent	**issue**	make sth known formally
		fresh	new
pursue	continue to discuss sth, find out about or be involved in sth	**float**	suggest an idea or plan for others to consider

4 Is the pronunciation of the underlined letters the same or different? Write *S* or *D*. Use the 🅰️ to help you.

1 s<u>oa</u>r fl<u>oa</u>t ....
2 c<u>li</u>mb host<u>i</u>le ....
3 pl<u>u</u>nge pl<u>u</u>mmet ....
4 c<u>o</u>llapse p<u>u</u>rsue ....
5 c<u>ou</u>p f<u>ou</u>nd ....
6 cou<u>p</u> clim<u>b</u> ....

5 Replace the underlined word(s) with a word or phrase that keeps the same meaning.

1 The price has <u>gone up very quickly</u>. ....
2 Sales have <u>fallen very quickly</u>. ....
3 The value has reached its <u>highest point</u>. ....
4 We could do with some <u>new</u> ideas. ....
5 There has been a <u>sudden and violent change of government</u>. ....
6 The share price has started to <u>increase in value</u>. ....
7 Problems started <u>following</u> the resignation of the chairman. ....
8 The company is still <u>continuing to discuss and find out about</u> a possible deal. ....

6 Complete the dialogues in a suitable way.

1 It's been a great year for sales.
2 Why has it been so disastrous?

3 Have the profits definitely fallen?

4 The shareholders don't want this to happen.
5 Are tax rises definite?

6 Prices fell in the summer.

7 It's a rich country.

8 Are sales at their highest point now?
9 Are they still involved in discussions about a merger?

~ Yes, they have .... this year.
~ The market .... after the rise in oil prices.
~ Yes, the chairman has .... a statement.
~ No, it's a .... takeover.
~ No, but the minister has .... the idea several times.
~ True, but they are starting .... again now.
~ Yes, but since the .... , the economy has been very unstable.
~ Yes, I would say they've ....
~ No, they've decided not to ....

📘 TEST YOURSELF

Gecko Headgear Ltd is a designer and **manufacturer** of **safety helmets** for use at sea. The company was **founded** in 1993 by Jeff Sacree and it started by selling **surfboards**. However, surfing is a seasonal business, and Jeff realized he needed to **diversify**. Fortunately, he was able to **exploit** a **gap in the market**.

'As a surfer, I could see the **potential** for a light helmet that gave **protection** and **retained** heat.' He made one and sold a few to other **surfers**. He then did some research and discovered that **lifeboat crews** might also be interested in his helmet. It would have to be **adapted for** their use, and for that he needed **investment**. So, he **took out** a **bank loan** and employed more staff. 'A good relationship with the bank is crucial if you're developing an **innovative** product. In our **case** the process took three years.' The new safety helmets were **launched** in the late 90s.

After the **contract** to supply helmets for the lifeboats was successful, Jeff developed different types of helmet for different uses, and the **firm** has always used customer **feedback** to **refine** the products.

'A good **partnership** with suppliers has also been a key factor in our success. We've worked closely with different manufacturers, and this has helped us to **keep ahead** of our **rivals**.'

safety helmet

surfboard
surfer

lifeboat

GLOSSARY

manufacturer	a person or a company that makes things using machines SYN **producer**; **manufacture** v
found v (often passive)	start an organization. A person is a **founder**.
diversify	introduce a wider range of products **diversification** n
exploit	make the best possible use of sth **exploitation** n
gap in the market	an opportunity to create a new product which has not been produced by other companies
potential	the possibility of becoming successful in the future
protection	the act of keeping sb/sth safe so it or they are not harmed or damaged
retain	keep or continue to have sth **retention** n
crew	all the people who work on a boat, ship, aircraft, etc.
adapt sth (for sth)	change sth so you can use it in a different situation

investment	the activity of putting money into sth, hoping that you will make more money as a result **invest in sth** v
loan	money that sb/sth lends you: **take out a (bank) loan**
launch	start sth new or show sth for the first time **launch** n
innovative	introducing new ideas **innovate** v; **innovation** n
case	a situation (see spotlight)
contract	a written legal agreement: **sign a contract**
firm	a business company
feedback	information and comments from people who have used sth: **give sb feedback (on sth)**
refine	change sth a little to make it better
partnership	a relationship between two organizations
keep ahead (of sb/sth)	remain in a stronger position compared to sb/sth
rival	a person or thing that is competing with you SYN **competitor**

SPOTLIGHT phrases with *case*

in some cases in some situations
- *I got a reply immediately, but **in some cases** you have to wait weeks.*

in that case if that is the situation
- *I'm busy on Monday. ~ OK, **in that case**, I'll call you on Tuesday.*

in any case whatever happens or has happened; anyway
- *The traffic will be bad. **In any case**, we'll be there on time, so don't worry.*

1 Read the text again quickly if necessary, then answer these questions.

1 What is Gecko Headgear? _____
2 When was it founded? _____
3 Why did Jeff need to diversify? _____
4 What qualities did the helmet have to have? _____
5 Were the helmets immediately suitable for lifeboat crews? _____

6 How did he get the money for extra staff? _____
7 What happened in the late 1990s? _____
8 What information has he used to refine the products? _____
9 What was a key factor in his success? _____

2 Complete the table.

VERB	NOUN	VERB	NOUN
retain	_____	innovate	_____
invest	_____	exploit	_____
diversify	_____	launch	_____

3 Change the order of the letters to make words. Use the definitions to help you.

1 TOCCARNT _____ a written legal agreement
2 NATERI _____ keep or continue to have something
3 ONPIRCTNEOT _____ keeping someone safe from harm
4 EFKABEDC _____ comments from people who use something
5 VINVONITEA _____ introducing new ideas
6 REDYFIVIS _____ introduce a wider range of products
7 PERITNSARPH _____ a relationship between two organizations
8 LOPENITAT _____ the possibility of becoming good in the future

4 Circle the correct answer(s). Sometimes both answers are possible.

1 They are the main *producers / manufacturers*.
2 If we can't use the product like that, we may have to *exploit / adapt* it.
3 You can't compete in Europe. ~ In *that case / any case*, we'll look outside Europe.
4 We have to *keep ahead of / retain* our competitors.
5 She *invested / founded* the company ten years ago.
6 We need to know what our *rivals / competitors* are doing.

5 Replace the underlined words with a single word that has the same meaning.

1 You have to make the best possible use of your strengths. _____
2 The introduction of new ideas was crucial. _____
3 The product needed to be improved a little bit. _____
4 My partners were prepared to put money in the company. _____
5 They signed a written legal agreement. _____
6 I knew the product had the possibility to become better. _____
7 We try to get information and comments on our products. _____
8 They wanted to introduce a wider range of products. _____

6 Complete the sentences.

1 They were lucky because they saw a _____ in the market.
2 I needed extra money so I _____ a bank _____ .
3 They _____ washing machines, but mostly sell them abroad.
4 You need people who are willing to _____ you feedback.
5 The company will need more _____ if it wants to diversify.
6 Many of the _____ on a lifeboat have worked at sea in other jobs.
7 In some _____ people take out a loan, but I borrowed money from my parents.
8 Innovation helps a company to _____ ahead of its _____ .
9 Carol Simmons was the _____ of the company. Her decision to sell the _____ four years later was a surprise.
10 We plan to _____ the new design in Paris at the end of the month.

TEST YOURSELF

A Success

A Maximo, your restaurant chain has been **thriving** now for over 20 years. What's the **secret of your success**?

B There's no secret really, and it hasn't always been successful. Life was tough at the beginning, and, as you would expect with a new business, we've had various **obstacles** to **overcome**. But I guess the big **breakthrough** was winning the *Master Chef* competition on TV, and since then we've **gone from strength to strength**. However, I don't want to **boast** about myself. The main reason for the success, I think, is the **dynamic** team of young chefs I have working for me. They are **passionate** about what they do and **aspire to** be the best. And you can never be **satisfied** with where you are, never relax. **Forward planning** is essential …

GLOSSARY	
thrive	grow or develop well SYN **flourish**
the secret of your success	a way of doing things that has brought you success
obstacle	a situation or event that makes it difficult for you to do sth
overcome	manage to control or deal with a problem
breakthrough	an important development that may lead to an achievement or agreement: *make a breakthrough*
go from strength to strength	become more and more successful
boast	talk with too much pride about sth you have done or can do **boast** n
dynamic	(of a person or a business) full of energy and ideas **dynamism** n
passionate	showing very strong feelings
aspire (to sth / to be sth)	have a strong desire to do or be sth
satisfied	pleased because you have done what you wanted to do OPP **dissatisfied**
forward planning	planning for the future

1 **Good or bad? Write *G* or *B*.**

1 We went from strength to strength. ………
2 I've overcome all obstacles. ………
3 I'm still waiting for a breakthrough. ………
4 Their business is flourishing. ………
5 I've never aspired to anything. ………
6 He's always boasting. ………
7 The company has been thriving for years. ………
8 They're a dynamic business. ………
9 We've had so many obstacles. ………
10 She is easily satisfied. ………

2 **Complete the questions with a suitable word from the top of the page.**

1 Can businesses ………………………… without a lot of hard work and a bit of luck?
2 In life, is it important to be ………………………… about what you do and the way you do it?
3 Is ………………………… planning important if you want to be successful at anything?
4 Is there something that you particularly ………………………… to do in your own future?
5 Have there been any particular obstacles in your life that you've had to ………………………… ?
6 Would you say that ………………………… is an essential quality for success in business – and life?
7 Do you think it's possible to talk about the things you have done or achieved without ………………………… ?
8 Are there positive things you've done where you nevertheless feel a bit ………………………… for some reason?
9 Think of someone who is very successful. What is the ………………………… of their success?
10 Can you think of a recent ………………………… in the area of either medicine or technology?

3 ABOUT YOU **Write answers to the questions in Exercise 2, or ask another student.**

………
………
………

 TEST YOURSELF

B Failure

Is the business **going downhill**?

~ Yeah, it's a real **struggle**. Marek thinks he's a **failure**.

Carla **came bottom** in the exams.

~ Yes, and I only just **scraped through**.
Mum says we've **let her down**.

Why did you **drop out** of the course?

~ Oh, it was **hopeless**. I was **getting nowhere**.

Callum and Natalie are always having **rows**.

~ I know, and I don't want to **interfere**,
but I doubt the marriage will **last**.

SPOTLIGHT *last*

Last often means 'continue for a period of time'.
- The lesson **lasts** 45 minutes.

It can also mean 'continue to exist, function or survive'.
- I don't think their relationship will **last**. (as above)
- The good weather won't **last**.
- These shoes should **last** a long time.

Finally, **last** can mean 'be enough for what sb needs'.
- The money will **last** me a couple of weeks.

GLOSSARY

go downhill	get worse in quality, health, etc. SYN **deteriorate**
struggle	sth that is very difficult to do or succeed in **struggle** v
failure	a person or thing that is not successful OPP **success**
come bottom	receive the lowest score in an exam OPP **come top**
scrape through (an exam)	only just succeed in passing an exam
let sb down	make sb disappointed because you haven't behaved well or done what you said you would do
drop out (of sth)	leave a course or stop doing sth before you have finished
hopeless	giving no hope that sth/sb will be successful or get better
get somewhere/ nowhere (with sth/sb)	make/not make progress with sth/sb
row (about/over sth)	(pronounced like *now*) a noisy argument or serious disagreement between two or more people **row** v
interfere (in sth)	get involved in a situation that does not involve you and where you are probably not wanted **interference** n

4 Circle the correct word(s). Sometimes both words may be correct.

1 Unfortunately, I *got / came* bottom in the end of year progress tests.
2 I don't want to *interrupt / interfere in* their relationship.
3 The film *continues for / lasts* an hour and a half.
4 She said she'd help but didn't, so she let us *down / out* badly.
5 Basically, the campaign has been a *fail / failure*.
6 Her health has been *going downhill / deteriorating* for some time.
7 I heard they had a terrible *row / argument*.
8 Jeans usually *last / wear* a long time.

5 Two words are missing in each dialogue. What are they? Where do they go?

1 The business is downhill. ~ Yeah, it's been for a while now. ....
2 What was the about? ~ Kate got annoyed because of Sonny's in her project. ....
3 Did Mia top in the exam? ~ Yes, but Tom only just through. ....
4 Do you think the relationship will long? ~ No. Not if Kieran keeps her down. ....
5 Why did she drop of the course? ~ She told me it was. ....
6 Why did you in their cooking? ~ I just felt they were nowhere with it. ....

6 Complete the questions.

Have you ever …

1 .... top in anything?
2 just .... through an exam?
3 .... out of a course or class because you you didn't like it, or because it was too easy?
4 done something or achieved something that you thought was a real .... ?
5 had a serious .... with another person? What was it about? Do you have a good relationship with them now?
6 stopped doing something because you felt you were getting .... ?

7 ABOUT YOU Write answers to Exercise 6, or ask another student the questions.

....

....

TEST YOURSELF

A Problems in general

A number of adjectives are used with *problem*: a **minor** problem (= small; OPP **major**), a **growing** problem (= getting bigger all the time), an **urgent** problem (= needs attention now) and an **insoluble** problem (= cannot be solved).

There are also many verbs that are commonly used with *problem*:

If problems **arise**, they start to exist.

If you **raise** a problem, you mention it so that people can discuss it or deal with it.

If you **address** a problem, you start to think about how to solve it.

If you **confront** a problem or difficult situation, you deal with it. SYN **face (up to) sth**

If you **tackle** a problem, you make a big effort to deal with it.

If you **resolve** a problem, you find a solution to it. SYN **solve**

If you **overcome** a problem, you succeed in dealing with a problem that has prevented you from achieving something.

If you **exaggerate** a problem, you make it seem bigger than it is.

If a problem **escalates**, it gets bigger or worse. SYN **grow**

If problems **multiply**, they increase very much in number.

1 **Replace the underlined word(s) with a single word that keeps the same meaning.**

1   Anxiety about weight is <u>increasing</u> among teenage girls. ....
2   She's had to <u>face up to</u> her fear of flying. ....
3   How did the problem <u>first occur</u>? ....
4   Our problems have <u>more than doubled</u> since last year. ....
5   Funding has become an <u>impossible</u> problem. ....
6   Unemployment is a problem, but we mustn't <u>make it seem bigger than</u> it <u>is</u>. ....
7   Can we easily <u>find a solution to</u> plastic recycling? ....
8   They've been <u>making a big effort to solve</u> the problem of knife crime for years. ....

2 **Complete the dialogues with a single word.**

1   Have they made the problem worse? ~ Yes, it has been .... for months .
2   Is he aware of the problem? ~ No, but he'll have to .... it soon.
3   Is it an .... problem? ~ No, we can deal with it later.
4   Have they discussed finance? ~ Yes, I .... it at the last meeting.
5   Has she .... her shyness? ~ Yes, and the difference is amazing.
6   Have they solved the problem? ~ No, but they're working hard to .... it.
7   It's an .... problem, isn't it? ~ It seems to be: we just don't know what to do.
8   Are they .... the problem? ~ Yes, I think they're making a real effort.
9   Is it a major issue? ~ No, it's just a .... problem, really.
10 Do we need to deal with it now? ~ Yes, otherwise it could ....

3 ABOUT YOUR COUNTRY **Are these things problems in your country? If so, which adjectives and verbs above might describe the problem, and what is the government doing about them? Write your answers, or talk to another student.**

litter on the streets   graffiti on walls   increasing household rubbish
pollution in town centres   parking in town centres   bullying in schools

....
....

TEST YOURSELF

B Teenage problems and solutions

How parents can tackle teenage problems

1 Teenagers are never satisfied with their appearance, and this can be very **damaging** for their **self-esteem**. Don't **play down** these worries, even if they seem **insignificant** to you. Explain that others don't notice the details that we notice in ourselves.

2 Some teenagers can **accept** failure, while others let it **get them down**. Help your teen to **keep things in perspective**. Explain that everyone has **setbacks** in life, and **reassure** them that you**'re behind** them 100%, **regardless of** what happens.

3 Some teenagers – boys especially – find it difficult to identify and **articulate** how they feel. Keep **channels of communication** open at all times and respect their ideas.

GLOSSARY	
damaging	having a bad effect on sb/sth **damage** v
self-esteem	the way you feel about yourself: **have high/low self-esteem**
play sth down	try to make sth seem less important than it really is OPP **take sth seriously**
insignificant	not big enough to be considered important OPP **significant; significance** n
accept	continue in a difficult situation: **accept the fact that …**
get sb down	If sth **gets you down**, it makes you feel sad or depressed.
perspective	the ability to think about problems and decisions without exaggerating their importance: **keep sth/things in perspective**
setback	a problem that delays or prevents progress
reassure	say or do sth that makes sb less worried
be behind sb/sth	give your support to sb/sth
regardless of sth	without being affected or influenced by sth
articulate formal	express your thoughts clearly in words **articulate** adj (Listen to the different pronunciation of the verb and adjective on the APP.)
channel	a system or method for sending or obtaining information: **a channel of communication**

4 **Complete the sentences.**

1 His poor exam results have not been good for his self-............................ .

2 It's upsetting, but she mustn't let it .... her ....

3 She's clever and can .... her ideas very clearly.

4 His mother will support him .... of what he does, because she loves him.

5 Bullying is not an .... issue; it's a serious problem.

6 Parents must ensure there is an open .... of communication with their kids.

7 Some boys cannot .... the fact that they're not good enough to be professional footballers.

8 I'm always telling my son to work harder, but he doesn't take me ....

9 Air pollution is very .... to people's health.

10 The government is not optimistic, and is .... any hopes of a settlement.

5 **Complete the conversation with a suitable word or phrase.**

A: One of the teachers told Carrie that she wasn't good enough to study medicine at university, and it has really **(1)** .... her confidence.

B: I'm sure it has. And Carrie tends to let things **(2)** .... her .... , doesn't she?

A: Yes. And when you're her age, it's difficult to keep things in **(3)** ....

B: I guess so. But I'm sure her mother has supported her.

A: Oh yes, she has. She's been right **(4)** .... her all along, and is constantly **(5)** .... her that everything will be OK. But it's been a **(6)** .... for her.

B: And is there any **(7)** .... in what the teacher is saying? Do you think he's right?

A: Possibly. But Carrie is clever and very **(8)** .... There are plenty of things she could do where good communication is important.

6 ABOUT YOU **Have you experienced any of the teenage problems above, either as a teenager yourself or as a parent? What other problems do teenagers often have, and how should parents respond? Write your answers, or talk to another student.**

....

....

 TEST YOURSELF

A A barn conversion

Friends of mine **converted** an old barn that had **formerly** been used for **domestic** animals. They bought it for **next to nothing**, and were **fortunate** that parts of it were still quite **well-preserved**. They **estimated** they could convert the barn for about £200,000, but the council then made them **modify** their building plans so the original **estimate turned out to be** a bit optimistic. Nevertheless, they now have a **magnificent contemporary** four-bedroom home.

barn

barn conversion

GLOSSARY

convert (sth) (into sth)	change from one form, system, or use into another **conversion** n	**estimate**	calculate the size, cost, etc. of sth approximately **estimate** n
formerly	in the past; before now **former** adj	**modify**	change sth slightly
domestic	(of animals) kept as pets or on a farm	**turn out (to be sth)**	prove to be
next to nothing	very little money, etc: **buy sth for next to nothing**	**magnificent**	extremely impressive and attractive SYN **splendid**
fortunate	lucky OPP **unfortunate**	**contemporary**	of the present time; modern
preserve	keep sth safe and in good condition: *a well-preserved 18th century table*		

1 Circle the odd one out based on the pronunciation of the underlined letters. Use the ⓐ to help you.

   1 c<u>o</u>nvert m<u>o</u>dify d<u>o</u>mestic
   2 contemp<u>o</u>rary f<u>o</u>rmerly f<u>o</u>rtunate
   3 estim<u>ate</u> v estim<u>ate</u> n fortun<u>ate</u>
   4 conv<u>er</u>t pres<u>er</u>ve form<u>er</u>ly

2 Replace the underlined word(s) with another word or phrase that keeps the same meaning.

   1 They were <u>not very lucky</u> with that house.
   2 It's a <u>magnificent</u> apartment.
   3 It's a hotel now, but <u>in the past</u> it was a bank.
   4 It's an old house but it's <u>in good condition</u>.
   5 They've just bought a <u>very modern</u> house.
   6 It was a small cottage, but it's been <u>changed slightly</u> over the years.
   7 We thought it would be quite grand, but <u>in the end it was</u> rather small.
   8 They have <u>calculated</u> they will need about £10,000.
   9 It cost <u>very little</u>.
  10 The barn is for our <u>cows, sheep, etc.</u> in the winter.

3 Complete the dialogues. More than one word may be correct.

   1 The building used to be a prison, didn't it?   ~ No, it's a .... hospital.
   2 Did they throw out all the old furniture?   ~ No, they thought it was worth ....
   3 Is it an old cottage they've bought?   ~ No, it's a barn ....
   4 How big is it?   ~ The agent .... it is about 300 square metres.
   5 Are you keeping to your original plan?   ~ No, we've had to .... it a bit.
   6 The conversion is very impressive.   ~ Oh yes, the house is really .... now.
   7 Do they want to keep all the old features in the house?   ~ No, they want something more ....
   8 Are they keeping the barn as it is?   ~ No, they're .... it into a music studio.

TEST YOURSELF

B Old and new objects

Innovative anti-snore **device** – **clips** onto sleeper's nose for a good night's sleep

Up-to-date guidebook to Korea – **second-hand** but **good as new**

Genuine antique grandfather clock. The 8-day **mechanism** is in perfect condition.

Reproduction of **Ancient** Egyptian statue of the goddess Bastet

Fully **reconditioned** exercise bike with original **packaging** and instructions

SPOTLIGHT *second-hand* and *new*

If something is **second-hand**, it is not completely new. If something is completely new, we usually say **brand new**. **(As) good as new** can be used to describe something that is not new but appears to be.

---

4 **Is the pronunciation of the underlined letters the same or different? Write *S* or *D*. Use the 🔊 to help you.**

1 an̲cient an̲tique ....
2 mech̲anism rec̲onditioned ....
3 genu̲ine dev̲ice ....
4 g̲enuine packag̲ing ....
5 an̲tique authen̲tic ....
6 inn̲ovative repr̲oduction ....

5 **Complete the phrase in each sentence.**

1 This email list is .... of date.
2 I need a paper .... for this document.
3 The sofa is .... as new.
4 The data is up to ....
5 My car is brand ....
6 I usually buy second-..................... books.

6 **Complete the sentences with a suitable word.**

1 A battery charger is an extremely useful energy-saving ....
2 It's a beautifully made, 18ᵗʰ century .... clock.
3 There were earrings like it thousands of years ago in .... Greece, and now they make .... of them and sell them in tourist shops.
4 We bought a second-hand hoover – it was fully .... and fantastic value.
5 I don't want a copy of the clock: I want a .... antique.
6 Shops often sell more goods if they're displayed in attractive ....
7 Our small factory .... antique dolls, and we sell them on the internet at a great profit.
8 They want the technology to be really .... to date, and they're awarding a prize for the most .... design.
9 This old clock has a very complex .... inside, but it still works perfectly.
10 If you .... the photo to your letter, then you can send the two together.

TEST YOURSELF

A Thinking about time

- **Time flies** when you get older.
- I get depressed **from time to time**.
- **It's about time** I started a pension.
- **At one time** I wanted to be a journalist.
- I do everything **at the last minute**.

- **In retrospect**, I wish I'd gone to university.
- **For the time being**, I'm happy where I am.
- I think **punctuality** is a great **virtue**.
- I live on a **day-to-day basis**.
- **With hindsight**, I should've worked harder.

GLOSSARY

time flies	time seems to pass very quickly	**for the time being**	for a short period of time, but not permanently
from time to time	sometimes but not regularly SYN **now and again**	**punctuality**	the fact of doing sth at the agreed or correct time and not being late
it's about time (that)	used to say that sth should happen soon or should have happened already. Notice that the past tense is used. SYN **it's high time (that)**		**punctual** adj
at one time	in the past, but not now	**virtue**	a particular good quality or habit OPP **vice**
do sth at the last minute	do sth at the latest possible time before sth else happens SYN **leave sth to/till the last minute**	**day-to-day**	planning for only one day at a time: *do sth on a day-to-day basis*
in retrospect	thinking about the past now, often with a different view from the one you had then SYN **looking back**	**with hindsight**	with the ability to understand a situation only after it has happened: *with the benefit of hindsight*

1 **Find eight time phrases in the box.**

leave sth	one time	flies	from time	with	in	day	time	at
for the time	-to-day	hindsight	retrospect	being	to time	to the last minute		

....

....

2 **Rewrite the sentences starting with the words given. Keep the same meaning.**

1 Looking back, I didn't enjoy it.   In ....
2 He leaves things till the last minute.   He does ....
3 It was an ambition in the past but not now.   It was an ambition at ....
4 I go there now and again.   I go there from ....
5 I don't think about the future.   I live on a ....
6 I'm OK here at the moment.   I'll be OK here for ....

3 **Complete the sentences.**

1 Looking .... , I don't think I made the most of my time at university.
2 With the benefit of .... , it was probably a mistake for me to leave my last job.
3 The trouble with Angel is that he .... everything till the last ....
4 Listen, it's .... time you started taking these exams seriously.
5 I'm always .... , never late. For some people though, ... doesn't matter.
6 The time has .... since I've been in Greece. I've loved every minute of it.
7 For most people, patience is a great .... Unfortunately, I'm very impatient, but I have worse .... than that!
8 This dictionary will be big enough .... the time ....

4 ABOUT YOU **Read the statements at the top of the page again. Are any true for you? Do you agree with any of them? Write your answers, using the phrases in bold, or talk to another student.**

....

....

....

TEST YOURSELF

B Memories

Some people have very **vivid** memories of their early childhood and can **recall** events in **extraordinary** detail. I have a few **unforgettable** memories. One of them is when I **slipped** and fell off a wall, and **landed** on a four-**inch** nail. It was still **stuck in** my foot when they took me to hospital. **Broadly speaking**, though, when I **look back on** that period of my life, I don't have many **lasting** or vivid memories; most are quite **vague**.

GLOSSARY	
vivid	(of memories, a description, etc.) very clear; producing a strong picture in your mind
recall *formal*	remember sth from the past **recollection** *n*
extraordinary	surprising, unusual and not what you expect SYN **incredible**
unforgettable	If sth is **unforgettable**, you cannot forget it, usually because it is beautiful, surprising or interesting.
slip (over/on sth)	slide a short distance by accident so that you fall or nearly fall
land	come down to the ground after falling or being thrown
inch	a measure of length, equal to approximately 2.5 cm
stick (in sth)	become fixed in one position and impossible to move
broadly speaking	used to show that what you are saying is true in general ALSO **generally speaking, on the whole**
look back (on sth)	think about sth in your past
lasting	continuing to exist or have an effect for a long time
vague	not clear in a person's mind: *a vague memory/recollection*

5 **Underline the correct answer(s). Both answers may be possible.**
1 I only have a *vague / vivid* memory; it was a long time ago.
2 She's had an *extraordinary / incredible* life.
3 I don't *remember / recall* the occasion very well.
4 It was ages ago, but I still have a very *vague / vivid* memory of it, as if it was yesterday.
5 *On the whole / Broadly speaking*, my recollections are quite vague.
6 He *slipped / stuck* on the ice and fell over.
7 I made a number of *lasting / vivid* friendships when I was at university.
8 Sam fell off the wall but managed to *slip / land* on his feet.

6 **Replace the underlined words with a word or phrase that keeps the same meaning.**
1 <u>Broadly speaking</u>, my memory isn't very good. ....
2 Climbing that mountain was an <u>incredible</u> experience. ....
3 I'm good at <u>remembering</u> events from my past. ....
4 She has a vague <u>memory</u> of the accident. ....
5 I don't remember <u>hitting the ground</u> after I fell. ....

7 **Complete the text with suitable words.**
I'm a keen climber and one of my most **(1)** .... memories was when I attempted to climb part of Mount Snowdon in Wales. I was quite near the top when I **(2)** .... on some loose rock. I must've fallen about five metres before I **(3)** .... on a narrow piece of rock. It was only about 18 **(4)** .... wide, so I could hardly move. Worse still, there was something **(5)** .... in my back (I later discovered it was part of my equipment), and the pain was terrible. I was there for three hours before being rescued. **(6)** .... on the incident, it was an **(7)** .... piece of luck that I wasn't seriously injured. It's an **(8)** .... memory, though not something that I **(9)** .... with pleasure.

8 ABOUT YOU **Complete the three questions, then write your own answers, or talk to another student.**
1 What is your earliest .... ? ....
2 What is your most .... memory of childhood? ....
3 Generally .... , do you think you .... events in your past clearly, or are your recollections quite .... ? ....
4 Do you often look .... on things from your past? Why / Why not? ....

TEST YOURSELF

A Written and spoken

Here are some link words from both written and spoken English.

*Some people can work to music **while/whereas** others find it very difficult.*

***While** the situation is not ideal, we'll have to manage.*

*It's not a serious problem. **Nonetheless/Nevertheless**, we'll have to do something about it.*

*People respect the minister for her knowledge of education. **Furthermore/Moreover**, they trust her.*

*You can withdraw £250 a day, **provided/providing** that you have the money in your account.*

*I'd better shut the window, **otherwise** it'll get cold in here.*

*Isabella failed her maths exam. **Consequently**, they wouldn't give her a place at the college.*

*I wasn't very keen on the idea of flying to Australia. **Besides**, I couldn't afford it.*

*Regular exercise strengthens the heart, **thereby** reducing the risk of heart attack.*

GLOSSARY	
while	used to compare or contrast two people, things, situations, etc. SYN **whereas**
while	(at the beginning of a sentence) although; despite the fact that …
nonetheless *formal*	despite this fact SYN **nevertheless**
furthermore *formal*	(used especially to add a point to an argument) in addition to what has just been said SYN **moreover** *formal*
provided (that)	used to say what must be done or happen to make sth else possible; only if SYN **providing (that)**
otherwise	used to state what the result would be if sth didn't happen or the situation were different
consequently	as a result; therefore
besides	in addition to what has just been said
thereby *formal*	used to introduce the result of the action or situation mentioned

1 Circle the correct answer(s). Sometimes both answers are possible.

1 The students are happy with the course. *Furthermore / Nonetheless* they want to carry on next term.
2 My father was there for two days, *whereas / while* the recommended stay is three.
3 We left early, *otherwise / consequently* we would've missed the bus.
4 Neither of us had an umbrella. *Consequently, / Therefore*, we both got rather wet.
5 I don't really want to go. *Nevertheless, / Besides*, it's too late now.
6 *While / Although* the weather wasn't great, we still managed to have a good time.
7 I can stay at the hotel *providing / while* I book well in advance.
8 The company will offer compensation, *thereby / nevertheless* ending the dispute.

2 Complete the sentences with a suitable link word or phrase.

1 I found the work quite difficult .... my brother thought it was easy.
2 It is one of the best places to stay. .... , it's not that expensive.
3 You can borrow the car .... that you return it by the weekend.
4 We both found the walk very tiring. .... , we carried on till the end.
5 It's a long way to go just for the evening. .... , I'm not that keen on opera.
6 The government reduced spending on arms, ... increasing funds available for health.
7 We had to stay and wait for my mother, and .... we missed our train.
8 I'll have to work on Saturday , ... I'll never finish this project on time.

3 Complete the sentences in a logical way.

1 I don't really want to go abroad this summer. Besides, ...
2 My brother is always late whereas ....
3 I missed the bus and consequently ....
4 You can watch me practise provided that ....
5 We'd better lock the door, otherwise ....
6 It wasn't the greatest film I've ever seen. Nevertheless, ...

 TEST YOURSELF

B More formal link words

… It is our understanding that the residents of Alton Court received a full apology from the Council in writing **prior to** the meeting of 7 June. **In view of** the limited **inconvenience** they suffered, this was felt to be **adequate**; **thus** no further action was taken.

With regard to Mr Wilson, however, some damage was caused to his property, and he **was obliged** to move out while the damage was being repaired. **Since** the council accepts full responsibility for this, it has agreed to pay Mr Wilson the full costs of the repair and a further £200 **in compensation**.

In conclusion, we hope this brings an end to the matter.

Yours …

GLOSSARY	
prior to sth *formal*	before sth
in view of sth *formal*	SYN **considering sth**
inconvenience	a quality of not being easy or suitable OPP **convenience**
adequate	acceptable; good enough OPP **inadequate**
thus *formal*	therefore; for this reason SYN **hence** *formal*
with regard to sb/sth *formal*	connected with sb/sth SYN **regarding sb/sth** *formal*
oblige (*usually passive*)	force sb to do sth
since	as; because
compensation	money you pay to sb because you have injured them, or lost or damaged their property
in conclusion	used in writing or a formal speech to show that you are about to finish what you are saying

4 **Underline the stress on these words. Use the APP to help you.**

considering   inconvenience   adequate
conclusion   inadequate   compensation

5 **Replace the underlined word(s) with a more formal word or phrase.**
1 He was only seven years old, <u>so</u> he could not be held responsible for his actions. ....
2 We were told <u>before</u> the meeting. ....
3 His performance was extraordinary <u>considering</u> his advancing years. ....
4 <u>As far as</u> the other climbers <u>are concerned</u>, we have no further information. ....
5 <u>So, to finish what I was saying</u>, there is still a lot of research we need to do. ....
6 In the end, they <u>had</u> to release the men ....

6 **Complete the sentences.**
1 I wasn't happy with her apology. I didn't think it was .... at all.
2 They did not have valid tickets, ... they were not allowed to board the train.
3 .... our conversation yesterday, I had not met either man.
4 Work on the new extension will commence next month. .... the roof, the contractors have assured us that necessary repairs will be carried out immediately.
5 .... the complaints received, we will need to speak to the director.
6 .... , the board would like to thank everyone for attending the meeting and for making such a positive contribution.
7 As the rail company lost all our luggage, we are asking them for ....
8 I didn't have enough money to pay the fare, so I was .... to get off the train.
9 The building work made life difficult, but the neighbours did apologize for the ....
10 We decided to go home early .... we had already done everything we planned to do.
11 The heating on the train was .... , so I complained to the rail company.
12 They provided additional seats for the .... of the customers.

TEST YOURSELF

A Public examinations

Exam requirements

Some public examinations in English consist of a written paper in which candidates are required to produce a piece of **extended** writing. They may be asked to **present** and develop an **argument**, **evaluate** ideas, **summarize** information, etc. Candidates are **assessed** on a number of **criteria**, including their ability to write in an organized and **coherent** way, their **command of** a range of **stylistic** features, and their ability to write in an appropriate **register**. Some tasks may ask students to write a **narrative**.

GLOSSARY	
extended	long or longer than usual or expected
argument	a set of reasons that sb uses to show that sth is true or correct
evaluate	form an opinion of sth after thinking about it carefully **evaluation** *n*; SYN **assess** *v*; **assessment** *n*
summarize	give a short statement that brings together the main points of sth **summary** *n*
criterion (*pl* **criteria**)	a standard or principle by which sth is judged
coherent	(of ideas, arguments, etc.) logical and well organized; clear and easy to understand OPP **incoherent**; **coherence** *n*
command of sth	a knowledge of sth and an ability to use it well
stylistic	connected to the way a writer or artist does sth **style** *n*
register	the words, grammar and style that sb uses in a particular situation: *a formal/informal register*
narrative	a description of connected events; a story. A person is a **narrator**.

SPOTLIGHT *present* v

Present (stress on second syllable) can mean 'show, offer or describe something for others to look at and consider'.
- *She's presenting a talk at the conference.* (SYN **give a presentation** *n*)
- *They want to present their ideas at the meeting next week.*

It is also used when you give something to somebody, especially at a ceremony.
- *The mayor presented the prizes to the winners.*

---

1 **Underline the stress on these words. Use the 🔊 to help you.**

argument	evaluate	evaluation	criterion	incoherent
present *v*	narrative	narrator	stylistic	summarize

2 **Circle the correct answer(s). Sometimes both answers may be possible.**
1. He asked me to *summary / summarize* the main points.
2. Having read her essay, what is your *command / assessment* of it?
3. The events in the novel are described by a *narrative / narrator*.
4. We had to *assess / evaluate* the different ideas.
5. The single most important *criterion / criteria* was experience.
6. The chairman came to my *criterion / presentation* and thanked me afterwards.
7. It was an interesting *argument / register*, but I'm not sure I agree with it.
8. You have to be able to *summarize / present* your argument on paper.

3 **Complete the sentences with a suitable word.**
1. I decided to write a .... because I'm quite good at telling stories.
2. You should provide a brief .... of your ideas at the end of the talk.
3. What was your .... of the essay? I found it .... and couldn't follow it.
4. The use of metaphors is an important .... feature of her writing.
5. What are your .... for choosing the best essay?
6. To write an academic essay, you need a very good .... of the language.
7. Most academic essays are written in a formal style and ....
8. I didn't think the .... he put forward in his essay was very convincing.
9. The head will .... the prize for the best piece of .... writing.
10. You have to develop an ...., which is completely ...., so the reader can understand it.

 **TEST YOURSELF**

B The basics of academic writing

In a piece of academic writing, the writer will do at least some of the following:

- **outline** their main ideas
- **explore** certain ideas in greater depth
- **illustrate** their ideas .
- **adopt** a particular **stance** or point of view
- **draw conclusions**

They may also compare and contrast, **condemn** or **condone**, explain, describe, analyse, evaluate, summarize, **assert**, **justify**, and – to the annoyance of some people – **sit on the fence**.

GLOSSARY	
outline	give a description of the main points involved in sth **outline** n
explore	examine sth carefully: **explore an idea**; **exploration** n
illustrate	make the meaning of sth clearer by giving examples **illustration** n
adopt	take a particular point of view, or use a particular method
stance (on sth)	an opinion that sb has about sth and expresses publicly SYN **position**
conclusion	a decision that you make about sth after thinking about it, discussing it and looking at any evidence: **draw/reach/come to a conclusion (about sth)**
condemn	say publicly that you think sth/sb is bad or wrong **condemnation** n
condone	accept behaviour that most people think is wrong
assert	state clearly that sth is true **assertion** n
justify	show that sth is right or reasonable **justification** n
sit on the fence	avoid deciding or saying which side of an argument you support

4 The pronunciation of the underlined letters is the same in seven of the words. Which word is different? Use the (APP) to help you.

a̲dopt   a̲ssert   c̲onclusion   c̲ondemn   c̲ondone   ju̲stify   illu̲strate   po̲sition

5 Which of these words clearly show a particular point of view?

condemn   outline   condone   assert   explore   justify   adopt a stance   illustrate

....

6 Complete the sentences with a form of the word in capitals.

1	There was universal .... of the attack.	CONDEMN
2	What .... did you draw about the reason for the delay?	CONCLUDE
3	I thought he gave a good .... of his point.	ILLUSTRATE
4	The book is an .... of the human mind.	EXPLORE
5	He was correct in his .... that the man was guilty.	ASSERT
6	What was his .... for the government's position?	JUSTIFY

7 Replace the underlined words with a word or phrase that keeps the same meaning.

1 She <u>gave a general picture of</u> her ideas.　　She .... her ideas.
2 She was <u>very critical of</u> his behaviour.　　She .... his behaviour.
3 She <u>went on to analyse</u> the idea in more depth.　　She then .... the idea in more depth.
4 She wouldn't <u>accept or tolerate</u> his behaviour.　　She wouldn't .... his behaviour.
5 She didn't <u>take and support</u> a clear <u>position</u>.　　She didn't .... a clear ....　.
6 She couldn't <u>show</u> her ideas <u>were reasonable</u>.　　She couldn't .... her ideas.
7 She <u>gave examples of</u> her ideas.　　She .... her ideas.
8 In the end, she <u>wouldn't agree or disagree</u>.　　In the end, she ....　.
9 She continued to <u>state very clearly</u> that she was innocent.　　She continued to .... that she was innocent.
10 He didn't <u>come to any final decisions or judgement</u>.　　He didn't ....　.

 TEST YOURSELF

Far from the Madding Crowd
by Thomas Hardy

Summary: After **inheriting** her uncle's farm, Hardy's heroine, Bathsheba Everdene, becomes an independent woman. Her beauty attracts many admirers: farm worker Gabriel Oak, landowner William Boldwood, and handsome soldier Frank Troy, whom she later marries. However, Troy is a selfish and **evil** man who allows his earlier love, Fanny Robin, to die in poverty while giving birth to his child. Boldwood hates Troy, and later in the novel he kills him in a jealous **rage**. Gabriel asks for **mercy** to be shown him, and Boldwood escapes death but is sent to prison instead. The novel ends with Bathsheba marrying Gabriel.

Commentary: Incidents, such as Fanny's **pregnancy** and her terrible death, and Boldwood's act of murderous violence, **convey** Hardy's growing taste for **tragedy**. But unlike Tess in the later *Tess of the D'Urbevilles*, **fate** still favours Bathsheba, as she finally finds happiness with Gabriel, who **embodies** the best qualities of the rural community in its fight against industrialization*, which Hardy found so **alien**.

Hardy **exposes** the dangers **inherent** in romantic love: relationships based on romantic love are by nature **irrational**, unstable and at risk of **betrayal**. In contrast, he **implies** that the true basis of a happy marriage is **companionship** and a common interest.

For some it is also an early example of **feminist** literature. Bathsheba is **portrayed** as an independent woman with the courage to **defy convention** and run a farm by herself. Her passionate nature leads her into errors of judgement, but Hardy gives her the qualities of strength, intelligence and good luck to overcome the mistakes of youth.

*industrialization = the development of new manufacturing processes in Britain from the late 18th century into the 19th century

GLOSSARY

inherit	receive property, money, etc, from sb who has died **inheritance** *n*	**expose**	tell the true facts about sth and show it to be bad or wrong
evil	morally bad; causing harm to people **evil** *n*	**inherent (in sth)**	If sth is **inherent in** sth, it is a natural part of it and cannot be removed from it.
rage	a feeling of violent anger that is difficult to control	**irrational**	not logical or sensible OPP **rational**
mercy	a kind or forgiving attitude towards sb you have the power to harm or the right to punish	**betrayal**	the act of being disloyal to sb who trusts you **betray** *v*
commentary	a written explanation or discussion of sth such as a book	**imply**	suggest sth in an indirect way without actually saying it **implication** *n*
incident	sth that happens, especially sth that is unusual or unpleasant	**companionship**	a friendly and comfortable relationship between people
pregnancy	the state of being **pregnant** (= expecting a baby)	**feminist**	having the belief that women should have the same rights and opportunities as men
convey sth (to sb)	communicate ideas and feelings to sb	**portray**	describe sb/sth in a piece of writing SYN **depict**
tragedy	a very sad event, especially one that often involves death	**defy**	refuse to obey a law, a rule or a person **defiant** *adj*
fate	a power that is believed to control everything and that cannot be changed	**convention**	the behaviour and attitudes that most people consider to be normal and right **conventional** *adj*; OPP **unconventional**
embody *formal*	be a good example of sth		
alien	strange, difficult to understand, and often unacceptable		

1 Mark the stress on these words. Use the 🅐 to help you.

expose   imply   defy   convey   portray   embody   inherit   inherent

2 Add the related words.

betray .... *n*   inherit .... *n*   pregnancy .... *adj*
portray .... *n*   defy .... *adj*   convention .... *adj*
imply .... *n*   evil *n* .... *adj*   .... *adj*

3 Circle the correct answer.

1 A commentary on a novel is *a summary / an explanation* of the main events.
2 If something is alien to you, it is *easy / difficult* to understand.
3 Unconventional beliefs are considered to be *strange / normal*.
4 Fate is considered to be *within / beyond* our control.
5 If you expose someone, you tell *the truth / lies* about them.
6 If you inherit something, it usually comes from someone you *know / don't know*.
7 An implication is *a direct / an indirect* way of saying something.
8 If you are defiant, you *agree / refuse* to do something.

4 Replace the underlined word(s) with a word (or words) that has a similar meaning.

1 She is <u>portrayed</u> as a very honest character.   ....
2 Martha is <u>expecting a baby</u>.   ....
3 The best man's speech is one of the <u>traditional parts</u> of a wedding.   ....
4 You could see he was full of <u>violent anger</u>.   ....
5 She is able to <u>communicate</u> a lot of feeling through her gestures.   ....
6 His attitude is <u>not logical or reasonable</u>.   ....
7 She <u>is a good example of</u> optimism and positive thinking.   ....
8 She misses <u>the enjoyment of being with Ellen</u>.   ....

5 Complete the dialogues with a suitable word.

1 Did he say Callum was responsible? ~ He didn't actually say it, but he .... it.
2 Do you often wear black? ~ No, but it's fairly .... to wear black at funerals.
3 How did you feel living in New York? ~ At first it felt very ....
4 Did she write about the rights of women? ~ Yes, she wrote some of the earliest .... literature.
5 What's the book about? ~ Basically it's about the conflict of good and ....
6 Did her parents leave her the house? ~ Yes, that was part of her ....
7 Is there a risk with this kind of company? ~ Yes, there's an .... risk with any new business.
8 Are there any evil characters? ~ Yes, and she .... their evil and cruelty throughout the novel.
9 Was the .... a surprise? ~ Yes, nobody knew they wanted a baby.
10 Was he ever violent? ~ Yes, I remember one .... when he attacked somebody.

6 Complete the summary of the novel with words from the box, in the correct form.

fate	tragedy	mercy	portray	
embody	convey	defy	betray	embodiment

Tess is the heroine of Hardy's novel that bears her name: *Tess of the D'Urbervilles*. She is **(1)** ....
in the novel as a daughter of nature, and **(2)** .... many noble qualities that make her such a
sympathetic character. But time and again she has to endure suffering from the brutal Alec D'Urbeville, who is the
(3) .... of evil in the novel. The other man in her life is Angel Clare, an intelligent young man who
(4) .... convention and is happy to work on a farm rather than go to university. He and Tess fall in
love and marry, but when Tess tells him that she has previously had a child by Alec, Angel feels **(5)** ....
and leaves her. **(6)** .... is sometimes kind to Hardy's heroines, but not in this case. Tess goes back to
Alec, but when Angel returns from Brazil and forgives her, she stabs Alec to death. Unlike Boldwood at the end of
Hardy's earlier novel *Far from the Madding Crowd*, Tess is shown no **(7)** .... She is executed for her crime,
although the final **(8)** .... is only **(9)** .... to us by a black flag being waved over the prison.

TEST YOURSELF

a painting by J.M.W. Turner, after whom the Turner Prize is named

The Turner Prize is awarded **annually** to a British visual artist for **outstanding artistic merit**. The winner also receives £25,000, although the amount has **varied depending on** the **sponsor**. The public can **submit** an artist **nomination**, and the **panel** of judges then selects a **shortlist** of three or four from their own nominations and those of the public. They select a winner on the day of the award ceremony, and the **venue alternates between** Tate Britain and galleries outside London.

Although it remains one of the most **prestigious** European art awards, it is also extremely **controversial**, and **splits** opinion in the art world. Some critics believe it **demonstrates** the most **pretentious** aspects of contemporary British art, while others think the Turner **deserves** respect for rewarding art which is **bold, challenging** and **imaginative**.

GLOSSARY			
annually	every year ALSO **monthly/daily**, etc.	**prestigious**	respected and admired as very important or of high quality
outstanding	extremely good SYN **excellent**	**controversial**	causing a lot of angry public argument and disagreement **controversy** n
artistic	connected with art or artists; showing a natural skill in or enjoyment of art		
merit	the quality of being good and deserving admiration	**split**	divide, or make a group of people divide, into smaller groups with different opinions **split** n
vary	change or be different according to the situation **variable** adj	**demonstrate**	show sth clearly by your actions SYN **display**
depending on sb/sth	used for saying that you are not certain of sth until other things have been considered	**venue**	a place where people meet for an organized event, e.g. a concert, ceremony, conference, etc.
sponsor	a person or company that pays for sth, e.g. a sporting or cultural event, usually in return for advertising	**alternate (between A and B)**	change from one thing to another and back again
submit	give a document, proposal, etc. to sb in authority so they can study it	**pretentious**	trying to be important, intelligent etc. or sth you are not in order to impress people
nomination	the act of suggesting or choosing sb as a candidate in an election, or for a job or award **nominate** v	**deserve**	If sb **deserves** sth, it is right they should have it because of the way they have behaved or what they are.
panel	a group of specialists who are asked to give their opinion on sth	**bold**	(of people and the things they do and create) brave and confident; not afraid to take risks
shortlist	a small number of candidates for a job, award, etc. that have been chosen from all those who applied or were nominated	**challenging**	difficult in an interesting way
		imaginative	having or showing new and exciting new ideas

1 Underline the stress on these words. Use the 🅰🅿🅿 to help you.

outstanding	depending	submit	nominate	nomination	controversial
alternate *v*	venue	prestigious	imaginative	pretentious	controversy

2 Circle the correct answer(s). Sometimes both answers are possible.

1 The quality of his work *varies / alternates*.
2 He *deserves / displays* the award for the way he has helped younger artists.
3 I think this is an *excellent / outstanding* work of art.
4 There aren't any new ideas in the work, but it's still quite *challenging / imaginative*.
5 The Turner Prize is a *bold / prestigious* award; that's why people want to win it.
6 Some paintings *split / divide* opinion among art critics.
7 She *displays / demonstrates* her love of Matisse when she paints in oil.
8 They *nominated / submitted* several people for the award.

3 Replace the underlined words with a single word that keeps the same meaning.

1 The prize is awarded <u>every year</u>.
2 A <u>group of specialist people</u> will make the final decision.
3 The <u>place where they hold the event</u> changes from year to year.
4 We need to find a <u>person with money who will support us</u>.
5 The award often causes a lot of <u>public argument and disagreement</u>.
6 I think she has <u>shown clearly by her actions</u> why she deserves to win.
7 The winner will be chosen from a <u>small number of the candidates who applied</u>.
8 I think Rothko's paintings are quite <u>interesting but difficult to understand</u>.

4 Complete the sentences.

1 *Guernica* is possibly Picasso's greatest _____ achievement.
2 Several sponsors have _____ a proposal for a new kind of art scholarship.
3 Lucian Freud received two _____ for the Turner Prize but never won it.
4 In the end the judges were _____ down the middle: two for and two against.
5 I think the art world is full of _____ people who are just trying to impress people and give the impression they are cleverer than they really are.
6 Antony Gormley is a very _____ sculptor. He takes on brave subject matter and on a large scale.
7 I've looked at most of his paintings and I can't see much artistic _____ at all.
8 Goldsmiths is one of the UK's most _____ institutions and attracts thousands of applications for Fine Art degrees each year.

5 Complete the sentences on the right. Keep the same meaning as the sentences on the left.

1 It changes from Melbourne to Sydney.   It alternates _____ .
2 The quality of the work varies.   The quality of the work is _____ .
3 Colours change according to the season.   Colours change depending _____ .
4 The paintings have lots of exciting new ideas.   The paintings are very _____ .
5 Her work attracts a lot of controversy.   Her work is very _____ .
6 They nominated three people.   There were three _____ .

6 ABOUT YOU Look at some examples of contemporary art (since 2000) online. Focus on five different works of art and decide what you think about them. Are they bold, imaginative, challenging, controversial, pretentious or variable in quality? Write your answers, or talk to another student.

_____

_____

_____

📖 TEST YOURSELF

A Research

Scientific method

Scientific research proposes **hypotheses** as explanations of **phenomena**, and then designs **experimental** studies to gather **empirical** evidence and test them out. It is important these procedures can be repeated in order to predict future results with some certainty. A feature shared by other fields of enquiry is the **conviction** that the process must also be **objective** in order to reduce a **biased** interpretation of the results. Another basic expectation is to make all the data available for **scrutiny** by other scientists. This provides the opportunity to **conduct** further **experiments** to try to **verify** the results.

GLOSSARY	
hypothesis (*pl* **hypotheses**)	a possible explanation of sth, based on a few facts but not yet proven: *formulate/confirm a hypothesis*; SYN **theory**
phenomenon (*pl* **phenomena**)	sth that happens or exists, especially sth that is not fully understood
experimental	connected with scientific experiments
empirical *formal*	based on experiments or experience rather than ideas: *empirical evidence/knowledge/research*
conviction	a strong opinion or belief: *a political/moral conviction*
objective	based on fact and not influenced by personal feelings or opinion OPP **subjective**; **objectivity** *n*
biased	influenced by personal feelings OPP **unbiased**
scrutiny	careful and thorough examination: *come under close scrutiny* SYN **inspection**; **scrutinize** *v*
conduct *formal*	organize and/or do a particular activity: *conduct an experiment / a survey*
verify	check or show that sth is true and accurate **verification** *n*

1 The pronunciation of the underlined letters is the same as in *sit* in six words, and the same as in *site* in the other three. Divide into them two groups. Use the (APP) to help you.

hypothesis   experimental   empirical   objective   scrutiny
biased   scrutinize   verify   conviction

....

....

2 Replace the underlined word(s) with a word that keeps the same meaning.
1 I don't think the results are <u>influenced by personal feelings</u>.   ....
2 The results will come under very close <u>examination</u>.   ....
3 At the moment it's just a working <u>theory</u>.   ....
4 His views are completely <u>objective</u>.   ....
5 It is their personal <u>belief</u> that this new drug is completely safe.   ....
6 They are hoping to <u>carry out</u> a similar experiment.   ....

3 Complete the sentences.
1 Violence in society is not a new ....
2 By repeating the experiment, we can see if we are able to .... the results.
3 Do you have any .... evidence to support your theory?
4 I'm pleased that the results .... my hypothesis.
5 It's a very .... report and lacks objectivity.
6 We will need to .... the results carefully.
7 They need to carry out further .... studies to confirm the results.

4 Answer the questions.
1 What's the opposite of *objective*? ....
2 What's the plural of *phenomenon*? ....
3 What noun is formed from *objective*? ....
4 What's the opposite of *biased*? ....
5 What's a synonym for *theory*? ....
6 What noun is formed from *verify*? ....
7 What nouns can be used with *conduct*? ....
8 What nouns can be used with *empirical*? ....
9 What verbs can be used with *hypothesis*? ....
10 What adjectives can be used with *conviction*? ....

📖 TEST YOURSELF

B Genetics

GENE THERAPY: *Genes* are the **units** which control the particular qualities inside a living thing. The process of passing these qualities on from parents to their children is known as **heredity**. *Gene therapy* is a technique for correcting **defective** genes responsible for diseases. It works by **inserting** a normal gene into the *genome* (the complete set of genes in a living **cell**) to replace an **abnormal** gene. A carrier **molecule** called a *vector* must be used to deliver the normal gene to the patient's target cells. But there are many **limitations**:

- the **rapidly** dividing nature of many cells means that gene therapy may be **short-lived**

- the normal gene may be attacked by the patient's **immune system**

- gene therapy works best on disorders **arising** from the **mutation** of a single gene.

GLOSSARY

therapy	the treatment of a physical problem or an illness
heredity	as explained in the text **hereditary** adj
defective	having a fault or faults SYN **faulty**; **defect** n
insert (sth into sth)	put sth into sth else, or between two things **insertion** n
cell	the smallest unit of living matter that can exist; all plants and animals are made up of **cells**: **blood/brain cells**
abnormal	different from what is expected, and often harmful or unwanted
molecule	the smallest unit (of two or more *atoms*) that a substance can be divided into, without changing its chemical nature **molecular** adj
limitation (usually pl)	a limit on what sb/sth can do or how good they/it can be
rapidly	very quickly **rapid** adj
short-lived	only lasting for a short time OPP **long-lived**
immune system	the system in your body that produces substances to help it fight against infection and disease **immunity** n
arise	(especially of a problem) start to happen or exist SYN **occur**
mutation	(in biology) a process in which genetic material changes in structure when it is passed on **mutate** v

SPOTLIGHT *unit*

A **unit** can be a thing, person or group that is complete in itself but can also form part of something larger.
- *The **basic unit** of society is the family.*
- *a **maternity unit** in a hospital*
- *the **central processing unit** of a computer*

---

5 **Underline the stress on these words. Use the ⏺ to help you.**

therapy   hereditary   abnormal   molecule   molecular   immune   mutate   defect n

6 **Circle the correct answer.**
1. The unit is *defective / defaulty*.
2. Is this particularly *unnormal / abnormal*?
3. The ward is in the maternity *unit / system*.
4. Arthritis can be *heredity / hereditary*.
5. The effects are *short-living / short-lived*.
6. a healthy *immune / immunity* system
7. The fault's in the central *processor / processing* unit.
8. The spread of the disease is a *rapid / rapidly* process.
9. Happily, the benefits are *short / long*-lived.
10. This vaccine provides *immunity / heredity*.

7 **Complete the sentences.**
1. Gene .... has been used to restore the function of ageing brain .... in monkeys.
2. The problem was caused by the .... of the genes as they were passed on.
3. The doctor .... a tube into the patient's stomach.
4. Cancer .... are constantly dividing, and that can happen very ....
5. Problems can .... when there is a .... in one or more genes in the body.
6. If an illness can be passed from parents to their children, it's a problem of ....
7. The technique involves the .... of genes for nerve growth into the brain.
8. In .... science, a .... is a stable unit comprising two or more atoms.

 TEST YOURSELF

skyscrapers

crane

REACHING FOR THE SKY

An architect starts with an **aesthetic** vision of what a **skyscraper** will look like, and an engineer then turns this **unique** concept into a safe and practical building. For skyscrapers, which have more **physical constraints** than the average building, this is no easy task. To **comply with** building **regulations**, any structure reaching high into the sky has to be capable of **supporting** its considerable weight and able to **withstand** high winds and earthquakes. They have to **undergo** a **thorough** process of testing, and if results indicate there may be **excessive** movement, engineers have to find ways to restrict this **motion** and ensure the building will be **structurally** sound.

A skyscraper will also have many users – e.g. office workers, residents, hotel guests – so it must **meet** their various **needs,** as well as the strict rules concerning protection from fire and flooding.

The **construction** of a skyscraper begins with laying the **foundations** on rock deep beneath the ground. Steel or **reinforced concrete** columns are **inserted** into holes within the foundations, and concrete is then poured around them. Large **cranes** erect the vertical columns of the building's **framework**, after which **girders** are attached horizontally between them. It is this structure that gives **support** to the enormous **load** the building must bear. **Panels** made of materials such as glass or metal are built onto the framework to complete the skyscraper's exterior.

GLOSSARY

aesthetic	made in an artistic way and beautiful to look at
unique	very special and unusual
constraint	a thing which limits your freedom to do sth: *physical/financial/political constraints* SYN **restriction; restrict** v
comply (with sth)	obey a rule, order, law, etc.
regulation	an official rule made by a government or other authority
support	hold sth in position or prevent sth from falling **support** n
withstand	be strong enough not to be hurt or damaged by extreme conditions, the use of force, etc. SYN **resist; resistance** n
undergo	experience sth, especially a change or sth unpleasant
thorough	done completely; with great attention to detail
excessive	more than is reasonable, appropriate, or permitted
motion	the act or process of moving: *The train is already in motion.*
structurally	the way in which sth is built or organized **structure** n
meet the needs of sb/sth	satisfy the needs of sb/sth
construction	the process or method of building or making sth, especially roads, bridges, etc. **construct** v
foundation (usually pl)	the bricks, concrete, etc. that form the solid underground base of a building
reinforced	made stronger, especially by the addition of another material
concrete	a building mixture of sand, cement, small stones and water
insert	put sth into sth else, or between two things
framework	the parts of a building or an object that supports its weight and gives it shape
girder	a long piece of wood or metal, used to support weight
load	the amount of weight or pressure that is pressing against or down on sth: *a building's vertical load*
panel	a square or rectangular piece of wood, glass or metal that forms part of a larger surface, such as a door or wall

1 **Is the pronunciation of the underlined letters the same or different? Write S or D. Use the 📱 to help you.**

1 c<u>o</u>ncrete   c<u>o</u>nstruct   ....
2 s<u>u</u>pport   c<u>o</u>mply   ....
3 th<u>o</u>rough   <u>u</u>ndergo   ....
4 thor<u>ou</u>gh   f<u>ou</u>ndation   ....

5 concr<u>e</u>te   r<u>ei</u>nforced   ....
6 un<u>i</u>que   res<u>i</u>st   ....
7 <u>ae</u>sthetic   un<u>i</u>que   ....
8 compl<u>y</u>   structurall<u>y</u>   ....

2 **Match 1–8 with a–h.**

1 meet   ....
2 comply with   ....
3 resist   ....
4 undergo   ....
5 construct   ....
6 insert   ....
7 support   ....
8 restrict   ....

a the horizontal load adequately
b a number of changes
c one tube inside the other
d the effect of strong winds
e the architect's freedom
f the regulations
g the needs of the users
h the road going under the bridge

3 **Circle the odd one out.**

1 a) restriction   b) construction   c) constraint
2 a) detailed   b) thorough   c) reinforced
3 a) panel   b) girder   c) concrete
4 a) framework   b) motion   c) movement
5 a) rule   b) law   c) regulation
6 a) withstand   b) resist   c) comply
7 a) regulation   b) framework   c) structure
8 a) base   b) foundations   c) concrete

4 **Replace the underlined word(s) with a word or phrase that keeps the same meaning.**

1 They've added <u>sand, cement, stones and water</u> to the foundations.   ....
2 The foundations will need to be <u>made stronger</u>.   ....
3 We will wait until the process is <u>moving and happening</u>.   ....
4 I'm not sure these girders can support the <u>amount of weight</u>.   ....
5 Most architects have to operate within various financial <u>restrictions</u>.   ....
6 Basically, the fence comprises six <u>rectangular pieces of wood</u>.   ....
7 The building has <u>experienced</u> a number of changes of use. ·   ....
8 High-rise buildings have to comply with <u>detailed</u> safety checks.   ....
9 The amount of force was <u>greater than is reasonable or appropriate</u>.   ....
10 There are an increasing number of <u>very tall buildings</u> in the city centre.   ....

5 **Complete the text.**

After the building has been designed, the **(1)** .... of the building is the responsibility of the enginers, and they have to ensure that the design is **(2)** .... sound. This involves testing the **(3)** .... of the building to the effects of strong winds, and if the movement is too great, the engineers have to find various ways to restrict its **(4)** .... This may bring the engineer into conflict with the architect, who might feel the **(5)** .... quality of his design is being reduced.

6 **What can you remember from the text on the other page? Write answers to the questions, or talk to another student.**

1 What are the two physical constraints that affect skyscrapers?   ....
2 What does a skyscraper need to satisfy apart from the needs of the users?   ....
3 Why do skyscrapers have to undergo thorough tests?   ....
4 What is the purpose of wind tunnel tests?   ....
5 What is inserted into the foundations of the building?   ....
6 What is then poured on top?   ....
7 How are the vertical supports put in position?   ....
8 What are placed between the vertical supports?   ....
9 How are the exterior walls then constructed?   ....

TEST YOURSELF

The words and phrases below are all commonly found in everyday spoken language, and some of them are informal.

~ Where's Karl?
~ We're **short of** milk, so he **went off to** get some. He'll be back **any minute**.

~ Can you **give us** all **a lift**?
~ Sure. I can take **up to** four people, and you can **stick** your stuff in the boot.

~ I **bet** Elsa will be exhausted after yesterday. It's not **like her** to walk six miles.
~ Well, **no doubt** she'll tell us what **made** her decide to do it. **I mean**, she didn't have to, did she?

~ What are you and Beata doing for her birthday?
~ Well, **it's up to** her really, isn't it? I don't know **whether or not** she has any plans.

~ Dominic said he'd be here at 9. He's not going to **make it**, is he? And the concert was an **absolute disaster** last time without him.
~ Don't worry. He'll **turn up** – he needs the money.

~ Do you **reckon** we'll still get tickets for the Mozart concert?
~ Oh yeah, we**'re bound to** – there's still three weeks **to go**.

~ I bet Kian **makes a mess of** organizing this festival. I don't know why I put him in charge.
~ True, but **you never know**, he may surprise us.

GLOSSARY

short (of sth)	not having enough of sth	whether	used to express a doubt or choice between two possibilities: *whether or not*
go off (to do sth)	leave a place, especially in order to do sth	disaster *inf*	a complete failure: *an absolute / a total disaster*
(at) any minute (now)	very soon	turn up	**1** (of a person) arrive, especially in a way that is unexpected (as above)
give sb a lift	give sb a free ride in your car		**2** be found, especially by chance, after being lost
up to sth	as far as a particular number, level, etc.		
stick *inf*	put sth in a place, especially quickly or carelessly	reckon *inf*	think sth or have an opinion about sth
I bet (that) … *inf*	used to say that you are almost certain sth is true or that sth will happen	be bound to do/ be sth	be certain or likely to happen, or do or be sth
it's (not) like you/him/ her, etc.	used to show what is usual or typical for sb	to go	remaining; still left
no doubt	used when you are saying that sth is probable	mess	a situation that is full of problems, usually because of bad organization or mistakes that sb has made: *make a mess of sth*
make sb/sth do sth	cause sb/sth to do or be sth	you never know *inf*	used to say that you can never be certain about what will happen in the future, especially when you are suggesting that sth good might happen
I mean *inf*	used to explain or correct what you have just said		
be up to sb	be sb's responsibility; be for sb to decide		

SPOTLIGHT *make it*

Make it can mean:
1 succeed in reaching a place, especially when it is difficult (as above)
2 be present at a place: *I'm afraid I can't make it this evening.*
3 be successful in a career: *Liam will never make it as a pop star.*
4 survive after a serious accident or illness; deal successfully with a difficult experience: *The doctors think he'll make it.*

1 Form eight phrases by using a word or phrase from each box.

no	whether	give me	make		disaster	it tonight	to you	or not
a total	at any	short	it's up		of money	a lift	doubt	minute

....

....

2 Good news or bad news? Write *G* or *B*.

1 She made a mess of the exam. ....
2 Dad made it through the operation. ....
3 The ceremony was an absolute disaster. ....
4 The accident was bound to happen. ....
5 Martina's not short of money. ....
6 The plane will take up to five, and we're seven. ....
7 Surprisingly, Daniel turned up on the right day. ....
8 Failing the test made her work harder. ....

3 Replace the underlined word(s) with a word or phrase that keeps the same meaning.

1 You can just <u>put</u> those books in the study. ....
2 <u>I'm sure</u> Caitlin will want to stay with us. ....
3 Darren's very clever; I'm sure he'll <u>be successful</u> in business. ....
4 We'll never win. There are only two minutes <u>remaining</u> before the final whistle. ....
5 Sophy's not feeling at all well, so she's <u>very likely</u> to be at home tonight. ....
6 I <u>think</u> the café will be shut by the time we get there. Let's go tomorrow instead. ....
7 Reuben just <u>left</u>, heading for the woods to try and find the dog. ....
8 The train goes in five minutes. Lena's not going to <u>get here in time</u>. ....

4 Rewrite the sentences on the left, starting with the words given. Keep the same meaning.

1 Could I go in your car? | Could you give ....?
2 Felix will be here very soon. | Felix will be here any ....
3 That's not typical of Vicky. | That's ....
4 It's your decision. | It's ....
5 He's not expected to come. | I don't think he ....
6 He created a lot of problems with the task. | He made ....
7 The traffic might be heavy; you can't be certain. | The traffic might be heavy – you ....
8 Has anyone found the documents yet? | Have the documents ....?
9 I haven't got much money left. | I'm a bit ....
10 Why did she change her mind about the car? | What ....?

5 Complete the dialogues in a suitable way.

1 **A** What are the chances that Alana will .... it as a film actor?
 B I .... that'll be a struggle. I ...., with so little experience and just a couple of parts in some TV adverts, the competition is .... to be tough. Still, you never .... – we might just see her in a Hollywood movie one day. Unless she becomes famous, though, no .... she'll have many periods waiting for work.

2 **A** Robbie seems rather depressed at the moment, and that's not .... him.
 B I know. I think he's finding his course really difficult. To be honest, I don't know what .... him think medicine was right for him. He's not very hardworking and he isn't very interested in people.
 A Well, he's got another three years to .... on the course. It's entirely up .... him whether or .... he finishes it or changes to something else.

3 **A** Where's Taki? He asked me to give him a .... to the stadium, and it's 6.30 already.
 B Well, he was here ten minutes ago, but he .... off to try and get a sandwich. He'll be here .... minute now – don't worry.

4 **A** Caro has lost the ring Ali bought her. It'll be a total .... if she can't find it.
 B I .... she's .... it somewhere safe and forgotten about it. It'll .... up, I'm sure.

6 These verbs have different meanings, apart from those given in the glossary. What are they? Use the 🔤 to help you.

reckon .... stick .... bet ....

 TEST YOURSELF

A Phrasal verbs with more formal equivalents

PHRASAL VERB	MORE FORMAL EQUIVALENT
If you **get** your ideas **across** to someone,	you **communicate** them to sb successfully.
If you **bring up** a topic in conversation,	you **raise** the topic. = introduce it into the conversation
If you **look up to** someone,	you **respect** them. = have a high opinion of them
If you **own up to** something,	you **confess to** it. = admit you did sth wrong
If you **get over** a problem	you **overcome** it. = find a way to solve it
If you **put** something **off**,	you **postpone** it. = arrange for an event etc. to take place at a later time
If you **put forward** a plan,	you **propose** it. = suggest it for discussion
If you **call off** a meeting,	you **cancel** it. = decide that sth that has been arranged will not take place
If you **make up for** something,	you **compensate for** it. = provide sth good to balance or reduce the bad effects of damage, loss, etc.
If you are **taken in** by someone,	you **are deceived** by them. = are made to believe sth that isn't true
If a book **comes out**,	it **is published**. = is produced for sale

1 Match the verbs on the left with the phrasal verbs on the right with the same meaning.

propose	compensate	cancel
postpone	deceive	confess
communicate	overcome	

take sb in	call sth off	put sth off
own up to sth	get sth across	get over sth
make up for sth	put sth forward	

....

....

2 Rewrite the sentences using the word in capitals at the end as part of a phrasal verb.

1 I never expected him to confess to the crime.   UP ....
2 Nothing can compensate for the loss of earnings.   MAKE ....
3 Will someone raise the topic at the meeting?   UP ....
4 Who proposed the plan?   FORWARD ....
5 The inspector isn't easily deceived.   IN ....
6 Why did they cancel the meeting?   OFF ....
7 He has always respected his uncle.   UP ....
8 When was the new dictionary published?   OUT ....
9 The match has been postponed for a week.   OFF ....
10 We have to communicate our message more clearly. ACROSS ....

3 Complete the responses using a suitable phrasal verb

1 Elena Ferranti is writing a new novel. ~ Great! When will .... ?
2 We need to discuss staff holidays. ~ Yes, at the next meeting, I'm going to ....
3 This is such an unhappy situation. ~ Yes, but in time, I'm sure ....
4 Do you think a lot of your grandparents? ~ Yes, I really ....
5 Damian seems so charming and friendly. ~ Be careful: don't be ....
6 Oh, no! I've got a dental appointment tomorrow and I'm going away! ~ Well, you'll just have to ....
7 Do they know who stole the painting? ~ Yes, one of the gallery guides has ....
8 The transport strike is coming to an end, isn't it? ~ Yes, they've decided to ....

 TEST YOURSELF

B Multiple meanings

One of the difficulties with phrasal verbs is that some have more than one meaning.

My brother **gets through** a lot of money.
(= use up a large amount of sth)
I tried calling the bank several times, but couldn't **get through** (to anyone). (= make contact by phone)
We couldn't **get through to** the village because of snow. (= reach somewhere)

Could you **set up** a meeting?
(= arrange for sth to happen)
I had to **set up** the computer for them.
(= make equipment or machinery ready for use)
The police have **set up** more roadblocks.
(= build sth or put sth somewhere)

I'm **taking over from** Sarah Miles next week.
(= begin to have responsibility for sth, especially in place of sb else)
The army has **taken over** the country.
(= gain control of a political party, country, etc.)

My mum **went through** a difficult period when my dad died. (= experience or suffer sth)
I **went through** the evidence carefully.
(= examine sth carefully, especially to find sth)
You have to **go through** various security checks.
(= perform a series of actions)

4 **What is the meaning of the phrasal verb in each sentence? Write your answer at the end.**

1 UN supply trucks are now trying to get through to the refugee camps. ....
2 Who will take over when the manager retires? ....
3 Do you need someone to set up the recording equipment? ....
4 I went through my emails but couldn't find any record of the meeting. ....
5 I got through to someone in the Accounts department, and they were very helpful. ....
6 We went through a terrible time when our baby was ill, but, fortunately, he recovered. ....
7 The region has been taken over by rebel soldiers. ....
8 If you've never set up a tent before, have a look at some online videos. ....

5 **Circle the correct word.**

1 I finally *went through / got through* to the doctor after 20 minutes on the phone.
2 The police have *gone through / set up* a traffic-free area in front of the parliament.
3 The lawyers are *going through / setting up* the documents, looking for clues to the disappearance of the money.
4 We are worried about who will *set up / take over* when the old leader resigns or dies.
5 The boys are home from university, so we're *getting through / going through* a mountain of food.
6 Nobody should have to *go through / take over* such terrible medical treatment.
7 The person who *got through / set up* the meeting sent out the wrong date to everyone.
8 Could you *go through / take over* the shop for a minute while I go and get a coffee?

6 **Complete the phrasal verbs in the questionnaire.**

Have you ever:

1 had problems _____ _____ to a place because of really bad weather? What happened?
2 _____ _____ a tent in pouring rain?
3 _____ _____ the driving when the person you were with was ill or too tired to carry on?
4 _____ _____ a terrible experience in a plane or on a train? What was it?
5 been stopped and questioned when you were_____ _____ passport control?
6 been involved in_____ _____ a festival?
7 had to help someone_____ _____ their PC or mobile phone?
8 known someone who_____ _____ money faster than they can earn it?

7 ABOUT YOU **Write your answers to the questionnaire in Exercise 7, or tell another student.**

 TEST YOURSELF

A Discussing problems

GLOSSARY

when it comes to sth ...	when it is a question of sth
go in one ear and out the other	be forgotten very quickly
my mind is/goes a complete blank	suddenly I cannot remember sth
the minute (that) ...	as soon as ...
get there	achieve your aim
could do with sth *inf*	used to say you need or would like to have sth
have sb/sth in mind	be thinking of sb/sth for a particular purpose
off the top of my head	without thinking about sth carefully
your/the best bet	used to tell sb the best action to take to get the result they want
as far as I know	used to say that you think you know sth, but you are not sure if it is true
might/may as well (do sth)	do sth because it seems the best in the situation, although you may not really want to do it

You know, my English should be quite fluent by now, but **when it comes to** foreign languages, what I learn in class **goes in one ear and out the other**, and **my mind goes a complete blank the minute** I open my mouth.

Well, it takes time to learn a language, but you'll **get there** in the end.

I **could** probably **do with** some extra lessons.

Perhaps. Do you **have anyone in mind**?

Off the top of my head, no.

Well, I think **your best bet** is to talk to your teacher.

As far as I know, she doesn't give private lessons, but you're right: I **might as well** ask her. Thanks.

SPOTLIGHT idioms

An **idiom** is a group of words whose meaning is often different from the meaning of the individual words in it, e.g. if someone is feeling **under the weather**, it means they don't feel well. It is sometimes easier to guess the meaning, e.g. **let me see/ think** is used when you are thinking or trying to remember something.
- Now **let me see** – where did he say he lived?

1 **Correct the mistakes in each sentence.**

1 I don't know the answer from the top of my head.
2 The information just goes in one ear and out of another.
3 Are you free on Friday? ~ Help me see what I've got on that day.
4 When it goes to science, I'm hopeless.
5 I think he's feeling below the weather.
6 It's no good to worry about it.
7 When I try to remember his name, my mind goes a big blank.
8 What do you have in the mind for New Year's Eve?

2 **Complete the idioms in the dialogues.**

1 We need someone for the extra work. ~ True. Do you have anyone in .... ?
2 Do you think we should leave? ~ We might .... I doubt they'll come now.
3 Did she ask you a question? ~ Yes, and my mind went a complete ....
4 What shall I do? ~ Your best .... is to ring the station.
5 They're making very slow progress. ~ Yes, but they'll get .... eventually.
6 Are you thirsty? ~ Yes, I could .... a drink.
7 Does the bank close at four? ~ Yes, as far ....
8 Can you remember the instructions? ~ No. They went in one ear ....
9 Does Emma know about the concert? ~ No, but I'll tell her the .... she comes in.

3 ABOUT YOUR LANGUAGE **How would you translate these idioms into your own language? Write a translation, or talk to someone who speaks your language.**

4 **A common word like *mind* is used in a number of idioms. If you don't know these idioms, use a dictionary to complete them.**

1 .... **your mind** decide sth
2 .... **sth in mind** remember/don't forget sth
3 .... **my mind** in my opinion
4 .... **your mind** say what you think

TEST YOURSELF

B Responses

A number of idioms are often used as responses in spoken English.

Idiom	Meaning
*I'm going to do the essay again. ~ **What for**?*	for what purpose or reason
*Are you going to the party? ~ **You bet**!*	used to emphasize that you are keen to do sth
*I've got my exam today. ~ OK. **(The) best of luck**.*	used to wish sb success in what they are going to do ALSO **all the best**
I'll be there as soon as I can. *~ It's OK – **take your time**.*	used to tell sb there is no hurry
Where's Poppy? *~ **Don't ask me**.*	used to emphasize that you don't know sth SYN **I haven't the faintest (idea)/ Goodness knows**
It must've been an awful evening. *~ **On the contrary**, I really enjoyed it*	used to introduce a statement that says the opposite of the last one
Are you ready? *~ **Hang on**.* *I'll be with you **in a minute**.*	wait a minute/moment very soon
Rani's going out with a film star. *~ **You're kidding**!*	*inf* used to show that you are very surprised at what sb has just said
I think you owe me some money. *~ **How come**?*	*inf* used to say you do not know how something can happen and would like an explanation
*Can we go in if we aren't members? ~ **No way**!*	*inf* used to say that sth is not at all possible or not allowed SYN **no chance**

5 **Circle the correct answer.**

1 If you answer **you bet**, you *want to do something / don't mind doing something*.
2 If you reply **don't ask me**, it means you *don't know the answer / don't want to answer*.
3 If you say **you're kidding**, you think the other person is *being / not being* serious.
4 **No way** means it's not *practical / possible*.
5 **Goodness knows** means *I'm sorry / I don't know*.
6 If you ask someone to **hang on**, you want them to *help you / wait for you*.

6 **Combine words from each box to form eight idioms.**

you're	no	how	what		of luck	bet	on	come
don't	hang	best	you		ask me	way	for	kidding

....

....

7 **Complete the idiom in each response.**

1 I've just won the lottery!   ~ You're ....!
2 Could I borrow your dad's car?   ~ No ....!
3 Why did they leave so early?   ~ Goodness ....
4 I'll be with you in two minutes.   ~ It's ok, take ....
5 Are you going to the party?   ~ Yes, you ....
6 I've got my driving test tomorrow.   ~ Well, best ....
7 The college said we have to apply again.   ~ What? How .... ?
8 I'm going to repeat the course.   ~ What .... ?
9 Where have they all gone?   ~ I haven't the ....
10 I heard the lecture was really boring.   ~ No, on the ....

[TEST YOURSELF]

A Commenting on a situation

Some idioms are commonly used to express an opinion about a situation.

> I can borrow money if necessary, but that would be **a last resort.**

> If I could get a job in TV, it would be **a dream come true.**

> We enjoyed Cyprus and, **as a matter of fact,** we think we'll go back next year.

> I haven't got a chance of getting that job, but never mind – **that's life.**

> Don't worry about your keys. **As it happens,** I have a spare set in my office.

> It's a lovely flat. **If only** I had £1m to spend on a place to live.

> You can eat what you like and drinks are free. **Sounds too good to be true**, doesn't it?

> The place is full now. It's **a good thing** we got here early.

> I would've gone to the match **but for** the weather.

> Carla wouldn't admit her mistake because she didn't want to **lose face.**

GLOSSARY

(as) a last/final resort	an action you will take if there is no other option SYN **if all else fails**	**if only**	used to say that you wish sth was true or that sth had happened
a dream come true	a wish or hope that becomes a reality	**(sound) too good to be true**	used to say that you cannot believe that sth is as good as it seems
as a matter of fact	used to add a comment on sth that you have just said, often sth you think will be interesting and possibly surprising	**be a good thing (that) ...**	be lucky that ... SYN **be a good job that ...**
that's life *inf*	used when you are disappointed about sth but know you must accept it	**but for sth/sb**	if it were not for sth/sb
as it happens	used when you say sth surprising, or sth connected with what sb else has just said	**lose face**	be less respected or look stupid because of sth you have done

1 **Write the last word in each of these idioms.**

1 if all else .... 3 it's a dream come .... 5 too good to be .... 7 if ....
2 as a matter of .... 4 lose .... 6 as it .... 8 a last ....

2 **Replace the underlined words with an idiom that keeps the same meaning.**

1 <u>I wish</u> I had more time. ....
2 It's <u>very fortunate</u> we booked the tickets last week. ....
3 If I get to the final, it will be <u>everything I've always wanted</u>. ....
4 I may not be selected for the team, but <u>I just have to accept that</u>. ....
5 Toby knows he's wrong but he won't admit it because he doesn't want to <u>look stupid</u>. ....
6 I can always sell my flat if <u>there are no other options</u>. ....
7 He would've played last week <u>if it had not been for</u> his injury. ....
8 He was born yesterday. And <u>it will surprise you that</u>, they've named him after you. ....

3 **Complete the idioms / set phrases in these dialogues.**

1 I'm afraid they gave you the wrong price. ~ Right. I thought it sounded ....
2 Can you raise the money for the trip? ~ Not sure. I may have to use my savings as ....
3 Are you disappointed you couldn't buy the flat? ~ Yes I am, but ....
4 We're going to be stuck here for hours! ~ Oh, ... I'd brought a book to read.
5 The shop will have to close. ~ Yes, it would have survived .... the high rent.
6 You haven't got a small screwdriver, have you? ~ Well, ... I have.
7 It looks as if it's going to rain. ~ Yes, it's .... I brought my umbrella.
8 Do you think you can win? ~ I'd love to. It would be a ....

🗂 TEST YOURSELF

B Adding tone and emphasis

Some idioms are used to add extra politeness or emphasis, and to prepare the listener for what you are going to say.

Do you know if they're married, **by any chance**?	used especially in questions to ask if sth is true or possible
I wouldn't mind a cup of tea, if it's no trouble.	used to say politely that you would very much like sth / to do sth
I'd love to go. **The (only) thing is**, I promised to help my dad in the garden.	used to introduce an explanation, and often one that suggests there is a problem
I didn't like it **at all**. / I'm not **at all** keen on it.	used to emphasize a negative statement (used after a verb but before or after an adjective)
You should read it. It's **by far** his best book.	used to emphasize what you are saying
Smoking is very bad for your health, **not to mention** the cost.	used to introduce extra information and emphasize what you are saying
Guess what! Ed and Sal are moving to Kenya.	used before giving sb surprising or exciting news
Believe it or not, he asked if he could live with us.	inf used to introduce information which is true but surprising
He's been working since 7 o'clock this morning, so **no wonder** he's tired.	inf used to emphasize the fact that sth is not surprising
Where **on earth** did you get those boots?	used after wh- questions to indicate surprise, and sometimes annoyance, about sth
I'd like to ask you a few questions, **if you don't mind**.	used to check that sb does not object to sth that you want to do, or ask sb politely to do sth SYN **if you wouldn't mind**
The room is empty but, **for some reason**, we're not allowed to use it.	used to say, often with slight annoyance, you don't know the reason for sth or don't understand it

4 **Cross out one wrong word in each sentence.**

1 That's by very far the worst article.
2 Believe it or believe not, he's a politician.
3 The only bad thing is, I can't afford to go.
4 Guess you what – I'm getting married.
5 Who on the earth gave you that tie?
6 I'd like to borrow this if that you don't mind.
7 He's bad at the job, not to be mention lazy.
8 I wouldn't really mind a lift, if that's OK.

5 **Complete the idiom or set phrase in each sentence.**

1 .... what! I've got a new job.
2 I'd love to go to Brazil in December, but the .... is, my exams are in January.
3 What on .... are you doing here this morning? It's Saturday!
4 I made a special trip to the post office, but for .... reason, they closed early.
5 I'm not hungry, but I .... mind a glass of water if that's OK.
6 He won all his matches, so no .... he's delighted.
7 Have you got any string I could use by any .... ?
8 The book was great, but I wasn't at .... impressed with the film; it was far too long.

6 **Add a suitable idiom or set phrase to these sentences.**

1 It didn't work.
2 Do you know if it's open?
3 Melinda's going to marry a famous pop star.
4 Why are you wearing gloves in the summer?
5 Jacob looks about 20, but he's only 13.
6 He's been very ill, so he looks thin.
7 They have a large apartment here, a farm in Wales and a house on the coast.
8 We said we were members, but they wouldn't let us in.
9 It is his most violent film.
10 I'd like to know more about your background.

 TEST YOURSELF

These phrases consist of two main words, usually joined by *and* or *or*. The word order is almost always fixed, i.e. **backwards and forwards** (NOT ~~forwards and backwards~~). Most are made up of near synonyms or opposites, and they are more common in spoken English.

Examples	Meaning
We've been going **backwards and forwards** all day.	move from one place to another and then back again, many times SYN **back and forth**
First and foremost we need a plan.	more than anything else
They'll be here **sooner or later**.	at some time in the future, probably soon
We're considering **the pros and cons** of moving.	the reasons for and against doing sth
I learnt how to use a computer by **trial and error**.	trying different ways of doing sth until you find the best one
It costs £300 a month, **more or less**.	1 approximately
I've **more or less** finished this book.	2 almost
I see my cousins **now and again**.	sometimes but not often; occasionally SYN **now and then, on and off**
Who is responsible for **law and order**?	a situation in which people obey the law
The children got home **safe and sound**.	safely; not harmed, damaged, lost, etc.
I'm **sick and tired of** this weather.	bored with or annoyed about sth, and wanting it to stop SYN **sick to death of sth**
I've almost finished packing except for a few **odds and ends**.	inf small things of little importance SYN **bits and pieces**

1 Form ten phrases using words in the box, adding either *and* or *or*.

trial	more	the pros	back	sick	sooner	odds	safe	ends	on
law	cons	forth	less	order	tired	later	off	error	sound

....

....

2 Complete the phrase in each sentence.
1 I'm sick to .... of these exams. Thank goodness there is only one more.
2 I've collected most of my stuff. I just have to get a few more bits and ....
3 We had a class discussion looking at the pros and .... of Esperanto.
4 First and .... , we have got to establish where we want to go.
5 It was a terrible flight, but we finally got here safe and ....
6 I'm moving stuff into my flat, and I've been going backwards and .... all day.
7 I think we've got more or .... everything we need.
8 It's a matter of law and .... , so the decision rests with the police.

3 Complete the dialogues with a suitable phrase.
1 It looks like they're not coming. ~ No, they'll be here ....
2 You look miserable. ~ Yes, I'm .... of the noise.
3 How did you assemble that bookcase without instructions? ~ Basically just ....
4 Do you go to that restaurant a lot? ~ No, but we like to go ....
5 How many came in the end? ~ Oh, I'd say 20 ....
6 Have you got everything ready for the party? ~ Yes, except for a few ....

4 ABOUT YOUR LANGUAGE **Do you have expressions like these in your language? How would you translate the examples at the top of the page?**

 TEST YOURSELF

We form most similes with: **(as) + adjective + as + noun** and a smaller number with: **verb** OR **noun + like + noun**
Similes with **as** emphasize the meaning of the adjective, so they are often easy to understand. They are more common in spoken English, and the first **as** is usually omitted.

(Main) noun	Simile	(Main) noun	Simile
gold	The children were **as good as gold** today. (= well behaved)	beetroot	Sian went **as red as a beetroot**. (= very embarrassed)
feather	I picked up the little girl – she was **as light as a feather**. (= very light)	bone	The ground is **as dry as a bone** at the moment. (= very dry)
bat	I'm afraid I'm **blind as a bat**. (used humorously)	cake	The new model is **selling like hot cakes**. (= selling very quickly or in large numbers)
post	My father is **deaf as a post**. (used humorously)	log	I **slept like a log** last night. (= slept very well)
rake	My sister's **as thin as a rake**. (= very thin)	dream	The plan **worked like a dream**. (= was very successful)
sheet	Sammy went **as white as a sheet**. (= white with fear or from illness)	sieve	Sometimes I've got **a memory/mind like a sieve**. (= a bad memory)

1 Complete the similes.

1 My poor uncle is deaf as a ....
2 This computer game will sell like hot ....
3 The sheets are dry as a .... after hanging in the hot sun.
4 Surprisingly, the suitcase was light as a ....
5 My father sleeps like a ....
6 Honestly, she's got a mind like a ....
7 He realized his mistake and went red as a ....
8 The printer is working like a .... now.
9 James is blind as a .... without his glasses.
10 She heard someone downstairs and went white as a ....

2 Choose a suitable simile to describe these people and things.

1 My grandfather can't hear a thing. ....
2 My grandmother can't see a thing. ....
3 My girlfriend needs to put on weight. ....
4 The plan was very successful. ....
5 She looked really ill. ....
6 The children behaved very well. ....
7 She was very embarrassed. ....
8 He often forgets things. ....
9 The little girl weighed almost nothing. ....
10 Everyone is buying the new phone. ....

3 ABOUT YOUR LANGUAGE Do you have similes in your language. Can you find equivalent expressions for the similes above?

....
....
....

TEST YOURSELF

I'm not very keen on the flat, or the area. **Mind you**, it's better than my last place. **Incidentally**, do you know how Pavel's getting on in his new flat?

Sam   The company is likely to move its headquarters to Brussels. **As for** Deborah, she may have to get a job with another insurance firm.

Tanya Yes, or **alternatively**, she could stay with the company here, but in a different branch.

Sam   OK, but **in the end**, she may decide that a change of company would **do her good**.

It's true that Peter was only trying to help. **Even so**, he shouldn't have got involved – it just made the problem a lot worse.

Mind you …
Incidentally …
As far as I am concerned …
In the end …

It's true …
Even so …
Alternatively …
In any case …

Brad   Do you think you'll go back to the same hotel?

Asma Well, as a matter of fact we were a bit disappointed the last time we were there. **By and large** the staff were still great, but the place was starting to look a bit tired, and the food wasn't quite as good.

I don't think Ali should apply for the job in Munich. He doesn't have that much experience and, **in any case**, he doesn't speak German.

MOTHER George wants to spend the summer in France **so as to** improve his French.

FATHER Well, **as far as I'm concerned**, that's fine, but I hope he's not expecting us to pay for it.

GLOSSARY	
mind you *inf*	used to add sth to what you have just said, especially sth that makes it less strong SYN **still**
incidentally	used to change the conversation to a different topic SYN **by the way**
as for sb/sth	used to start talking about sb/sth
alternatively	used to introduce an idea that is a second choice or possibility
in the end	after everything has been considered
do sb good	have a positive effect on sb; help sb
it's true (that) …	used to admit that a fact or statement is correct, although you think sth else is more important
even so	despite that; used for introducing a new idea, fact, etc. SYN **all the same / nevertheless**
by and large	used when you are saying sth that is generally but not completely true SYN **to a large extent / on the whole / broadly speaking**
in any case	whatever happens or may have happened; often used to introduce the most important reason, argument, etc. SYN **anyway, besides**
so as to do sth	with the intention of doing sth
as far as I'm concerned	used to give your opinion about sth

1 **Match 1–10 with a–j.**

1	mind	....	a	case	6	in any	....	f	speaking
2	by and	....	b	extent	7	broadly	....	g	I'm concerned
3	even	....	c	the way	8	by	....	h	so
4	as far as	....	d	you	9	to a large	....	i	same
5	on the	....	e	large	10	all the	....	j	whole

2 **Correct the mistake in each sentence.**

1 Broad speaking, it was very interesting.

2 We had a fantastic time. All same, I was glad to get home.

3 We left very early such as to avoid the rush hour.

4 I don't like her going in the sea because the water is dirty. In every case, she can't swim very well.

5 As far I'm concerned, the neighbours can have a street party if they want to.

6 You might get an interview for the job but, at the end, it's just a question of luck.

7 We've got most things organized for the picnic, and so for food, we'll all bring our own.

8 She seems very tired; I think a holiday would make her good.

9 I thought all the students did well. By my way, what's the Italian boy called?

10 I got some help from my father. Even, it was a very difficult task.

3 **Replace the underlined word(s) with a word or phrase that keeps the same meaning. More than one answer is often possible.**

1 I think he was from the Czech Republic. <u>By the way</u>, do you know Michaela from Prague?

2 <u>To a large extent</u>, you can get by without speaking the language.

3 I'm disappointed with my broadband speed. <u>Still</u>, it's faster than it was before.

4 We can't give Fergus a lift – he lives miles away. <u>In any case</u>, we haven't got room in the car.

5 <u>I agree</u> some of the definitions could be a bit shorter. <u>Nevertheless</u>, it's a good dictionary.

6 We could go for a nice long walk. ~ <u>Or</u> we could just stay here and chat.

7 I'm sure the exercise will <u>have a positive effect on them</u>.

8 I paid for the tickets in advance <u>in order to</u> get a good discount.

9 <u>If you ask me</u>, the government has got its policy on health care completely wrong.

10 We thought about getting a cat but, <u>after considering it for some time</u>, we decided not to.

4 **Complete the sentences and dialogues with a suitable word or phrase.**

1 Nuria said it wasn't likely to rain. _____ , I'm still taking my umbrella.

2 We were thinking we might buy a tent and go to a camping site. _____ , we could just stay in a B&B.

3 I took a different route home _____ avoid seeing Mr Pedder; he never stops talking.

4 Do you speak English at home? ~ Yeah, to a large _____ .

5 I've packed lots of jumpers so I'm prepared for the cold weather. ~ Good, you'll need them. _____ , what time does the plane leave?

6 I've been told there's a very good Chinese restaurant in the main square. _____ somewhere to stay, I'm afraid I can't help you.

7 You won't want to climb that hill – it's very steep. And, _____ , it's too far away.

8 We'd planned to move in the spring, but _____ we decided it was more sensible to stay here.

9 There are a few problems in my neighbourhood, but _____ , it's a good place to live.

10 _____ that a lot of people drop litter, which is very anti-social. _____ , you can't start sending people to prison for that kind of offence.

TEST YOURSELF

Sayings are well-known phrases that express things about life that most people believe are wise and true. They are more common in spoken English.

We must do something, we must do something, we must do something.

Nice to see you this morning, James.

Example	Meaning
Tonia still finds playing the piano difficult, but **practice makes perfect**.	If you do sth repeatedly, you will become very good at it.
I haven't heard from my son for weeks, but usually **no news is good news**.	If you haven't had any news, then nothing has gone wrong, and things are probably fine.
I know innocent people suffer in war, but sometimes **the end justifies the means**.	Bad or unfair methods of doing sth are acceptable if the results of the action are good or positive.
Are tickets available? ~ Yes, but it's **first come, first served**.	people will be dealt with, served, seen, etc. in the order in which they arrive
How's the course going? ~ **So far, so good**.	used to say that things have been successful up until now, and you hope that will continue
Can we come as well? ~ Of course. **The more the merrier**.	the more people or things there are, the better the situation will be, or the more fun people will have
Do you believe in **an eye for an eye**?	used to say that you should punish sb by doing to them by what they did to you or sb else
They finally turned up at 8.30, but **better late than never**.	It is better to arrive late or achieve sth late, than not arrive or achieve sth at all.
The mountain road is dangerous so go slowly – **better safe than sorry**.	It is better to be careful than to take a risk or act too quickly and later regret it.
I've always believed that **prevention is better than cure**.	It is better to stop a problem before it occurs than let it happen and then have to do sth about it.
I met two of your old flatmates today. **It's a small world**, isn't it?	used to express your surprise when you are talking to sb and find out that you both know the same person
They should actually do something. **Actions speak louder than words**.	what a person does means more than what they say they will do
Calvin is never satisfied. **The grass is always greener on the other side (of the fence)**, you know.	said about people who are never happy with what they have and always think other people have a better situation than them
I know he doesn't look great but **don't judge a book by its cover**.	You should not form an opinion about sb/sth from their/its appearance only.
What they did to you was awful, but I don't think you should take revenge. **Two wrongs don't make a right**.	used to say that if sb does sth bad to you, the situation will not be improved by doing sth bad to them
I know it's not a great job, but **beggars can't be choosers**.	used when there is no choice so sb should just accept what is available
Could you help me with this? **Two heads are better than one**.	used to say that two people can achieve more than one person working alone

1 **Cover the opposite page and correct the mistakes.**

1 So far, no good. ....
2 Two brains are better than one. ....
3 It's a little world. ....
4 First come are served. ....
5 Practice makes better. ....

6 No news is no news. ....
7 The more the happier. ....
8 Don't judge a book by the number of pages. ....

2 **Which sayings are illustrated at the top of the opposite page?**

1 ....
2 ....
3 ....
4 ....

5 ....
6 ....
7 ....
8 ....

3 **Complete these sayings.**

1 Better late than ....
2 Better safe than ....
3 No news is ....
4 The more ....
5 Practice makes ....

6 The end justifies ....
7 Two wrongs don't ....
8 Beggars can't ....
9 Prevention is ....
10 Don't judge a book ....

4 **Use a suitable saying to respond to each of these situations.**

1 I came down slowly – I didn't want to fall over. ~ Well, ...
2 He works on his English for three hours every day. ~ Well, ...
3 Shall we do the maths homework together? ~ Yes, ...
4 My son has been away for two months but hardly ever phones. ~ Well, ...
5 Do you think people should take revenge? ~ No, I don't believe in ....
6 How are you getting on now you're in London? ~ Well, ...
7 Gabi is never happy, is she? ~ No, I'm afraid with her the ....
8 They finally got here, but they missed the first part. ~ Well, ...
9 It's not a nice flat but it's all they can afford. ~ Well, ...
10 Can anyone go the exhibition? ~ Yes, but be quick. It's ....
11 If he steals my bag, I'll keep his phone. ~ Oh, come on. ....
12 If we stop giving a small number of people expensive drugs, we can actually treat more people and save more lives. ~ You're saying that the ....

5 ABOUT YOU **Write answers to these questions, or talk to another student.**

1 Are there any sayings on page 184 that you think are particularly true?
....
....

2 Are there any sayings that you do not think are true?
....
....

6 **Here are six more sayings in English. Can you guess what they mean? See page 184 for answers.**

1 Beauty is only skin-deep. ....
2 Love is blind. ....
3 Charity begins at home. ....
4 Put all your eggs in one basket. ....
5 Once bitten, twice shy. ....
6 Absence makes the heart grow fonder. ....

TEST YOURSELF

We generally use **vague** language in spoken English when we aren't able to be precise, or don't want or need to be.

How long will you be away?
~ Three weeks **or so.**

He earns **loads of** money, doesn't he?
~ Probably, somewhere **in the region of** £100,000.

He's **something to do with** TV, isn't he?
~ Yes, **something like that.**

She doesn't look well. Is she ill **or something?**
~ I don't know. I am **sort of** worried about her.

We'll buy that car **somehow or other.**
~ Well, I've got £1000, **give or take** a bit.

I've got loads of **stuff** to prepare. How many are coming?
~ Oh, fifty **odd,** I think.

GLOSSARY	
vague	not clear or detailed
or so	You add **or so** after a number, quantity, etc. to show that it is approximate. SYN **or thereabouts**
loads (of sth) *inf*	a large quantity of sth SYN **tons/piles (of sth)** *inf*
in the region of	used when you are giving a number, price etc. to show that it is not exact: *He paid **somewhere in the region of** £500.* SYN **approximately**
something to do with sth	in some way connected with sth
or something *inf*	used when you are not exactly sure about a thing, person or place ALSO **or somebody/ somewhere;** SYN **something/ somebody/ somewhere or other**
sort of *inf*	to some extent, but in a way that is hard to explain SYN **kind of**
somehow	in some way or by some means, although you don't know exactly how: **somehow or other**
give or take sth	used for talking about numbers which are not exact: *We'll have 100 guests, **give or take ten**.*
stuff *inf*	used to refer in a general way to things people say, do, or think, etc: *They played **some great stuff**. I don't believe **all that stuff**.*
odd (after a number) *inf*	approximately or a little more than the number mentioned: **30 odd** students

> **SPOTLIGHT** *something like that,* etc.
>
> We can use can use these phrases when we are being vague.
> - She's a doctor **or something like that.**
> - He works in publishing I think. ~ Yeah, **something along those lines.**
> - He said they advise importers. **Something of that sort.**

1 **Replace the underlined word(s) with a word or phrase that keeps the same meaning.**

1 We've got <u>loads</u> of food. _____
2 It cost £200 or <u>so</u>. _____
3 I am <u>sort</u> of glad she went. _____
4 She's an optician or something <u>like that</u>. _____
5 I think he's 50 <u>or just over</u>. _____
6 It's <u>in the region of</u> 400 miles. _____
7 I'll get there <u>by some means</u>. _____
8 He was <u>not clear</u> about how to get there. _____
9 I'll give the book to Susana or <u>one of the other girls</u>. _____

2 **One word is missing in each sentence. What is it, and where does it go?**

1 She was just sort pretending to be ill; I don't think she actually was. _____
2 We seem to have of rice, so I might make a paella. _____
3 He's a chief executive something; I'm not too sure. _____
4 We'll leave at seven, give take a few minutes, so don't be late. _____
5 I've got a meeting tonight but I'll finish my essay by tomorrow or other. _____
6 The whole trip cost somewhere the region of £400. _____

3 **Rewrite the sentences using the word in capitals to make each sentence more vague.**

1 We invited a hundred to the wedding. — SO _____
2 He looks depressed. — SORT _____
3 Her job is in marketing. — DO _____
4 There were a lot of good groups and comedians at the festival. — STUFF _____
5 It's 300 miles. — REGION _____
6 We could go to France. — SOMEWHERE _____
7 I've got £500. — GIVE _____
8 We could get him a book for his birthday. — SOMETHING _____

4 ABOUT YOUR LANGUAGE **Translate the dialogues at the top of the page. Do you have similar phrases in your language?**

_____
_____

 TEST YOURSELF

A number of verbs are commonly used in the passive, especially in certain contexts (see the spotlight).

The man **is said to be** carrying a weapon.
The boat **is reported** to be a mile from shore.
The teenager **is known as** a troublemaker.
She **is known for** her work as a therapist.
They **were meant** to stay together.
The meeting **is scheduled** for next week.
Four **have been short-listed** for the prize.
Residents **are empowered** by the new law.
The body will **be cremated**, not buried.
The man **has been jailed** for the robbery.
I **was overcome with** grief.
Two girls **have been suspended from** school.
We **were caught up in** a traffic jam.

GLOSSARY

be known as sth/sb OR **for sth**	have a reputation as sth/sb or for sth
be meant (for sth / to do sth)	be intended for sth / to do sth
be scheduled (for sth)	be arranged to happen at a particular time
be short-listed (for sth)	be part of a small list for a prize, award, etc, chosen from all the people who applied for it. The winner is sb from that list.
be empowered (to do sth) *formal*	have or be given the power or authority to do sth SYN **be authorized (to do sth)**
be cremated	(of a dead body) be burnt, especially as part of a funeral ceremony
be jailed	be sent to prison
be overcome (with sth)	be strongly affected by sth, especially sth emotional
be suspended sb (from sth)	be officially stopped from doing your job, going to school, etc.
be caught up (in sth)	be involved in sth, especially when you do not want to be

SPOTLIGHT using passives

The use of the passive is more impersonal and commonly found in news reports, etc, where these passive phrases are common.
- *The minister **is said to be** considering resignation.*
- *Food supplies **are reported to be** arriving in the country.*

1 **Complete the sentences with a suitable verb.**
1 The helicopter carrying the prince is _____ to be nearing the country.
2 Most of the survivors were _____ with emotion when they greeted their families.
3 The civil servants were _____ for giving secret information to journalists.
4 When I die, I want to be _____ , not buried.
5 The courts are _____ to give longer prison sentences if they wish.
6 She is _____ as a rather difficult boss.
7 The meeting is not _____ to start until 2 p.m.
8 Sorry I'm late. I was _____ in the debate about education and couldn't leave.

2 **Rewrite the sentences in the passive, using a suitable verb from the top of the page.**
1 People tell me he is dangerous. — He is _____ .
2 The judge sent him to prison for five years. — He was _____ .
3 They're going to put the film on at 9.00 p.m. — The film is _____ .
4 They considered four people from the nominations. — Four people were _____ .
5 We spent ages in a traffic jam. — We were _____ .
6 The school told the girls to leave. — The girls were _____ .
7 People know her because of her charity work. — She is _____ .
8 It wasn't my plan to join the army. — I wasn't _____ .
9 He was very emotional when he saw her. — He was _____ .

3 **Other verbs, taught elsewhere in the book, are also commonly used in the passive. Use the Word List if you don't know these verbs or can't remember what they mean.**

be charged (with sth)	be entitled to sth	be surrounded (by sth)	be accused of sth
be wounded	be stranded	be convicted (of sth)	be trapped

 TEST YOURSELF

A With adjectives

Un-, **in-** and **dis-** are some of the prefixes used with adjectives, usually to give a negative meaning.

You will already know some of these adjectives when they are used without negative prefixes. The glossary explains the words you are less likely to know.

un-	He's **unqualified** to drive that car. They chose an **unknown** actor for the part. I'm **unfamiliar** with this keyboard. It was an **uncharacteristic** mistake. The workers have called an **unofficial** strike. The project is still **unfinished**.
in-	Ben is **incapable of** making a decision. I'm afraid this passport is **invalid**. The food was **insufficient** for our needs. They got divorced because they were **incompatible**. The treatment of some refugees is **inhuman**.
dis-	The Prime Minister will fire any **disloyal** ministers. One **disobedient** child was removed from the class.

GLOSSARY

unqualified	not having the right knowledge, experience or qualifications to do sth OPP **qualified**
uncharacteristic (of sb/sth)	not typical of sb; not the way they usually behave OPP **characteristic**
unofficial	does not have permission or approval from sb in authority OPP **official**
invalid	not legally or officially acceptable OPP **valid**
insufficient	not enough for a particular purpose OPP **sufficient**
incompatible	Two people who are **incompatible** are very different from each other and not able to work or live happily together. OPP **compatible**
inhuman	lacking the qualities of kindness and pity
disloyal (of sb) (to sb/sth)	not loyal or faithful to your friends, country, etc. OPP **loyal**
disobedient	failing or refusing to obey OPP **obedient**

SPOTLIGHT *un- and under-*

There is a difference between **un-** and **under-**. An **unemployed** person doesn't have a job; an **underemployed** person doesn't have enough work to do, or not all of their skills are not made use of. Other examples are **uncooked** and **undercooked**, or **unpaid** and **underpaid**.

1 *Un-, in-, or dis-?* Cover the table and complete the words.

1	............known	4	............obedient	7	............finished	10	............familiar
2	............capable	5	............characteristic	8	............loyal	11	............compatible
3	............human	6	............valid	9	............employed	12	............sufficient

2 Match the adjectives on the left with the nouns on the right.

an unofficial	an incompatible	an invalid	insufficient		ticket	money	dog	couple
an unqualified	a disobedient	inhuman	an unfamiliar		conditions	name	strike	teacher

....
....
....

3 Complete the dialogues using a word beginning with *un-, in-, dis-,* or *under-*.

1	The family were cruel and treated him like a slave.	~ I know, it was ....
2	Did you know the performers?	~ No, they were all ....
3	Has she got a job?	~ No, she's ....
4	What were the vegetables like?	~ OK, but a bit ....
5	Have they completed the roadworks?	~ No, they're still ....
6	Does she know what she's going to do?	~ No, she's .... of making a decision.
7	Is it voluntary work?	~ Yes, it's ....
8	It's very unusual for Moira to make that mistake	~ Yes, very ....
9	Do you know the town?	~ No, I'm .... with the area.
10	It was awful of Teri just to walk out and leave us with no support.	~ Yes, it was very ....

🗂 TEST YOURSELF

B With verbs

These prefixes can be used with some verbs, with particular meanings. You will already know some of these verbs when used without a prefix.

mis-	= badly; incorrectly	**misunderstand** **miscalculate** **mislead**	**mistreat** **misjudge**
re-	= again	**rewrite** **reassess** (e.g. the cost of sth, an exam candidate)	**redo** (e.g. a piece of work)
un-	= doing the opposite of sth	**unwrap** (e.g. a present). **undo** (e.g. your jacket) **unwind** (e.g. a bandage)	**unpack** (e.g. a suitcase) **untie** (e.g. your shoelaces)
over-	= too much	**overcharge** (e.g. in a shop) **overestimate** (e.g the amount of food you need) **oversleep** (= sleep longer than you want) **overdo it** (= work too hard)	

GLOSSARY

mistreat	treat a person or animal in a cruel, unkind or unfair way
misjudge	form a wrong opinion about a person or situation, especially in a way that creates a problem
mislead	give sb the wrong impression and make them believe sth that is not true
unwind	open up/out sth that has been wrapped into a ball or around sth

4 Cross out the wrong answer.

1	I think he was **mis**_____ .	a) treated	b) advised	c) led
2	Could you **un**_____ this for me?	a) charge	b) wrap	c) tie
3	I think I **over**_____ him.	a) estimated	b) charged	c) calculated
4	I shall have to **re**_____ what I have done.	a) write	b) judge	c) assess
5	I **over**_____ this morning.	a) bought	b) did it	c) slept
6	She completely **mis**_____ me.	a) judged	b) understood	c) believed

5 Circle the correct form(s). Sometimes both words are possible.

1 He *miscalculated / mistreated* the length of the room.

2 I'm going to *redo / rewrite* my essay.

3 When I get to the hotel, I will *unpack / unwrap* my suitcase.

4 I think she completely *misled / misunderstood* what I said.

5 I'm trying to *untie / unwind* the string from around this post.

6 I *overcharged / overdid it* this morning, and now I'm worn out.

6 Complete the sentences.

1 I'm going back to that shop: I think they _____ me for those earrings.

2 They _____ me when they said they would help; they've done nothing really.

3 I love seeing the children _____ their presents on their birthdays.

4 The doctor asked me to _____ my shirt and sit on the bed.

5 I thought Ben couldn't do this job but I was wrong; I _____ him.

6 I can't stand seeing people _____ animals.

7 We _____ the time it would take, and so we arrived an hour early.

8 I need to _____ the policy because it clearly isn't working.

 TEST YOURSELF

The suffixes **-ion**, **-ment** and **-al** can be added to verbs to form related nouns with the same basic meaning. You will notice there are sometimes small spelling changes.
The words in bold are the forms which have not been taught elsewhere in the book or series.

Suffix	Verb → Noun	Meaning
-ion	**accommodate** → accommodation	*v* provide sb with a room or place to sleep
	create → **creation**	*n* the act or process of making sth that is new, or of causing sth to exist that didn't exist before
	appreciate → **appreciation**	*n* the feeling of being grateful for sth
	collaborate → collaboration	*v* work together with sb to produce or achieve sth
	complete → **completion**	*n* the act or process of finishing sth
	hesitate → **hesitation**	*v* be slow to speak or act because you are uncertain or nervous
	inspect → inspection	*v* look at sth closely, especially to check it is correct
	detect → **detection**	*v* discover or notice sth, especially sth that is not easy to see, hear, etc.
	object → **objection**	*v* say that you disagree with or oppose sth
	resign → **resignation**	*n* the act of giving up your job
-ment	accomplish → **accomplishment**	*n* an impressive thing that is done or achieved after a lot of work
	acknowledge → **acknowledgement**	*v* accept that sth is true
	encourage → **encouragement**	*n* the act of encouraging sb to do sth
	measure → **measurement**	*n* the size, length or amount of sth
	settle → **settlement**	*n* an official agreement that ends an argument
-al	**deny** → **denial**	*v* say that sth is not true
	dismiss → **dismissal**	*n* the act of dismissing sb from their job
	propose → **proposal**	*n* a formal suggestion or plan
	refuse → **refusal**	*n* an act of saying or showing that you will not do, give or accept sth

> **SPOTLIGHT** different meanings
>
> The addition of a suffix to a verb sometimes creates a noun with a meaning that is further from that of the verb.
> - *I **edit** the magazine.* (= prepare it for publication by correcting mistakes, making changes, etc.)
> - *We now have an online **edition** of the magazine.* (= the form in which a book is published)

1 Complete the correct noun forms.

1 settle / ....
2 refuse / ....
3 acknowledge / ....
4 complete / ....

5 measure / ....
6 resign / ....
7 propose / ....
8 object / ....

9 deny / ....
10 appreciate / ....

2 Organize the words under the two headings below.

| encouragement | dismissal | refusal | appreciation | objection |
| collaboration | accomplishment | denial | settlement | |

POSITIVE MEANING

....
....
....

NEGATIVE MEANING

....
....
....

3 Complete the sentences with a suitable verb.

1 I .... because I wasn't quite sure what to say.
2 The civil servant .... talking to the press, and said he would never do that.
3 Several neighbours are unhappy and have .... to the council's plans.
4 The paper .... that some of the information was wrong, and has issued an apology.
5 We should be able to .... a couple more people in the flat if necessary.
6 The gas company is .... the property to check for any leaks.
7 How long have you .... that particular magazine?
8 The two companies have decided to .... in the hope of finding a solution.
9 What's the purpose of the tests? ~ They are designed to .... the disease early.
10 Do your neighbours mind you building an extension? ~ Yes, one person has .... to it.

4 Find five pairs of words in the box that have a connection. Briefly explain the connection.

| refusal | inspection | cooperation | denial | agreement |
| dismissal | collaboration | resignation | settlement | examination |

.... / .... / ....
.... / .... / ....
.... / ....

5 Rewrite the sentences on the left starting with the words given. Keep the same meaning.

1 We encouraged him.   We gave ....
2 We finally settled the matter.   We finally reached ....
3 They will inspect it next week.   There will be ....
4 She hesitated at the beginning.   She began after some ....
5 Do you know what the room measures?   Do you know the ....
6 Marc resigned yesterday.   Marc handed in ....
7 We can accommodate three more.   We can provide ....
8 I left after they created the new company. I left after the ....

6 Complete the dialogues with a suitable noun.

1 Were there strong disagreements with the policy? ~ Yes, there were several ....
2 Has anyone put forward a plan?   ~ Yes, there has been one ....
3 Does the company accept this is true? ~ I hope so, but there has been no public ....
4 When will the builders finish?   ~ Next Friday is the earliest date for ....
5 I hear a couple of people were fired. ~ Yes, in actual fact, there were three ....
6 He claimed he didn't steal the bike.   ~ I know, but nobody believes his ....
7 I hope people thanked you for your help. ~ Yes, they all showed their ....
8 Where did you see the article?   ~ It was in last month's ....
9 Did you find or notice anything wrong? ~ No, but problems often escape ....

📖 TEST YOURSELF

A Suffixes that form adjectives

The suffixes **-able**, **-al** and **-ive** can be added to some nouns and verbs to form adjectives. There are sometimes minor spelling changes.

The new **agricultural** scheme is a **cooperative** venture among farmers in South Wales, but it would be **logical** to extend it to the whole of Wales.

The company has become increasingly **profitable** in recent years. It makes very simple **functional** clothes which are hard-wearing and **affordable**.

The army worked throughout the night to put up **protective** barriers, but the **destructive** force of the storm has still caused considerable **structural** damage to the town.

The school is proud of its **progressive educational** policy, but some parents still believe they are being too **selective** regarding entry requirements.

GLOSSARY	
agricultural	connected with the practice of farming
cooperative	doing sth together or working together with others towards a shared aim **cooperation** n
logical	seeming natural, reasonable or sensible **logic** n
profitable	that makes or is likely to make money
functional	(of clothes, furniture, etc.) practical and useful; with little or no decoration
affordable	cheap enough that people can afford it
protective	providing or intended to provide protection
destructive	causing destruction or damage
structural	connected with the way in which sth is built
progressive	in favour of new ideas and modern methods
educational	connected with education
selective	careful about what or who you choose

1 Underline the stress on these words. Use the APP to help you.

agricultural	cooperative	affordable	profitable
progressive	structural	destructive	cooperation

2 Rewrite the sentences using suitable adjectives. Keep the same meaning.

1 They have the means to buy these houses.   These houses ....
2 He's given us his full cooperation.   He's been very ....
3 The company is making a lot of money.   The company is very ....
4 The earthquake caused massive damage.   The earthquake was very ....
5 Parts of the building are damaged.   There was some .... damage.
6 Do they have a policy on farming?   Do they have an .... policy?
7 Is the army careful about who they choose?   Is the army .... ?
8 Did it seem a sensible thing to do?   Did it seem very .... ?

3 Complete the sentences.

1 As a father he has always been very .... towards his children.
2 It's a very forward-thinking company with lots of .... ideas.
3 When we asked for their help, the children were all very ....
4 Their furniture is not beautiful, but it's ....
5 We have to consider the .... needs of all the children, not just the clever ones.
6 Hundreds applied for places, but the company are very ....
7 I fail to see the .... behind his argument. It didn't make any sense at all.
8 I can't organize the talks alone. I need their .... to get everything done.

4 Do you know or can you guess the adjectives formed from these nouns and verbs?

architecture	innovation	believe	experiment	administration
clinic	accept	constitution	communication	excuse

....

....

🗒 TEST YOURSELF

B Suffixes that form verbs

The suffixes **-en**, **-ize** and **-ify** can be added to some nouns and adjectives to form verbs. In most cases, the meaning is easy to guess if you already know the nouns and adjectives.

Verb	Meaning
They need to **strengthen** the bridge	make sth/sb stronger
This story will **weaken** the President's position.	make sb/sth less strong or powerful
I'm going to **shorten** this dress.	make sth shorter
He is **authorized** to make the payments.	give official permision for sth, or for sb to do sth
We need to **maximize** our efficiency.	increase sth as much as possible OPP **minimize**
They **specialize in** computer technology.	be or become an expert in a particular area of work or study
The government must **stabilize** the currency.	become or make sth become firm and steady; become or make sth stable
We have to **clarify** the situation.	make sth clearer and easier to understand
This story will **intensify** speculation.	increase or make sth increase in degree and strength SYN **heighten**
We need to **simplify** the rules.	make sth easier to do or understand
You must **specify** your name in full.	state sth giving an exact measurement, time, instruction, etc.

5 The stress on the verbs above is on the first syllable, with one exception. What is the verb that has the stress on the second syllable? Use the (APP) to help you. ....

6 Write the verbs related to these nouns and adjectives.
1 maximum ....
2 strength ....
3 simple ....
4 authority ....
5 short ....
6 specific ....
7 weak ....
8 stable ....
9 clear ....
10 specialist ....

7 Replace the underlined words with a verb ending in -en, -ize or -ify, and make any other necessary changes in word order. Keep the same meaning.
1 The builder said he would <u>make</u> the wall <u>stronger</u>. ....
2 We need to <u>make</u> our position on this issue <u>clearer</u>. ....
3 He <u>is an expert</u> in this field of medicine. ....
4 The presence of the police <u>heightened</u> the concern in the crowd. ....
5 <u>Do you have the authority</u> to replace the tickets? ....
6 I need to <u>increase</u> the time available to us <u>as much as possible</u>. ....
7 This is too complicated. We need to <u>make</u> the instructions <u>much easier</u> for students. ....
8 You must <u>give</u> the <u>exact</u> details on the form. ....
9 Engineers are trying to <u>make</u> the bridge <u>more stable</u>. ....
10 This result <u>makes</u> her position <u>less strong</u>. ....

8 Do you know or can you guess the verbs related to these adjectives and nouns? Check the meanings in the (APP).
tight / .... legal / .... modern / .... visual / ....
pure / .... economy / .... equal / .... peace / ....

📓 TEST YOURSELF

Many words can be used as a noun or verb with the same base form, and often with a closely related meaning. You will already know many of these words in one or other form.

1 **in the shade**

2 **a bad tackle**

VERBS	NOUNS
He **leads** the race by five seconds.	He has a **lead** of five seconds in the race.
I'm **drafting** a letter.	I'm writing the first **draft** of a letter.
I was **shaded** by the trees.	We sat **in the shade**[1] of the trees.
Our luggage is being **transported** by sea.	They are using sea **transport** for our luggage.
Everyone **cheered** loudly.	There was a loud **cheer** from everyone.
We use a device to **filter** water.	We use a water **filter**.
He **tackled** the player badly.	It was a bad **tackle**[2].
I **paused** for a moment, then continued.	There was a **pause** for a moment, then I continued.
They **tortured** some of the men.	Some of the men suffered **torture**.
We really had to **battle** to win the game.	It was a real **battle** to win the game.

In some cases, the meanings of a noun and verb with the same base form are further apart.

I **deposited** the money in the bank.	I have to leave a **deposit** of £200.
We must **combat** this threat to the environment.	The weapons are used **in combat**.
We need to **extract** as much information as possible.	He asked me to read an **extract**.
I hope to **mate** the two dogs.	Bryn has lots of good **mates**.
We **traced** him to an address in York.	They found no **trace** of the money.
The shareholders have **disputed** the figures.	The countries have had a long **dispute**.

GLOSSARY

lead	the position ahead of others in a race, competition or contest **lead** v
draft	write the first version of sth such as a letter, speech or book **draft** n
transport	take sth/sb from one place to another in a vehicle **transport** n
cheer	a shout of joy, support or praise **cheer** v
filter	a device containing paper, chemicals, etc. that a liquid or gas is passed through in order to remove unwanted material **filter** v
pause	stop talking or doing sth for a short time before continuing **pause** n
torture	the act of causing sb severe pain in order to punish them or make them say sth **torture** v
battle (with/for/ against sth)	a big effort that sb makes to solve a problem or succeed in a difficult situation **battle** v
deposit n	a sum of money that is given as the first part of a larger payment
deposit v	put money into a bank account

combat n	fighting, especially during a time of war
combat v	stop sth harmful or unplesant from happening, or from getting worse
extract n	a short piece from a book, piece of music etc, that gives you an idea what the whole is like
extract v	obtain money, information, etc, often by taking it from sb who is unwilling to give it
mate n inf	a friend
mate v	(of two animals or birds) have sex in order to produce young
trace n	a mark or sign that sth existed or happened
trace v	find sb/sth by looking carefully for them/it SYN **track sb/sth down**
dispute n	an argument or a disagreement between two people, groups or countries
dispute v	question whether sth is true and valid

1 Underline the stress on these words. Use the APP to help you.

transport *n*	transport *v*	combat *n, v*	extract *n*
extract *v*	deposit *n, v*	dispute *n, v*	torture *n, v*

2 Match 1–8 with a–h

1	He tackled	....		**a**	for a moment, then carried on.
2	She drafted	....		**b**	loudly when they scored.
3	He paused	....		**c**	the player without the ball.
4	She sat	....		**d**	some distant members of her family.
5	He deposited	....		**e**	with alcoholism for years.
6	She's traced	....		**f**	a couple of emails.
7	He battled	....		**g**	in the shade to stay cool.
8	She cheered	....		**h**	most of the money in a bank account.

3 Rewrite these sentences using the noun instead of the underlined verb.

1 The speaker <u>paused</u>, then sat down.　　There ....
2 The table was completely <u>shaded</u>.　　The table ....
3 We have a device to <u>filter</u> the oil.　　We have ....
4 The Liberals are <u>leading</u> by five points.　　The Liberals ....
5 We could hear the crowd <u>cheering</u>.　　We could ....
6 They <u>tortured</u> two of the prisoners.　　Two of the prisoners ....
7 How will they <u>transport</u> the goods?　　What .... ?
8 It will be a <u>battle</u> to get the idea approved.　　They will ....

4 Complete the sentences with a suitable noun or verb.

1 He read a short .... from his new play.
2 I'd like you to meet a .... of mine. His name is Patrick.
3 I'm trying to .... the family who used to live in our house.
4 The landlord wants a .... of one month's rent.
5 Several soldiers were killed or wounded in ....
6 Police recovered the money but there was no .... of the stolen jewellery.
7 Doctors are looking for a way to .... the spread of the disease.
8 Where can I .... the money?
9 The government have released the figures, but the opposition are .... them.
10 The player was .... just outside the penalty area.

5 ⬛ ABOUT YOU Write answers to the questions, or talk to another student.

1 Who is your best mate? ....
2 Have you ever been in dispute with an organization. If so, what was it about? ....
3 Have you ever tried to trace your family history? ....
4 Have you ever had to battle really hard to achieve something? If so, what? ....
5 When was the last time you deposited money in a bank account? How much was it for? ....
6 Do you prefer sitting in the sun or in the shade? Why? ....
7 Do you often cheer at sports events or social events? If so, what particular events? ....
8 Have you ever had to pay a deposit for something? If so, what, and when? ....

6 Look at this list of verbs. Which ones can also be used as nouns with the same form?

abuse	accept	alert	adjust	applaud
support	bid	bow	coincide	chase

....
....

TEST YOURSELF

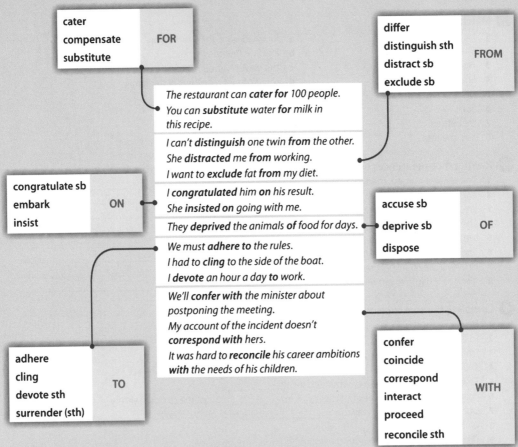

cater compensate substitute	FOR

differ distinguish sth distract sb exclude sb	FROM

The restaurant can **cater for** 100 people.
You can **substitute** water **for** milk in this recipe.

I can't **distinguish** one twin **from** the other.
She **distracted** me **from** working.
I want to **exclude** fat **from** my diet.

congratulate sb embark insist	ON

I **congratulated** him **on** his result.
She **insisted on** going with me.

They **deprived** the animals **of** food for days.

accuse sb deprive sb dispose	OF

We must **adhere to** the rules.
I had to **cling to** the side of the boat.
I **devote** an hour a day **to** work.

We'll **confer with** the minister about postponing the meeting.
My account of the incident doesn't **correspond with** hers.
It was hard to **reconcile** his career ambitions **with** the needs of his children.

adhere cling devote sth surrender (sth)	TO

confer coincide correspond interact proceed reconcile sth	WITH

GLOSSARY

confer (with sb) (on/about sth) *formal* discuss sth with sb in order to exchange opinions or get advice

interact (with sb) communicate with sb, especially when you are with them

proceed (with sth) continue doing sth that has already started

coincide (with sth) (of two or more events) take place at the same time

correspond (with sth) be the same as or match sth

reconcile sth (with sth) find an acceptable way of dealing with two or more ideas, needs, etc. that seem to be opposed to each other

adhere to sth *formal* behave according to a particular law, rule, set of instructions, etc.

surrender (to sb) admit you have been defeated and want to stop fighting

cling (on) to sth/sb hold on tightly to sth/sb

devote sth to sth give an amount of time, attention, etc. to sth

deprive sb/sth of sth prevent sb from having or doing sth, especially sth important

dispose of sth get rid of sth that you do not want or cannot keep

accuse sb (of sth) say that sb has done sth wrong or is guilty of sth

distinguish sth (from sth) recognize the difference between two people or things

exclude (sth from sth) deliberately not include sth in what you are doing

differ (from sth/sb) be different from sth/sb

distract sb/sth (from sth) take sb's attention away from what they are trying to do

insist (on sth / doing sth) demand that sth happens or that sb do something

embark on sth *formal* start to do sth new or difficult

congratulate sb (on sth) tell sb you are pleased about their success

cater for sth/sb provide food and drinks for a social event

compensate sb (for sth) provide sth good to balance or reduce the bad effects of damage, loss, etc. SYN **make up for sth**

substitute (sth) (for sth/sb) take the place of sth/sb; use sth/sb instead of sth/sb else

1 Underline the stress on these words. Use the 🅐🅟🅟 to help you.0

| proceed | interact | exclude | correspond | embark |
| reconcile | congratulate | distinguish | adhere | substitute |

2 Organize the verbs below into two groups: verbs which have a positive sense or suggest moving forward; and verbs which have a more negative sense or suggest that something is being removed.

| deprive | embark | interact | dispose | exclude |
| congratulate | proceed | surrender | confer | reconcile |

MORE POSITIVE   **MORE NEGATIVE**

....

....

....

3 Complete the sentences with the correct preposition.

1   It wasn't necessary but he insisted .... helping us.
2   Their views differ .... mine.
3   The children were deprived .... adequate food and clothing.
4   This letter corresponds .... what they said in their email.
5   The party will coincide .... my birthday.
6   I couldn't distinguish one trumpet .... another.
7   They accused me .... lying.
8   When are the team planning to embark .... their polar expedition?

4 Replace the underlined word(s) with another word that keeps the same meaning.

1   I will have to <u>discuss this</u> with colleagues before I can give you an answer.   ....
2   My aunt has for years <u>given</u> all her time to her sick elderly father.   ....
3   I can't <u>tell</u> an American accent from a Canadian one.   ....
4   We can <u>carry on</u> with our plan.   ....
5   It's difficult to <u>communicate</u> with so many children at the same time.   ....
6   We are going to <u>get rid</u> of that furniture.   ....
7   I can't <u>provide food and drink</u> for that many people.   ....
8   We must <u>stick firmly</u> to the rules and regulations set by the committee.   ....
9   The lovely cucumbers we've grown will <u>make up</u> for the tomatoes we had to throw away.   ....
10 The little boy had to <u>hold on tightly</u> to his mother's coat.   ....

5 Complete the sentences with the correct verb.

1   Most of the rebel soldiers have .... to the army and are now prisoners.
2   How do you .... increased air travel with the need to protect the environment?
3   When my brother plays loud music, it really .... me from working.
4   It was my treat, and I .... on paying for everything.
5   If you are .... of certain vitamins, your health will eventually suffer.
6   I .... Sarah on her exam results. She was very pleased.
7   Nothing can really .... for the loss of a loved one.
8   They often .... me from their conversations. It makes me feel very lonely.
9   The type of cheese isn't important: you can .... cheddar for parmesan.
10 Both parents .... all of their free time to their children.

6 Write the prepositions that usually follow these verbs. They are not only the prepositions used above, but the verbs have been taught elsewhere in this book. Use the Word List if necessary.

cope .... sth	relate .... sb	subtract sth .... sth
impose sth .... sb	stare .... sb	reflect .... sth
stem .... sth	opt .... sth	

📖 TEST YOURSELF

Do you usually have **confidence in** your ability to do things?

Should you always **take advantage of** opportunities to earn more money?

Is it true that any **exposure to** radiation can be harmful?

Do you need **reminders of** people's birthdays, or do you always remember them?

Would you like greater **involvement in** politics or charity work?

Is it true there is no **substitute for** hard work if you want to be successful?

With the exception of a flat or car, what is the most expensive thing you've ever bought?

If the government imposed **limitations on** air travel for environmental reasons, would you support that?

Do you think society is better since the **emergence of** social media?

Is there anyone that you feel **contempt for**?

GLOSSARY	
confidence (in sth/sb)	the feeling that you can trust, believe in and be sure about the abilities or good qualities of sb/sth
take advantage of sth	make use of sth well; make use of an opportunity
exposure (to sth)	the state of being in a place or situation where there is usually no protection from sth harmful or unpleasant
reminder (of sth)	sth that makes you think about or remember sb/sth that you have forgotten, would like to forget or might accidentally forget
involvement (in sth)	the act of participating in sth and giving time to it
substitute for sth	a person or thing that you use or have instead of one you normally use or have
with the exception of sth	except; not including
limitation (on sth)	a rule, fact or condition that limits sth SYN **restraint (on sth)**
emergence (of sth)	the fact of starting to exist or become known for the first time
contempt (for sb/sth)	the feeling that sb/sth is without value and deserves no respect

1 **Circle the correct preposition.**

1 the emergence *of* / *for* democracy
2 restraints *of* / *on* the use of alcohol
3 my involvement *on* / *in* the project
4 take advantage *of* / *for* the sun
5 no substitute *in* / *for* love
6 limitations *on* / *in* the use of cars
7 a reminder *to* / *of* how dangerous cars are
8 confidence *on* / *in* the justice system

2 **Complete the dialogues with a suitable noun.**

1 Can they work 12 hours a day? ~ No, there are _____ on the number of hours they are permitted to work.
2 Did everyone do their homework? ~ Yes, with the _____ of Reuben, as usual.
3 Clara's very well qualified. ~ I agree, but there's no _____ for practical experience.
4 There are still guards outside. ~ Indeed. It's a _____ of the danger still around us.
5 Luca thinks he's going to fail the test. ~ That boy has no _____ in his abilities.
6 Do you use sunblock? ~ Yes, I'm worried about _____ to too much sun.
7 Jonas doesn't respect even his own MP. ~ I agree. He shows complete _____ for Parliament.
8 They've given me a great opportunity. ~ Yes, make sure you take _____ of it.

3 **Complete the sentences with the correct noun and preposition.**

1 Living near the nuclear plant, I'm worried about _____ _____ radiation.
2 Teachers generally encourage parents' _____ _____ their children's education.
3 We are seeing the _____ _____ new democracies around the world.
4 The government have imposed serious _____ _____ public spending during the crisis.
5 We enjoyed the meal, with the _____ _____ Carla, who hated every mouthful.
6 The critic was very rude and showed _____ _____ the director's new ideas.
7 The smashed car on the side of the road is a _____ _____ the dangers of drinking and driving.
8 I'm planning to take _____ _____ of our neighbours' absence to hold a big party.

4 ABOUT YOU **What are your answers to the questions at the top of the page? Write them down, or ask another student.**

 TEST YOURSELF

You are more **liable to** injury if you don't warm up before exercise.

The air traffic controllers appear **intent on** causing maximum disruption, and most flights will be **subject to** long delays.

Some of the new computers are no longer **compatible with** existing software and, as a result, technological problems are now **inherent in** the system.

Some of the workers remain **resistant to** change, but they are no longer **representative of** the majority.

Jasmina is **dedicated to** her husband; he is totally **dependent on** her.

I am very **sceptical of** the claim that a single vaccination could make people **immune to** a wide range of diseases.

Eight kilometres is roughly **equivalent to** five miles.

GLOSSARY

liable (to sth)	likely to be affected by sth	**representative of sth/sb**	typical of a particular group or thing
intent (on/upon sth / doing sth)	determined to do sth	**dedicated (to sb/sth)**	working hard at sth because it is very important to you
subject (to sth)	likely to be affected by sth, especially sth bad	**dependent on sb/sth**	needing sb/sth in order to survive or be successful
compatible (with sth)	able to be used or exist with sth without causing problems	**sceptical (of/ about sth/sb)**	having doubts that a claim or statement is true or that sth will happen
inherent (in sth/sb)	that is a basic or permanent part of sth/sb and that cannot be removed	**immune (to sth)**	that cannot catch or be affected by a particular illness or disease
resistant (to sth)	opposed to sth and not wanting it to happen	**equivalent to sth**	equal in number amount etc, to sth else

1 Underline the stress on these words. Use the ⒶⓅⓅ to help you.

intent   subject   compatible   inherent   resistant   liable

representative   dedicated   dependent   sceptical   immune

2 Complete the prepositions.

1 She's dedicated .... her job.
2 I'm sceptical .... this article.
3 Is he representative .... the group?
4 Why is he so dependent .... them?
5 The timetable is subject .... change.
6 He's intent .... completing this task.

7 20% is equivalent .... a fifth.
8 The company is resistant .... new ideas.
9 This app is not compatible .... my device.
10 There are risks inherent .... his plan.

3 True or false? Write *T* or *F*. If false, say why.

1 Someone who is immune to a disease has a good chance of getting it.   ....
2 A feature which is inherent in a system can be removed from it.   ....
3 Software which is compatible with a computer can easily be used with it.   ....
4 Someone who is dedicated to their work usually leaves the office early.   ....
5 If an agreement is subject to approval, it is definitely going to happen.   ....
6 If someone is dependent on you, they need you to help them survive.   ....
7 A qualification that is equivalent to a degree is higher than a degree.   ....
8 An area which is liable to flooding is very likely to flood.   ....

4 Replace the underlined words with an adjective and preposition. Make any other changes that are necessary.

1 Transport in this area is <u>likely to be affected by</u> disruption because of road works.
2 Some of the players were <u>opposed to</u> the system brought in by the new manager.
3 Because of vaccinations, most people are <u>unlikely to catch</u> measles.
4 2.5cm is <u>the same as</u> one inch.

5 The manager is <u>determined to</u> ensure that the players are well looked after.
6 I'm rather <u>doubtful about</u> conspiracy theories: the world just isn't that well organized.
7 Do you think the results of the survey are <u>typical of</u> the population as a whole?
8 Some of the techniques are <u>basic features of</u> this particular art form.

A Phrases with *at*, *in*, *on* and *by*

I wrote out the paragraph **in full**.
Really? You didn't do that **by choice**, did you?
Certainly not. I was made to do it.

I can normally get theatre work **on the basis of** my experience, but **at present** there's absolutely nothing, so I've been helping out behind the bar at my local pub. I'm hoping something will come up **in the near future**, but it's **by no means** certain.

Do you have to travel **at short notice**?
Yes, I get a call and have to leave **at once**.

You didn't ignore Suki **on purpose**, did you?
No, Suki and I are **on good terms**, but I just didn't see her.

GLOSSARY	
in full	including the whole of sth
by choice	because you have chosen (to do sth)
on the basis of sth	because of sth
at present	now; at the moment
in the near future	soon
by no means	not at all
at short notice	with very little warning ALSO **at a moment's notice**
at once	immediately SYN **right away**, **straight away**
on purpose	not by accident; deliberately
on good/friendly/ bad, etc. terms (with sb)	have a good/friendly/bad, etc. relationship (with sb)

1 Circle the correct word.

1 He came *in / at* a moment's notice.
2 I'm sure she did it *by / on* purpose.
3 She's busy *at / in* present.
4 I completed the application *in / by* full.
5 I got the job *on / in* the basis of my qualifications.
6 We have to leave right *way / away*.
7 They're not *on / in* friendly terms.
8 The solution is *at / by* no means clear.

2 Replace the underlined words with a prepositional phrase. Keep the same meaning.

1 We can give you an appointment <u>with very little warning</u>.
2 The doctor is very busy <u>right now</u>, but he'll ring you later.
3 They gave me the job <u>because</u> of my qualifications.
4 The papers think that Ellis will win the election, but it is <u>not at all</u> certain.
5 Call the emergency services <u>immediately</u> if you think you are in danger.
6 It is believed that the fire was started <u>deliberately</u> in order to claim insurance.
7 Louise is moving to the countryside <u>because she wants to</u>, not because she has to.
8 Are the brothers <u>getting on well</u> these days, or are they still arguing?

3 Complete the sentences with a suitable prepositional phrase.

1 I drive to work, but I'd never do it .... if I could avoid it.
2 When it is ready, take the pie out of the oven and serve it ....
3 I may need more teachers soon, but .... we're OK.
4 We haven't made a profit yet, but we're hoping to do so ....
5 I left the money on the table .... to see if Kia would steal it, but she didn't.
6 Luke and Dan aren't speaking to each other. I don't know why they're .... with each other.
7 It may be difficult to find someone to do the job .... , but we'll try.
8 You can't just put your initials. You have to write your name ....
9 I finally managed to calm them down, but it was .... easy.
10 The products were all very similar so I just chose one .... price.

 TEST YOURSELF

B Phrases in headlines

Government **out of touch with** public mood

Tunnel named **in honour of** football coach

Mystery illness **on board giant** cruise ship

Gene therapy trial **on hold**

COUPLE FOUND **IN POSSESSION OF** COCAINE

COMPANY **UNDER INVESTIGATION** FOR USING WORKERS AS **SLAVE LABOUR**

TRAFFIC FLOW IMPROVED **BY MEANS OF** BETTER PUBLIC TRANSPORT

Unions work hard to keep government **in office**

Film release delayed **out of respect for bereaved** family

GLOSSARY

out of touch (with sth)	no longer having recent knowledge or information about sth
tunnel	a passage built underground, e.g. to allow a road or railway to pass through
in honour of sb/sth	in order to show respect and admiration for sb/sth
on board	on or in a ship, an aircraft or a train
giant	very large **giant** *n* a very large and powerful organization
on hold	delayed until a later time or date
in possession of sth *formal*	having or holding sth
slave labour	work that is done by slaves. A **slave** is a person who is owned by another person and forced to work for them: **treat sb like a slave**
by means of sth *formal*	with the help of sth
in office	in a position of authority, especially in government ALSO **in power**
out of respect (for sb)	done because you care for sb/sth or think they are important
bereaved	If sb is **bereaved**, a close friend or relative has recently died.

SPOTLIGHT *under*

Under can mean 'in the process of something'.
under investigation in the process of being investigated
Other examples are:
under discussion **under construction** **under attack**

---

4 Combine the prepositions on the left with the nouns on the right to form eight phrases. You can use some of the prepositions more than once.

in	under		hold	investigation	respect	possession of
by	on	out of	office	attack	touch	means of

....

....

5 Circle the words which are possible.
1 The government has been *in power / on board / in office* for five years.
2 Following the accusations of slave labour, several men are now *under investigation / under construction / on hold*.
3 The suspect was found *in honour of / in possession of / by means of* stolen goods.
4 I attended the ceremony *in honour of / out of respect for / out of touch with* those who died.
5 She is *out touch with / in possession of / under attack* the feelings of the general public.
6 The bridge is *under attack / under discussion / under construction*.

6 Complete the sentences.
1 We have had to put our holiday plans on .... for the moment because of work.
2 Hundreds came to the funeral out of .... for the .... family.
3 I can't help as I'm really out of .... with this area of research nowadays.
4 If you are caught in .... of drugs, you will be in trouble.
5 The mile-long .... running under Solsbury Hill has been under .... for years and is still not finished.
6 He works for a .... multinational company, with offices in 12 countries.
7 She opened the can by .... of a special device designed for the disabled.
8 The servants are treated like .... in that house. It's shocking.
9 The aircraft can take off when everyone is on ....
10 The statue is in .... of Ada Lovelace, who was the first computer programmer.

 TEST YOURSELF

A Synonyms and opposites

Marcus Campion was a man of **exceptional** talent, who had been one of the most **eminent** lawyers of his generation. He was not a **conventional** lawyer, though, and had a reputation for defending men and women accused of the most **brutal** crimes. However, even he felt uneasy as he considered his latest case. 'This Mabbutt is a **bizarre** character, and I admit I haven't formed a wholly **favourable** impression of him,' remarked Campion to his colleagues. "But I'm still **reluctant** to accept he might've killed his own children just to take revenge on their mother." Campion had defended **wicked** men in the past, but this was a most **disturbing** case, and he sat down to start preparing his case with a heavy heart.

GLOSSARY

exceptional	unusually good SYN **outstanding**
conventional	tending to follow what is done or considered acceptable by society in general OPP **unconventional**
brutal	violent and cruel SYN **vicious**; **brutality** n
bizarre	very strange and unusual SYN **weird**, **peculiar**
favourable	making people have a good opinion of sb/sth OPP **unfavourable**
reluctant	hesitating before doing sth because you don't want to do it or you are not sure it is the right thing to do SYN **unwilling** OPP **willing**
wicked	bad and morally wrong SYN **evil**
disturbing	making you feel anxious and upset or shocked SYN **upsetting**

SPOTLIGHT *eminent and notorious*

Someone who is **eminent** is famous and respected, often for being good at a profession. If someone or something is **notorious**, they are / it is famous for being bad. SYN **infamous**
- *a notorious criminal*

1 Underline the stress on these words. Use the APP to help you.

brutal	bizarre	favourable	upsetting	peculiar	conventional
reluctant	vicious	outstanding	eminent	notorious	infamous

2 Circle the words which have a positive meaning.

outstanding	brutal	notorious	favourable	wicked	weird	
disturbing	upsetting	eminent	evil	exceptional	vicious	infamous

3 Find seven pairs of synonyms in the box.

evil	exceptional	brutal	reluctant	wicked	notorious	bizarre
disturbing	infamous	unwilling	outstanding	vicious	upsetting	weird

.... / .... / .... / ....
.... / .... / .... / ....
.... / ....

4 Complete the sentences.

1 He was an .... man and responsible for the deaths of many innocent people.
2 There's a .... story in the paper about a man who lives underwater.
3 She's an .... scientist as well as being a well-known writer.
4 It's become a/an .... road because of the number of fatal accidents on it.
5 To see my sister shouting and screaming at me like that was very ....
6 He lives in a wooden hut without any electricity; it's a very .... lifestyle.
7 He had an .... game, and was easily the best player on the pitch.
8 It was a .... attack, and the man needed 12 stitches for a head wound.
9 I was .... to help, but I wish they'd made clear how big the job was.
10 It's a fairly .... family: husband, wife and two children.

🗄 TEST YOURSELF

B Adjectives easily confused

Adjective	Examples	Meaning
comparable	The economic situation in this country is not really **comparable** to China.	similar to another thing, situation or person, and able to be compared to it
comparative	I've produced a **comparative** analysis of the two social care systems.	connected with studying things to find out how similar or different they are
naked	The child was almost **naked**.	not wearing clothes
bare	They walked in **bare** feet along the beach.	(of a part of the body) not covered by clothes: **bare arms/legs**
deadly	It's a **deadly** snake.	causing or likely to cause death
deathly	There was a **deathly** silence in the room.	like a dead person; suggesting death
comprehensive	I need a **comprehensive** list of the hotels.	full, and including all necessary details
comprehensible	It's a **comprehensible** story.	able to be understood OPP **incomprehensible**
super	We had a **super** meal at Gino's.	inf, becoming old-fashioned extremely good
superb	Kaufmann's performance was **superb**.	excellent; of very high quality
superior	This model is **superior to** the others.	greater or better in quality than sth/sb else
childlike	My brother has a **childlike** enthusiasm.	approving having qualities typical of a child
childish	My sister's behaviour is very **childish**.	disapproving behaving in a silly way
tasty	The dish was really **tasty**.	(of food) full of flavour OPP **tasteless**
tasteful	It's a very **tasteful** room.	(of clothes, furniture, etc.) attractive and of good quality OPP **tasteless**

5 **Correct the mistakes. Two sentences have no mistakes.**

1 In some countries, women can't walk around with naked arms. ....
2 A comparative house in the south would cost twice as much. ....
3 My mother always wears very tasteful clothes. ....
4 The police found a bare body in the lake. ....
5 Some of these plants can be deathly and kill you in minutes. ....
6 I thought the beds were far super in the first hotel we stayed at. ....
7 He can be very childish if he doesn't get his way – it's very annoying. ....
8 The food is always very tasteful at Amy's. ....

6 **Complete the sentences. The words in capitals at the end will give you some help.**

1 I've done some research on the subject, but we'll have to wait for a more .... study.   COMPLETE
2 She still has a .... quality about her, which is lovely.   INNOCENT
3 I really enjoyed the orchestra, and the soloist was ....   EXCELLENT
4 The woman was .... pale and looked extremely unwell.   LIKE A DEAD PERSON
5 Anyone could follow her instructions: they were entirely ....   EASY TO UNDERSTAND
6 The soup was awful: very thin and ....   WITH NO FLAVOUR

7 **Complete the questions, then write your answers, or talk to another student.**   ABOUT YOU

1 Why do you think people might study .... religion? ....
2 What type of place are you forbidden to enter with .... arms or legs? ....
3 Why do some people find the instructions for electronic gadgets .... ? ....
4 What kind of decoration in a home do you consider .... ? ....
5 Why do you think adults sometimes suddenly behave in a .... way? ....
6 Why do some people believe that a vegetarian diet is .... to a meat diet? ....
7 Where might it be acceptable for someone to swim in the sea .... ? ....
8 Where might you expect to see a .... spider? ....

TEST YOURSELF

100) Adverbs

A Commenting

A I can't believe that Maurice still **commutes** to London every day – it's an awful journey.

B I know. But **apparently** he really likes his job. And **presumably** he earns a lot more working in London.

A True. **Ultimately** though, I think he does it more for his career than the money.

B **Fair enough.**

A **Frankly**, I think he's mad.

B I don't **entirely** agree with you.

A **Basically** that is where we are different. For us family life is more important, but for Maurice, his career means **practically** everything to him.

B Yes, I know. **Strangely**, he wasn't all that ambitious when we were at school.

GLOSSARY	
commute	travel regularly by train, car, etc. between your home and your place of work **commuting** n
apparently	according to what you have heard or read SYN **evidently**
presumably	used to say that you think sth is probably true
ultimately	finally; when everything has been considered
fair enough *inf*	used to say that an idea or suggestion seems reasonable
frankly	used to show that you are saying what you really think about sth SYN **to be (perfectly) honest**
entirely	in every way possible; completely: *I **entirely** agree. It's **entirely** different.*
basically	used when giving the most important fact SYN **essentially**
practically	almost SYN **virtually**
strangely (enough)	used to show that sth is surprising SYN **oddly (enough)**, **curiously (enough)**

1 **Circle the correct answer(s). Both answers may be possible.**

1 He promised to come, so *apparently / presumably* he'll turn up later.
2 The boys are coming home *basically / essentially* because they've run out of money
3 The class are consulted but *ultimately / curiously* the teacher makes the final decision.
4 Others disagree, but *entirely / frankly* I thought it was an excellent idea.
5 We're expecting *virtually / practically* everyone to be there.
6 I don't know if the books will help us but *practically / apparently* we have to read them.

2 **Replace the underlined word(s) with another word or phrase that keeps the same meaning.**

1 Sian rang a couple of minutes ago. <u>Apparently</u>, the others missed the train. ....
2 They said the restaurant was always busy, but <u>surprisingly</u> it was almost empty. ....
3 <u>Virtually</u> all the shops were closed when I got into town. ....
4 There are various options, but <u>in the end</u> we will have to see what is most practical. ....
5 We got there early <u>essentially</u> because we weren't sure when it started. ....
6 I got her a ticket but <u>frankly</u>, I don't think she's interested. ....
7 I thought Will's comments were <u>quite reasonable</u>. ....
8 Entry is free, so <u>it's likely</u> they will all be here. ....

3 **Complete the sentences with a suitable word or phrase.**

1 .... we can't get tickets until tomorrow. That's what he told me.
2 Max wanted to talk about salaries as well, but that's an .... different matter.
3 She said she'd come if she can finish work early. ~ OK, that's ....
4 I know he won't be happy, but .... I don't care what he thinks.
5 I usually feel nervous before I give a talk, but .... I felt fine today.
6 I know they missed yesterday's class but .... they'll be here today.
7 The bar is usually very busy, but today it was .... empty.
8 I try to help the boys but .... they are responsible for their actions.

4 ABOUT YOU **Would you be prepared to spend more than two hours a day commuting to work if it gave you the opportunity for a better job and more money? Write your answer, or talk to another student.**

 TEST YOURSELF

B Multiple meanings

I **briefly**[1] worked in the tax office.

I **briefly**[2] explained the **concept** to him.

She said she came to my training **session purely** out of interest, but that wasn't **strictly**[1] true.

Smoking is **strictly**[2] prohibited in here.

I don't know **precisely**[1] how it happened, but I could see she was **truly**[1] sorry about it.

He's very young; that's **precisely**[2] why he needs my help.

She was a **truly**[2] remarkable woman.

The restaurant is **invariably** full, but it's **primarily** for tourists.

Do go and see the play: the acting was **simply**[1] brilliant.

He explained the rules **simply**[2] and clearly.

GLOSSARY	
briefly	**1** for a short time **2** in a few words
concept	an idea or principle that is connected with sth abstract
session	a period of time that is spent doing a particular activity
purely	completely and only: *purely by chance*
strictly	**1** exactly and completely **2** used to emphasize that sth must happen in all circumstances
precisely	**1** exactly and correctly **2** used to emphasize that sth is very true or obvious
truly	**1** sincerely **2** really
invariably	used to emphasize that sth is always true or always happens
primarily	mainly SYN **chiefly**, **predominantly**
simply	**1** used to emphasize a statement SYN **absolutely** **2** in a way that is easy to understand

5 Replace the underlined word(s) with another word that keeps the same meaning.

1 I did it <u>only</u> for the money. ....
2 He is <u>sincerely</u> sorry. ....
3 Her view was <u>exactly</u> the same as mine. ....
4 He's <u>mainly</u> vegetarian. ....
5 I went there <u>for a short time</u>. ....
6 He is <u>always</u> late. ....
7 Gravity is a difficult <u>principle</u> to understand. ....
8 I do about three forty-minute <u>periods of activity</u> in the gym each week. ....
9 What I said wasn't <u>exactly and completely</u> true. ....

6 Circle the correct answer(s). More than one may be possible.

1 She studies physics *chiefly / invariably / purely* because she enjoys it.
2 I'm not sure she is being *strictly / precisely / briefly* honest.
3 I was in town and met her *invariably / primarily / purely* by chance.
4 He spoke *purely / briefly / chiefly* about his childhood.
5 I'm always punctual, but she's *precisely / invariably / primarily* late.
6 His voice is *simply / predominantly / truly* remarkable.
7 Camping here is *truly / purely / strictly* forbidden.
8 He explains the procedure *simply / purely / strictly*, so you know exactly what you have to do.

7 Complete the sentences with a suitable adverb.

1 They do sell some records, but it's .... a bookshop.
2 I'm unlucky with the weather. It .... rains when I go on holiday.
3 She came to stay with us .... last year – just for a few days.
4 I care about them. That's .... why I'm always worried if they're late.
5 They talked .... about the holiday and didn't say much.
6 I was .... sorry to hear about her mother's accident.
7 Pavel knows .... what we need, so he's the best person to do the job.
8 We didn't have time to go back and help; it was .... impossible.
9 We stayed in the same hotel .... by chance.
10 Fishing is .... forbidden along this part of the river.

TEST YOURSELF

Answer key

Unit 1

1
1. accurate
2. synonym
3. synonymous
4. ambiguous
5. ambiguity
6. interpret
7. interpretation
8. self-explanatory

2
1. D
2. S (*Pupils are usually at primary school.*)
3. D
4. S
5. S
6. D
7. S
8. D

3
1. ambiguity
2. precision
3. synonymous
4. accuracy
5. interpretation
6. self-explanatory
7. virtually

4
1. *Huge* means 'very big/large'.
2. *Acquire* is much more restricted because it has one main sense. *Get* has many different meanings.
3. Yes, it is self-explanatory: a waiting room is a room where people wait, e.g. in a railway station or a doctor's surgery.
4. The two words are not exactly synonymous because *slim* means 'thin in a positive way', whereas *thin* is often used to suggest that someone needs to put on more weight, so it is not used positively.
5. It's not entirely accurate because a pupil could be at a secondary school or a primary school, and it's actually more common to use the word about children at primary school.
6. *Pick up* has different senses, so the sentence could mean: 1) I physically picked up the bag from the ground, a chair, etc, or 2) I collected the bag from somewhere.

5 **Negative words**: insulting, disapproving, offensive, inappropriate, swearing

Some **slang** words may also have a negative meaning, but most slang is not negative.

Irony may also be used with a negative intention, but not usually.

6
1. literal
2. Both are possible.
3. Irony
4. gold
5. inappropriate
6. ironic
7. an insult
8. offensive

7
1. disapproving
2. figuratively/ metaphorically
3. insulting/offensive
4. slang
5. golden
6. metaphor
7. swore
8. literally

Unit 2

1
1. You're not gonna believe this but I lost.
2. How can I get out of doing this homework?
3. I'm in two minds about going to Greece.
4. University is the last thing on my mind.
5. It was sweet of him to take us.

2
1. second thoughts
2. on my mind
3. get out of
4. believe this
5. sweet
6. two minds
7. struck
8. tied up
9. crawling
10. thick

3
1. crawling
2. thick
3. sweet
4. tied up
5. striking
6. get out of
7. thought
8. mind

4
1. How did you **get** him
2. These batteries **come** in
3. that will **make** it
4. fishing that **brings** most people
5. I'll **see** what they think
6. it won't **keep** after today
7. to **put** them into words
8. that will **do** for

5
1. brings
2. get
3. come
4. leave
5. see
6. do
7. make
8. leave
9. see
10. get
11. push

Unit 3

1 proble*ma*tic like*li*hood require*me*nt benefit bene*fi*cial worth*while* recog*ni*tion compa*ra*ble apo*lo*gize irre*pla*ceable apolo*ge*tic house*hold* hu*ma*nity humani*ta*rian po*sse*ss

2
1. irreplaceable
2. inclusive
3. noticeable
4. comparable
5. humanitarian
6. worthwhile
7. apologetic
8. housing

3
1. He was a worthy winner.
2. What is the likelihood (that) we'll win? (*also possible*: How likely is it (that) …?)
3. Most households earn more than in the past.
4. Is it noticeable that he's lost a lot of weight?
5. It's an interesting vase but it's worthless.
6. There is no recognition of the importance of the measures.
7. It was a very worthwhile conference.
8. The tablets were beneficial.

4
1. housing
2. guidelines
3. apologetic
4. inclusive
5. problematic
6. humanity
7. replacement
8. handling

5
1. guidance
2. humanitarian
3. certainty
4. inclusion
5. possesses
6. mistook
7. comparable
8. uncertainty

6 *possible answers, from somebody in the UK:*
1. In England they do, and should make it clear if they don't.
2. Yes, we haven't built enough new homes for many years, and there is now a shortage in some parts of the country.
3. They are fairly comparable with prices in other European countries, though some countries are cheaper, e.g. Portugal, and some are more expensive, e.g. Norway.
4. Yes, you normally have to achieve certain grades in your A level examinations. The grades will often depend on the university you want to go to, and the subject you want to study.
5. Though there have been some improvements over the last forty years, unfortunately, racism is still a problem.
6. I don't really have any degree of certainty about my future career, but I'm optimistic.

Unit 4

1 1 Yes 3 No 5 No 7 Yes
    2 Yes 4 Yes 6 No 8 No

2 1 treats them with respect
    2 keep it a secret
    3 spreading a rumour
    4 get the credit
    5 roared with laughter
    6 set a good example; make an effort
    7 broke the news
    8 passes the buck; take the blame
    9 take responsibility

3 **take**: control of sth; pleasure in doing sth; tablets; a look at sth
    make: an impression, a profit, an offer; a noise
    set: a limit; sth on fire; the standard

4 1 c 3 f 5 b 7 d
    2 h 4 e 6 g 8 a

5 1 perfect example 4 brief description
    2 strong accent 5 exact opposite
    3 principal concern 6 chaos OR nonsense

6 1 utter nonsense
    2 complete opposite
    3 narrow escape
    4 main concern
    5 pure silk/cotton, etc.
    6 brief/detailed description
    7 familiar faces
    8 strong accent
    9 close friends
   10 utter chaos

Unit 5

1 1 cut 5 expectancy
    2 polish/varnish 6 pin
    3 self- 7 clips
    4 barbed 8 spare

2 1 tongue 5 cuts
    2 licence 6 model
    3 certificate 7 nail
    4 loyalty 8 junk

3 *possible answers, for a British person*:
    1 My mother tongue is English. I also speak reasonable Spanish and some French.
    2 Yes, just over ten years.
    3 I think it's in one of the drawers of my bedside table.
    4 Yes, I have a loyalty card for one department store and also one for a café I use a lot.
    5 Yes, I often take a shortcut when I'm walking into town, and another one when I'm driving towards the motorway about ten miles from where I live.
    6 I think my older brother has been the most influential role model in my life so far.
    7 No, I don't.
    8 I try not to eat junk food. I don't buy it to eat at home, but I sometimes eat junk food when I'm out and I'm hungry, such as fish and chips or a hamburger.

4   greetings card (= a card with a picture on the front and a message inside that you send to sb on a particular occasion such as a birthday) ; identity card; credit card; railcard; postcard; debit card; SIM card (= a plastic card inside a mobile phone that stores information to identify the phone and person using it); gift card (= a card that is worth a particular amount of money that can be exchanged for goods and services, usually given to sb as a gift)
        bus pass
        boarding pass/card

5 1 no use 4 last a long time
    2 at the last possible moment 5 exhausted
    3 determined 6 forgetful

6 long-standing, worn out, well behaved, narrow-minded, self-righteous, bad-tempered

7 1 self-righteous
    2 last-minute
    3 long-standing
    4 single-minded
    5 bad-tempered
    6 broad-minded/open-minded

8 well known; well behaved; well dressed (= wearing attractive clothes); well informed (= knowing a lot about a particular subject)
    self-confident; self-conscious (= worrying about what others think of you); self-service (of restaurants); self-employed

Unit 6

1 1 counting (3)
    2 reflect (4)
    3 absorbed (1)
    4 counted (2)
    5 absorb (4)
    6 counts (1)
    7 reflected (1)

2 1 do 5 comment
    2 count 6 circumstances
    3 take 7 favour
    4 favour 8 owes

3 1 We could see our faces reflected **in** the water.
    2 She proposed **that we** leave the children behind. OR She proposed **leaving** the children behind.
    3 You can take dogs into shops in certain circumstances.
    4 There were ten people there, **not** counting the two of us.
    5 I'll need to reflect **on** what he said.
    6 He proposed **that we** take the car. OR He proposed **taking** the car.

4 1 count 4 reflected
    2 in favour of 5 comment
    3 circumstances 6 counts

5 1 You **inform sb of sth** or **about sth**: e.g. *Please inform us of any changes of address. The boss has informed us about the new guidelines.*
    2 **Observe** is *formal* in four of the five senses: e.g. *Have you observed any changes lately?*
    3 **Finding** is usually *plural*: e.g. *Our research findings indicate that pregnant women benefit from this treatment.*
    4 **Immune** is followed by the preposition *to*: e.g. *Adults are immune to German measles.*

6 *possible answers*:
    face: bury your face in your hands, red in the face, sb's face fits / doesn't fit, sb's face is like thunder, face to face (with sb/sth), face up/down, etc.
    head: nod your head, shake you head, hang your head in shame, turn your head, head injuries, per head, etc.
    take: sb can take it or leave it, have (got) what it takes, take sb aback, take after sb, take against sb/sth, take sb/sth apart, etc.

Unit 7

1 You would probably be happy to be described as: glamorous (especially if you are a woman), gorgeous, slim, stunning.

You would probably be unhappy to be described as: bald (especially if you are a woman or young man), full of wrinkles, hideous, overweight.

You might be unsure if you were described as: chubby, cute or skinny.

2 Cheeks are often described as *chubby*.
Gorgeous and *stunning* are synonyms.
Overweight is similar to *fat*.
Wrinkles affect your skin.
Babies are often cute.
People wear make-up.

3
1	tattoo	6	cute
2	getting on for; figure	7	hideous OR gorgeous
3	cheeks	8	glamorous
4	slim/slender	9	stunning/gorgeous
5	wrinkles	10	wear

4 con<u>ceal</u>, cre<u>ate</u>, en<u>hance</u>, ex<u>agger</u>ate, exagge<u>ra</u>tion, <u>guide</u>lines, hori<u>zon</u>tal, il<u>lu</u>sion, <u>vert</u>ical

5
1	true	5	more
2	help you	6	wide
3	positive	7	better
4	vertical	8	can't

6
1	features	6	exaggeration
2	hips	7	conceal
3	stripes; heels	8	unflattering
4	key	9	broad; waist
5	draw	10	guidelines

Unit 8

1
1	B	3	G	5	B	7	G
2	B	4	G	6	G	8	B

2
1	jumping	6	necessarily
2	look	7	gestures
3	observe	8	combination
4	fingernails	9	sweat
5	interpret	10	constantly

3 *possible answers*:
1 I think British people use gestures less than some nationalities, but I make some gestures a lot: put my head to one side when I'm thinking; avoid eye contact if I'm not telling the truth; move about a lot if I'm bored or restless, etc.
2 Generally, yes.
3 No, I'm not and I hardly ever notice what people are wearing.
4 No, I don't bite my fingernails. I think I scratch my head when I'm nervous.
5 I don't blush easily, but I do go red if I think I've said something embarrassing.
6 Yes, I do that quite a lot. It's interesting to wonder what kind of lives other people have.

4 *These words are correct*:
1	with	5	towards
2	make	6	arms
3	fist	7	signal
4	legs	8	someone

5
1	flirting	5	fist; anger
2	leant/leaned; fancied/ fancies	6	signal
3	defensive	7	generalizations
4	fold; cross	8	display

6 *possible answers*:
1 I often fold my arms, sometimes when I'm being defensive and sometimes when I'm bored. I think I cross my legs mostly out of habit. I'm not sure what it means.
2 Yes, that's definitely true. But I also lean back sometimes when I'm thinking about something they've said.
3 Yes, I think I do flirt quite a lot with members of the opposite sex. It's fun and is sometimes quite exciting.
4 I think I hold eye contact longer than is normal, stroke my lips with my thumb and forefinger, and move closer to them.

Unit 9

1
1	D	3	D	5	S	7	S	9	D
2	S	4	D	6	D	8	S	10	S

2
1	begged; begged
2	swept; swept
3	tore; torn
4	shook; shaken
5	nodded; nodded
6	kneeled/knelt; kneeled/knelt
7	sewed; sewed
8	put; put
9	leaned/leant; leaned/leant
10	spilt/spilled; spilt/spilled

3
1	in	5	in
2	against	6	down
3	in/into	7	on
4	on	8	for

4
1	door	6	blanket
2	towel	7	water
3	body	8	drinks
4	lipstick	9	shoulders
5	toaster	10	carpet

5
1	begging	6	kneeled/knelt
2	pray	7	tore
3	shook	8	fold
4	crawling	9	drag
5	plug; socket	10	nodding

6 *possible answers*:
1 I have spilt things but not often.
2 Never. I just run my hands through my hair and that's it.
3 No, I don't. I prefer a natural look.
4 I can sew buttons on quite well, but that is the limit of my sewing talents!
5 No, I don't – I'm not religious.
6 I'm not bad at diving, but I haven't actually tried for a long time.
7 Yes, it does.
8 There are quite a lot, especially in big cities.
9 Yes, kettles are the most common way of boiling water for hot drinks.

Unit 10

1
1	soldiers
2	thieves
3	the police
4	*possible answers*: a bull, an elephant, a rhinoceros, etc.
5	Usually because they are in a hurry and need to be somewhere quickly.
6	Because they don't see something in their way, or perhaps they aren't looking.
7	Usually because they have nothing particular they want to do.
8	in the countryside, in the mountains, etc.

2
1 hiking
2 charged/marched
3 rush
4 Correct.
5 ran
6 chase
7 strolled/wandered
8 Correct.

3
1 rushed
2 stumbled/ tripped over
3 stroll
4 ran off
5 chasing
6 flat out
7 wandered

4 Group 1: stiff, agility, motivated, demanding
Group 2: agile, devise, widen, vital
Group 3: crucial, essential

5
1 stiff
2 bend
3 Both are possible.
4 down
5 Both are possible.
6 stretch
7 workout
8 agile

6
1 constant
2 think up / devise
3 bend
4 press-ups; motivated
5 bent
6 strengthen
7 works out
8 motivation
9 demanding
10 agility

Unit 11

1 The four that are different are: vision, optician, strain and eyesight.

2
1 Both are possible.
2 adjust
3 eliminate
4 concentrate
5 ease
6 tear
7 Both are possible.
8 optician's

3
1 eye strain.
2 to ease the pain.
3 a small adjustment.
4 you can't completely eliminate. OR you can't eliminate completely.
5 The optician said
6 can irritate your eyes.
7 a bit blurred if
8 tears in her eyes
9 a lot of people blink.
10 powers of concentration.

4 *possible answer:*
I once had a problem with tear production.
My eyes became very dry, and that caused irritation. I went to the optician's and she gave me some drops for my eye. It solved the problem within days, and I haven't had it since.

5
1 spectacular
2 suspiciously
3 barely
4 still; invisible
5 glimpse
6 glanced

6
1 invisible, misty
2 visible, spectacular
3 suspicious
4 caught a glimpse of, spotted
5 stand, keep
6 glanced at
7 only just, barely

7
1 He sat still while I drew him
2 I could just make out the boat on the horizon.
3 They were both gazing at me; I don't know why.
4 Those stars are invisible without a telescope.
5 We could only just see the trees through the mist.
6 After a while I spotted Leo in the crowd.
7 The thief ran out of the building and vanished into thin air.
8 I caught a glimpse of Blanca as she left the shop.
9 Please keep still.
10 I had a suspicion he wasn't telling the truth.
(OR I had a suspicion he was lying.)

Unit 12

1
1 noise
2 laughing
3 in tears
4 overhear
5 whispering
6 snores

2 background noise, in tears, catch a cold, in a whisper, burst out laughing

3
1 sneeze
2 blind
3 deaf
4 catch
5 whisper
6 cheered; booed
7 snore
8 sighs
9 overheard
10 irritating

4 no noise: silence
a noise: crack, sigh, footsteps
a loud noise: bark, yell, scream, slam, crash (*also possible*: crack)

5
1 c   2 e   3 a   4 b   5 d

6
1 silence
2 yelling
3 nightmares
4 footsteps
5 slammed the door
6 crash
7 cracks
8 screamed

7
1 horns
2 barks
3 yelling
4 slamming
5 nightmare
6 sigh
7 relief

Unit 13

1
1 No   3 No   5 Yes   7 No
2 Yes   4 No   6 Yes   8 No

2
1 No
2 No
3 Yes
4 No
5 Yes
6 No
7 Yes
8 No (if it's a glass bottle) / Yes (if it's a plastic bottle)

3
1 squeezed
2 gave; tap
3 grabbed
4 gave; hug
5 slapped
6 rubbed
7 punched
8 scratch

4 gentle: stroke, slide, pat
usually vigorous: apply pressure, stimulate
A *massage* can be gentle or vigorous.

5
1 cheeks
2 forehead
3 fingertips
4 jaw
5 eyebrows

6
1 pat/massage
2 massage
3 stroking
4 pressure
5 scalp; vigorously/ energetically
6 applied
7 fingertips
8 tension
9 stimulate
10 slide
11 lightly (*also possible*: gently)
12 firmly

Unit 14

1 1 D 3 S 5 S 7 D
   2 S 4 D 6 S 8 S

2 1 allergic; rash
   2 commonly
   3 cancer; potentially
   4 allergy
   5 fever; minor
   6 potential; diabetes; attack
   7 fatal
   8 inability; potentially

3 Hay fever is caused by pollen.
Diabetes is the inability to control the sugar in the blood.
Asthma causes breathing difficulties.
Breast cancer is an illness in which a lump grows in the breast.
An allergy sometimes results in / causes a rash on the body.

4 1 T
   2 F – You can open it.
   3 T
   4 F – A disorder is an illness to a part of the body; it is not used about machines.
   5 F – It continues.
   6 T
   7 T
   8 F – If you consult someone, you ask them for information or advice about something.

5 1 dose
   2 term
   3 date
   4 excess
   5 effects
   6 enclosed

6 1 leaflet
   2 disorder
   3 enclosed
   4 dose/dosage
   5 persist
   6 date

7 1 dissolves
   2 persistent; consult
   3 discard
   4 short-term
   5 exceed
   6 consultation

Unit 15

1 1 Yes 3 Yes 5 No 7 Yes
   2 No 4 No 6 Yes 8 No

2 *possible answers:*
   1 A fractured skull is very serious, and the person could die.
   2 A dislocated elbow requires hospital treatment.
   3 A twisted ankle is painful, and it may be difficult to walk on it for a couple of days.
   4 A black eye is not serious but looks bad and may last for a few days or even a week.
   5 A bruise on the arm may be quite painful and last a few days.
   6 A blister can be painful, but you can put a special plaster on it so it doesn't hurt.

3 1 hundreds/masses
   2 unconscious
   3 eye
   4 dislocated
   5 bruises
   6 blisters
   7 fractured
   8 wrist, ankle

4 *possible answers:*
   1 I've had a black eye once or twice, bruised myself hundreds of times, twisted/sprained my ankle once or twice, and been stung by a wasp a few times. That's it! I've never fractured or dislocated anything, and luckily I've never been unconscious from an illness or injury.
   2 You would have to go to hospital for a fractured skull and a dislocated shoulder. You might go and see a doctor for one or two of the other injuries.

5 1 D 3 D 5 D 7 S 9 S
   2 S 4 S 6 D 8 D 10 D

6 1 aid
   2 swollen
   3 bleeds
   4 heal
   5 thoroughly
   6 place
   7 bacteria; virus
   8 wounded
   9 bleeding
   10 wrap; swelling

7 1 To give simple medical treatment to somebody, often before a doctor comes or before the person can be taken to a hospital.
   2 Bathe it thoroughly.
   3 A plaster
   4 To prevent infection
   5 It holds a dressing in place, and provides protection / helps keep the wound clean.
   6 A few days to a week.
   7 To reduce the swelling in a part of your body.
   8 It can travel easily from person to person.

Unit 16

1 1 D 3 S 5 S 7 D
   2 D 4 S 6 S 8 D

2 1 passionate **about**
   2 not very **decisive**
   3 assert **himself**
   4 great **enthusiasm**
   5 has a **lively** personality
   6 **dynamic**
   7 a passion **for**
   8 **truly** passionate

3 1 passionate
   2 introvert
   3 dynamic
   4 assertive
   5 enthusiastic
   6 talkative
   7 decisive
   8 lively
   9 extrovert

4 *possible answers:*
My brother is an extrovert, which is quite strange because his twin brother is an introvert. They get on quite well, though.
My mum is very talkative, and dynamic too. She never sits still.
My friend Caren is truly passionate about horses – she spends all her free time riding and looking after her horse, Romeo.
My cousin Philip is very assertive.
My brother-in-law Jack is very enthusiastic about cars: old cars, new cars – any cars!

5 1 P 3 P 5 P 7 P 9 N
   2 P 4 N 6 N 8 N 10 P

6 1 showing off
   2 affectionate
   3 sensible
   4 sincere
   5 Decent
   6 ethic
   7 saint

7 1 considerate
   2 affection
   3 show
   4 boast
   5 Decent
   6 inconsiderate
   7 genuine/sincere
   8 integrity

8 *possible answers, from Argentina:*
   1 In my country, you are expected to give your seat to the elderly, pregnant women and people with special needs. The front seats on buses and trains are designated for that purpose, and drivers and conductors can enforce the rule if necessary. I think everybody would agree that it's considerate to give your seat to someone who needs it, but the regulation exists so that even those who are unwilling to give up their seat must do it.

2 In general terms, showing affection for your partner in public is acceptable in our society, although of course some people are more reserved than others and prefer not to show their feelings so openly.

3 Many people would agree that if you need to show off, you are seeking attention because you lack confidence.

4 Nowadays, travelling to far-off places is much more common than in the past, particularly for the young. People share those experiences – mostly on social media – but it's not considered boastful. In fact, most people are eager to hear about expensive holidays!

5 I think we used to be kinder and more friendly towards strangers and foreigners in the past. Nowadays, because of the rise in crime rates, most people are wary of strangers.

6 I'm afraid that in my country we are notorious for not being punctual! Therefore, we are used to being kept waiting.

7 Not all shop assistants are genuinely friendly, but some customers can be really rude and tiresome.

8 Most politicians are perceived as lacking integrity, so they are not trusted.

Unit 17

1

NOUN	ADJECTIVE
arrogance	arrogant
confidence	confident
efficiency	efficient
charm	charming
motivation	**motivated**
potential	**potential**
knowledge	**knowledgeable**
idiot	**idiotic**

2 1 S   3 S   5 S   7 D
    2 S   4 D   6 D   8 S

3 1 well informed   5 struggle
    2 straightforward   6 ridiculous
    3 immature   7 timid
    4 efficient   8 capable

4 1 What did you make of Aaron?
    2 Josie struggled to explain what she meant.
    3 Lawrence was lacking in charm.
    4 I didn't take to Rollo at first.
    5 Parminder came over/across very well in the interview.
    6 Rupert struck me as capable.
    7 I think that Ariana has potential.
    8 Vicky didn't seem (to be) very motivated.

5 *possible answers*:
    1 I'm well informed about politics and economics.
    2 I think that people who are conscientious are very important, and we need people like that in our schools, health service and industry.
    3 If people are charming towards me, I'm usually charming back to them.
    4 I feel confident when I am in control and know what I want to say.
    5 It's sometimes a struggle for me to remember people's names when I first meet them, so I can seem rude when I meet them again.
    6 If I meet someone who is arrogant, I spend as little time with them as possible.
    7 If someone doesn't take me seriously, I don't worry too much. It's their problem, not mine.
    8 I don't take to people who are arrogant and immature.
    9 In an interview situation, I think I probably come across as quite well informed, but perhaps a bit shy and lacking in confidence.

10 If someone says something ridiculous in an interview, I think it could be because they're nervous or don't know what they're talking about.

Unit 18

1 1 P   4 P   7 N   10 N
    2 N   5 N   8 P   11 P
    3 N   6 P   9 P/N   12 N

2 1 astounded   5 ecstatic
    2 over the moon   6 in tears
    3 heartbroken   7 delighted
    4 disgusted   8 desperate

3 1 astounded/astonished   6 delighted/ecstatic/
    2 shocked   thrilled
    3 desperate   7 tears
    4 devastated   8 disgusted
    5 ashamed

4 reveal; vulnerable; anxiety; worsen; severe; disclose; psychological; intense; anxious; psychology; psychologist; suppress

5 1 psychology   5 severe
    2 reveal   6 handling
    3 vulnerable   7 intense
    4 worsened   8 anxiety

6 1 handle   6 depression
    2 vulnerable   7 anxious
    3 psychologists   8 bottle up
    4 suppress   9 reveal
    5 intense   10 psychology

7 *possible answers*:
    1 The best ones handle stress well. Some athletes try to handle stress by taking drugs, and that's a terrible idea.
    2 I don't think they should show that they're vulnerable, but I do think they should apologize for mistakes and be prepared to change their ideas where necessary.
    3 I think psychologists have been looking at the effects of social media on how we feel about ourselves and communicate with each other, as well as the effects of internet porn (pornography) on young people.
    4 I think at work, it's sensible to suppress your emotions sometimes. You can't say how you feel all the time.
    5 They need to reach out and try to meet people – join a club or talk to their neighbours, for instance. It's not easy to solve, though.
    6 I think doctors often suffer from depression, as well as people on low wages whose lives are difficult.
    7 Breathe deeply; sit quietly and relax; do yoga or go for a run.
    8 Yes, I think it does: your heart and blood pressure can suffer.
    9 Yes, to friends or family.
    10 No, I haven't ever studied psychology.

Unit 19

1 1 N   3 N   5 N   7 P   9 P
    2 P   4 P   6 N   8 N   10 N

2 1 regret
    2 dislike
    3 blame
    4 strain
    5 respect
    6 stare
    7 forgave
    8 stuck

3 I've been having a **tough** time at work recently. A young man joined the department and for some reason **took** an instant dislike to me. His desk was close to mine, and he just sat and **stared** at me without saying a word, which made me feel uncomfortable. Over time, he started to shout at me and became more and more **aggressive** until I felt quite nervous being near him. It put a big **strain** on me, and my work began to suffer. One day, I decided it was time to stick **up** for myself, so I told him his behaviour was terrible. I was shocked when he suddenly started crying and of course, I **regretted** what I had said to him. He thought that I **blamed** him for the poor results in the department, when in fact, that wasn't the case. Eventually, things **settled** down, and we got on much better.

4
1 S	3 D	5 S	
2 S	4 D	6 S	

5
1	reluctance	5	fault
2	initial	6	strict
3	sensitive	7	looking up
4	caring		

6
1	fault	6	patience
2	reluctant	7	accepted
3	is strict	8	looking up
4	Initially	9	nasty/mean
5	accepts	10	bond

Unit 20

1
1 D	3 D	5 S	7 D
2 D	4 S	6 D	8 S

2
1	courageous	5	dignity
2	heroine	6	heroic
3	bravery	7	inspirational
4	inspires/inspired	8	spiritual

3
1 inspiration/heroine; courageous
2 look/looked; captain; inspired; hero
3 heroine; courage; dignity

4 *possible answers:*
1 When I was growing up, my hero was Ronaldo because I'm a great Manchester United fan, and he played for them when I was in my teens.
2 I now look up to my boss at the charity where I work. She has always been very calm and dignified, even when difficult decisions have had to be made.
3 My mother was very courageous, especially at the end of her life when she died from cancer at the relatively young age of 50.

5 rebel, detest, despise, lose (your temper), disapprove, loathe, bully

6
1	disapproval	6	greedy
2	loathe	7	can't bear
3	despicable	8	of
4	rebellious	9	fame
5	misery	10	principles

7
1	bully	6	against
2	principle	7	disapprove
3	temper	8	values
4	can't bear	9	greedy
5	rebel; rebellious	10	despise; villain

8 *possible answers:*
1 I think both are possible, but I certainly saw my brother bully my sister when we were young. They're great friends now, though.
2 I won't eat rabbit or small birds.
3 No, not very often.
4 I can't bear drivers who drive too close behind me.
5 Yes, I was. As a man, I had long hair, wore strange clothes, and often went on political demonstrations.
6 No, it isn't, but I've never done it.

7 Yes. I disapprove of my sister's boyfriend. He drinks too much and doesn't treat her well. I hope she leaves him soon.
8 Yes, they often do. My parents have a different way of living: more serious, more religious than I am, but we agree on basic values such as honesty, integrity and loyalty.
9 Yes, some of them are, but there are also some like Bill and Melinda Gates who are very generous and have spent many millions trying to eradicate malaria.
10 I won't name names, but there are one or two politicians, in this country and abroad, that I despise because I think they are responsible for causing a great deal of harm to society.

Unit 21

1 peer pressure, nature or nurture? play a part, a broken home, a deprived childhood, a beneficial effect

2
1 P	3 N	5 P	7 N
2 P	4 N	6 P	8 N

3
1	home	5	impact
2	deprived	6	model
3	pressure	7	crucial
4	nature	8	incentive

4 *possible answers:*
I'm sure parents play a very important role, but sometimes teenagers are very influenced by their friends, which can be a good or bad thing. I know my aunt and uncle played a crucial role in my childhood.

Peer pressure is very significant, I agree, particularly with social networking. It can be dangerous, too.

In general, I think positive incentives, such as praise or the possibility of more freedom, are better for young people.

I know two or three people who either came from a broken home or had a deprived childhood. One has done brilliantly in life, and one has had a few problems , but is doing his best to deal with them. So I agree, these factors don't necessarily have a damaging effect.

5
1	sympathetic	5	pace
2	teenager	6	consistent
3	through	7	adulthood
4	adolescence	8	grown-up

6
1	wise	7	wisdom
2	cope	8	time; pace
3	phase	9	adult
4	supportive	10	sympathy
5	transition	11	conduct
6	consistent		

7
1 Yes, that's always true.
2 No, I think the best way to cope with problems is to think about solutions in a positive way.
3 I don't think so. I think middle age is a difficult phase.
4 Yes, that's crucial.
5 No, it's very difficult. Adolescents have so much to learn and so many pressures.
6 I think that's true.
7 On the whole, I agree.
8 I'm not sure about this. Sometimes you have to take time to think, but occasionally it's not possible. Making mistakes isn't bad if you learn from them.
9 Yes, I agree.
10 I agree. Life can be difficult for them, but in the end, things get better.
11 I think that's true, but it doesn't mean we should always accept bad conduct from teenagers. They must also take some responsibility for their actions.

Unit 22

1 tendency (3) resemblance (3) criticism (4)
widower (3) alike (2) apparent (3)
personally (3, or 4 if characteristic (5)
you pronounce the 'a')

2
1	D	3	D	5	S
2	S	4	S	6	S

3
1 in her teens
2 (very) alike
3 resembles / takes after
4 siblings
5 hard to say
6 case
7 passed away / passed on
8 characteristics

4
1 widow
2 personally
3 resemblance; alike
4 However
5 apparent/obvious
6 criticized
7 takes
8 presence
9 picked
10 tendency

5
1 remind you of
2 criticism
3 in her father's footsteps
4 brought up / raised
5 hard to say
6 stepfather
7 personally
8 late

6 *possible answers:*
1 I think I resemble my father more than my mother.
2 No, not really. I can see characteristics in both my mother and father which I share.
3 I have a sister, and we are alike in that we both have brown hair, brown eyes and fair skin. Our characters are completely different, though.
4 All the members of my family are very punctual and get very impatient if anyone else is late.
5 I think there is perhaps some truth in the idea that daughters become more like their mothers and sons become more like their fathers. However, living in different times also makes us different from our parents in terms of our attitudes to things.
6 If we're honest, I don't think anyone likes being criticized, but I it's something people learn to accept a bit more as they get older. That has been my case, I think.

Unit 23

1
1 unsophisticated
2 inoffensive
3 downwards
4 discourteous
5 unacceptable
6 bad manners

2
1 sophistication
2 offend
3 customary
4 unacceptable
5 courteous
6 inoffensive

3
1 customary
2 manners
3 considered
4 viewed
5 discourteous
6 rude
7 sophisticated
8 split
9 lick; stick

4 *possible answers, from India:*
1 Yes, it is quite customary to eat chicken legs or wings with your fingers at home in India. However, when eating outside, at a restaurant or somebody else's home, we use cutlery.
2 Yes, Indian parents think it's important for children to have good table manners.
3 No, in India it is not considered bad manners to eat everything you are given. Usually, we are encouraged to take as much food as we can eat. Wasting food is considered bad manners.
4 Yes, it is viewed as polite to offer food to the elderly first.
5 Yes, it is discourteous to start eating your food before others have been served.

6 Yes, as a guest, it would be offensive to criticize the host's food.
7 Talking with your mouth full might not be considered very sophisticated in India.
8 It is customary among young people, especially among friends, to split the bill in restaurants in India.
9 Yes, it is viewed as rude to lick your knife, fork or spoon when you have finished eating, or stick your own knife, fork or spoon into dishes of food for the whole table.

5
1	H	3	U	5	H	7	H
2	U	4	U	6	U	8	H

6
1 outstanding / on his best behaviour
2 All three are possible.
3 poor/good
4 exception to / offence at
5 exceptional/ outstanding
6 offensive/upsetting
7 All three are possible.
8 impressed me / was exceptional

7
1 impress
2 good/exceptional
3 behaviour
4 foot
5 offence
6 deeply
7 remark/comment
8 exception
9 judgement
10 humorous

Unit 24

1
1	D	3	S	5	S	7	S
2	D	4	S	6	D	8	S

2
1 mango
2 aubergine
3 beetroot
4 avocado
5 raspberry
6 asparagus
7 watermelon
8 courgette
9 grapefruit
10 spinach
11 apricot
12 broccoli

3
1 vegetable
2 herb
3 nut
4 dried
5 spice
6 pulse

4
1 avocado, mango, apricot
2 All the vegetables can be eaten cooked. *Celery* and *spinach* are also eaten raw in the UK in salads. *Courgette* and *broccoli* can be eaten raw, but that is rare in the UK.
3 To add flavour.
4 They are both considered to be healthy.

5 *possible answers, from Argentina:*
1 All of these are usually grown in my country, Argentina:
mangoes grapefruit
aubergines spinach
beetroot apricots
avocados broccoli
raspberries lentils
asparagus basil
watermelons nuts
courgettes almonds
2 I have tried everything!
3 **fruit:** tangerines, oranges, apples, quinces, grapes, pears
vegetables: Brussels sprouts, carrots, onions, cauliflower, cabbages, leeks
nuts: hazelnuts
herbs: bay leaves
dried fruit: dried figs
spice: saffron

6 frying pan; lemon squeezer; kitchen scales; food processor; carving knife; deep-fat fryer

7
1 colander
2 casserole
3 corkscrew
4 food processor (OR a sharp knife)
5 whisk
6 (kitchen) scales
7 carving knife
8 frying pan

8
1 lemon/orange/lime
2 cheese
3 potatoes (for chips / French fries), fish, other vegetables
4 flour, sugar, sometimes rice or large pieces of meat
5 bread, ham, other meat, some vegetables
6 meat
7 meat
8 some vegetables and some fruit, e.g. carrots, potatoes, apples, pears

9 *possible answers, from Argentina:*
I have a casserole, a food processor, a whisk, a colander, a grater, a peeler, a lemon squeezer, a corkscrew, kitchen scales and a carving knife.
I don't have a frying pan or a deep-fat fryer, but they wouldn't be useful because I don't like fried food!!

Unit 25

1
1 lean, tender
2 sweet, rich
3 tasteless, bland
4 fresh, stale
5 salty
6 rare, well done, tough
7 greasy
8 tasteless, sweet, ripe

2
1 stale
2 ripe
3 tough
4 bitter
5 fattening /rich
6 appetizing

3
1 appetite
2 spicy
3 salty
4 lean
5 raw
6 rare
7 bland
8 greasy
9 rich

4
1 opener
2 service
3 up
4 yourself
5 less
6 lunch

5
1 treating
2 Instant
3 mug
4 tray
5 care
6 takeaway
7 popped
8 self-service

6
1 instant
2 mug
3 cereal
4 packed
5 canteen
6 heat up
7 takeaway
8 treat
9 lap

7 *possible answers:*
1 Always real coffee.
2 Usually a cup, but sometimes a mug.
3 I hardly ever eat cereal. I usually have toast and coffee for breakfast.
4 I sometimes take a packed lunch if I'm travelling.
5 I work from home so I never eat in a canteen now – but I used to.
6 I usually eat fresh food, but I probably heat up prepared food once or twice a week.
7 No, hardly ever.
8 I go to one of two or three of my favourite restaurants in town.
9 No, never. I always eat at the table, but I used to eat on my lap a lot when I was a teenager and a student at university.

Unit 26

1
steering wheel
pedestrian crossing
windscreen wiper
road sign
number plate
wing mirror
parking meter
traffic warden

2
1 tyre
2 windscreen
3 pavement
4 kerb / pay and display machine
5 number plate
6 pedestrian/zebra crossing

3
1 steering wheel
2 boot
3 windscreen wipers
4 headlights
5 wing mirror
6 road sign

4 *possible answers, from China:*
1 There are some zebra crossings in my city, Hong Kong. Motorists always stop for pedestrians.
2 I don't drive, so I don't use pay and display machines. My friends who drive usually pay by a stored-value smart-card. Some people still pay with coins if the machine allows.
3 There are very few traffic wardens in Hong Kong. If there is one to direct the traffic due to special conditions, drivers and pedestrians must follow their instructions.
4 We do not fit special tyres on our car in the winter because it does not snow here.
5 Automatic headlights and windscreen wipers are helpful, especially windscreen wipers as it rains quite often here.
6 Some people park on the pavement here, though it is not allowed.

5
1 moving
2 hand
3 attention
4 suddenly
5 direction
6 lost

6
1 accelerate
2 reverse
3 hazard
4 potential
5 overtake
6 lookout
7 swerved
8 pull away

7
1 overtake
2 steer
3 down; brake / put on the brakes / put the brakes on
4 alert / on the alert
5 potential
6 gear
7 automatic

8 *possible answers:*
1 Yes, I agree and I don't try to overtake on a bridge.
2 No, you shouldn't, but sometimes I do.
3 Yes, I agree and, where possible, I always do.
4 Of course you should, but I think many motorists carry on driving when they are tired.
5 That's true.
6 That sounds like good advice. Fortunately, I've never been in that situation. I have skidded, but only for a moment, and I've never lost control of the car.
7 Personally I agree, but people who like driving often prefer manual cars.

Unit 27

1 The four that are different are: collide, collision, pile-up and via.

2 blocked (1), casualty (3), via (2), exit (2), scattered (2), chaos (2), ambulance (3), helicopter (4)

3 **transport:** lorry, ambulance, helicopter
people: eyewitness, casualties
roads: lane, exit, junction
accidents: collide, pile-up, casualties, ambulance
(also possible: eyewitness)

4
1 T
2 F – There were eyewitnesses.
3 T
4 F – The lorry spilled a load of wood (logs).
5 F – One person died at the scene of the accident.
6 F – A helicopter took the driver to hospital.
7 F – There were six or seven other casualties.
8 F – Two lanes of the motorway are now blocked.
9 T
10 F – Police are advising motorists to exit via Junction 12.

5
1 If you pull out in a car, you drive away from the side of the road.
2 A junction is a place where two roads meet.
3 Correct
4 A lane is a section of the road that is marked by white lines to keep traffic separate.
5 Casualties are people who are killed or injured in accident (or war).
6 Correct
7 If you collide with sth, you do hit it.
8 Correct
9 Correct
10 If you block somebody, you do not let them pass.

6
1 service station
2 lane
3 load
4 blocked; incident
5 via; chaotic/chaos
6 junction
7 extensive
8 logs
9 pile-up; critical
10 exit

Unit 28

1
1 bitterly cold
2 They are the same.
3 hot and humid
4 a chilly day
5 They are the same.
6 a dull day
7 scattered showers
8 quite wet, to say the least

2
1 scattered
2 spell
3 bitterly
4 torrential
5 thick/dense
6 chilly
7 mild
8 odd

3
1 downpour (*possible but less likely*: shower)
2 flashes
3 least
4 rainbow
5 humidity
6 bitterly
7 chilly
8 dull
9 showers

4
1 D
2 S
3 S
4 D
5 D
6 D

5
1 too much
2 light
3 causes
4 need
5 strong winds
6 large
7 future
8 period

6
1 forecast
2 standstill
3 disruption
4 closely
5 dependent
6 heatwave
7 drought
8 shortages
9 gales
10 significant
11 widespread

7 *possible answers, from Australia*:
1 The weather in Australia varies enormously depending on what part of the country you live in. In Sydney, where I live, winters are mostly mild. The summers are generally long and hot, and can be quite humid. Torrential rain and thunderstorms with lots of lightning are quite common.
2 The long summers and mild winters make it easy to spend a lot of time outdoors, and I think make people more relaxed than in cold countries.
3 It's never bitterly cold in Sydney, and thick fogs are rare. It can be cloudy and dull, but is more often sunny.

Unit 29

1 *probable answers*:
1 men
2 both
3 women
4 both
5 more women, but some men, too
6 both
7 women
8 both
9 men

2
1 waistcoat
2 loose-fitting
3 high-heeled
4 plain
5 check(ed)
6 sandals
7 sleeved
8 cap
9 straps
10 tight

3 *possible answers (for a man)*:
1 Nothing in silk, but I have a brown suede jacket and a pair of black suede shoes.
2 I do wear sandals if it is hot, but I don't like them very much.
3 I don't wear short-sleeved shirts much. I usually just roll up the sleeves on my long-sleeved shirts.
4 Nobody in my family wears a cap, but my grandfather used to when he was alive.
5 I've got a couple of check shirts and a couple of striped shirts, but the majority are plain.
6 I don't wear V-neck jumpers much, but I've got a woollen sleeveless cardigan and a black and grey waistcoat.

4
1 S
2 D
3 S
4 D
5 S
6 D
7 D
8 S

5
1 a wig
2 an apron
3 a fancy-dress party
4 a bucket of water
5 kilts
6 shiver
7 flip-flops
8 a badge
9 dress up
10 a barbecue
11 glamorous
12 an outfit

6 *possible answers (for a woman)*:
1 I went to one hen party. I was the oldest person there and I felt a bit embarrassed because they all made a lot of noise and drank a bit too much.
2 I went to one fancy-dress party dressed as a soldier. People thought that was a bit strange because I'm more of a pacifist.
3 I don't get that many chances to dress up nowadays, so when I do, I really enjoy it.
4 I tend to buy outfits for special occasions, like weddings or parties, but most of the time I just buy individual items of clothing.
5 Yes, I do. I generally wear a top and maybe a jumper, jeans and trainers.
6 I like barbecues because they are usually very casual affairs, and you can wear what you like.

Unit 30

1
1 D
2 S
3 D
4 S
5 S
6 S
7 D
8 D

2 bunk beds, vacuum cleaner, bookcase, central heating, dustbin, smoke alarm, doorbell, ironing board, chest of drawers, letter box

3 *suggested answers (others may be possible)*:
one hand: doorbell, plug
two hands: broom, dustbin (one hand to open the lid and one to put the rubbish into it)
one or two hands: hoover / vacuum cleaner
no hands: doormat, radiator, socket (using one hand to put a plug in the socket)

4
1 broom
2 radiator
3 stool
4 socket
5 (door)mat
6 dustbin
7 drawers
8 hoover
9 bunk
10 box

5 *possible answers:*

I've got all of those things in my house except for bunk beds. I've got two smoke alarms: one in the kitchen and one in the hall. I've got a letter box, but it isn't in the front door: it's on the wall next to the front door.

6
1	D	3	S	5	S
2	D	4	D	6	D

7
1 half a dozen
2 loo
3 spare
4 get hold of
5 plumber
6 estimate
7 greasy

8
1 hold
2 outside/exterior
3 steps
4 grease
5 porch
6 dripping
7 dozen
8 blinds

Unit 31

1
1 exhausted / worn out
2 nightie/nightdress
3 sleeping pills
4 oversleep
5 nightmare
6 have a lie-in
7 a sleeper
8 yawn
9 sleeping bag
10 snore

2
1 exhausted / worn out
2 fell asleep
3 fast asleep
4 nightmare
5 get back to sleep
6 went off
7 overslept
8 sleepy

3
1 heavy; light (OR light; heavy)
2 pyjamas / a nightie
3 alarm
4 wide
5 lie-in
6 snore
7 pills
8 bag

4 *possible answers:*
1 I'm a fairly heavy sleeper.
2 I own a pair of pyjamas, but I usually wear shorts and a T-shirt in bed.
3 I hardly ever set an alarm because I always wake up about the same time.
4 It's quite unusual, but yes I do. I usually wake up and get up almost immediately.
5 No, I never have a lie-in.
6 Yes, my wife tells me I snore sometimes.
7 I have taken sleeping pills to help me on long plane or train journeys.
8 I never go camping so I don't own a sleeping bag.

5 The pronunciation is different in: provided and insomnia.

6 The pronunciation is different in: as long as.

7 have a nap, sleep like a log, suffer from insomnia, have a restless night, in total darkness, have something on my mind

8
1 irritable
2 as long as / provided that
3 like a log
4 stick
5 restless
6 my mind
7 establish
8 restricted
9 disturbed

9 *possible answers:*
1 I usually sleep like a log, but not in different beds, e.g. on holiday.
2 That's true for me – I often have a restless night if I eat very late.
3 I don't work late so that doesn't restrict the amount of time I sleep.
4 I don't get irritable after just one bad night, but I'm not nice to be around after two!

5 I think it is important to establish a good routine for sleep.
6 No, that's not true for me – I don't need to be in total darkness to sleep.
7 I don't suffer from insomnia, but I feel sorry for those who do.
8 I used to have a nap in the afternoon, but not any longer.
9 Yes, I don't sleep as well if I have things on my mind.

Unit 32

1
1	D	3	D	5	S
2	S	4	D	6	S

2
1 unaware; debit; statements; transactions
2 sum; credit; promptly
3 outgoings/expenditure; overdrawn; debts
4 ignores; put money into

3
1 withdrew
2 overdrawn
3 outgoings/expenditure/transactions
4 mount/build
5 cautious
6 prompt
7 income
8 awareness

4 *possible answers:*

I don't keep a record of my outgoings, but I check my bank statements online a couple of times a week so I know more or less what I spend.

I always keep my account in credit; I'm never overdrawn.

I have an arrangement with my bank so that my credit card bills are paid automatically at the end of the month.

I do check my bank statements but I don't always look carefully at all the different transactions.

I wouldn't say I was cautious with money, and I do waste money on food that I buy and don't always eat. However, I don't think I waste large sums of money.

5 **money**: budget, owe, economize, subsidize, pay sth off, deficit
numbers: calculate, work something out, subtract, take sth away

6
1	D	3	S	5	S
2	S	4	D	6	D

7
1 *Surplus* is different; *shortfall* and *deficit* mean an amount that is less than you need.
2 *Calculation* is different; *shortfall* and *shortage* both mean not having enough of something.
3 *Economize* is different; *take away* and *subtract* mean to take one number from another.
4 *Subsidize* is different; *economize* and *make cutbacks* mean to reduce the amount you spend.
5 *Budget* is different; *deficit* and *shortage* both mean you don't have enough of something.
6 *Pay sth off* is different: *work out* and *calculate* mean to find the total number/amount of something.

8
1 shortages
2 shortfall
3 subsidy
4 work out / calculate
5 deficit/shortfall
6 economize / make cutbacks
7 budget/economize
8 owing
9 subsidized

Unit 33

1 *suggested answers:*
involves violence: manslaughter, rape
may involve violence: mugging, kidnapping, arson
(if people are killed or injured in the fire)
doesn't involve violence: shoplifting, bribery, fraud

2 **usually involved with money:** fraud, mugging, bribery, blackmail, kidnapping, shoplifting (stealing goods which are worth money)

3
1 shoplifter
2 blackmailer
3 arsonist
4 kidnapper
5 rapist
6 mugger

4
1 mugged
2 manslaughter
3 kidnapped
4 shoplifters
5 threatened
6 raping
7 bribed
8 deliberate/intentional
9 blackmailed
10 fraud

5 *suggested answers:*
a negative meaning: slum, gang, abuse, neglect, penalty, harsh

6
1 slum
2 neglected
3 discipline
4 gang
5 abuse
6 offenders
7 morals
8 attraction

7
1 parental responsibility
2 suffered abuse (*also possible:* been abused)
3 discipline
4 moral issue
5 harsher penalties
6 drifted into crime
7 neglect
8 attraction

8 *possible answers, from Kenya:*
I disagree. Crime rates are high in estates where the middle class live as well as in slum areas. Gadgets such as mobile phones, tablets and laptops are easy targets for criminals. Many criminals blame parental neglect, yet it is a lack of discipline on their part. There have been instances of pickpockets making away with gadgets such as mobile phones on busy streets and laptops stolen from public offices.

Crimes are also committed by people who aren't poor because they offer an easy way to make money and live a good life. People who abuse alcohol and drugs often drift into crime because they steal to get money to buy their next dose. What is needed are harsh penalties for offenders which will discourage others and prove that crime does not pay.

Unit 34

1 *suggested answers:*
usually negative: regret, filthy, litter, depressing, homeless
These words can be negative, but it depends on the context: abandon, damp, hang around, graffiti, concerned

2
1 dirty
2 poor
3 sorry
4 ground
5 wet
6 worried
7 sad
8 writing and/or drawing

3
1 homeless
2 passage
3 concern
4 youths
5 graffiti
6 depressing
7 hanging
8 regretted

4 *possible answers, from Poland:*
litter on the ground: Interestingly, I often see litter on the ground near dustbins in a park near my home during weekends. I suppose the park cleaning service doesn't work at weekends and this is the reason why there is so much abandoned litter. And obviously, such a sight is a drawback of walking in the park on Sunday. A real shame. But on the whole, I don't think we have much litter in the street, not compared to some other countries.

graffiti: Yes, quite a lot. Some of it falls under the category of murals. They are a nice artistic expression. But actually there are quite a lot of spray 'signatures', not representing anything – just lines, not meaning anything – a rather depressing sight. Another category is often linked with supporting e.g. a football team or degrading/disrespecting it. Some texts on walls are political statements.

homeless people sleeping in the street: One can see homeless people in the streets but not sleeping. They sleep in parks or deserted houses but not really in the streets. You can sometimes see homeless people sitting in passages in the city centre.

filthy pavements: Yes, where filth is created by unfavourable weather conditions such as melting snow, or mud because of torrential rain.

gangs of youths: I suppose in some very specific districts of a bigger city, but on the whole gangs of youths hanging around are not a big problem in Poland.

5
1 S
2 D
3 D
4 S
5 D
6 S
7 D
8 D (In the UK, a *district* can be in any part of a town, but a *suburb* is only outside the centre of a town.)

6
1 built-up
2 suburb/district
3 surrounded; drawback/disadvantage/shame/pity
4 handy/convenient; surrounding
5 district; nearby; go on
6 lively; drawback/disadvantage/shame/pity; decent
7 on the whole/in general
8 desirable

7 *possible answers:*
1 It's quite built-up because it's not far from the centre, but many houses have a garden, and there are two parks, so there is still a feeling of space.
2 It's surrounded by garden on three sides, with a road on the fourth side.
3 We have quite a few shops nearby: a chemist's, a florist's, a small supermarket, a deli, and one or two others.
4 It's very convenient for me because I can walk into town in ten minutes.
5 I suppose the main drawbacks are that it is on a hill so the walk home is all uphill, and many residents complain about the shortage of parking.
6 As time goes on I think the district will improve because councils are more aware of the environment than they used to be, and I've noticed that the shops are gradually getting better.

Unit 35

1
1. meadow
2. frequent
3. outskirts
4. shallow
5. occasionally
6. nevertheless
7. swap
8. stream

2
1. swap
2. stream
3. spot
4. isolated
5. infrequent
6. meadow
7. beyond
8. occasionally
9. nevertheless
10. outskirts

3
1. shallow
2. isolation
3. frequent
4. Nevertheless
5. rural
6. outskirts
7. frequency
8. beyond
9. spot
10. deep

4 arable farm; cereal crop; mixed feelings; physical labour; earn a living; herd of cows

5
1. grow crops
2. herd of cows
3. mixed farm
4. arable farm
5. dairy farm
6. does he do for a living?
7. pass on the farm to my son
8. crops

6
1. combination
2. increasingly
3. keep
4. crops
5. earn
6. pass
7. labourers/labour; labourers/labour
8. mixed

7 *possible answers, from China:*
1. There are very few farms in Hong Kong, where I live. Since the farms here are not very large, they usually grow a small range of crops.
2. They only use machines to do some work. Most of the work is done by hand.
3. Farmers here keep cows, pigs, chickens, ducks and fish.
4. Most farms here grow vegetables, such as Chinese kale, Tientsin cabbage and green cucumber. Some grow fruit, such as guava, green papaya and red dragon fruit. Very few of them grow cereals.
5. Very few people here earn a living from farming.
6. There is no shortage of labour here, but not many people want to do farming work.

Unit 36

1
1. undergone
2. flourishing
3. remarkably
4. unique
5. unspoilt
6. remote
7. resort
8. delight

2
1. thriving
2. stunning
3. diverse
4. unique
5. remote
6. remarkable
7. unwind/take it easy
8. restored

3
1. easy
2. beaten track
3. restoration
4. resort
5. laze
6. wander
7. remarkably
8. away from it

4 ~~beautiful~~ views **stunning**
~~unusual and surprising~~ city **remarkable**
~~keep~~ so much **retain**
~~varied~~ architecture **diverse**
~~flourishing~~ European **thriving**
managed to ~~repair~~ **restore**
~~casually walk~~ around **wander**
~~exciting~~ nightlife **vibrant**
you can ~~relax~~ **unwind**

5 *possible answers:*
1. No. I like city breaks but I'm not looking for anything particularly vibrant or exciting.
2. I like to unwind, but not on a beach: it's usually too hot for me.
3. Sometimes I do; at other times I like to be in a busy city.
4. No, I'm not a very adventurous person.
5. Yes, that's my idea of a perfect holiday, along with good weather and good food.

Unit 37

1 <u>ju</u>stify <u>va</u>cancy <u>lu</u>xury in ad<u>va</u>nce <u>mi</u>serable guaran<u>tee</u> lu<u>xu</u>rious ex<u>clu</u>sive <u>pre</u>ferably fully-<u>booked</u>

2 *suggested answers:*
1. G
2. B
3. G
4. G
5. either
6. B
7. G
8. Probably B, but could be either.

3
1. Having said that
2. preferably
3. in advance
4. guaranteed
5. justify
6. vacancy; fully-booked
7. impressed
8. luxury

4 *possible answers:*
1. Yes, well in advance. I'm very organized.
2. No, not luxurious hotels, but I like something reasonably comfortable.
3. I haven't ever used Airbnb, but have stayed in a B&B on a few occasions.
4. No, I much prefer city breaks where I can visit museums, art galleries, etc.
5. No, I don't think they do.
6. Convenience, reasonable comfort and good value.

5
1. flexibility
2. given
3. generous
4. going away
5. expense
6. youth hostel or a caravan
7. appeal
8. strict

6
1. He's (very) mean.
2. If it's a cheap place, it enables us to stay a bit longer.
3. We have a limited budget.
4. The date is (very) flexible.
5. We opted for something quite simple.
6. I want to live in comfort.
7. A room with a balcony is an extra expense.
8. A caravan isn't (very) appealing to/for me.

7 *possible answers:*
1. I stayed in a caravan when I was a child. I remember they were very small but quite exciting for children. I have never stayed in a youth hostel but have friends who use them all the time.
2. I think I prefer to have a bit of comfort.
3. I don't go on holiday much so I'm prepared to spend quite a lot, though there is still a limit on what I can afford.
4. Yes, I do. I try to forget about work completely unless there's something urgent.
5. Flexibility is quite nice.
6. Yes, they always wanted us to do things together as a family, and not go off on our own.

Unit 38

1
1. spacious–late
2. detached–flat
3. staircase–care
4. entrance–camera
5. mortgage–damage
6. overall–saw

2
1. basically
2. staircase
3. exterior; interior
4. largely
5. mortgage
6. bonus
7. overall
8. decorating
9. spacious
10. put in

3
1. terraced; semi-detached
2. hall
3. plan
4. take out
5. decorating
6. put in / install

4 possible answers, from the Czech Republic:
1. Yes, especially terraced houses. They've been here for centuries: the old ones are usually single-storey buildings forming a line along the main street in a village and having a large garden or even an orchard behind the house; the modern ones are higher, often two-storey buildings, sometimes with an attic and a tiny front and a small back garden where the families relax and enjoy barbecues and meals in the summer. Semi-detached houses are less common, but we do have them, especially on the outskirts of cities. Their bonus is more privacy than in the terraced houses but, of course, the prices are usually higher.
2. No, not really. The entrance hall is mostly small, even tiny, with a lot of doors and is simply furnished with a wall rack and a shoe rack or cupboard.
3. Open-plan design is not very popular in our homes. In most homes, there's one large room, which serves as a living-room, dining-room and a kitchen, and a number of smaller rooms which provide privacy to the family members. Open-plan flats are usually very modern and spacious and are often built in reconstructed areas of big cities. They are either offered for rent or for sale, but because of the high prices, the buyer normally applies for a mortgage.
4. Yes, a lot of people do, especially young people. But to get the mortgage you need to prove you have a permanent job and the amount of the mortgage depends on how much you earn.
5. Some people still do the decorating themselves – either because they enjoy doing things on their own, or because of the cost. But nowadays, more and more people have the decorating, and cleaning afterwords, done for them.
6. It depends, of course. If a young couple buy a home, they often need to save before they can make some bigger changes. A lot of bathrooms and kitchens are installed in old high-rise blocks of flats, which are in a somewhat dilapidated condition. Sometimes the young people move into a home which used to be owned by their grandparents, so they refurbish the whole place. Also, a lot of people decide to replace their old kitchen or bathroom when their family situation changes, for example when they look after an old relative or their children leave home, or they decide to extend their living area because a child marries and/or has a baby.

5 rental, attic, landlord, extend, unfurnished, flatmate, contract, deposit

6
1. rental
2. Both
3. Both
4. flatmate
5. storage
6. lease
7. sign
8. extend

7
1. contract
2. flatmates
3. storage
4. deposit
5. extension
6. furnished
7. rental property
8. storey (also possible: floor)

8 possible answers, from the Czech Republic:
1. Yes, it is, especially in big cities. People usually want to buy a flat or house if they believe it's for a lifetime. If they come to the city to work or study, they usually rent a flat. Young people often live in rented flats until they start a family, then they look for a place to buy. And, of course, there are people who can never afford to buy a place of their own.
2. In the past, almost all the flats offered for rent were unfurnished. But with the changing lifestyle, a lot of flats, especially in big cities, are offered furnished and with all modern conveniences.
3. No, the length of contracts varies. It depends on the renter and landlord's agreement. The contract can be signed for a few months and for many years. But included in the contract, there are always conditions under which any of the parties can terminate the contract, and also a common condition is a deposit of three months' rent which can be used to cover the cost of any damage caused by the renter.
4. Yes, usually they are, on condition the renter has caused no problems and and the landlord has no other plans with the flat, of course.

Unit 39

1
1. pond
2. Both are possible.
3. scenery
4. tropical
5. Both are possible.
6. nature
7. wildlife
8. countryside

2
Frogs live in ponds.
You keep tools in a shed.
Birds build nests.
Nature consists of all kinds of wildlife.
Trees have roots.

3
1. scenery
2. roots
3. woods
4. acquire
5. intended
6. species
7. slope
8. tropical
9. greenhouse
10. hollow

4
1. B
2. G
3. G
4. B
5. B
6. G
7. G
8. B

5
1. spade
2. put my feet up
3. mow the lawn
4. cut back this bush (cut this bush back)
5. compost to the soil
6. lawnmower
7. hedge round the field
8. some weeding

6
1. to make the soil more fertile
2. It makes the ground wet and more difficult to dig.
3. Yes, because the weeds are not wanted and can make the garden very untidy.
4. Perhaps once a week or once a fortnight, depending on the season and the weather.
5. Cut them back.
6. To sit on and relax/put your feet up.
7. Yes, otherwise it will probably get too big.
8. Cleaning tools, cleaning the shed, tidying the garden, etc.

Unit 40

1
1. scroll
2. icon
3. launch
4. browse
5. install
6. prompt
7. settings
8. storage

2
1. key sth (in)
2. tap
3. switch
4. launch
5. browser
6. storage
7. scroll up

3 1 installed
2 browsing
3 prompt
4 tap
5 scroll
6 settings
7 launched
8 icon

4 1 D 3 S 5 D
2 S 4 S 6 S

5 1 No, you can't. It's too badly damaged.
2 You turn it off and then on again immediately.
3 Yes, you are.
4 It has many components.
5 A mouse is an external component.
6 No, it's very unwise. Without a backup, you risk losing all of your data.
7 Yes, it does.

6 1 freeze 3 damp 5 update 7 back up
2 antivirus 4 downwards 6 plug 8 unplug

7 *possible answers:*
1 My old computer used to freeze a lot, so I got a new one which doesn't.
2 Yes, I have – it's very important.
3 Not very often. I know I should do it more often than I do.
4 I don't think about it – I just wipe it! I didn't know you had to wipe it downwards.
5 I update my software every time the device prompts me to do so.
6 I usually plug it in when I get home in the evening.
7 My data updates automatically all the time.
8 Very occasionally I shut it down, but I think I only unplug it when I go away on holiday.

Unit 41

1 climax
underestimate
opponent
contender
relatively
priority
opposition
overestimate

2 1 quite easy
2 a difficult game
3 a team you are playing against
4 No, a contender is somebody taking part who might/could win it.
5 very important
6 judge them well
7 at the end
8 many teams.

3 1 opponents; tough (*also possible*: challenging)
2 priority
3 underestimate
4 League
5 relatively
6 contenders
7 home; away
8 reaching
9 titles

4 1 qualification
2 victory
3 inconsistent
4 domination
5 transformation
6 consistency

5 1 P 3 N 5 N 7 N 9 P
2 P 4 P 6 P 8 N 10 P

6 1 chance
2 pitch
3 boost
4 row
5 throw
6 consistency
7 qualify
8 pressure; sort
9 defeats
10 stand a chance

7 *possible answers:*
I support Chelsea. They have done quite well this season, but there have been too many home defeats and draws against teams we really should dominate easily. We were a bit inconsistent, and the manager was under pressure for a lot of the time because Chelsea supporters always expect a lot. In the end, though, we qualified for the Champions League, so that's not bad.

Unit 42

1 1 D 3 S 5 S 7 D 9 D
2 S 4 D 6 S 8 D 10 S

2 *Rhythm, tune, catchy, sing along, melody, chorus, hit single* and *lyrics* are associated with music.
Genre can be used in connection with music, but also with the other arts, e.g. literature, painting.

3 1 determination
2 complex
3 irrelevant
4 criterion
5 encounter
6 unforgettable

4 1 catchy (*also possible*: memorable)
2 tune (*also possible*: melody)
3 hit singles
4 chorus
5 lyrics
6 complicated/complex
7 relate to
8 rhythm

5 1 criteria
2 tune/melody (*also possible*: chorus)
3 genre
4 encountered
5 relevant; relate
6 engage
7 memorable (*also possible*: unforgettable)
8 relevance
9 determine
10 surface

6 *possible answers, from Argentina:*
1 I think that, as with all art forms, what matters is how we relate to the piece – what the song means to us personally. There are many reasons why a song might be considered great – it might be the rhythm, the lyrics, the melody, or a combination of all three.
2 A great pop song should be relevant to the listeners, which means that audiences can personally engage with the feelings evoked in the song. That is why most hits deal with basic human emotions, like love in all its forms.
3 As I'm not a musician myself I tend to focus on the lyrics.
4 I'm always humming or singing along to my favourite songs.
5 I think the sentiment behind a song is what can make a song truly popular. But of course there are exceptions to this – some very repetitive and simple songs have become hits.
6 I would say most songs by The Beatles have stood the test of time. If I had to write a list, I would include:
We can work it out (The Beatles)
I guess that's why they call it the Blues (Elton John)
Under my skin (Frank Sinatra)
Suspicious Minds (Elvis)
There must be an angel (Eurythmics)
Land of Confusion (Genesis)
Yesterday (The Beatles)

Unit 43

1 **actor:** fabulous, classic, unanimous
play: sensational, praise
far: cast
hair: scare
caught: applause, audience
theatre: adapt

2 1 set
2 death
3 effects
4 Both are possible.
5 classic
6 adaptation
7 ghost
8 applaud
9 tension

3 1 to death / stiff
2 adaptation
3 cast
4 unanimous
5 praise
6 applause
7 classic
8 tense

4 aspect   sequence
   blockbuster   somewhat
   con<u>vin</u>ced   sub<u>ti</u>tles
   expec<u>ta</u>tion   unpre<u>dic</u>table
   screen<u>play</u>

5 1 Yes   3 Yes   5 No
   2 No   4 Yes   6 No

6 1 predictable   5 somewhat/rather
   2 convincing   6 screenplay
   3 expectations   7 dubbed
   4 sequence   8 blockbusters

7 1 poor   5 subtitles
   2 exceeded my   6 unpredictable
      expectations   7 originality
   3 convinced (either)   8 somewhat confusing
   4 aspect (either)

Unit 44

1 <u>time</u>-consuming, con<u>tri</u>bute (In British English, <u>contribute</u> is also possible.), contri<u>bu</u>tion, dis<u>po</u>sable, be<u>fore</u>hand, <u>gate</u>crasher, get <u>go</u>ing, liven <u>up</u>

2 1 hosts   5 beforehand
   2 disposable   6 liven
   3 away   7 contribution
   4 time-consuming   8 prospect

3 1 preparation   5 going
   2 beforehand   6 livened up
   3 contributed   7 clear up
   4 gatecrashers

4 *possible answers, from Argentina:*

   I would say that in my country, sometimes parties are prepared beforehand, which of course gives the hosts the chance to enjoy the party more, but sometimes gatherings are kind of improvised.

   Guests usually contribute with drinks or snacks. I have never seen bouncers in private parties, but it sounds like a good idea – now with people posting everything on social media, gatecrashing is a risk.

   If people know one another, things get going quickly. Music can certainly liven up any event, particularly live music!

   Of course, there is always a lot to clear up afterwards, but if you feel your guests have had a good time, it's really worth it.

5 1 in company
   2 you fancy doing?
   3 have a good/great time (*also possible*: have a laugh)
   4 better be off (now)
   5 awkward (with people)
   6 warm welcome
   7 own company
   8 accompany you
   9 welcome (at her place)
  10 pop round/over/in / call round

6 1 good company   6 good of him
   2 popped/called   7 company
   3 welcome   8 open arms
   4 own company   9 call/pop
   5 socialize   10 be off

Unit 45

1 1 restoration   4 reversal
   2 amendment   5 evolution
   3 transformation

2 1 transform   4 reform/amend
   2 restore/reverse   5 adapt/adjust
   3 evolve   6 alter

3 1 transformed   6 alter (*also possible:*
   2 restore   adjust)
   3 evolution   7 adapt/adjust
   4 reversal   8 amend
   5 reform (*also possible:*   9 alterations
      amend)   10 transition

4 1 B   2 B   3 G   4 B   5 G   6 G

5 1 subtle   6 bring about
   2 sweeping/major/   7 resisted
      wholesale   8 implementation
   3 refreshing   9 an ongoing
   4 enforce   10 facilitate
   5 put into practice

6 1 pursue   6 welcome
   2 sweeping/radical/   7 ongoing
      major/wholesale   8 consultation
   3 resistance   9 implemented
   4 enforce/impose   10 obvious
   5 consulted

Unit 46

1 ap<u>pli</u>ance   in the <u>long</u> run
   better <u>still</u>   on <u>standby</u>
   con<u>serve</u>   tumble <u>dry</u>er
   dis<u>pos</u>al   conser<u>va</u>tion
   energy-saving

2 1 B   3 G   5 B   7 B   9 B
   2 B   4 G   6 G   8 G   10 G

3 1 short-term   7 long term
   2 labour-saving   8 landfill sites
   3 solar panels   9 batteries
   4 on standby   10 switch
   5 tumble   11 toxic
   6 eco (ecological)   12 dispose
      disaster

4 1 dryer   7 batteries; still; charger
   2 charge (up)   8 saving
   3 monitor   9 consumer
   4 consume   10 investment
   5 appliances   11 generated
   6 conserve   12 savings

5 *possible answers:*
   1 No, I haven't, so I can obviously manage without one.
   2 Occasionally, but not often.
   3 We have a device that tells us how much electricity we use, but I don't bother to look at it very often.
   4 No, I don't.
   5 an oven, a fridge, a washing machine, a dishwasher, a kettle, a toaster, a coffee machine, food mixer and radio.
   6 Yes, I usually do.
   7 I use rechargeable batteries for a number of things: my laptop, phone, toothbrush and e-reader.
   8 I use energy-saving light bulbs and rechargeable batteries. I've got solar panels (14 of them) and haven't got a tumble dryer.
   9 I've no idea, but probably above average because I work from home a lot of the time.
   10 I think they are a great investment.
   11 In 2019, about 3% of electricity was generated by solar energy in the UK.
   12 Keeping a car is expensive, but some public transport could be a lot cheaper – the trains in particular. I've made significant savings, though, in using my bike more.

Unit 47

1
1	S	3	S	5	D	7	S
2	D	4	D	6	D	8	S

2
1 danger 3 natural 5 verge
2 out 4 in 6 species

3
1 out; extinct
2 cleared; deforestation
3 extinction; decline
4 regions
5 habitat
6 endangered; instance
7 conservation
8 declining; die
9 pointing
10 considered

4
1 ~~divested~~ diverted
2 ~~feed~~ breed
3 ~~puts~~ poses
4 ~~civic~~ civil
5 ~~kill~~ wipe
6 ~~over~~ after
7 ~~decorational~~ decorative
8 ~~threaten~~ threat

5
1 civil
2 horn
3 divert
4 after
5 up
6 poses
7 out
8 threat

6
1 likelihood
2 territory
3 poaching
4 under threat
5 territorial
6 tiger poacher
7 breed
8 ended up

Unit 48

1
1	D	3	D	5	D	7	D	9	D
2	S	4	D	6	S	8	D		

2
revolutionary
restriction
surgical
vaccination; vaccinate
diagnose; diagnostic
transplant
infect; infectious

3
1	No	3	Yes	5	Yes	7	Yes
2	No	4	No	6	No	8	Yes

4
1 theatre
2 advances
3 supplements
4 era
5 rate
6 procedure
7 donor/transplant
8 minerals
9 cure
10 medicine

5
1 eradicated / wiped out; wiped out / eradicated
2 restricted; transplant
3 vaccinate; vaccine
4 conventional; advances
5 infection
6 operate; procedure/operation; confined
7 revolutionary/radical; resume
8 enabled

Unit 49

1
1	S	3	S	5	D	7	S
2	D	4	S	6	D	8	S

2
1 emigration
2 seek
3 ethnic
4 refuge
5 Both are possible.
6 fled
7 Both are possible.
8 Both are possible.

3
1 There's no limit on the number of people given political **asylum** in this country.
2 Racial and sexual **discrimination** is against the law in matters of employment.
3 Economic **migration** to richer countries has existed for centuries.
4 There are over 2,000 **refugees** seeking political asylum in this country.

5 Nearly half a million people were forced to **flee** their homes during the civil war, and many of them **took** refuge in the mountains, away from the fighting.
6 My neighbour has always had a **prejudice** against people whose skin is a different colour.
7 Asians only form a small **minority** within the population.
8 There has been a lot of **racial** tension between different ethnic groups.

4 culture shock, live in peace, religious faith, have no desire to do sth, have a part to play, country of origin

5
1 ~~for~~ towards
2 in part~~ly~~
3 ~~nostalgic~~ nostalgia
4 ~~stereoscope~~ stereotype
5 ~~integrity~~ integration
6 ~~natural~~ native

6
1 native
2 faith
3 shock
4 part
5 stereotypical
6 desire
7 for
8 integrate
9 hostile
10 peace
11 nostalgic

Unit 50

1
ide<u>o</u>logy
ideo<u>log</u>ical
<u>ca</u>pitalism
con<u>ser</u>vative
status <u>quo</u>
op<u>pose</u>
opp<u>o</u>sition
ex<u>tre</u>mism
as<u>so</u>ciate
associ<u>a</u>tion
dis<u>tri</u>bute
distri<u>bu</u>tion

2
ideological
conservative;
  conservative
socialist; socialist
liberalism; liberal
association; associated
extremism; extreme
distribution

3
1 F – A **communist** economy ...
2 T
3 T
4 F – A liberal believes in economic freedom and **gradual** political change.
5 F – The Conservative party in Britain believes in **capitalism**.
6 F – **Communists** believe that everyone should own the means of production.
7 F – Extremists tend to have **extreme** beliefs.
8 T

4
1 right-wing
2 wealthy
3 opposed to it
4 status quo
5 moderate
6 in the centre
7 the opposition
8 communist (also possible: socialist)

5
1 distribution
2 favour
3 ownership
4 associate
5 maintain
6 wealthy
7 extent
8 prominent
9 partly
10 association/connection

6 *possible answers, from Hungary*:
1 We have many different parties showing the whole spectrum of political views from right-wing to left-wing. Fortunately, extremist parties are not among the major political players and do not have seats in the Parliament.
2 It depends on the particular issue we are talking about. If I find it necessary, I cannot refrain from calling/voting for radical change.
3 In many cases maintaining the status quo would be quite boring. When it comes to politics, I can imagine situations where radically changing the existing order is the only way out.

4 I am not that much into politics so I cannot really say. What I find unacceptable is when people criticize the existing government just because they are in power. I believe in studying a given issue from as many aspects as possible and forming an informed opinion based on facts rather than on my emotions.
5 Yes, I strongly believe in personal and economic freedom, and am quite tolerant towards people whose views differ from mine.
6 Absolutely, I always have my ID card and my driving licence on me.
7 I live in a big city – Budapest – so we have practically all types of public transport. The most common are bus, tram and the underground, but you can also take a suburban train or cycle around on the many newly-built cycle paths. The latest craze is the electric scooter but, personally, I find it rather dangerous.

Unit 51

1
1 resident
2 ensure
3 voluntary
4 council
5 allocate
6 manifesto
7 councillor
8 volunteer

2
1 ~~manifest~~ manifesto
2 ~~to~~ in
3 ~~make~~ take
4 ~~volunteer~~ voluntary
5 ~~for~~ of
6 ~~out~~ up
7 ~~assure~~ ensure
8 ~~grand~~ grant

3
1 councillors; behalf
2 volunteers; sector
3 have
4 stick/stand; take
5 grant
6 resident; citizen
7 green
8 allocated
9 ensure
10 council

4
1 budget / funding
2 committee / authorities
3 spokesperson / chairman
4 profile
5 All are possible.
6 All are possible.
7 mayor/head
8 chairs / sits on

5
1 police
2 eligible OR ineligible
3 chair
4 authority/authorities
5 budget
6 committees
7 mayor
8 heads
9 profile
10 funding

6 *possible answers, from the Czech Republic:*
1 Yes. Each town has a mayor. In big cities they are called Lord Mayor. Elections take place every four years. In these local elections, people vote for the future members of the council. Then, at their first meeting, the elected councillors choose the mayor. He/She is usually the head of the party who won the majority of seats and his/her deputies are heads of the coalition parties.
2 Yes, it is. The bigger the town, the more influence the mayor has.
3 The mayor cannot decide much on their own. They always act in compliance with the decisions of the town council. They take decisions on the town's development, approve its budget, and establish and abolish organizations such as the local police, technical services which look after the cleaning of the town, collection and sorting of rubbish, parks and other green spaces, cultural centres, and sports centres and facilities. They are also responsible for kindergardens and basic schools, and a lot more. The mayor is the one to sign the most important documents and bears the responsibilty for matters they refer to.

Unit 52

1 free of charge, health care, clinical trial, strictly confidential, cosmetic surgery

2
1 specialist
2 confidential
2 surgery
4 prescribe
5 if; care
6 register; enrolled
7 refer; specialist
8 participants; trial

3
1 care
2 register
3 prescription
4 of charge
5 specialist
6 referred
7 confidential
8 suspect

4 *possible answers, from Poland:*
Yes, you do need to register with a GP.
Your GP refers you to a specialist
You get a free prescription for some drugs but some are paid for. People who are insured get some discount. I also think you get some discount if you are a pensioner.
When you suspect that a doctor has made a mistake and it is too late to have it fixed by him/her, you can sue the doctor for negligence, damages, etc.
In order to become a participant in a clinical trial, you need to be referred by your GP or a specialist.
I think in certain cases you can have cosmetic surgery for free, e.g. when it is treatment after an accident or an operation.
Yes, all medical records are strictly confidential.

5
1 feet
2 no
3 admitted
4 old self
5 Both are possible.
6 kept
7 Both are possible.
8 Both are possible.
9 recuperation
10 dedicated

6
1 no notice of me
2 me informed
3 off my feet
4 real self
5 recuperate/convalesce
6 miserable
7 well-being
8 dedicated

7
1 admitted; ward
2 kept
3 rushed
4 well-being; prime
5 junior
6 absolute
7 convalescence
8 discharged

8 *possible answers, from Poland:*
1 Yes.
2 Yes, I think they are.
3 Yes, very much so.
4 Yes, according to the law.
5 That depends on the hospital, but probably on the whole it is true.
6 Yes, they do.
7 It may differ from case to case but, on the whole, that is the case, usually.
8 No, patients (or their families) will have to buy their medicines from a pharmacy.

Unit 53

1
detain
suspect *v*
suspect *n*
offence
invalid
magistrate
custody
solicitor
remand
convict
acquit
constable

2
1 in
2 for
3 with
4 of
5 of
6 to

3
1 constable/sergeant/ inspector
2 offence
3 issue/grant/refuse
4 custody
5 grant
6 acquit

4
1 a magistrate OR a judge
2 the police
3 a solicitor
4 a judge OR a magistrate
5 the person awaiting trial / the prisoner
6 the police officer who arrests the suspect
7 a police constable
8 an inspector
9 the chief constable
10 a judge

5
1 rank
2 warrant
3 remanded
4 procedure(s); valid
5 suspect; offence
6 caution

6
1 about
2 constable/officer
3 detained
4 custody
5 suspect
6 solicitor
7 charged
8 offences
9 magistrate
10 granted
11 convicted
12 sentenced

Unit 54

1
abolish
abolition
capital punishment
deterrent
rehabilitate
rehabilitation
reoffender
occupational
hazard
justify
justification
justifiable

2
1 up
2 me as a friend
3 capital punishment for some crimes
4 justifiable (*also possible*: justified)
5 imprisonment
6 abolition of the law
7 occupational hazard
8 reoffenders
9 revenge (on him)
10 crisis

3
1 rehabilitate
2 reoffend
3 deterrent
4 capital
5 abolish
6 justification; revenge
7 crisis
8 justice; justice

4 *possible answers:*
1 I don't know the answer to that, but I think we could rehabilitate more offenders than we do at present.
2 There are many possible reasons: not enough support from friends, family or the state; the person can't get a job and is short of money, mixing with the wrong kind of people; crime becomes a way of life, etc.
3 Clearly it isn't a very effective deterrent if a significant number reoffend.
4 No, I have never believed in capital punishment.
5 I would like like to abolish solitary confinement.
6 The answer is probably 'no', but I can understand people wanting revenge; it's human nature in some situations and circumstances.
7 Yes, I believe it is. I think we currently lock up more people in the UK than any other European country. The prisons cannot cope with the numbers; they are overcrowded.
8 I believe in the need for the criminal justice system, but justice – the fair treatment of people – is not easy to achieve.

5
1 confinement
2 Both are possible.
3 assessment
4 Both are possible.
5 Both are possible.
6 Both are possible.
7 Both are possible.
8 institution

6
1 therapy
2 segregation
3 catering
4 cells
5 consent
6 proportion
7 mutual
8 principle
9 confinement
10 exclusively

7 *possible answer:*
I think we should have more prisons based on these principles. It wouldn't work for everyone and perhaps not a majority, but it could be successful in rehabilitating a good proportion of offenders because it works on the principle that if you treat people like decent human beings, there is a good chance they will then behave like decent human beings.

Unit 55

1
1 Encompass is different.
2 These three are pronounced like *bit*: civilian, encompass, enlisted.
These three are pronounced like *bet*: deadly, differentiate, weapon.
3 The three that are different are: comprise, diverse, missile.

2
unarmed combat
the vast majority
the armed forces
lethal weapon
military service
serve your country
make a distinction
be in command
military aircraft

3
1 vast
2 military
3 consists
4 fundamental
5 combat
6 diverse
7 guard
8 enlisted
9 deadly
10 distinguish/differentiate
11 encompasses
12 compulsory
13 commands
14 (a large military) operation

4
1 armed
2 made up
3 command
4 serve
5 reserves
6 diverse
7 branch
8 weapons
9 comprise/consist of

5 *possible answers, from India:*
1 Yes, India has got a professional military in place. The Indian Armed Forces consist of three uniformed services – the Indian Army, the Indian Navy and the Indian Air Force.
2 Yes, India has a reserve army.
3 Yes, India has many institutions that provide military service.
4 Yes, the police are usually armed in India.
5 No, I have never stood next to a tank.
No, I have never owned or used a deadly weapon.
No, I have never been in a professional army.
Yes, I have flown in a helicopter a few times.
No, I have never dropped from a parachute.
No, I have never enrolled for military service.

Unit 56

1
1 D
2 D
3 S
4 D
5 D
6 S
7 S
8 S

2
1 B
2 B
3 G
4 B
5 G
6 G
7 G
8 G (for the army) B (for the criminals)

3
1	f	3	j	5	h	7	e	9	d
2	c	4	a	6	g	8	b	10	i

4
1 New arms deal
2 Government pledges/vows to back new hospital
3 Go-ahead for rail scheme
4 Company chief axed
5 Boost for big banks (*also possible*: Backing for big banks)
6 Latest statistics a blow for the economy
7 Kidnappers demand ransom
8 Ministers urge delay
9 Motorcyclist cleared of child's death
10 PM rules out further tax cuts

5
1 Blast wrecks new shopping centre
2 Senators rule out more international aid
3 Shareholders bid to axe chairman
4 Officers foil prison escape plot
5 Bid to change law on hunting (OR Bid to change hunting law)
6 New food alert (OR New alert about certain foods)

Unit 57

1 mass; blank; precious; instant; specialist; opening

2
1	D	3	S	5	S	7	S
2	S	4	D	6	S	8	D

3
1 blank
2 opening
3 tone
4 assume
5 quoting/citing
6 talk
7 pace
8 assumption
9 part

4
1 I went to the opening of the exhibition.
2 You must grab the reader's attention.
3 I can recognize his style instantly.
4 It was a mistake on my part.
5 We must leave now, otherwise we'll be late.
6 There is mass unemployment
7 Did you quote/cite her?
8 Freedom is precious.

5
1 publication
2 specialist
3 mass
4 commodity
5 opening
6 Quotes

6
1 It determines the style of writing.
2 You can assume a greater level of knowledge on the part of your readers.
3 Don't use difficult words and long sentences, but don't talk down to your readers.
4 The most precious commodity is space, and it is precious because it is always in short supply.
5 It has to engage the reader instantly; summarize the story, and state why you are writing it; set the tone for the rest of the story.
6 Quotes should be short, otherwise the story may lose pace and direction.

7 *possible answers for the UK:*
The most specialist newspaper is *The Financial Times*. Specialist magazines include *The Spectator* and *The New Statesman*.
Mass-market papers include *The Sun*, *The Mirror* and *The Daily Mail*.
The Prime Minister of the United Kingdom, the President of the US, and famous celebrities such as sportsmen and women are commonly quoted in newspapers and on TV.

Unit 58

1 con<u>cern</u>ing, de<u>bate</u>, conflict, di<u>vide</u>, contest
(Note that the verb **con<u>test</u>** is stressed differently.), turnout, ne<u>go</u>tiate, refe<u>ren</u>dum, e<u>lec</u>torate

2
1 concerning/regarding
2 a narrow majority
3 has divided
4 electorate
5 turnout
6 negotiate / take part in negotiations

3
1 referendum
2 will
3 negotiation(s)
4 debate
5 closely; contest
6 conflict

4
1 A referendum
2 It was concerning Britain's continued membership of the EU.
3 It deeply divided opinion in the nation.
4 A narrow majority in favour of leaving the EU.
5 72% of the total electorate
6 There was a long period of negotiation.

5
1	D	3	D	5	S	7	S
2	D	4	S	6	D	8	D

6
1 govern
2 cooperate
3 advocate
4 compromise
5 philosophy
6 multiple
7 coalition
8 dominance/dominant
9 consensus

7
1 two or more political groups working together
2 everyone
3 a lot of control
4 for it
5 more powerful
6 give up some of the things you wanted for a solution both sides can accept

8
1 multiple
2 compromise
3 govern
4 dominant
5 cooperate
6 core; philosophy
7 advocate
8 coalition

Unit 59

1 re<u>bell</u>ion, minimise, pro<u>tes</u>ter, up<u>hold</u>, demonstrators, a<u>vert</u>, e<u>rect</u>, occupy, demon<u>stra</u>tion, <u>mean</u>while, pro<u>test</u>, diso<u>be</u>dience

2 demonstration, disruption, rebellion, disobedience, resistance, occupy

3
1 T
2 F – If someone upholds the law, they obey it.
3 F – If you avert an accident, you prevent it from happening.
4 F – If you tolerate something, you allow it to continue.
5 F – A building which is occupied contains protesters or people who are currently living or working in it.
6 T
7 F – If you minimize something, you reduce it to the lowest possible level.
8 F – A rebellion is opposition to authority by an organized group.

4
1 barriers
2 disobedience
3 activists/ demonstrators/ protesters
4 disruption
5 resistance
6 movement
7 called on
8 staging
9 entire
10 tolerate

5 1 like human **beings**
2 have called **on** activists
3 to **minimize** the disruption
4 in **connection** with the events
5 have been **occupied**
6 to **avert** any potential danger
7 a group of **activists/demonstrators/protesters**
8 avert **disruption**
9 no longer **put** up with
10 who **erected** the barriers

6 1 movement
2 mission
3 disobedience
4 avert
5 occupying
6 tolerated
7 activists/
   demonstrators/
   protesters
8 demonstration/
   protest
9 activists/
   demonstrators/
   protesters
10 calling
11 beings
12 stage

Unit 60

1 Evacuate is the exception.

2 1 collapsed
2 numerous
3 evacuated
4 trapped inside their
   homes
5 strike/hit
6 death toll
7 considerable
8 rescued
9 scale
10 significantly

3 1 strikes/hits
2 collapse
3 trapped
4 evacuation
5 rescue/save
6 maintain
7 tremors
8 considerable/
   significant
9 scale
10 toll

4 devastate firefighter casualty precaution deliberate
suspect assessment courage courageous intensity
intentional suspicion

5 1 suspect
2 intensity
3 assessment
4 courageous
5 devastation
6 precaution
7 casualties
8 tackling

6 1 blaze
2 deliberately
3 brigade
4 bravery (also possible:
   courage)
5 assessment
6 praise
7 suspicious
8 intense

7 1 casualties
2 brigade
3 intense
4 praised
5 assess
6 suspicion

Unit 61

1 1 S
2 D
3 D
4 S
5 D
6 S

2 1 formally (Note that
   the most natural word
   order is: They formally
   announced it.)
2 confirmation
3 drowned
4 floated
5 fragments
6 estate
7 assistance
8 notify

3 1 acre
2 fragments
3 formally
4 floating
5 notify
6 confirmation
7 lord
8 drowned

4 possible answers, from China:
1 Acre and hectare are commonly used to describe an
   area of land in our language. For smaller areas, we often
   use square foot and square metre.
2 We don't have any large estates in my city, Hong Kong.
3 There is no equivalent of a lord in our country.
4 Hong Kong is divided into districts. Our country is
   divided into provinces, and in each province there are
   many cities and counties.
5 We should call the emergency line if someone dies at
   home of natural causes. Police then come to confirm the
   case. And an ambulance is sent to collect the body and
   provide all the necessary assistance.

5 regulator network edit distress in the public
interest live stream commentator prejudice delicate
balancing act

6 network, broadcaster, clip, edit, live stream
(You can have a media regulator, but regulators also operate
throughout other business and industries.)

7 a public library; a balancing act; a media regulator; in the
public interest; a film clip; racial prejudice

8 1 clips
2 broadcast
3 distress
4 edited
5 live stream
   (also possible:
   live broadcast)
6 public; delicate
7 prejudice
8 commentator;
   regulator

Unit 62

1 1 revealing, exposing
2 carried out,
   conducted
3 pry into
4 All three are possible.
5 contrasts with
6 emerge
7 be revealed, emerge
8 Coverage
9 findings, revelations
10 deserve

2 1 carried
2 revealed
3 findings
4 deserve
5 emerged
6 eye
7 contrast
8 privacy

3 1 tabloid
2 prying; public
3 privacy
4 celebrity

possible answers:
1 Yes, we do.
2 Yes, they do it all the time.
3 I think the families of celebrities deserve privacy, but it
   is difficult for people in the public eye to avoid publicity
   and keep their privacy. There are times when celebrities
   actually enjoy being in the public eye.
4 The advantages are often wealth, status and being able
   to enjoy privileges that ordinary people don't have.
   The disadvantages are the lack of privacy, and that is
   sometimes accompanied by stress.

4 1 D
2 D
3 S
4 D
5 D
6 D
7 S
8 D

5 1 Allegedly, he has lost all his money.
2 They acted in her defence. / They rallied to her defence.
3 They say she has a fortune / is worth a fortune.
4 Jason has custody of his son.
5 He's been through hell recently.
6 She's had support from (her) fellow workers.

6 1 rumour
2 allegation
3 scandal
4 rock
5 hell
6 alleging
7 rehab
8 fortune
9 custody
10 fellow
11 rally
12 defend

Unit 63

1 severe; direct; remaining; mysterious; stuck; rapid; delicate

2
1 tip
2 Both are possible.
3 severe
4 mysterious
5 Both are possible.
6 do
7 Both are possible.
8 remaining
9 ever since

3
1 bear / put up with
   (*also possible in formal*
   English: endure)
2 delicate
3 dare
4 (ever) since
5 dare
6 mysterious
7 rapid/speedy recovery
8 dare
9 directly
10 stuck

4
1 S
2 D
3 D
4 D
5 S
6 S
7 D
8 S

5
1 kill you
2 die
3 see
4 chance
5 fall
6 clearly

6
1 panic
2 swamp
3 spotted
4 tale
5 stay put
6 stranded
7 lower limit
8 any chances

Unit 64

1
1 D
2 D
3 S
4 D
5 S
6 D
7 D
8 D
9 S
10 D

2 apprentice handyman executive entrepreneur
lucrative librarian electrician nowadays
civil servant vacancy bodyguard self-employed

3
1 jeweller
2 handyman
3 civil servant
4 barman/barmaid
5 apprentice (plumber)
6 bodyguard
7 carpenter
8 plumber
9 librarian
10 butcher
11 accountant
12 housewife/
   househusband

4 (*Answers may vary from country to country.*)
   In the UK, these jobs are generally quite well-paid:
electrician, civil servant, accountant
   **These jobs can be quite well paid but often they
aren't**: manual worker, librarian, casual work
   These jobs aren't well paid: barman/barmaid,
apprentice, housewife

5
1 seeking
2 senior
3 lucrative
4 nowadays
5 manual
6 employed
7 vacancies
8 executive
9 tough
10 incentive
11 post/position; vacant
12 civil service

6 *possible answers*:
1 Yes, I used to do manual work in my holidays when I was
   at university, and I've been self-employed for a number
   of years.
2 I think it would be fun to be a handyman: working for
   yourself, doing varied jobs, and often spending time
   solving problems for other people.
3 I am self-employed and prefer it that way.
4 I don't need an incentive to work hard if I enjoy what
   I'm doing. If I didn't enjoy my job, then I would need
   incentives, such as a good salary or long holidays.
5 No, I'm not very good at it, but I quite like it for short
   periods of time.
6 Yes, I think it might be fun.
7 I think they're a great idea, and it would help young
   people if there were more apprenticeship schemes in
   this country.

8 No, I don't think I would be happy only doing
   housework unless it was for a very short period of time.
9 I wouldn't mind a low-status job if it was temporary, but
   I would be less happy if I had a permanent job which
   had low status.

Unit 65

1 qualifications
administration
manufacturing
market research
   (*also possible*: market research)
human resources
finance
recruitment
insurance

2
1 market research
2 human resources
3 retail
4 insurance
5 manufacturing
6 administration
7 finance
8 recruitment / HR / human resources

3
1 registered
2 qualification(s)
3 finance
4 sector
5 manufacturing

4 *possible answers*:
   My experience has been in retail. I've worked for Marks
& Spencer now for 15 years. Initially, I was a shop-floor
manager for a number of years, and then I retrained and
now work in human resources, where I spend a lot of my
time looking at ways for other staff members to move on in
their careers and develop new skills. I find human resources
a very rewarding sector to work in.

5
1 D
2 S
3 D
4 D
5 D (They might be
   the same, but not
   necessarily.)
6 S
7 D
8 S
9 S
10 D
11 D
12 S

6
1 challenging
2 department
3 prospects
4 promoted
5 elsewhere
6 unemployed
7 fire/sack
8 resign/quit
9 appointed
10 promotion
11 redundant
12 quit (*also possible*:
   resign)

7 *possible answers*:
1 True
2 Not true
3 True (I think, so but I'm not sure.)
4 True
5 Not true (at the moment)
6 Not true (I was once out of work for nearly six months.)
7 True (I don't think I could do it.)
8 True (Probably, but again I'm not sure.)
9 Not true (I wasn't sure I would like the job when I was
   appointed.)
10 Sometimes true and sometimes not. (People are
   sometimes promoted because they are talented, and
   sometimes promoted because they are the most senior
   member of staff.)
11 Not true. I have never been made redundant.
12 Not true. I have never resigned because I didn't like
   my job.

Unit 66

1 <u>free</u>lance   guaran<u>tee</u>
   ac<u>cou</u>ntable   ad<u>di</u>tional
   <u>in</u>sight   en<u>cou</u>nter

2
1 encountered
2 degree
3 accountable to no one
4 insight into
5 balance
6 pros and cons
7 an extent
8 gets in the way of

3
1 freelance
2 boss
3 solely
4 encountered
5 degree
6 better
7 in the way
8 guaranteed
9 additional

4 *possible answers:*

I was a freelance illustrator for four years. I enjoyed similar advantages such as being able to choose what work to take on and being my own boss. Occasionally I encountered a degree of isolation as my work often got in the way of my social life. Over the years, I came to appreciate that my income was not guaranteed and that I had to take on extra work when it was available. I was able to take care of my family, open a restaurant, which my wife runs, and buy a car. I don't miss the additional benefits of a regular job because I have health insurance and I am enrolled in a pension scheme.

5
1 P   3 N   5 P   7 N
2 N   4 P   6 N   8 P

6
1 fit in
2 use her initiative
3 of collaboration
4 away with it
5 enterprise
6 mutual respect

7
1 valued
2 part; spirit
3 foster/promote/ encourage
4 diverse
5 disruptive
6 suppress; fulfilling/ rewarding

8 *possible answers:*

In general, I agree with the pros and cons above, although a good team shouldn't suppress individual enterprise and initiative.

Other advantages of working in a group:
1 It can improve your communication skills.
2 Individuals can learn from other members of the group and improve their skills.

Other disadvantages are:
1 Some individuals become very competitive with other individuals, and this can damage the effectiveness of the team.
2 If members of the team do not agree on the goals, it can be hard to make progress.

Unit 67

1 dispute, give in, break down, halt, closure

2
1 set
2 settle
3 ballot
4 set
5 halt
6 step up
7 give in
8 broken down

3
1 closures
2 stake
3 dispute
4 precedent
5 have broken down / broke down
6 inclined
7 wages
8 ballot

4 minimum wage; fringe benefit; maternity leave; state pension; dental treatment; go on strike; trade union

5
1 maternity
2 union
3 bonus
4 go on
5 leave
6 entitled; pension
7 right; trade; strike
8 commission
9 right
10 minimum; leave

6 *possible answers:*
1 In my job, I don't get a commission because I'm not a salesman, and I don't get health or dental insurance either. However, I get the other perks mentioned. The annual bonus varies from year to year, but we usually get one. The other benefit I get is the opportunity to eat in a subsidized canteen, where the food is quite good and very cheap. The most important benefit for me is the company pension because it's worth the most money.
2 I enjoy all the rights mentioned, and I believe everyone should have those rights.
3 *(answer from a 17-year-old still at school)* I like the sound of an annual bonus, especially if it comes at Christmas when I need more money. I would also like paid sick leave if I was ill. I don't know much about pensions but my parents are always telling me they're important, so that would be good too.

Unit 68

1 re<u>min</u>der, pri<u>ori</u>tize, ac<u>com</u>plish, an<u>ti</u>cipate, <u>dead</u>line, <u>de</u>legate

2
1 prioritized
2 remind
3 Both are possible.
4 basis; wherever
5 anticipated
6 stick
7 Both are possible.
8 priority

3
1 basis
2 sticks
3 anticipate
4 reminder
5 delegate
6 make a note
7 matter
8 accomplished/ achieved
9 deadlines
10 note it down
11 at a time

4 *possible answers:*

I think it is a good idea to make a note of tasks you need to do, but I don't think it is necessary to put reminders everywhere. Prioritizing is also important, but setting deadlines for every task is very difficult. I think it's also difficult sometimes to stick to one thing at a time. Sometimes you just have to do two things at the same time. I try to stick to my priorities. That's important. And you should always delegate if you can. Anticipating problems is not easy.

5
1 prompt
2 overwhelming
3 Both are possible.
4 stream
5 Both are possible.
6 flood
7 frustrated
8 Both are possible.

6
1 Our spending has got out **of** control.
2 My **nerves** are on edge.
3 Fortunately, the situation is **under** control.
4 I was overwhelmed **by** the response.
5 There's so much work. I'm **stressed** out.
6 He keeps **interrupting** me when I'm working; it's annoying.

7
1 interruptions
2 productive
3 productivity
4 promptly
5 stressed
6 endless

8 *possible answers:*
1 Fortunately, I don't get a constant stream of interruptions, but I find that even one or two can be a bit frustrating.
2 I'm usually quite productive in the morning, but less so in the afternoon.

3 I think my productivity would be improved if we had air conditioning. In the summer it gets very hot where I work, and it makes me feel a bit sleepy.
4 Personally, I like to reply to emails promptly, otherwise they build up and become overwhelming.
5 I don't think I get stressed out, but I do sometimes worry a bit that I don't have enough time.
6 No, I don't think so, but I know several friends who think like that.

Unit 69

1 *possible answers:*
1	soon	5	control
2	result	6	past
3	start	7	support
4	owns	8	agreement

2
1	strike/make/conclude	5	imminent
2	bid	6	takeover/acquisition
3	set	7	agenda
4	mount	8	corporate

3
1	former boss	6	outcome
2	his leadership	7	another bid / a higher
3	backing		bid
4	a deal	8	merger
5	shareholders		

4 1 D   2 S   3 S   4 S   5 D   6 S

5
1	soared/rocketed	5	coup
2	plunged/plummeted	6	climb
3	peak	7	in the wake of
4	fresh	8	pursuing

6
1	soared/rocketed	5	floated
2	collapsed (*also possible*: plunged/ plummeted)	6	to climb
		7	coup
		8	reached a peak
3	issued	9	pursue it
4	hostile		

Unit 70

1
1 A designer and manufacturer of safety helmets for use at sea.
2 1993.
3 Because surfing was a seasonal business.
4 It had to be light, give protection and retain heat.
5 No, he had to adapt them.
6 He took out a bank loan.
7 He launched the new safety helmets.
8 Feedback from his customers.
9 A good partnership with suppliers.

2 retention; investment; diversification; innovation; exploitation, launch

3
1	contract	5	innovative
2	retain	6	diversify
3	protection	7	partnership
4	feedback	8	potential

4
1	Both are possible.	4	keep ahead of
2	adapt	5	founded
3	that case	6	Both are possible.

5
1	exploit	5	contract
2	Innovation	6	potential
3	refined	7	feedback
4	invest	8	diversify

6
1	gap	7	cases
2	took out; loan	8	keep; rivals/ competitors
3	manufacture		
4	give	9	founder; firm
5	investment	10	launch
6	crew		

Unit 71

1
1	G	7	G
2	G	8	G
3	B	9	B
4	G	10	Probably B because it's not considered good if you are satisfied too easily, especially in the competitive world of business.
5	B		
6	B		

2
1	thrive/flourish	6	dynamism
2	passionate	7	boasting
3	forward	8	dissatisfied
4	aspire	9	secret
5	overcome	10	breakthrough

3 *possible answers:*
1 I think you need hard work or luck (and probably both) to thrive for a long time.
2 I think it's good if you are passionate about what you do. I'm not sure it's essential in order to be successful, though.
3 Forward planning is certainly important in business or a career.
4 I'd like to feel that I had fulfilled my potential. In other words, I aspire to be the best I can be in my field.
5 I had a motorbike accident when I was 21 and couldn't really walk for about three months.
6 I'm not sure dynamism is that important, though it probably helps.
7 Yes, I think it is possible to talk about your own achievements without boasting, but you need to be careful about how you do it, and also how much you do it.
8 Yes, I have passed exams where I still felt dissatisfied because I could've done better.
9 Penelope Cruz is very successful, and I think her secret is that she combines being very talented with being very beautiful.
10 There are breakthroughs every year in the treatment of different cancers.

4
1	came	5	failure
2	interfere in	6	Both are possible.
3	lasts	7	Both are possible.
4	down	8	last

5
1 The business is **going** downhill. ~ Yeah, it's been **deteriorating** for a while now.
2 What was the **row** about? ~ Kate got annoyed because of Sonny's **interference** in her project.
3 Did Mia **come** top in the exam? ~ Yes, but Tom only just **scraped** through.
4 Do you think the relationship will **last** long? ~ No, not if Kieran keeps **letting** her down.
5 Why did she drop **out** of the course? ~ She told me it was **hopeless**.
6 Why did you **interfere** in their cooking? ~ I just felt they were **getting** nowhere with it.

6
1	come	4	struggle
2	scraped	5	row
3	dropped	6	nowhere

7 *possible answers:*
1 Yes, I have come top in a few exams over the years.
2 Yes, I just scraped through an important maths exam when I was 16.
3 No, but I dropped out of a Spanish course because I was too busy with work.
4 Actually, passing my driving test was a struggle because I failed the first time.
5 Yes, I had a serious row with someone at work because they didn't give me an opportunity to apply for a job that I wanted. We have a better relationship now, but for a long time we didn't.
6 Yes, I stopped doing yoga because I didn't think think I was getting any better.

Unit 72

1
1. escalating/growing
2. confront
3. arise
4. multiplied
5. insoluble
6. exaggerate it
7. resolve
8. tackling

2
1. escalating/growing
2. address (confront/ face up to are also possible)
3. urgent
4. raised
5. overcome
6. tackle/resolve
7. insoluble
8. tackling/confronting
9. minor
10. escalate

3 *possible answers*:

Litter on the streets is not a major problem, but it's not an easy problem to resolve because some people will always drop litter. It's a question of education, I think.

Graffiti is a major problem in some places, but where I live they are tackling it quite successfully. If you see graffiti, you can call a number, and they will send a team to clean it off. It seems to work.

Household rubbish is a growing problem and will only be resolved when we stop using so much plastic and packaging around everything we buy.

Some cities are now seriously starting to address the problem of pollution by introducing charges for vehicles with high pollution levels.

Parking is another growing problem as we increase the number of cars in society. Most cities in England are tackling it by increasing out of town parking areas to encourage people to get buses into the town centre.

Bullying has always been present, especially in schools. More schools are facing up to the problem now with both punishments for offenders and counselling for victims.

4
1. esteem
2. get her down
3. articulate
4. regardless
5. insignificant
6. channel
7. accept
8. seriously
9. damaging
10. playing down

5
1. damaged
2. get her down
3. perspective
4. behind
5. reassuring
6. setback
7. significance
8. articulate

6 *possible answers*:

I think teenagers are often unhappy about their appearance (I was), and this is bad for their self-esteem. I also agree that it is difficult to accept any kind of failure, and equally difficult to keep things in perspective.

Another problem for teenagers now is the significance of social media. This causes massive peer pressure to do what others do. It is easy in these circumstances for teenagers to exaggerate the significance of various problems.

Unit 73

1
1. modify
2. contemporary
3. estimate v
4. formerly

2
1. unfortunate
2. splendid
3. formerly
4. well-preserved
5. contemporary
6. modified
7. it turned out to be
8. estimated
9. next to nothing
10. domestic animals

3
1. former
2. preserving
3. conversion
4. estimates
5. modify
6. splendid
7. contemporary
8. converting

4
1. D   2. S   3. D   4. S   5. D   6. S

5
1. out
2. clip
3. (as) good
4. date
5. new
6. hand

6
1. device
2. antique
3. Ancient; reproductions
4. reconditioned
5. genuine
6. packaging
7. reproduces
8. up; innovative
9. mechanism
10. clip

Unit 74

1 leave sth to the last minute, in retrospect, with hindsight, at one time, from time to time, for the time being, time flies, day-to-day

2
1. In retrospect, I didn't enjoy it.
2. He does things at the last minute.
3. It was an ambition at one time.
4. I go there from time to time.
5. I live on a day-to-day basis.
6. I'll be OK here for the time being.

3
1. back
2. hindsight
3. leaves everything till the last minute
4. about/high
5. punctual; punctuality
6. flown
7. virtue; vices
8. for the time being

4 *possible answers*:

I think time definitely flies when you're older.

I wouldn't say I get depressed generally, but certain events make me depressed from time to time, such as political events, social issues or family isues.

That's not true for me because I started a pension some years ago. However, it's probably about time I increased the amount of money I put into my pension.

I never wanted to be a journalist, but at one time I wanted to be a professional rugby player.

No, that's not true. I do certain things at the last minute such as sending people birthday cards, but in general I'm quite organized.

That's not true for me because I went to university.

In general that's true, though I sometimes think about how I might be happier.

I am very punctual but I'm not sure it's a great virtue.

No, that's not true for me. I often plan for the future.

I'm sure that's true. I can think of several times in my life when I didn't work as hard as I should've done.

5
1. vague
2. Both are possible.
3. Both are possible.
4. vivid
5. Both are possible.
6. slipped
7. lasting
8. land

6
1. On the whole
2. extraordinary
3. recalling
4. recollection
5. landing

7
1. vivid/unforgettable
2. slipped
3. landed
4. inches
5. stuck
6. Looking back
7. extraordinary/ incredible
8. unforgettable
9. recall

8
1. recollection
2. vivid/unforgettable
3. speaking; recall; vague
4. back

possible answers, from Hungary:

1 To be honest, I find it hard to recall true memories of my early childhood. My parents were keen photographers so they got a shot of practically every step my sister and I took. Whenever I try to look back on my childhood, I can mostly recall the photos I have seen many times since then. This feels sad because I will never know if the memory would have faded had it not been for the photo immortalizing the moment.

2 I would say it is the Christmas Eves we used to have when I was a child. We would wait outside the living room for my father to ring the bell, which meant we were allowed to go in and have a look at the glistening tree and the neatly wrapped presents underneath. We would step in and with my mother taking the lead we would start singing. It was pure magic for me back then.

3 It depends on the emotion attached to the event. I tend to avoid recalling embarrassing situations or events that went particularly badly for me. What I remember most vividly is situations where I excelled in something or achieved my goals, however insignificant they appear now.

4 I prefer looking ahead, but now and again certain smells or sights or people I happen to meet evoke some memories, and in those moments I do enjoy looking back and recalling things that I have experienced or places I have been to. It's also great to reminisce in the company of old friends and have a laugh about the past we shared. I'm obviously talking about good memories. As for the unpleasant ones, they're probably not worth dwelling on, so I just try to erase them from my memory.

Unit 75

1
1 Furthermore
2 Both are possible.
3 otherwise
4 Both are possible.
5 Besides
6 Both are possible.
7 providing
8 thereby

2
1 while/whereas
2 Furthermore/Moreover/Besides
3 provided/providing
4 Nevertheless/Nonetheless
5 Besides (*Furthermore* and *Moreover* have the same meaning, but are too formal for this context.)
6 thereby
7 consequently
8 otherwise

3 *possible answers*:
1 I can't afford it.
2 I'm very punctual.
3 I was late for work.
4 you keep quiet.
5 someone could get in.
6 I'm glad I saw it.

4
considering
inconvenience
adequate
conclusion
inadequate
compensation

5
1 thus/hence
2 prior to
3 in view of
4 With regard to the other climbers / Regarding the other climbers
5 In conclusion
6 were obliged

6
1 adequate
2 thus/hence
3 Prior to
4 With regard to / Regarding
5 In view of
6 In conclusion
7 compensation
8 obliged
9 inconvenience
10 since
11 inadequate
12 convenience

Unit 76

1 argument evaluate evaluation criterion incoherent present *v* narrative narrator stylistic summarize

2
1 summarize
2 assessment
3 narrator
4 Both are possible.
5 criterion
6 presentation
7 argument
8 Both are possible.

3
1 narrative
2 summary
3 asessment/evaluation; incoherent
4 stylistic
5 criteria
6 command
7 register
8 argument
9 present; extended
10 argument; coherent

4 Justify is different.

5 The words which most clearly show a point of view are: condemn, condone, assert, justify, and adopt a stance.

6
1 condemnation
2 conclusion
3 illustration
4 exploration
5 assertion
6 justification

7
1 outlined
2 condemned
3 explored
4 condone
5 adopt; stance
6 justify
7 illustrated
8 sat on the fence
9 assert
10 draw any conclusions

Unit 77

1 expose imply defy convey portray embody inherit inherent

2
betrayal
portrayal
implication
inheritance
defiant
evil
pregnant
conventional; unconventional

3
1 an explanation
2 difficult
3 strange
4 beyond
5 the truth
6 know
7 an indirect
8 refuse

4
1 depicted
2 pregnant
3 conventions
4 rage
5 convey
6 irrational
7 embodies
8 Ellen's companionship

5
1 implied
2 conventional
3 alien
4 feminist
5 evil
6 inheritance
7 inherent
8 exposes
9 pregnancy
10 incident

6
1 portrayed
2 embodies
3 embodiment
4 defies
5 betrayed
6 Fate
7 mercy
8 tragedy
9 conveyed

Unit 78

1 outstanding depending submit nominate nomination controversial alternate venue prestigious imaginative pretentious Controversy and controversy are both possible.

2
1 varies
2 deserves
3 Both are possible.
4 challenging
5 prestigious
6 Both are possible.
7 Both are possible.
8 nominated

3
1 annually
2 panel
3 venue
4 sponsor
5 controversy

6 demonstrated (*also possible*: displayed)
7 shortlist
8 challenging

4
1 artistic
2 submitted
3 nominations
4 split
5 pretentious
6 bold
7 merit
8 prestigious

5
1 It alternates between Melbourne and Sydney.
2 The quality of the work is variable.
3 Colours change depending on the season.
4 The paintings are very imaginative.
5 Her work is very controversial.
6 There were three nominees.

Unit 79

1 sit: experimental, empirical, objective, scrutiny, verify, conviction
site: hypothesis, biased, scrutinize

2
1 biased/subjective
2 scrutiny/inspection
3 hypothesis
4 unbiased
5 conviction
6 conduct

3
1 phenomenon
2 verify
3 empirical
4 confirm
5 biased/subjective
6 scrutinize
7 experimental

4
1 subjective/biased
2 phenomena
3 objectivity
4 unbiased
5 hypothesis
6 verification
7 experiment/survey
8 evidence/knowledge/ research
9 formulate/confirm
10 political/moral

5 therapy
hereditary
abnormal
molecule
molecular
immune
mutate
defect

6
1 defective
2 abnormal
3 unit
4 hereditary
5 short-lived
6 immune
7 processing
8 rapid
9 long-lived
10 immunity

7
1 therapy; cells
2 mutation
3 inserts/inserted
4 cells; rapidly
5 arise; defect
6 heredity
7 insertion
8 molecular; molecule

Unit 80

1
1 D
2 S
3 S
4 D
5 S
6 D
7 S
8 D

2
1 g
2 f
3 d
4 b
5 h
6 c
7 a
8 e

3
1 construction
2 reinforced
3 concrete
4 framework
5 law
6 comply
7 regulation
8 concrete

4
1 concrete
2 reinforced
3 in motion
4 (vertical) load
5 constraints
6 panels
7 undergone
8 thorough
9 excessive
10 skyscrapers

5
1 construction
2 structurally
3 resistance
4 motion
5 aesthetic

6
1 climate and geology
2 the aesthetic objectives of the owner and architect
3 because each one is unique
4 to see if the building can resist/withstand the effects of strong winds
5 steel or reinforced concrete columns
6 concrete
7 by a crane
8 girders
9 by attaching panels of material, such as glass or metal, to the framework

Unit 81

1
1 no doubt
2 whether or not
3 give me a lift
4 make it tonight
5 a total disaster
6 at any minute
7 short of money
8 it's up to you

2
1 B
2 G
3 B
4 B
5 G
6 B
7 G
8 G

3
1 stick
2 bet
3 make it
4 to go
5 bound
6 reckon
7 went off
8 make it

4
1 me a lift?
2 minute.
3 not like Vicky.
4 up to you.
5 he'll turn up.
6 a mess of the task.
7 never know.
8 turned up yet?
9 short (of money).
10 made her change her mind about the car?

5
1 make; reckon; mean; bound; know; doubt
2 like; made; go; to; not
3 lift; went off; any
4 disaster; bet/reckon; stuck; turn

6 *These are some other meanings:*
RECKON
1 **be reckoned** be generally considered to be sth: *He's reckoned to be quite good on the piano.*
2 *inf* expect to do sth: *We reckon to get there about seven.*
STICK
1 push sth sharp into sth: *The nurse stuck the needle in my arm.*
2 fix something to something else with glue, etc. *I stuck the stamp on the envelope.*
BET
1 risk money on a race or an event by predicting the result: *I bet £50 on the result of the cup final.*
Look at the APP for more.

Unit 82

1 propose – put sth forward
compensate – make up for sth
cancel – call sth off
postpone – put sth off
deceive – take sb in
confess – own up to sth
communicate – get sth across
overcome – get over sth

2 1 I never expected him to own up to the crime.
   2 Nothing can make up for the loss of earnings.
   3 Will someone bring the topic up at the meeting?
   4 Who put forward the plan?/ put the plan forward?
   5 The inspector isn't easily taken in.
   6 Why did they call off the meeting? / call the meeting off?
   7 He has always looked up to his uncle.
   8 When did the new dictionary come out?
   9 The match has been put off for a week.
   10 We have to get our message across more clearly.

3 1 it come out?   5 taken in (by him).
   2 bring it up.   6 put it off.
   3 we'll get over it.   7 owned up to it.
   4 look up to them.   8 call it off.

4 1 reach somewhere
   2 begin to have the responsibility for sth, especially in place of sb else
   3 make equipment ready for use
   4 examine sth carefully, especially to find sth
   5 make contact by phone
   6 experience or suffer sth
   7 gain control of a country, etc.
   8 build sth or put sth somewhere

5 1 got through   5 getting through
   2 set up   6 go through
   3 going through   7 set up
   4 take over   8 take over

6 1 getting through   5 going through
   2 set up   6 setting up
   3 taken over   7 set up
   4 gone through   8 gets through

7 *possible answers*:
   1 Yes. I was driving in the south of France near the border with Spain, and suddenly there was an incredible rainstorm. The road flooded and all the cars were stuck; the water came halfway up the door. We waited for about half an hour, and then the water started to go down, but it was quite frightening.
   2 No. I've only put up a tent in a hot country in summer.
   3 Yes, I took over from my husband once when he was feeling very ill.
   4 No, I haven't, fortunately.
   5 Yes, once. I was told my passport had nearly run out, and I should make sure I renewed it when I got back home.
   6 No, I'm pleased to say I haven't!
   7 I've helped someone set up their phone, but not a computer.
   8 I do. My cousin is hopeless with money and always spends anything he gets immediately. It means by the end of the month he always wants to borrow from me.

Unit 83

1 1 **off** the top of my head
   2 in one ear and out **the other**
   3 **Let** me see
   4 When it **comes** to science
   5 **under** the weather
   6 no good **worrying** about it
   7 my mind goes a **complete** blank
   8 What do you have **in mind**?

2 1 mind   6 do with
   2 as well   7 as I know
   3 blank   8 and out the other
   4 bet   9 minute
   5 there

4 1 make up your mind   3 to my mind
   2 bear in mind   4 speak your mind

5 1 want to do sth   4 possible
   2 you don't know   5 I don't know
   3 not being serious   6 wait for you

6 you're kidding; no way; how come; what for; you bet; don't ask me; hang on; best of luck

7 1 kidding   6 of luck
   2 way/chance   7 come
   3 knows   8 for
   4 your time   9 faintest (idea)
   5 bet   10 contrary

Unit 84

1 1 fails   5 true
   2 fact   6 happens
   3 true   7 only
   4 face   8 resort

2 1 If only   5 lose face
   2 a good thing (that) 6 all else fails
   3 a dream come true   7 but for
   4 that's life   8 as a matter of fact

3 1 too good to be true 6 as it happens/as a
   2 a last/final resort   matter of fact
   3 that's life   7 a good thing (that)
   4 if only   8 a dream come true
   5 but for

4 1 by ~~very~~ far   5 Who on ~~the~~ earth
   2 Believe it or ~~believe~~ 6 if ~~that~~ you don't mind
      not   7 not to ~~be~~ mention
   3 The only ~~bad~~ thing 8 I wouldn't ~~really~~ mind
   4 Guess ~~you~~ what

5 1 Guess   5 wouldn't
   2 thing   6 wonder
   3 earth   7 chance
   4 some   8 all

6 1 It didn't work **at all**. / **Believe it or not**, it didn't work.
   2 Do you know if it's open, **by any chance**?
   3 **Guess what!** Melinda's going to … / Melinda's going to marry a famous pop star, **believe it or not**.
   4 Why **on earth** are you wearing gloves in the summer?
   5 Jacob looks about 20, but **believe it or not**, he's only 13.
   6 He's been very ill, so **no wonder** he looks thin.
   7 They have a large apartment here, **not to mention** a farm in Wales and a house on the coast.
   8 We said we were members but, **for some reason**, they wouldn't let us in … / … but, **believe it or not**, they wouldn't let us in.
   9 It's **by far** his most violent film.
   10 I'd like to know more about your background, **if you don't mind**. / **If you don't mind**, I'd like to know more about your background.

Unit 85

1 trial and error   sooner or later
   more or less   odds and ends
   the pros and cons   safe and sound
   back and forth   on and off
   sick and tired   law and order

2 1 death   4 foremost   7 less
   2 pieces   5 sound   8 order
   3 cons   6 forwards

3 1 sooner or later
   2 sick and tired / sick to death
   3 (by) trial and error
   4 now and again / now and then
   5 more or less
   6 bits and pieces / odds and ends

Unit 86

1
1	post	5	log	9	bat
2	cakes	6	sieve	10	sheet
3	bone	7	beetroot		
4	feather	8	dream		

2
1 He's deaf as a post.
2 She's blind as a bat.
3 She's thin as a rake.
4 It worked like a dream.
5 She went/was as white as a sheet.
6 They were as good as gold.
7 She went as red as a beetroot.
8 He's got a mind like a sieve.
9 The little girl was as light as a feather.
10 The new phone is selling like hot cakes.

Unit 87

1
1	d	3	h	5	j	7	f	9	b
2	e	4	g	6	a	8	c	10	i

2
1 **broadly** speaking
2 All **the** same
3 **so** as to
4 In **any** case
5 As far **as** I'm concerned
6 **in** the end
7 **as** for
8 **do** her good
9 by **the** way
10 Even **so**, …

3
1 Incidentally
2 On the whole / By and large / Broadly speaking
3 Mind you
4 Anyway/Besides
5 It's true; Even so / All the same
6 Alternatively
7 do them good.
8 so as to
9 As far as I'm concerned
10 in the end

4
1 All the same / Nevertheless / Even so
2 Alternatively
3 so as to
4 extent
5 By the way/ Incidentally
6 As for
7 besides / in any case / anyway
8 in the end
9 by and large / on the whole / broadly speaking / to a large extent
10 It's true; All the same / Even so / Nevertheless

Unit 88

1
1 So far, so good.
2 Two heads are better than one.
3 It's a small world.
4 First come, first served.
5 Practice makes perfect.
6 No news is good news.
7 The more the merrier.
8 Don't judge a book by its cover.

2
1 The grass is always greener on the other side (of the fence).
2 Actions speak louder than words.
3 First come, first served.
4 Better late than never.
5 Two heads are better than one.
6 Don't judge a book by its cover.
7 It's a small world.
8 An eye for an eye.

3
1 better late than never
2 better safe than sorry
3 no news is good news
4 the more the merrier
5 practice makes perfect
6 the end justifies the means
7 two wrongs don't make a right
8 beggars can't be choosers
9 prevention is better than cure
10 don't judge a book by its cover

4
1	better safe than sorry	8	better late than never
2	practice makes perfect	9	beggars can't be choosers
3	two heads are better than one	10	first come, first served
4	no news is good news	11	Two wrongs don't make a right.
5	an eye for an eye	12	end justifies the means
6	so far, so good		
7	the grass is always greener on the other side (of the fence)		

5 *possible answers:*
1 I agree that you shouldn't judge a book by its cover, and I think that prevention is better than cure. I also find there is a common human tendency to believe that the grass is always greener – it's very easy to look around and see people who have more than you. But if you look around it is also easy to find people who have less.
2 I think there are some circumstances when the end _never_ justifies the means, and I don't believe in an eye for an eye. I'm not sure why people say the more the merrier. It might be true sometimes, but quite often the opposite is true – having more people can spoil some things.

6
1 How a person looks is less important than their character.
2 When you love somebody, you cannot see their faults.
3 You should care for your own family first, before you start looking after others.
4 rely on one course of action for success rather than give yourself several different possibilities
5 After an unpleasant experience, you are careful to avoid something similar.
6 used to say that when you are away from somebody you love, you love them even more

Unit 89

1
1	tons/piles	5	odd
2	thereabouts	6	approximately
3	kind	7	somehow
4	of that sort / along those lines	8	vague
		9	somebody

2
1 sort of pretending to be ill
2 have loads/tons/piles of rice
3 executive or something
4 give or take a few minutes
5 tomorrow somehow or other
6 somewhere in the region

3
1 We invited a hundred or so to the wedding.
2 He looks sort of depressed.
3 Her job is something to do with marketing.
4 There was lots of good stuff at the festival.
5 It's in the region of 300 miles.
6 We could go to France or somewhere.
7 I've got £500, give or take a few pounds.
8 We could get him a book or something (like that / along those lines / of that sort) for his birthday.

Unit 90

1
1. reported/said
2. overcome
3. suspended/jailed
4. cremated
5. empowered/authorized
6. known
7. scheduled
8. caught up

2
1. said to be dangerous (*also possible*: be reported …)
2. jailed for five years
3. scheduled for 9.00 p.m.
4. short-listed (for the prize)
5. caught up in a traffic jam for ages
6. suspended from school
7. known for her charity work.
8. meant to join the army / meant for the army
9. overcome with emotion when he saw her.

Unit 91

1
1. unknown
2. incapable
3. inhuman
4. disobedient
5. uncharacteristic
6. invalid
7. unfinished
8. disloyal
9. unemployed
10. unfamiliar
11. incompatible
12. insufficient

2 an unofficial strike; an incompatible couple; an invalid ticket; insufficient money; an unqualified teacher; a disobedient dog; inhuman conditions; an unfamiliar name

3
1. inhuman
2. unknown
3. unemployed
4. undercooked
5. unfinished
6. incapable
7. unpaid
8. uncharacteristic (of her)
9. unfamiliar
10. disloyal (of him)

4
1. advised
2. charge
3. calculated
4. judge
5. bought
6. believed

5
1. miscalculated
2. Both are possible.
3. unpack
4. misunderstood
5. Both are possible.
6. overdid it

6
1. overcharged
2. misled
3. unwrap
4. undo
5. misjudged
6. mistreating/mistreat
7. overestimated
8. reassess

Unit 92

1
1. settlement
2. refusal
3. acknowledgement
4. completion
5. measurement
6. resignation
7. proposal
8. objection
9. denial
10. appreciation

2 **positive**: encouragement, appreciation, collaboration, accomplishment, settlement
negative: dismissal, refusal, objection, denial

3
1. hesitated
2. denied
3. objected
4. acknowledged
5. accommodate
6. inspecting
7. been editing / edited
8. collaborate
9. detect
10. objected

4 refusal / denial: Both are saying 'no' to something.
inspection / examination: Both involve looking at sth carefully.
cooperation / collaboration: Both involve working with others towards a common goal.
agreement / settlement: Both involve finding a solution to a conflict/problem that both parties can agree on.
dismissal / resignation: Both mean leaving a job (under different circumstances).

5
1. him (some / a lot of, etc.) encouragement
2. a settlement
3. an inspection next week
4. hesitation at the beginning
5. measurements of the room?
6. his resignation yesterday
7. accommodation for three more
8. creation of the new company

6
1. objections
2. proposal
3. acknowledgement
4. completion
5. dismissals
6. denial
7. appreciation
8. edition
9. detection

Unit 93

1 agri<u>cul</u>tural co<u>op</u>erative <u>affor</u>dable <u>prof</u>itable pro<u>gress</u>ive <u>struc</u>tural de<u>struc</u>tive coope<u>ra</u>tion

2
1. are affordable
2. cooperative
3. profitable
4. destructive
5. structural
6. agricultural
7. selective
8. logical

3
1. protective
2. progressive
3. cooperative
4. functional
5. educational
6. selective
7. logic
8. cooperation

4 architectural, innovative, believable, experimental, administrative, clinical, acceptable, constitutional, communicative, excusable

5 Answer: intensify

6
1. maximize
2. strengthen
3. simplify
4. authorize
5. shorten
6. specify
7. weaken
8. stabilize
9. clarify
10. specialize

7
1. The builder said he would strengthen the wall.
2. We need to clarify our position on this issue.
3. He specializes in this field of medicine.
4. The presence of the police intensified the concern in the crowd.
5. Are you authorized to replace the tickets?
6. I need to maximize the time available to us.
7. We need to simplify the instructions for students.
8. You must specify the details on the form.
9. stabilize
10. weakens

8 tighten, legalize, modernize, visualize, purify, economize, equalize, pacify

Unit 94

1 <u>trans</u>port *n*; trans<u>port</u> *v*; <u>com</u>bat *n*, *v*; <u>ex</u>tract *n*; ex<u>tract</u> *v*; <u>de</u>posit *n*, *v*; dis<u>pute</u> *n*, *v*; <u>tor</u>ture *n*, *v*

2
1. c
2. f
3. a
4. g
5. h
6. d
7. e
8. b

3
1. There was a pause, then the speaker sat down.
2. The table was (completely) in the shade / in complete shade.
3. We have an oil filter.
4. The Liberals have a five-point lead / have taken the lead by five points.
5. We could hear (the) cheers from the crowd.
6. Two of the prisoners suffered torture.
7. What transport will they use for the goods?
8. They will battle to get the idea approved.

4
1 extract
2 mate
3 trace
4 deposit
5 combat
6 trace
7 combat
8 deposit
9 disputing
10 tackled

5 *possible answers:*
1 My best mate is a guy called Tom, and I've known him ever since university.
2 Yes, I have been in dispute with a rail company trying to get money back for a journey that was cancelled.
3 No, I haven't but I know several people who have traced their families back over three or four generations.
4 Yes, I think I had to battle really hard to get to university. I missed one whole school term through illness and had to work incredibly hard to catch up.
5 Most money I earn is deposited automatically in my bank account, but I remember going to my bank about two weeks ago to deposit a cheque that somebody had given me.
6 I always sit in the shade because I burn easily if I sit in the sun.
7 I sometimes cheer even when I'm watching sport on TV, but I always cheer if I go to see live football matches when my team are playing.
8 Yes, I had to pay a deposit when I rented a room in my second year at university.

6 *Abuse, alert, support, bid, bow* and *chase* can all be used as nouns with no change in meaning. (But note that the the noun *abuse* is pronounced with an 's' sound, and the verb is pronounced with a 'z' sound.)

Unit 95

1 pro**ceed** inter**act** ex**clude** corre**spond** em**bark** re**concile** con**gra**tulate dis**tin**guish ad**here** **sub**stitute

2 **more positive**: embark; interact; congratulate; proceed; confer; reconcile
more negative: deprive; dispose; exclude; surrender

3
1 on
2 from
3 of
4 with
5 with
6 from
7 of
8 on

4
1 confer
2 devoted
3 distinguish
4 proceed
5 interact
6 dispose
7 cater
8 adhere
9 compensate
10 cling

5
1 surrendered
2 reconcile
3 distracts
4 insisted
5 deprived
6 congratulated
7 compensate / make up
8 exclude
9 substitute
10 devote

6
cope with sth
relate to sb
subtract sth from sth
impose sth on/upon sb
stare at sb
reflect on sth
stem from sth
opt for sth

Unit 96

1
1 of
2 on
3 in
4 of
5 for
6 on
7 of
8 in

2
1 limitations/restraints
2 exception
3 substitute
4 reminder
5 confidence
6 exposure
7 contempt
8 advantage

3
1 exposure to
2 involvement in
3 emergence of
4 limitations/restraints on
5 exception of
6 contempt for
7 reminder of
8 advantage of

4 *possible answers:*
I have confidence in my ability to manage my life in general, but no confidence in my ability to be successful in business.
I don't think you should take advantage of every opportunity. Sometimes more money just means more problems, and not all ways of making money are legal.
Yes, I think that's true.
I don't need reminders of people's birthdays; I can remember everyone's birthday in my family.
I'd like to have greater involvement in charity work; I will do more when I have time.
I think that's true. You can't have what you want without some effort.
The most expensive thing I've ever bought is a sofa, which I got in a sale.
Yes, I would support government limitations on air travel.
There are pluses and minuses, but on the whole, I think social media is allowing people to be more unkind and ruder to each other.
I feel contempt for certain corrupt and egotistical politicians.

Unit 97

1 in**tent** **subject** com**pat**ible in**her**ent re**sist**ant **liable** repre**sent**ative **dedicated** de**pend**ent **scep**tical im**mune**

2
1 to
2 about
3 of
4 on
5 to
6 on
7 to
8 to
9 with
10 in

3
1 F – Someone who is immune to a disease has little or no chance of getting it.
2 F – A feature which is inherent in a system cannot be removed from it.
3 T
4 F – Someone who is dedicated to their work doesn't leave their workplace early.
5 F – If an agreement is subject to approval, it might happen.
6 T
7 F – A qualification that is equivalent to a degree is similar to/like a degree.
8 T

4
1 liable to
2 resistant to
3 immune to
4 equivalent to
5 intent on/upon ensuring
6 sceptical of/about
7 representative of
8 inherent in

Unit 98

1
1 at
2 on
3 at
4 in
5 on
6 away
7 on
8 by

2
1 at short notice / at a moment's notice
2 at present
3 on the basis of
4 by no means
5 at once / right away / straight away
6 on purpose
7 by choice
8 on good terms / on friendly terms

3
1 by choice
2 at once / right away / straight away
3 at present
4 in the near future
5 on purpose
6 on bad terms
7 at short notice / at a moment's notice (also possible: at once, right away, straight away)
8 in full
9 by no means
10 on the basis of

4 in possession of, in office; under investigation, under attack; by means of; on hold; out of respect, out of touch

5
1 in power / in office
2 under investigation
3 in possession of
4 in honour of / out of respect for
5 out of touch with
6 under attack / under construction

6
1 hold
2 respect; bereaved
3 touch
4 possession
5 tunnel; construction
6 giant
7 means
8 slaves / slave labour
9 board
10 honour

Unit 99

1 brutal, bizarre, favourable, upsetting, peculiar, conventional, reluctant, vicious, outstanding, eminent, notorious, infamous

2 **positive meaning**: outstanding, favourable, eminent, exceptional

3 evil/wicked, exceptional/outstanding, brutal/vicious, reluctant/unwilling, notorious/infamous, bizarre/weird, disturbing/upsetting

4
1 evil
2 bizarre
3 eminent
4 notorious/infamous
5 disturbing/upsetting
6 unconventional
7 exceptional/outstanding
8 brutal/vicious
9 willing
10 conventional

5
1 **bare** arms
2 a **comparable** house
3 Correct.
4 a **naked** body
5 can be **deadly**
6 far **superior**
7 Correct.
8 always very **tasty**

6
1 comprehensive
2 childlike
3 superb
4 deathly
5 comprehensible
6 tasteless

7
1 comparative
2 bare
3 incomprehensible
4 tasteful/tasteless
5 childish
6 superior
7 naked
8 deadly

Unit 100

1
1 presumably
2 basically/essentially
3 ultimately
4 frankly
5 virtually/practically
6 apparently

2
1 Evidently
2 strangely (enough) / oddly (enough) / curiously (enough)
3 Practically
4 ultimately
5 basically
6 to be (perfectly) honest
7 fair enough
8 presumably

3
1 Evidently/Apparently
2 entirely
3 fair enough
4 frankly / to be (perfectly) honest (*also possible*: ultimately, basically)
5 curiously (enough)/ strangely (enough) /oddly (enough)
6 presumably
7 practically/virtually
8 ultimately

4 *possible answer*:
When I was in my twenties, I would've been prepared to commute every day for a better job with more money. Now in my forties, I'm not sure. I wouldn't see so much of my children, and I don't think I have the energy now to spend basically 12 hours a day working.

5
1 purely
2 truly
3 precisely
4 primarily/chiefly/ predominantly
5 briefly
6 invariably
7 concept
8 sessions
9 strictly

6
1 chiefly/purely
2 strictly
3 purely
4 purely/briefly/chiefly
5 invariably
6 simply/truly
7 strictly
8 simply

7
1 primarily/chiefly/ predominantly
2 invariably
3 briefly
4 precisely
5 briefly
6 truly
7 precisely
8 simply/absolutely
9 purely
10 strictly

The CEFR levels given in this Word list indicate the words and phrases which are from the 5000 Oxford. The numbers are unit numbers, not page numbers.

abnormal 79

abolish **C1** 54

abolition 54

about *as in* be about to do sth **B1** 53

absence **C1** *as in* absence makes the heart grow fonder 88

absent-minded 5

absolute **B2** 52

absolutely **B2** 100

absorb (= take in liquid, etc.) **B2** 6; (= understand) **C1** 6

abuse *n, v* **C1** 33

accelerate **C1** 26

accelerator 26

accept (= continue in a difficult situation) **B1** 72; (= agree to sth; allow sb to be part of a group) **B1** 19; accept responsibility for sth/sb 19

acceptable **B2** 23

accidentally **B2** 63

accommodate **B2** 92

accompany **B2** 44

accomplish **B2** 68

accomplishment **C1** 92

accountable (to sb) **C1** 66

accountant **B2** 64

accumulate **C1** 32

accuracy **B2** 57

accurate **B2** 1

accuse sb (of sth) **B2** 95

acknowledge **B2** 92

acknowledgement 92

acquire **B2** 39

acquisition **C1** 69

acquit sb (of sth) 53

acre **C1** 61

action **A1** *as in* actions speak louder than words 88

activist **C1** 59

adapt (to sth) **B2** 45

adapt sth (for sth) **B2** 70

adaptation **C1** 43

additional **B2** 66

address (a problem) **B2** 72

adequate **B2** 75

adhere to sth **C1** 95

adjust (= change sth slightly) **B2** 11; (= get used to sth) **B2** 45

adjustment **C1** 11; **C1** 45

administration **B2** 65

admit sb (to hospital) 52

adolescence 21

adolescent *n* **C1**, *adj* 21

adulthood 21

adopt (= take a point of view) **B2** 76

advance *n* advances (in sth) 48; in advance **B2** 37

advantage *as in* take advantage of sth 97

adventure **A2** 36

adventurous 36

advocate *n, v* **C1** 58

aesthetic **C1** 80

affair (= event/situation) **B2** 29

affection **C1** 16

affectionate 16

affordable **B2** 93

agenda **B2** 69

agile 10

agility 10

aggressive **B2** 19

agricultural **C1** 93

aid *n* **B2** 56

Airbnb™ 37

aircraft **B2** 55

alarm *n* **B1** *as in* set the alarm 31

alert *adj* **C1** 26

alert *n* **C1** 56; on the alert 26

alien *adj* **C1** 77

alike *adj* **C1** 22

all the same 87

allegation **C1** 62

allege **C1** 62

allegedly **C1** 62

allergic to sth 14

allergy 14

alert *as in* on the alert 26

allocate **C1** 51

almond 24

alter **B2** 45

alteration 45

alternate (between A and B) 78

alternatively 87

ambiguity 1

ambiguous 1

ambulance **B2** 27

amend *v* **C1** 45

amendment **C1** 45

ancient **A2** 73

anger **B2** 8

annually **B2** 78

anticipate **B2** 68

antique 73

antivirus 40

anxiety **B2** 18

anxious **B2** 18

anyway **A2** 87

apologetic 3

apparent **B2** 22

apparently **B2** 100

appeal (to sb) *v* **B2** 37

appealing **C1** 37

appetite **C1** 25

appetizing 25

applaud **C1** 43

applause 43

appliance 46

apply (pressure) 13

appoint **C1** 65

appreciation **C1** 92

apprentice 64

apprenticeship 64

appropriate **B2** 1

approval **B2** 20

approve of sb/sth **B2** 20

approximately **B1** 89

apricot 24

apron 29

arable 35

argument (= set of reasons) **B1** 76

arise **B2** 72

armed **B2** 55; the armed forces 55

arms **B2** 55, 56

arrogance 17

arrogant 17

arson 33

arsonist 33

articulate *v* **C1**, *adj* 72

artistic **B2** 78

as

a favour 6

a matter of fact 84

blind as a bat 86

deaf as a post 86

dry as a bone 86

far as I know 83

far as I'm concerned **B2** 87

for sth **B2** 87

good as gold 86

good as new 73

it happens 84

light as a feather 86

long as **B2** 31

red as a beetroot 86

thin as a rake 86

white as a sheet 86

ashamed **B2** 18

ask v as in ask (sb) a favour 6; don't ask me 83

asparagus 24

aspect **B2** 43

aspire (to (be) sth) **C1** 71

assert **C1** 76; assert yourself **C1** 16

assertion **C1** 76

assertive 16

assess **B2** 60, 76

assessment **B2** 60, 76

assistance **B2** 61

associated with sth/ sb **B2** 50

assume **B2** 57

assumption **B2** 57

asthma 14

astonished 18

astounded 18

asylum **C1** 49

at

a moment's notice 98

all 84

any minute (now) 81

home (= playing sport) 41

once **B2** 98

one time 74

present **B2** 98

short notice 98

stake 67

the scene (of sth) 27

your own pace 21

atom 79

attack n **A2** as in under attack 98

attic 38

attitude **B1** 16

attraction **B1** 33

aubergine 24

audience **A2** 43

authentic **C1** 73

authority **B2** (= organization) 51

authorize **C1** 93

authorized as in be authorized to do sth 90

automatic **B2** 26

avert 59

avocado 24

awareness (of sth) **B2** 32

away (= playing sport) 41

awkward **B2** 44

axe v 56

back sb/sth 56, 69

back and forth 86

back sth up 40

background noise 12

backing **C1** 69

backup **C1** 40

backwards **B1** as in backwards and forwards 85

bacteria **B2** 15

bad-tempered 5

badge **B2** 29

badly-hit 68

bail **C1** 53

balance (A with/and B) **B1** 66

balancing act 61

bald 7

ballot n **C1**, v 67

B and B 37

bank statement 32

barbecue n 29

bare **C1** 99

barely **B2** 11

bark v 12

barman/barmaid 64

barrier **B2** 59

basically **B2** 38, 100

basil 24

basis **B2** as in on the basis (of sth) 98

bathe 15

battle n **B1**, v **B2** 94

be

a good thing/job that … 84

about to do sth **B1** 53

authorized to do sth 90

behind sb 72

better/worse off 66

caught up in sth 90

confined to sth 48

cremated 90

empowered to do sth **C1** 90

getting on for sth 7

in two minds about sth 2

jailed **B2** 90

known as/for sth 90

meant for / to do sth 90

off (= leave) 44

on the lookout for sth/sb 26

overcome with sth **B2** 90

overdrawn 32

reported to be sth **C1** 90

said to be sth **C1** 90

scheduled for sth 90

short-listed for sth 90

stranded 63

suspended from sth 90

the last thing on sb's mind 2

tied up (= busy) 2

up to sb 81

/get out of control 68

bear v **B2** 63; can't bear sth/sb 20

beat (= mix quickly) **B2** 24

beaten as in off the beaten track 36

beauty as in beauty is only skin-deep 88

beetroot 24

beforehand 44

beg **B2** 9

beggar n as in beggars can't be choosers 88

behaviour **A2** as in on your best behaviour 23

behalf as in on behalf of sb / on sb's behalf **C1** 51

behind as in be behind sb **B1** 72

being **B2** 59

believe **A1** as in believe it or not 84; you're not gonna believe this 2

bench **C1** 39

bend v **B1** 10

beneficial **B2** 3, 21

bent adj **B2** 10

bereaved 98

besides **B2** 75, 87

bet (= believe sth is true) **B2** 81; you bet 83; your/ the best bet 83

betray **C1** 77

betrayal 77

better as in be better off 66

better late than never 88

better safe than sorry 88

better still 46

beyond **B2** 35

biased 79

bid *n* (= attempt) **C1** 56; (= offer) **B2** 69

bid *v* (= to attempt) **C1** 56; (= to offer) **B2** 69

birth certificate 5

bite *v* **B1** *as in* **bite your fingernails** 8

bit *n as in* **bits and pieces** 86

bitter (= sharp taste) **B2** 25

bitterly *as in* **bitterly cold** 28

bizarre **C1** 99

black eye 15

blackmail *n, v* 33

blackmailer 33

blame *n* **B2** *as in* **take the blame** 4

bland 25

blank *adj* **A2** 57

blanket **B2** 9

blast *n* **C1** 56

blaze *n* 60

bleed **C1** 15

bleeding 15

blind *adj* **B2** *as in* **(as) blind as a bat** 86

blind *n* (= for a window) 30

blink *v* 11

blister *n* 15

blizzard 28

block *v* 27

blockbuster 43

blow *n* (= shock/ disappointment) **B2** 56

blurred (vision) 11

blush *v* 8

board *n as in* **on board** **B2** 98

boast *v* **C1** 16, 71; *n* 71

bodyguard 64

bold (= of people) **B2** 78

bond *n* **B2** 19

bonus (= sth good you get) **C1** 38; (= extra money) **C1** 67

bookcase 30

boost *n* **B2** 41, 56; *v* **B2** 56

boot (= of a car) 26

bottle sth up 18

bound to do/be sth **B2** 81

bracelet 29

braise 24

brake *n, v* 26; *as in* **put on the brakes** 26

branch (= of an organization) **B1** 55

brand new 73

brave **B1** 20

bravery 20, 60

break down 67

break the news 4

breakthrough **C1** 71

breast cancer 14

breathe a sigh of relief 12

breed *v* **C1** 47

bribe *v* 33

bribery 33

brief (description) **B2** 4

briefly (= for a short time; in a few words) **B2** 100

bring (= cause sb to reach sth) **B1** 2

bring sb up **B2** 22

bring sth about **C1** 45

bring sth up **C1** 82

broad (shoulders) **B2** 7

broad-minded 5

broadcast *n, v* **B2** 61

broadcaster **B2** 61

broadly speaking 74, 87

broccoli 24

broken home 21

broom 30

browse *v* 40

browser **C1** 40

browsing 40

bruise *v, n* 15

brutal **C1** 99

bucket 29

budget *n* **B2** 32, 37, 51; *v* 32, 37, 51

build up 32

built-up 34

bully *n, v* 20

bunk bed 30

burst out laughing 12

bush **B2** 39

but **A1** *as in* **but for** 84

butcher 64

button **A2** 9

by

and large 87

any chance 84

choice 98

far 84

means of sth **C1** 98

mutual consent 54

no means **C1** 98

the way 87

cabinet **C1** 9

cable **B2** 40

calculate **B2** 32

calculation **C1** 32

call on sb **C1** 59

call sth off 82

can opener 25

cancel **B2** 82

cancer **B2** 14

canteen 25

can't *as in* **can't stand sth/sb** 20

cap (= for your head) **B1** 29

capable **B2** 17

capital punishment 54

capitalism **C1** 50

capitalist **C1** 50

captain **B1** 20

care *v* **A2** *as in* **couldn't care less (about sth/sb)** 25

caring *adj* 19

carpenter 64

carry *as in* **get/be carried away** 44

carry sth out **A2** 62

carve **C1** 24

carving knife 24

case (= situation) **A2** 70; **in any case** **C1** 70, 87; **in some cases** 70; **in that case** 70; **the case** (= true situation) **B1** 22

casserole 24

cast (= of a play/film) **B2** 43

casual (clothes) **B2** 29; **casual (work)** **C1** 64

casualty **C1** 27, 60

catch (a cold/flu) **B1** 12; **catch (a glimpse of sth/ sb)** **B2** 11; **be caught up in sth** 90

catchy 42

cater for sth/sb **C1** 95

caution **C1** 53

cautious **C1** 32

cease **C1** 56

ceasefire 56

celery 24

cell (= room in prison) **B2** 54; (= smallest unit of matter) **B2** 79

central heating 30

centre party 50

cereal 25, 35

certainty **B2** 3

chair (a committee) *v* **B2** 51

chairman **B2** / **chairwoman**/ **chairperson** 51

challenge *n* **B1** **65**

challenging **B2** 78

chance **A2** *as in* **a real/ good chance** 41; **by any chance** 84; **my last/big chance** 41; **no chance** 83; **take a chance (on sth)** 63

change *n* **A1** *as in* **a major change** 45;

change (gear) v A1 26

channel (of communication) 72

chaos C1 27

chaotic 27

characteristic n B2 22

characteristic of sb B2 22, 91

charge v (= run at sb) 10; charge sth (up) B1 46; charge sb (with sth) B2 53

charger 46

charity as in charity begins at home 88

charm n (= the power of pleasing or attracting people) C1 17; (= a pleasant or attractive quality or feature) 36

charming B2 17, 36

chase v B2 10

check/checked (shirt) 29

cheek (= on the face) B2 7, 13; (= rudeness) 23

cheeky 23

cheer v B2 12, 94; n B2 94

chest of drawers 30

chief n B2 56

chief constable 53

chief executive 64

chiefly 100

childish 99

childlike 99

chilly 28

choice A2 as in by choice 98

chop v B2 24

chorus 42

chubby 7

circumstance B2 6

cite B2 57

citizen B2 51

civil war 47

civil servant 64

civil service 64

civilian C1 55

clap v 43

clapping 43

clarify B2 93

classic adj B2 43

clear (= remove) B1 47; clear sb (of sth) B1 56

clear (sth) up 44

click (on sth) v B1 40

click n 40

climax n 41

climb (= increase in value/ amount) B2 69

cling (to sth) C1 95

clinical C1 52

clip n (= part of film) B2 61; (= for fastening) 73

clip v (= fasten) 73

closely B2 28; closely-fought/contested 58

closure C1 67

coalition C1 58

coherence 76

coherent 76

coincide (with sth) C1 95

colander 24

collaborate C1 92

collaboration (with sb) C1 66

collapse (= fall to the ground) B2 60; (= decrease suddenly in value) 69

collide with sth/sb 27

collision C1 27

comb v 9

combat n C1 55, 94; v C1 94

combination B2 8, 35

come (with/in sth) (= sold or produced with sth) B1 2; come to a standstill 28; come top/bottom 71

come across (as sth) 17

come out 82

come over (as sth) 17

comfort B2 37

command v (= be in charge of sth) B2 55

command of sth n (= knowledge/ability) 76

comment n A2 6, 23; no comment 6

commentary C1 77

commentator C1 61

commission B2 67

committee B2 51

commodity C1 57

commonly B2 14

communicate with sb A2 82

communism 50

communist adj C1, n 50

commute v 100

companionship 77

company (= being with people) B1 44

comparable C1 3, 99

comparative B2 99

compatible (= with people) 91; compatible with sth/ sb (= of a computer) 97

compelling C1 42

compensate (for sth/sb) C1 82, 95

compensation C1 75

completion B2 92

complex adj B1 42

complicate 42

complicated B2 42

comply (with sth) C1 80

component B2 40

compost 39

comprehensible 99

comprehensive B2 99

comprise B2 55

compromise n, v C1 58

compulsory B2 55

conceal C1 7

concentrate B1 11

concentration B2 11

concept B2 100

concern n B2 34; sb's main concern 4

concern v B2 34

concerned (about/for sth) B2 34

concerning prep 58

conclusion B1 76; in conclusion 75

concrete n B2 80

condemn C1 76

condemnation 76

condone 76

conduct v (= organize an activity) B2 62, 79

conduct n B2 21

confer (with sb) C1 95

confess B2 82

confidence (in sth/sb) B2 17, 97

confident B1 17

confidential 52

confine sb/sth in sth C1 54; be confined to sth 48

confinement 54

confirmation C1 61

conflict n 58

confront C1 72

congratulate sb (on sth) C1 95

connection B1 as in in connection with sth 59

conscientious 17

conscious B2 15

consensus C1 58

consent n C1 as in by common/mutual consent 54

consequently B2 75

conservation B2 47

conservatism 50

conservative adj, n B2 50

conserve C1 46

consider sb/sth to be sth / as sth B1 23, 47

considerable B2 60

considerate 16

considering *prep* 75

consist of sth **B1** 55

consistency **C1** 41

consistent **B2** 21, 41

conspiracy **B2** 56

constant **B2** 10

constantly **B2** 8

constraint **C1** 80

construct *v* **B2** 80

construction **B2** 80; **under construction** 98

consult **B2** 14, 45

consultation **C1** 14, 45

consume **B1** 46

consumer **B1** 46

consumption **B2** 46

contemporary **B2** 73

contempt for sth/sb **C1** 97

contender **C1** 41

contest *n* **B2** 58

contract *n* **B2** 38, 70

contrast (with sth) *v* **B1** 62

contrary *n* **C1** *as in* **on the contrary** 83

contribute **B2** 44

contribution **B2** 44

control *n* **A2** *as in* **be/get out of control** 68; **under control** 68

controversial **B2** 78

controversy **B2** 78

convalesce 52

convalescence 52

convenience **B2** 75

convenient **B1** 34

convention **B2** 48, 77

conventional **B2** 48, 99

conversion **C1** 73

convert (sth) (into sth) **B2** 73

convey (sth to sb) **B2** 77

convict sb (of sth) **C1** 53

conviction (= belief) **C1** 79

convinced **B2** 43

convincing **B2** 43

cooperate (with sb) **C1** 58

cooperation 93

cooperative **C1** 93

cope with sth **B2** 21

core *adj* **B2** 58

corkscrew *n* 24

corporate **B2** 69

correspond (with sth/ sb) **C1** 95

cosmetic surgery 52

could **A1** *as in* **could do with sth** 83; **couldn't care less (about sth/sb)** 25

council **B1** 51

councillor **C1** 51

count *v* (= say numbers) **A2** 6; (= calculate a number) **A2** 6; (= include) **B2** 6

county **B2** 61

coup **C1** 69

courage **B2** 20, 60

courageous 20, 60

courgette 24

courteous 23

courtesy **C1** 23

coverage **B2** 62

crack *v, n* **B2** 12

crash *n, v* 12

crawl (= on hands and knees) **C1** 9; (= move slowly of traffic) 2

creamy 25

create **B1** *as in* **create an illusion** 7

creation **B2** 92

credit *n* **B2** *as in* **in credit** 32

cremate *as in* **be cremated** 90

crew **B2** 70

crisis **B2** 54

criterion/criteria **B2** 42, 76

critical (= dangerous) **B2** 27

criticism **B2** 22

criticize **B2** 22

crop *n* **B2** 35

cross (your legs) 8

crucial **B2** 10, 21

cure *n, v* **B2** 48

curiously *as in* **curiously enough** 100

custody (= being in prison) **C1** 53; (= a legal right) **C1** 62

customary 23

cut sth back 39

cutback *as in* **make cutbacks** 32

cute **B2** 7

daily *adv* **B1** 78

dairy **B2** 35

damaging **C1** 21, 72

damp *adj* 34, 40

danger **A1** *as in* **in danger of extinction** 47

dare *v* **B2** *as in* **don't you dare** 63

darkness **B2** 31; **in total darkness** 31

day-to-day 74

deadline **B2** 68

deadly **B2** 63, 99

deaf 12; **(as) deaf as a post** 86

deal *n* **B1** 56, 69

death toll 60

deathly 99

debate *n* **B2** 58

debit card 32

debt **B2** 32

deceive 82

decent (= honest and fair) **B2** 16; (= good enough quality) **B2** 34

decisive **C1** 16

decline *v, n* **B2** 47

decorate **B1** 38

decorating 38

decorative 47

dedicate yourself to sth 20

dedicated to sb/sth **C1** 97

deep **A2** 35

deep *as in* **in a deep sleep** 31

deep-fat fryer 24

deep-fry 24

deeply **B2** 23

deer 11

defeat *n* **B2** 41

defect *n* **C1** 79

defective 79

defence **B2** 62

defend **B2** 62

defensive **C1** 8

defiant 77

deficit **C1** 32

defy **C1** 77

degree (= certain amount/ level of sth) **B2** 66

delegate (sth to sb) 68

deliberate **B2** 60

deliberately **B2** 60

delicate **C1** 61, 63

delight *n* 36

delighted **B2** 18

delightful 36

deliver (= give a message, etc.) **B1** 42

delivery **B2** 42

demanding 10

demonstrate (= protest) 59; (= show) **B2** 78

demonstration **B2** 59

demonstrator 59

denial **C1** 92

dense (fog) **C1** 28

dental 67

deny **B2** 92

department **A2** 65

dependent on sb/sth **B2** 28, 97

depending on sb/ sth **B1** 78

depict **C1** 77

deposit n **B2** 38, 94; v **C1** 94

depressed **B2** 18, 34

depressing **B2** 34

depression **B2** 18

deprivation 21

deprive sb (of sth) **C1** 21, 95

deprived 21

deserve **B2** 62, 78

desirable **C1** 34

desire n **B2** 49

desperate **B2** 18

desperation 18

despise 20

destructive **C1** 93

detailed (description) **B2** 4

detain **C1** 53

detect **B2** 92

detection **C1** 92

deter 54

deteriorate **C1** 71

determine **B2** 42

determination 43

deterrent 54

detest 20

devastate **C1** 60

devastated 18

devastation 60

device **A2** 73

devise **C1** 10

devote sth (to sth/ sb) **B2** 95

diabetes 14

diagnose **C1** 48

diagnosis **C1** 48

diagnostic 48

die out 47

differ (from sth/sb) **B2** 95

differentiate **C1** 55

dig v **B2** 39

dignified 20

dignity **C1** 20

directly **B1** 63

disadvantage **B1** 34

disapproval 20

disapprove of sb/sth 20

disapproving 1

disaster **A2** 81

discard **C1** 14

discharge sb (from hospital) **C1** 52

discipline **B2** 33

disclose **C1** 18

discomfort 11

discourteous 23

discrimination **C1** 49

discussion **A2** as in **under discussion** 98

disgust n 18

disgusted 18

dislike n **B1** as in **take an instant/immediate dislike to sb** 19

dislocate 15

disloyal 91

dismiss **B2** 65, 92

dismissal **C1** 92

disobedience 59

disobedient 91

disorder **B2** 14

display v **B2** 8, 78; n 8

disposable 44

disposal **C1** 46

dispose of sth **C1** 46, 95

dispute n **C1** 67, 94; v **C1** 94

disruption **C1** 28, 59

disruptive 66

dissatisfied 71

dissolve **C1** 14

distinction **C1** as in **make a distinction** 55

distinguish (between people or things) **B2** 55; distinguish sth/sb (from sth/sb) **B2** 95

distract sb (from sth) **B2** 95

distress n **C1** 20, 61

distribute **B2** 50

distribution **B2** 50

district **B2** 34

disturb **B2** 31

disturbing **C1** 99

dive (= into water) **B2** 9

diverse **B2** 36, 55, 66

diversification 70

diversify 70

diversity **B2** 55

divert sth/sb (from sth) **C1** 47

divide **B2** 58

division **B2** 58

do (= be enough/ acceptable) **B2** 2; **do sb a favour** 6; **do sb good** 87; **do sth at the last minute** 74

domestic (= of animals) **B2** 73

dominance **C1** 58

dominant **B2** 41, 58

dominate 41

domination 41

don't as in **don't ask me** 83; **don't judge a book by its cover** 88; **don't you dare** 63

donor **C1** 48

doorbell 30

dosage 14

dose **C1** 14

doubt n **B1** as in **no doubt** 81

downpour 28

downwards **B2** 23, 40

dozen **B2** 30

draft n, v **B2** 94

drag v **B2** 9

drain v **C1** 24

draw v **B2** as in **draw sb's attention to sth** 7

drawback 34

drawer 30

dream n **A2** as in **a dream come true** 84

dressing 15

dress up 29

drift into sth 33

dripping 30

driving licence 5

drop out (of sth) 71

drought **B2** 28

drown **C1** 61

dry adj **A2** as in **(as) dry as a bone** 86

dubbed **C1** 43

dull (= of weather) **C1** 28

dustbin 30

dynamic **B2** 16, 71

dynamism 71

early adj **A1** as in **an early night** 44

earth as in **what, etc. on earth** 84

earth tremor 60

ease v **C1** 11

easy as in **take it easy** 36

eco- (abbreviation of ecology) 46

economize 32

ecstatic 18

edit (a film, etc.) 61; (= prepare for publication) **B2** 92

edited 61

edition **B2** 92

educational **B1** 93

efficiency **C1** 17

efficient **B2** 17

effort **B1** as in **make an effort** 4

egg **A1** as in **put all your eggs in one basket** 88

electorate 58

electrician 64

elegant B2 29

eligible C1 51

eliminate B2 11

elimination 11

elsewhere B2 65

embark on sth 95

embody C1 77

emerge (= become known) B2 62; (= come out of a hidden place) B2 62; (= start to exist) B2 62

emergence of sth/sb C1 97

emigrate 49

emigration 49

eminent 99

empirical C1 79

empower C1 as in be empowered to do sth 90

en suite 38

enable sb to do sth B2 37, 48

enclosed 14

encompass C1 55

encounter v (= experience sth difficult) B2 66; (= meet unexpectedly) B2 42

encounter n B2 42

encounter v B2 66

encouragement C1 92

end n as in in the end A2 87; the end justifies the means 88

end up (doing sth) B1 47

endangered 47

endless C1 68

endure C1 63

energetically 13

energy-saving 46

enforce C1 45

enforcement C1 45

engage (= interest/attract) B2 42

enhance B2 7

enlist 55

enlisted 55

enough as in strangely/oddly/curiously enough 100

enrol on sth C1 52

ensure B2 51

enterprise C1 66

enthusiasm B2 16

enthusiastic B2 16

entire B2 59

entirely B2 100

entitle (sb to sth) C1 67

entrance hall 38

entrepreneur B2 64

equivalent to sth adj B2 97

era B2 48

eradicate 48

erect C1 59

escalate C1 72

essential B1 10

essentially B2 38, 100

establish (= start or create sth) B2 31; (= discover or prove the facts of a situation) B2 42

estate B2 61

estimate n B2, v B2 30, 73

ethic B2 16

ethical B2 16

ethnic B2 49

evacuate C1 60

evacuation 60

evaluate B2 76

evaluation B2 76

even as in even so 87

ever as in ever since B2 63

evidently 100

evil adj B2 77, 99; n B2 77

evolution B2 45

evolve B2 45

exact adj A2 1

exaggerate C1 7, 72

exaggeration 7

example B1 as in set an example 4

exceed (= do more than you are allowed to do; be greater than a particular number/amount) B2 14

excellent A1 78

exception as in take exception to sth 23; with the exception of sth/sb C1 97

exceptional C1 23, 99

excess C1 14

excessive B2 80

exclude sb (from sth) B2 95

exclusive C1 37

exclusively C1 54

executive n B2 64

exemplify 93

exhausted 31

exit (= of a motorway) n B2, v C1 27

expectation B2 43

expenditure C1 32

expense B2 37

experimental C1 79

expire C1 14

expiry date 14

exploit C1 70

exploitation C1 70

exploration B2 76

explore B2 76

expose (= show sth that is hidden) B2 62; (= tell the true facts about sth) B2 77

exposure to sth B2 97

extend B2 38

extended (= of a building) C1, (= of a piece of writing) 76

extension 38

extensive B2 27

extent B2 as in to a large extent 85; to some extent 50

exterior 30, 38

external adj B2 40

extinct 47

extinction 47

extract n B2 94

extract sth (from sb) v 94

extraordinary B2 74

extreme B2 50

extremism 50

extremist n C1, adj 50

extrovert n, adj 16

eye n as in an eye for an eye 88; eye contact 8; eye strain 11

eyebrow 13

eyesight 11

eyewitness 27

fabulous B2 43

face n as in a familiar face 4

face up to sth 72

facilitate C1 45

failure B2 71

fair enough 100

faith B2 49

fall v B1 as in fall asleep 31

fame B2 20

fancy dress 29

fancy sb B1 8; fancy (doing) sth B1 44

far as in by far 84

fast adv B2 as in fast asleep 31

fatal C1 14

fate C1 77

fattening 25

fault n B2 19

faulty 79

favour n (= sth that helps sb) B1 6; be in favour (of sth/sb) B1 50

favour v B2 50

favourable 99

feature n (= part of face/body) B1 7

feedback **B2** 70

fellow *adj* **B2** 62

feminist *adj* **C1** 77

fertile 39

figurative 1

figure (= body) 7

filter *n, v* **C1** 94

filthy 34

finance *n* **B2** 65

final *adj* **A1** *as in* a final resort 84

financial **B1** 65

findings **B2** 62

fingertip 13

fire *v* (= dismiss) **B1** 65

fire brigade 60

firefighter 60

firm *n* **B2** 70

firmly **B2** 13

first aid 15

first *adv as in* first and foremost 85; first come, first served 88

fist *as in* clenched fist 8

fit in (with sb/sth) 66

flash *n* **B2** 28

flatmate 38

flattering 7

flee **C1** 49

flexibility **C1** 37

flexible **B2** 37

flip-flop *n* 29

flirt (with sb) 8

float (= in water) **B2** 61; (= suggest an idea) 69

flood (= water) **B1** 68; (= a large quantity of sth) **B2** 68

flourish **C1** 71

flourishing 36

foil *v* 56

fold *v* **B1** 9; fold your arms 8

follow *as in* follow in sb's footsteps 22

food processor 24

foot *as in* put your feet up 39; put your foot in it 23

footstep 12

for *as in* for my part 49; for some reason 84 for the most part 49; for the time being 74

forehead 13

forgive **B2** 19

formally 61

former **B2** 69, 73

formerly **B2** 73

fortunate **B2** 73

fortune **B2** 62

forward planning 71

foster (= help/develop) **C1** 66

found *v* **B2** 70

foundation(s) (= of a building) **C1** 80

founder *n* **B2** 70

fracture *v* 15

fragment *n* **B2** 61

framework **B2** 80

frankly **C1** 100

fraud **B2** 33

free *as in* free of charge 52

freelance *adj, adv* 66

freeze *v* (= of a computer) 40

frequency **B2** 35

frequent **B2** 35

fresh (= new) **B2** 69

fringe benefit 67

frog **A2** 39

from *as in* from time to time 74

fruity 25

frustrated *adj* **C1** 68

frying pan 24

fulfil **B2** 66

fulfilling 66

full *as in* in full **C1** 98

fully-booked 37

functional **C1** 93

fundamental 55

funding **B2** 51

funds *n* **B2** 47

furnished 38

furthermore **B2** 75

future *n* **A1** *as in* in the near future **B2** 98

gain (wisdom) **B2** 21

gale 28

gallop 63

gang **B2** 33

gap *as in* gap in the market 70

gatecrasher 44

gaze at sth/sb 11

gear **C1** 26

generalization *as in* make generalizations 8

generally speaking 74

generate **B2** 46

generous **B1** 37

genre **B2** 42

gently 13

genuine (= real) **B2** 73; (= showing what you think) **B2** 16

gesture 8

get

(back) to sleep 31

(sb/sth to do sth) 2

away from it all 36

away with sth 66

carried away 44

going (= start to become enjoyable) 44

hold of sth 30

in the way of sth 66

on *as in* be getting on for sth 7

out of sth 2

over sth 82

sb down 72

somewhere/nowhere 71

sth across 82

the credit 4

the sack 65

there (= achieve your aim) 83

through (to sb) 82

through sth 82

ghost story 43

giant *adj* **B1** , *n* **B2** 98

ginger 24

girder 80

give *as in* give or take 89; give sb a hug/tap, etc 13; give sb a lift 81; give sb the sack 65

give in 67

given (that) 37

glamorous 7, 29

glance at sth/sb 11

glimpse *n* **C1** 11

go

away (= on holiday) **A2** 37

downhill 71

for a stroll 10

from strength to strength 71

hiking 10

in one ear and out the other 83

off (= leave a place) **B2** 81

off (= ring) **B2** 31

on (= happening) 34

on (= continue without changing) 34

on (= of time: pass) 34

red 8

through (a phase) 21

through sth (= examine sth; experience sth; perform a series of actions) 82

to sleep 31

go-ahead *n* 56

golden (opportunity) **B2** 1

good *adj as in* (as) good as gold 86; (as) good as new 73; good of sb (to do sth) 44

good *n as in* do sb good 85

goodness *as in* goodness knows 83

gorgeous **B2** 7

govern **B2** 58

grab *v* **B2** 13; grab sb's attention 57

graffiti 34

grand *adj* **B2** 37

grant *n* **B2** 51

grant (bail) *v* **B2** 53

grapefruit 24

grass *n* **A2** *as in* the grass is always greener (on the other side) 88

grate *v* 24

grater 24

greasy 25, 30

greed 20

greedy 20

green *adj* **B1** 51

greenhouse **B2** 39

grounds (for sth/doing sth) **B2** 53

group therapy 54

growing *adj* 72

guarantee *n* **B2** 37, 66; *v* **B2** 37, 66

guaranteed *adj* 66

guard *n* **B1**, *v* **B1** 55

guess *v as in* guess what 84

guest house 37

guidance **C1** 3

guidelines **B2** 3, 7

habitat **B2** 47

had *as in* had better **B2** 44

half **A1** *as in* in half 9; half a dozen 30

halt *v* **C1** 67

hand *v as in* hand in your notice 65

handle (emotions, etc.) **B2** 18

handling **C1** 3

handy **C1** 34

handyman 64

hang around/about 34

hang on **B2** 83

hard *adj* **A1** *as in* it's hard to say 22

hard-wearing 5

harsh **C1** 33

hate *v* **A1**, *n* **B1** 94

have *as in* have a (good) laugh 44; have a part to play (in sth) 49; have second thoughts (about sth) 2; have sth/sb in mind **C1** 83; having said that 37

hay fever 14

hazard *n* **C1** 26, 54

hazardous 26

head *n* (= of an organization) **A2** 51

head *v* (= be in charge) **B1** 51

headlight 26

heal **B2** 15

health care 52

heart **B1** *as in* a heart of gold 1

heart attack 14

heartbroken 18

heat (sth) (up) 25

heatwave 28

heaven **B2** 62

heavy (sleeper) **B1** 31

hedge *n* 39

heighten **C1** 93

helicopter **B1** 27, 55

hell (= in religion) **B2**; (= a very unpleasant experience) **B2**; (= a swear word) 62

hen party 29

hence 75

herb **B2** 24

herd **B2** 35

hereditary 79

heredity 79

hero **A2** 20

heroic 20

heroine 20

heroism 20

hesitate **B2** 92

hesitation 92

hideous 7

high *as in* a high profile 51

high-heeled shoe 29

hike *v* 10

hindsight *as in* with hindsight 74

hit (single) *n* **A2** 42

hit *v* **B1** 60

hold *n as in* on hold 98

hollow **B2** 39

holy **B2** 16

home *as in* at home (= playing sport) 41

homeless *adj* **B2** 34

honest **B1** *as in* to be (perfectly) honest 100

honour *n* **B2** *as in* in honour of sb/sth 98

hoover *n, v* 30

hopeless 71

horizontal 7

horn **C1** 12

host *n* **B1** 44

hostess 44

hostile (= unfriendly) **C1** 49; (= in business) 69

hostility 49

household 3

housewife/ househusband 64

housing **B2** 3

how *as in* How come? 83; how dare you 63

however *as in* however much/hard, etc. 22

hug *v, n* 13

human being 59

human race 3

human resources 65

humanitarian **C1** 3

humanity **C1** 3

humid 28

humidity 28

humorous **B2** 23

hundreds (of sth) **A1** 15

hunting **B2** 56

hypothesis **B2** 79

I *as in* I couldn't care less 25; I haven't the faintest idea 83; I mean **A2** 81; I wouldn't mind 84

icon **B2** 40

identity card 5

ideological **C1** 50

ideology **C1** 50

idiot **C1** 17

idiotic 17

if *as in* if all else fails 84; if only **B2** 84; if you don't/wouldn't mind 84

ignore **B1** 32

illustrate **B2** 76

illustration **B2** 76

imaginative 78

immature 17

immediate *adj* **B1** *as in* take an immediate dislike to sb 19

immigrant **B1** 49

immigration **B2** 49

imminent **C1** 69

immune system 79

immune to sth **B2** 97

immunity 79

impact *n* **B1** 21

implement *v* **B2** 45

implementation **C1** 45

implication **C1** 77

imply **B2** 77

impose sth on/upon 45

impress **B2** 23, 37

impressed **B2** 23

impressive **B1** 37

imprison **C1** 54

imprisonment **C1** 54

in

a deep sleep 31

a minute 83

a row 41

a whisper 12

advance 37

any case **C1** 70, 87

conclusion 75

connection with sth **C1** 59

credit 32

danger (of extinction) **A2** 47

decline 47

excess of sth 14

favour of sb/sth **B1** 50

full **C1** 98

half 9

honour of sth/sb 98

office 98

part **B2** 49

place **B2** 15

possession of sth 98

power 98

reserve 55

retrospect 74

some cases **A2** 70

tears 12, 18

that case 70

the end **A2** 87

the middle of nowhere 37

the near future **B2** 98

the public eye 62

the public interest 61

the region of sth 89

the short/medium/long term 46

the wake of sth **C1** 69

total darkness 31

view of sth 75

your own time 21

inability **C1** 14

inaccurate 1

inadequate **C1** 75

inappropriate **C1** 1

incapable 91

incentive **B2** 21, 64

inch n **B2** 63, 74

incident **B2** 27, 77

incidentally 87

inclined to do sth **C1** 67

inclusion **C1** 3

inclusive 3

incoherent 76

income **B2** 32

incompatible 91

incomprehensible 99

inconsiderate 16

inconsistent 41

inconvenience 75

increasingly **B2** 35

incredible **A2** 74

ineligible 51

inevitable **B2** 19

infamous **C1** 99

infect **C1** 48

infection **B2** 15, 48

infectious 15, 48

inflexible 37

influential **C1** 21

inform **B2** 52

infrequent 35

inherent (in sth) **C1** 77, 97

inherit (qualities/features) **B2** 22; (money/land) **B2** 77

inheritance 77

inhuman 91

initial adj **B2** 19

initially **B2** 19

initiative **B2** 66

inmate **C1** 54

inner (city) **B2** 34

innovate 70

innovation **B2** 70

innovative **B2** 70, 73

inoffensive 1, 23

insert (sth into sth) **B2** 79, 80

insertion **C1** 79

inside lane 27

insight (into sth) **B2** 66

insignificant 72

insist (on sth/doing sth) **B2** 95

insoluble 72

insomnia 31

inspect **C1** 92

inspection **C1** 79

inspector **B2** 53

inspiration **C1** 20

inspirational 20

inspire **B2** 20

install **B2** 40

installation 40

instance **B2** 47

instant (food) adj **B2** 25; take an instant dislike to sb 19

instantly **B2** 57

institute **B2** 54

institution **B2** 54

insufficient **C1** 91

insult n, v **C1** 1

insulting 1

insurance **B2** 65

integration (into sth) **C1** 49

integrity **C1** 16

intended (for sth) **B2** 39

intense **B2** 18, 60

intensify **C1** 93

intensity **C1** 60

intent on/upon sth / doing sth 97

intentional 60

interact (with sb) **B2** 95

interfere (in sth) **C1** 71

interference **C1** 71

interior n **C1** 38

internal **B2** 40

interpret **B2** (= explain the meaning of sth) **B2** 1; (= decide that sth has a particular meaning) **B2** 8

interpretation **B2** 1, 8

interrupt **B2** 68

introvert n, adj 16

introverted adj 16

invalid 91

invariably 100

invest in sth **B1** 70

investigation **B2** as in under investigation 98

investment (= sth worth buying) **B2** 46; (= investing money) **B2** 70

invisible **C1** 11

involvement (in sth) **C1** 97

ironic **C1** 1

ironically **C1** 1

ironing board 30

irony **C1** 1

irrational 77

irrelevant **C1** 42

irreplaceable 3

irritable 31

irritate 11

irritating 12

irritation 11

isolated **B2** 35

isolation **C1** 35

issue v (a fine, etc.) **B2** 53; (= make a statement) **B2** 69

it's as in it's a small world 88; it's about/high time 74; it's hard to say 22; it's true (that …) 87

jail *v* B2 *as in* **be jailed** 90

jaw 13

jeweller 64

jewellery A2 64

job *as in* **be a good job** 84

joy 18

joyful 18

judge *v* B1 *as in* **don't judge a book by its cover** 88

judgement B2 23

juicy 25

jump *v as in* **jump to conclusions** 8

junction C1 27

junior 52

junk food 5

justice (= the fair treatment of people; the legal system) B2 54

justifiable 54

justification C1 54, 76

justify B2 37, 54, 76

keep (= remain fresh) 2; **keep (animals)** 35; **keep sth a secret** 4

keep ahead (of sb) 70

kerb 26

kettle 9

key sth (in) B1 40

key to sth *n* (= an important thing) 7

kid *v as in* **you're kidding** 83

kidnap C1 33, 56

kidnapper 33, 56

kidnapping 33

kilt 29

kind of 89

kitchen scales 24

kneel down 9

know *v* A1 *as in* **be known as/for sth** B1 90; **you never know** 81, 84

knowledgeable 17

labour *n* (= people who work) B2 35

labourer 35

lacking (in sth) *adj* 17

land *v* A2 74

landfill 46

landlady 38

landlord C1 38

lane (= road) B2 27

lap C1 25

largely B2 38

last *adj* A1 *as in* **a last resort** 84

last *v* (= continue; be enough) A2 71

last-minute 5

lasting *adj* 74

late *adj as in* **a late night** 44; (= no longer alive) 22

laugh *n as in* **have a (good) laugh** 44

launch *v* (= start a computer program) B2 40; (= start an activity) B2 40, 70

law and order 86

lawnmower 39

laze around/about 36

lead *n, v* B1 94

leadership B2 69

leaflet B2 14

league B2 41

lean (towards sb) B2 8

lean against sth B2 9

lean *adj* 25

lease *n* 38

leave sth to/with sb B2 2; **leave sth to/till the last minute** 74

leave *n* (= holiday) B2 67

left-wing 50

legalize 93

lemon-squeezer 24

lentil 24

let me see/think 83

let sb down 71

letter box 30

liable to sth C1 97

liberal *adj, n* C1 50

liberalism 50

librarian 64

lick *v* 23

lie-in *as in* **have a lie-in** 31

life expectancy 5

lifeboat 70

lift *n* B1 *as in* **give sb a lift** 81

light *adj* A2 *as in* **(as) light as a feather** 86

light sleeper 31

lightly 13

like *prep* A1 *as in* **like me/you/him, etc.** 81

likelihood C1 3, 47

limitation (on sth) B2 97

literal 1

literally B2 1

litter B2 34

live *v* A1 *as in* **live in peace** 49

lively B2 16, 34

liven sth up 44

live stream *n* 61

live-stream *v* 61

living *n* (= money you earn) B1 35

load *v* B2 27

load *n* (= sth being carried) B2 27; (= the amount of weight/pressure) 80; **loads (of sth)** 89

loan *n* B2 70

loathe 20

lock sb up 54

loft 38

log C1 27

logic C1 93

logical B2 93

long-lived 79

long-standing C1 5

long-term B2 14

loo 30

look back (on sh) 74

look out for sth/sb 8

look up (= improve) 19

look up to sb 20, 82

lookout *as in* **be on the lookout for sb/sth** 26

loose-fitting 29

loosen 93

lord (= a title) B2 61; the Lords 56

lose *as in* **lose face** 84; **lose your temper** 20

love *n* A1 *as in* **love is blind** 88

lower *adj* 63

loyal B2 91

loyalty card 5

luck A2 *as in* **(the) best of luck** 83

lucrative 64

lump 14

lung cancer 14

luxurious 37

luxury B1 37

lyrics B2 42

magistrate C1 53

magnificent B2 73

main A1 *as in* **sb's main concern** 4

maintain (= in good condition) B2 39; (= at a certain standard) B2 60

maintenance C1 39

major (change) A2 45

majority B2 58

make

(= think or calculate) 2

a distinction 55

a note of sth 68

a speedy recovery 63

an effort 4

cutbacks 32

generalizations 8

it (= various meanings) 81

sth of sb 17

sb feel welcome 44

sb redundant 65

sb/sth do sth 81

sth/sb out 11

up (= comprise) 55

up (for sth/sb) 95

up for sth 82

make-up B2 7

mango 24

manifesto 51

manners A2 23

manslaughter 33

manual *adj* 26, 64

manufacture B2 70

manufacturer 70

manufacturing B2 65

march *v* C1 10, 29

market *n* B1 *as in* **on the market** 38

market research 65

mass *adj, n* B2 57; **mass-market** 57

massage *v, n* 13

massive B2 27

mat 30

matching B2 29

mate *n, v* B2 94

maternity 67

matter *as in* **as a matter of fact** 84; **no matter what/how, etc.** B2 68

mature *adj* (of behaviour) C1 17; (= fully grown) C1 39

maximize C1 93

may *as in* **may as well do sth** 83

mayor B2 51

meadow 35

mean *v as in* **be meant for / to do sth** 90

mean *adj* (= wanting to keep money) 37; (= unpleasant) 19

means (of sth / doing sth) B2 50; **by means of sth, by no means** 98

measurement B2 92

mechanism B2 73

medium *adj* B1 25

meet (the needs of sb/ sth) B2 80

melody C1 42

memorable B2 42

mention *v* A2 *as in* **not to mention** C1 84

mercy C1 77

merger C1 69

merit *n* C1 78

merry *as in* **the more the merrier** 88

mess *n* 81; **make a mess of sth** 81

metaphor B2 1

metaphorical 1

middle *n* A2 *as in* **in the middle of nowhere** 37

might *as in* **might as well do sth** 83

migrant 49

migration C1 49

mild (weather) B1 28

military *n, adj* B2 55

military service 55

mind *n* A2 *as in* **my mind is like a sieve** 86; **be in two minds about sth** 2; **have sth in mind** 83; **my mind is/goes a complete blank** 83; **on my mind** 31

mind *v as in* **mind you** 85

mineral B2 48

minimize C1 59

minimum *adj* B2 67

minister B2 56

minor *adj* B2 14, 72

minority (= within a community) B2 49

minute *n* A1 *as in* **(at) any minute (now)** 81; **do sth at the last minute** 74; **in a minute, the minute (that …)** 83

miscalculate 91

miserable (= making you feel very unhappy or uincomfortable) B2 37; (= very unhappy or uncomfortable) B2 52

misery C1 20

misinterpret 8

misjudge 91

mislead 91

missile C1 55

mission 59

mist 11

mistake sb/sth for sb/sth 3

mistreat 91

misty 11

misunderstand 91

mix *v* B1 24

mixed *as in* **mixed farming** 35; **mixed feelings** 35; **mixed race** 35

moderate *adj* C1, *n* 50

modernize 93

modify B2 73

molecular 79

molecule 79

moment A1 *as in* **at a moment's notice** 98

money A1 *as in* **put money into sth, take money out** 32

monitor *v* B2 46

monthly *adv* 78

moon *as in* **over the moon** 18

mop *n* 29

moral *adj* B2 33

morals *n* B2 33

more *as in* **more or less** B2 87

moreover B2 75

mortgage *n* B2 38

mother tongue 5

motion B2 80

motivated 10, 17

motivation B2 10, 17

mount *v* B2 69

mount up 32

movement B2 59

mow (the lawn) 39

mud B1 39

muddy 39

mug *n* 25

mug *v* 33

mugger 33

mugging 33

multiple *adj* B2 58

multiply B2 72

mutate 79

mutation 79

mutual C1 66

mysterious B2 63

mysteriously 63

naked B2 99

nap *n as in* **have a nap** 31

narrative *n* B1 76

narrator 76

narrow *adj* A2 7; **a narrow escape** 4

narrow-minded 5

nasty B2 19

native *adj* B1 49

nature (= character) B1 21; (= physical world) A2 39

near *adj* B1 *as in* **in the near future** B2 98

nearby B2 34

necessarily *as in* **not necessarily** B1 8

neglect *n, v* C1 33

negotiate B2 58

negotiation B2 58

nerves B2 68

nest C1 39

network B1 61

nevertheless **B2** 35, 75, 87

news **A1** *as in* **no news is good news** 88

next to (nothing) 73

nightdress/nightie 31

nightmare (= bad dream) **B2** 12, 31; (= bad experience) **B2** 12

no *as in* **no comment** 6; **no way** **A2**, **no chance** 83; **no matter what/ how, etc.** **B2** 68; **no wonder** 84

nod *v* **C1** 9

nominate **C1** 78

nomination **C1** 78

nonetheless **C1** 75

nostalgia 49

nostalgic 49

not *as in* **not necessarily** **B1** 8; **not to mention** **C1** 84

note *n* **A1** *as in* **make a note of sth** 68

note sth down 68

notice *n* **B1** *as in* **take no notice of sb/sth** 52

noticeable 3

notify **C1** 61

notion (of sth) **B2** 23

notorious **C1** 99

now *as in* **now and again** 85; **now and then** 85

nowadays **B2** 64

numerous **B2** 60

number plate 26

nurture *n, v* 21

nut **A2** 24

obedient 91

object *v* **B2** 92

objection **C1** 92

objective *adj* **B2** 79

objectivity 79

obligatory 55

oblige **C1** 75

observant 8

observation **B2** 8

observe **B2** 8

obstacle **B2** 71

obvious **B1** 22, 45

occasionally **B2** 35

occupational *as in* **occupational hazard** 35

occupy (= enter a place and take control of it) **C1**, (= fill or us a space / an amount of time) **B2**, (= live or work in a room, etc.) **C1** 59

occur **B1** 79

odd *adj* (= approximately) 89; (= not regular or fixed) 28

oddly *as in* **oddly enough** 100

odds and ends 85

off *adv* **A2** *as in* **be off** (= leave) 44

off *as in* **off the beaten track** 36; **off the top of my head** 83

offence (= a crime) **B2** 53; **take offence (at sth)** 23

offender **B2** 33

offensive *adj* **B2** 1, 23

office **B2** *as in* **in office** 98

official *adj* **B1** 91

on

a daily/weekly basis 68

and off 85

behalf of sb / on sb's behalf **C1** 51

board **B2** 98

good/friendly/bad, etc. terms (with sb) 98

hold 98

my mind 31

purpose 98

standby 46

the alert 26

the basis of sth **B2** 98

the contrary 83

the market 38

the part of sb / on sb's part **C1** 57

the whole 34, 87

once *as in* **at once** **B2** 98; **once bitten, twice shy** 88

one *as in* **one (thing) at a time** 68

ongoing **B2** 45, 47

only *as in* **only just** 11

open-minded 5

open-plan 38

opening (= beginning; the act of making sth open; a small hole) **B2** 57

operating theatre 48

operation (= surgery) **B1** 48; (= organized activity) **B2** 55

opponent **B2** 41

oppose **B2** 50

opposed to sth **B2** 50

opposite *n* **A1** *as in* **the exact/complete opposite** 4

opposition **B2** 50

opt for sth **C1** 37

optician 11

optional 55

or *as in* **or so** **B2** 89; **or something/ somewhere, etc.** 89; **or thereabouts** 89

organ (= of the body) **B2** 48

origin **B2** *as in* **country of origin** 49

originality 43

otherwise **B2** 57, 75

out *as in* **out of date** 73; **out of respect (for sb)** 98; **out of touch (with sth)** 98; **out of work** 65

outcome **B2** 69

outfit **B2** 29

outgoings 32

outline *v, n* **B2** 76

outside *n* **A2** 30

outskirts 35

outstanding (= excellent) **B2** 23, 78, 99

over *as in* **over the moon** 18

overall *adv* **B2** 38

overcharge 91

overcome (a problem) **B2** 71, 72, 82; **be overcome with sth** **C1** 90

overdo 91

overdrawn *as in* **be overdrawn** 32

overestimate *v* 41, 91

overhear 12

oversleep 31

overtake 26

overweight 7

overwhelmed (by sth) **C1** 68

overwhelming **C1** 68

owe **B2** 32; **owe sb a favour** 6

own up to sth 82

ownership **B2** 50

pace **B2** 21, 57; **at your own pace** 21

pacify 93

packaging 73

packed lunch 25

panel (= group of specialists) **B2** 78; (= piece of metal, glass, etc) **B2** 80

panic *n* **B2**, *v* 63

parachute 55

parental **C1** 33

part **A1** 66; **have a part to play (in sth)** 44; **in part** **B2** 49; **on the part (of sb) / on sb's part** **C1** 57

participant (in sth) **B2** 52

partly **B2** 50

partnership **B2** 70

pass *v as in* **pass the buck** 4

pass away/on 22

pass sth on 35

passage **B2** 34

passion **B1** 16

passionate **B2** 16, 71

pat *v* 13

patience **B2** 19

patient *adj* **B2** 19

pause *n, v* **B2** 94

pavement 26

pay and display machine 26

pay (sth) off 32

PC 53

peace **A2** *as in* live in peace 49

peak **C1** 69

peculiar **C1** 99

pedestrian crossing 26

peel *v* 24

peeler 24

peer pressure 21

penalty (= punishment) **B2** 33

pension **B2** 67

perfect (example) *adj* **A1** 4

perk *n* 67

persist **C1** 14

persistent **C1** 14

personally (= by a particular person) **B1** 22; personally speaking 74

perspective 72

phase *n* **B2** 21

phenomenon **B2** 79

philosophy **B2** 58

pick sth up (= get a skill, habit, etc.) 22

pile-up 27

pile *n as in* piles of sth 89

pinch *v* **B2** 13

pitch *n* **B2** 41

pity *n* **B2** 34; that's a pity, what a pity 34

place *n* **A1** *as in* in place **B2** 15

plague (= disease; serious problem) 68

plain **B2** 29

plaster *n* 15

play *as in* play a part (in sth) **B1** 21

play down 72

plea **C1** 56

pledge *n, v* **C1** 56

plot *n, v* **B2** 56

plug (sth) in 9, 40

plug *n* **C1** 30

plumber 30, 64

plummet 69

plunge **C1** 69

poacher 47

poaching 47

point sth out **B1** 47

police constable 53

police officer 53

police *v* 51

policing 51

pollen 14

pond **C1** 39

poor (= low quality) **B1** 43

pop in (to somewhere) 25

pop round/over/in 44

porch 30

portray **C1** 77

pose *v* **B2** 47

position (= job) **B2** 64; (= opinion) **B2** 76

possess **B2** 3

possession **B1** *as in* in possession of sth 98

post (= job) **B2** 64

postpone **C1** 82

potential *adj* (= may happen) **B2** 14, 26; (= can be successful) **B2** 17

potential *n* (= possibility of success) **B2** 17, 70

potentially **B2** 14

power *n* **A2** *as in* in power 98

practically 100

practice makes perfect 88

praise *v* **B2** 43

pray **B1** 9

precaution 60

precedent **C1** 67

precious **B2** 57

precise **B2** 1

precisely (= exactly and correctly; for emphasis) **B2** 100

precision **C1** 1, 57

predictable **B2** 43

predominantly **C1** 100

preferably 37

pregnancy **C1** 77

pregnant **B2** 77

prejudice *n* **C1** 49, 61

preparation **B2** 44

prescribe **C1** 52

prescription **C1** 52

presence (= of a person) **B2** 22

present *v* (= give sth to sb; show/describe) **B2** 76

present *n* **A1** *as in* at present 98

presentation **B1** 76

preserve **B2** 73

press-up 10

pressure *n* **B1** *as in* under pressure 41

prestigious **C1** 78

presumably **C1** 100

pretentious 78

prevention *as in* prevention is better than cure 88

primarily **B2** 100

prime *adj* **B2** 52

principal (concern) *adj* **B2** 4

principle **B2** 54

printing **B2** 57

prior to sth **B2** 75

prioritize 68

priority **B2** 41, 68

privacy **B2** 62

private (sector) *adj* **B1** 65

pro *n as in* the pros and cons 66, 86

probe *n, v* **C1** 56

problematic **C1** 3

procedure **B2** 53

proceed (with sth) **B2** 95

producer **B2** 70

productive **C1** 68

productivity **C1** 68

profitable **C1** 93

progressive **B2** 93

prominent **C1** 50

promote **B1** 65

promotion **B2** 65

prompt *adj* 32, 68

prompt *v* **C1** 40

promptly 32, 68

proportion **B2** 54

proposal **B2** 92

propose **B2** 6, 82

prospect *n* (= that sth will happen) **B2** 44; prospects (= chance of being succesful) **B2** 65

protection **B2** 70

protective **C1** 93

protest *n, v* **B1** 59

protester **B2** 59

provided (that) 31, 75

providing (that) 75

pry (into sth) 62

psychological **B2** 18

psychologist **B2** 18

psychology **B2** 18

public *adj* **A2**, **B1** 61; in the public eye 62; in the public interest 61; public appearance 61; public figure 61; public money 61; public sector 65

publication **B2** 57

publish **A2** 82

pull away (= drive off) 26

pull out (= of a car) 27

pulse 24

punch v, n **C1** 13

punctual 74

punctuality 74

pupil **B2** 1

pure (gold/silk/
cotton) **B2** 4

purely **B2** 100

purify 93

purpose **A2** as in on
purpose 98

pursue (= achieve sth over
time) **B2** 45; (= continue
with sth) **B2** 69

push (= make sb work
harder) **B2** 2

put

(= say or write sth) **B2** 2

a strain on sth/sb 19

all your eggs in one
basket 88

money into sth 32

on the brakes 26

sth aside 68

sth forward **B2** 82

sth in 38

sth into practice 45

sth off 82

sth on (clothes) **A2** 9

up with 63

your feet up 39

your foot in it 23

pyjamas 31

qualification (= in
a competition) 41;
qualification(s) (= exams
passed) **B1** 65

qualified adj **B1** 91

qualify **B1** 41

quit **B1** 65

quotation **B1** 57

quote n, v **B1** 57

racial **B2** 49

racism **B2** 3

racist adj, n **B2** 3

radiator 30

radical (= new and
different) **C1** 48; (=
wanting political change)
C1 50; (= complete) 45

rage n **C1** 77

rainbow 28

raise (a problem, topic,
etc.) **B2** 72, 82

raisin 24

rally (around/to sb/sth) 62

rank n **B2** 53

ransom n 56

rape n, v **C1** 33

rapid **B2** 79

rapidly **B2** 79

rapist 33

rare (= cooked a short
time) 25

rash n 14

raspberry 24

rate n **A2** 48

rather **A2** 43

rational **C1** 77

raw **B2** 25

rear-view mirror 26

reassess 91

reassure **C1** 72

rebel n **C1**, v 20

rebellion **C1** 59

rebellious 20

reboot v 40

recall v **B2** 74

reckon v **B2** 81

recognition **A2** 3

recollection 74

reconcile sth (with sth) 95

reconditioned 73

recovery **B2** as in make a
speedy recovery 63

recruit v **B2** 65

recruitment **B2** 65

recuperate 52

recuperation 52

red adj **A1** as in (as) red as
a beetroot 86

redecorate 38

redo 38, 91

redundant as in make sb
redundant 65

refer sb (to sth) **A2** 52

referendum **C1** 58

refine 70

reflect (= like a mirror) **B1** 6;
reflect (on sth) **B2** 6

reform v, n **C1** 45

refreshing (change) 45

refuge **C1** 49

refugee **B2** 49

refuse (bail) 53

refusal **C1** 92

regard sth/sb as sth **B2**
23, 54

regard n as in with regard
to sb/sth **C1** 75

regarding prep 58, 75

regardless of sth/sb **C1** 72

region **A2** 47; in the region
of sth 89

regional **B2** 47

register v (= put your name
on a list) **B2** 52, 65

register n (= a list) **B2** 65;
(= words/style that sb
uses) 76

regret v **B2** 19, 34; n **B2** 34

regulation **B2** 80

regulator **C1** 61

rehab (abbreviation of
rehabilitation) 62

rehabilitate 54

rehabilitation **C1** 54

reinforced (concrete) 80

relate to sth 42

relatively **B2** 41

release (tension) **B2** 13

relevance **C1** 42

relevant **B2** 42

reluctance 19

reluctant **C1** 19, 99
:

remaining adj 63

remand v as in be
remanded in custory 53

remark n **B2** 23

remarkable **B2** 36

remarkably **B2** 36

remind sb about sth **B1**
68; remind sb of sb/
sth **B1** 22

reminder of/about sth **C1**
68, 97

remote **B1** 36

rental (property) **C1** 38

reoffend 54

reoffender 54

replacement **C1** 3

report v **A2** as in be
reported to be sth **C1** 90

representative of sb/sth
adj **B2** 97

reproduce **C1** 73

reproduction **C1** 73

requirement **B2** 3

rescue n, v **B2** 60

resemblance 22

resemble **C1** 22

reserve n **B2** as in in
reserve 55; the reserve(s)
(= an extra force) 55

resident n **B2** 51

resign **B2** 65

resignation **C1** 92

resist (= refuse to accept
sth) **B2** 45; (= not be
harmed by sth) **B2** 80

resistance (= refusal to
accept sth) **C1** 45, 59; (=
ability not to be harmed
by sth) **C1** 80

resistant to sth 97

resolve **B2** 72

resort n (= a place for holidays) **B2** 36; **a last/final resort** 84

respect n **B1** as in **gain sb's respect** 19; **out of respect (for sb)** 98

respect v **B1** 82

responsibility **B1** as in **take responsibility** 4

restless as in **have a restless night** 31

restoration **C1** 36, 45

restore **B2** 36, 45

restrict **B2** 31, 48

restricted 1

restriction **B2** 48

resume **C1** 48

retail n **B2** 65

retain **B2** 36, 70

retention 36, 70

retrospect as in **in retrospect** 74

reveal **B2** 18, 62

revelation **C1** 62

revenge **C1** 54

reversal 45

reverse v (**a car**) **C1** 26; (= a change sth to the opposite) **C1** 45

revolution **B2** 48

revolutionary adj **C1** 48

reward n, v **B2** 65

rewarding 66

rewrite 91

rhythm **B2** 42

rich (= of food) **B2** 25

ridiculous **B2** 17

right n (= moral or legal claim) **B1** 67

right adv **B1** as in **right away** 98

right-wing 50

ripe adj 25

rival n **B2** 70

road sign 26

roar as in **roar with laughter** 4

rock v **C1** 62

rocket v 69

role model 5, 21

root (= of a plant) **B2** 39

rough (= approximate) **B2** 30

row1 n **B1** as in **in a row** 41

row2 n (= argument) 71

rub v **B2** 13

ruin v **B2** 40

rule sth out 56

rumour v **C1** 62

run v **A1** as in **run flat out** 10

run after sb/sth 10

run away 10

run off with sth 10

run sb/sth over 10

rural **B2** 35

rush v **B2** 10; **rushed off your feet** 52

sack v **C1** 65

safe adj **A2** as in **safe and sound** 85

safety helmet 70

saint **C1** 16

salty 25

sandal 29

satisfied **B2** 71

save (= rescue) **A2** 60

saving n **B2** 46

say v **A1** as in **be said to be sth** 90; **to say the least** 28

say n as in **have a say in sth** 51

saying 88

scale n **B2** 60

scalp 13

scandal **B2** 62

scanner 48

scare v **B2** as in **scare sb to death** 43

scatter 27

scattered (showers) **C1** 28

scene (= of an accident) **A2** 27

scenery 36

sceptical of/about sth **C1** 97

schedule v **B1** as in **be scheduled for sth** 90

scheme **B2** 56

scrape through (an exam) 71

scratch v, n **B2** 13

scream v, n **B2** 12

screenplay 43

screw v, n **C1** 9

scroll up/down 40

scrutinize 79

scrutiny **C1** 79

search warrant 53

second **A1** as in **have second thoughts (about sth)** 2

second-hand 73

secret n **A2** as in **the secret of your success** 71

sector **B2** 65

see (= find out) **B1** 2

seek **B2** 64

segregate 54

segregation 54

selective **C1** 93

self- (= of, to or by yourself) 54

self **B2** 52

self-assessment 54

self-catering 54

self-confidence 5

self-contained 54

self-employed 64

self-esteem 72

self-explanatory 1

self-righteous 5

self-service 25

sell v **A1** as in **selling like hot cakes** 86

semi-detached house 38

senior adj **B2** 52

sensational 43

sense **A2** as in **a sense of humour** 23

sensible **B1** 16

sensitive (= understanding feelings) **B2** 19; **sensitive (to sth)** (= easily affected by sth) **B2** 31

sentence sb (to sth) **B2** 53

sentiment **C1** 42

sequence 43

sergeant **B2** 53

seriously **B1** as in **take sb seriously** 17, 51, 72

serve (= do useful work) **B2** 55

service station 27

session **B2** 100

set v (= decide; fix sth for others to copy) **B1** 67; **set (an example)** **B1** 4; **set (the alarm)** **B1** 31

set n (= scenery in a film) 43

set sth aside 68

set sth off 69

set sth up (= arrange for sth to happen; make equipment ready for use; build/put sth somewhere) 82

setback 72

settings 40

settle (= end a disagreement) **B2** 67

settle down 19

settlement **C1** 92

severe **B2** 18, 63

sew sth (on) 9

shade n, v 94

shake (your head) **A2** 9

shallow **B2** 35

shame n (= the feelings of guilt, etc.) **B2** 18; **that's a shame, what a shame** 34

shareholder **C1** 69

shed n 39

shiver *v* 29

shock *n* **B2** 18, 49; *v* **B2** 18

shocked **B2** 18

shoplifter 33

shoplifting 33

short *as in* **at short notice** 98; **short (of sth)** **B2** 81

shortage **B2** 28, 32

shortlist *n* 78

short-listed *as in* **be short-listed for sth** 90

short-lived 79

short-sleeved 29

short-term **B2** 14

shortcut 5

shorten 93

shortfall 32

shortlist *n* 78

show off 16

show-off 16

shrug *v* **C1** 9

sibling **B2** 22

sick *as in* **sick and tired** 85; **sick to death of sth** 85

side effect 14

sigh *v* **C1** 12

sight *n* **B1** 11

signal *n* **B1**, *v* 8

significance **B2** 72

significant **B2** 28, 60, 72

significantly 60

silence *n* **B2** 12

silk **B2** 29

simplify 93

simply (= for emphasis; in a simple way) **B1** 100

since *conj* **B2** (= because) 75

sincere **B2** 16

sing *v* **A1** *as in* **sing along to sth** 42

single-minded 5

sit *v* **A1** *as in* **sit on the fence** 76

skid *v* 26

skinny 7

skirt *n* **A1** *as in* **a check(ed)/tight-fitting/ loose-fitting skirt** 29

skull **B2** 15

slam *v* **C1** 12

slang 1

slap *v* **C1**, *n* 13

slave *n* **B2** 98

slave labour 98

sleep *v* **A1** *as in* **sleep like a log** 31, 86

sleeper (= bed on a train) 31

sleeping bag 31

sleeping pill 31

sleepy 31

slender 7

slice *v* **B1** 24

slide *v* **B2** 13

slight (accent) **B2** 4

slim 7

slip (over/on sth) **B2** 74

slope *n* **B2** 39

slow down **B1** 26

slum 33

small *as in* **it's a small world** 88

smoke alarm 30

sneeze *v* 12

snore *v* 12, 31

so *as in* **so as to do sth** **B2** 87; **so far, so good** 88

soar **C1** 69

socialism 50

socialist *adj* **C1**, *n* 50

socialize (with sb) 44

socket 9, 30

soil *n* **B1** 39

solely **C1** 66

solicitor **C1** 53

solve **A2** 72

somehow **B2** 89

something *as in* **something like that/of that sort** 89; **something to do with sth** 89

somewhat **B2** 43

soon *as in* **sooner or later** 85

sophisticated **C1** 23

sophistication 23

sort of 89

sort sth out **B2** 41

sought after 47

soul **B2** 1

sound *adj* **C1** *as in* **safe and sound** 85

sound effect 43

spacious 38

spade 39

spare *adj* **B2** 30; **spare part** 5

specialist *adj* **B2** 52, 57

specialist *n* **B2** 52

specialize (in sth) **B2** 93

species **B2** 39, 47

specify **B2** 93

spectacular **B2** 11

speed up 26

speedy *as in* **make a speedy recovery** 63

spell *n* **C1** (= a period of time) 28

spice *n* **B2** 24

spicy **B1** 25

spill *v* **B2** 9, 27

spinach 24

spirit (= lives after death) **B2** 1

spiritual **B2** 20

splendid 73

split (= divide) **B2** 78; (= divide to share) **B2** 23

spokesperson **B2**/ spokesman **B2**/ spokeswoman **B2** 51

sponsor *n* **B2** 78

spot *n* (= particular area) **B1** 35

spot *v* **B2** 11, 63

sprain (your wrist/ ankle) 15

spread (a rumour) **B1** 4

squeeze *v* (= press) **C1** 13; (a lemon) **C1** 24

squeeze *n* 13

stabilize **C1** 93

stag party/night 29

stage *v* **B2** 59

staircase 38

stake *n* *as in* **at stake** 67

stale 25

stance **B2** 76

stand *as in* **stand a chance of (sth/doing sth)** 41; **stand still** 11; **stand the test of time** 42

stand up for sth/sb 51

standby *as in* **on standby** 46

stare (at sb/sth) **B2** 19

starve **B2** 63

status **B2** 64

status quo 50

stay *v* **A1** *as in* **stay put** 63

steadily **B2** 13

steer **C1** 26

steering wheel 26

step *n* **B2** 30

step sth up 67

stepfather/mother, etc. 22

stereotype **C1** 49

stereotypical 49

stew *v* 24

stick (in sth) (= become fixed) **B1** 74; (= put sth in a place) **B1** 81; (= put sth into sth) **B1** 23

stick to sth **B2** 31

stick up for sb/yourself 19, 51

stiff *adj* 10

still *adj* (= without moving) `B1` 11; (= adding to sth you have said) `B1` 85

stimulate 13

stool 30

storage (= space to keep things) `C1` 38; (= process of keeping information) `C1` 40

storey 38

straight away 98

straightforward 17

strain *n* `C1` 11; **put a strain on sth/sb** 19

strand *as in* **be stranded** 63

strangely *as in* **strangely enough** 100

strap *n* 29

stream (= small river) `B2` 35, 68; (= continuous flow of things) `B2` 68

strengthen `B2` 10, 93

stressed out 68

stretch *v* `B2` 10

strict `B2` 19, 37

strictly (= in all circumstances) **B**2, (= exactly/ completely) `C1` 100

strike *n* `B2` 67

strike (= of a disaster) `B2` 60; **strike sb** (= come to mind) `B2` 2; **strike sb as sth** `B2` 17

stroke *v* 13

stroll *n, v* 10

strong (accent) `B1` 4

structural `C1` 93

structurally 80

structure *n* `B2` 80

struggle *n* `B2`, *v* `B2` 17, 71

stuck (in sth) 63

stuff *n* `B2` 89

stumble *v* `C1` 10, 63

stunning `B2` 7, 36

style *n* `A2` 76

stylistic 76

subject to sth `B2` 97

subjective 79

submit `B2` 78

subsidize 32

subsidy `C1` 32

substitute sth/sb (for (sth/ sb) `C1` 95

substitute (for sth) *n* `C1` 97

subtitles 43

subtle `C1` 45

subtract sth from sth 32

suburb `B2` 34

success `A2` 71

suede 29

sufficient `B2` 91

sum (of sth) `B2` 32

summarize `B1` 76

summary `B1` 76

super *adj* `B2` 99

superb `C1` 43, 99

superior *adj* `C1` 99

supplement *n* `C1` 48

support *v* (= hold sth in position) `B2` 80

support *n* (= help) `A2` 69; (= sth that holds sth else) `B2` 80

supportive `C1` 21

suppress (feelings) `C1` 18; (= prevent sth from developing) `C1` 66

surface *n* 42

surfer 70

surgeon `B2` 48

surgery `B2` 48

surgical `C1` 48

surplus `C1` 32

surrender (to sb) `C1` 95

surround `B2` 34; **be surrounded by sth** 34

surrounding `B2` 34

survival (rate) `B2` 48

suspect *v* `B2` 52; **suspect sb of (doing) sth** `B2` 53

suspect *n* `B2` 53

suspend `B2` *as in* **be suspended from sth** 90

suspicion `C1` 11, 60

suspicious 11, 60

suspicious (circumstances) `C1` 6

suspiciously 11

swamp *n* 63

swap *v* 35

swear (= promise; use bad language) `B2` 1

swearing 1

sweat *v, n* 8

sweep *v* `B2` 9

sweeping (change) 45

sweet (of sb) 2

swelling 15

swerve *v* 26

switch (to sth) *v* `B1` 40, 46

swollen 15

sympathetic `B2` 21

sympathy `B2` 21

synonym 1

synonymous 1

tabloid *n* 62

tackle (a problem) `B2` 60, 72; (= in sport) *v* `C1` 94

tackle *n* `C1` 94

take

(no) notice of sb/sth 52

a chance (on sth) 63

advantage of sth `B2` 97

after sb 22

an instant/immediate dislike to sb 19

exception to sth 23

it easy 36

money out 32

offence (at sth) 23

over (from sb) `B2` 82

over sth `B2` 82

responsibility 4

sb in 82

sth in 6

sb/sth seriously 17, 51, 72

sth away from sth 32

the blame 4

to sb/sth 17

up sth `B1` 57

your time 83

takeaway 25

takeover 69

tale `B2` 63

talk down to sb 57

talkative 16

tank *n* `B2` 55

tap *v, n* `B2` 13, 40

tasteful 99

tasteless 25

tasty 99

tattoo *n* 7

team spirit 66

tear *n* (= water from the eye) `B2` 11, 18; **in tears** 12, 18

tear *v* `B2` 9

teens `B2` 22

tendency `B2` 22

tender `C1` 25

tension `B2` 13, 43

term *as in* **in the short/ medium/long term** 46; **on good/friendly/bad, etc. terms (with sb)** 98

terraced house 38

territory `B2` 47

territorial 47

that *as in* **that's a pity/ shame** 34; **that's life** 84

the *as in* **the (only) thing is …** 84; **the end justifies the means** 88; **the grass is always greener (on the other side)** 88; **the more the merrier** 88; **the secret of your success** 71

theory `B1` 79

therapy `B2` 54, 79

thereabouts *as in* **or thereabouts** 89

thereby **C1** 75

thick (= stupid) 2

thick (fog) **B1** 28

thin *adj* **A2** *as in* **(as) thin as a rake** 86

thing *as in* **be a good thing** 84; **be the last thing on sb's mind** 2; **the (only) thing is …** 84

think sth up 10

thorough **B2** 80

thoroughly **B2** 15

thoughtful **C1** 16

threat **B2** 47; **under threat** 47

threaten **B2** 33

thrilled **C1** 18

thrive **C1** 71

thriving 36

throw sth away (= remove; waste an opportunity) 41

thus **B2** 75

tie *v as in* **be tied up** (= busy) 2

tight-fitting 29

tighten **C1** 93

time *as in* **at one time** 74; **from time to time** 74; **in your own time** 21; **it's about/high time** 74; **take your time** 83; **time flies** 74

time-consuming 44

timid 17

tin opener 25

tip *n* (= thin point) 63

title (= position of winner) 41

to *as in* **to a large extent** 85; **to be (perfectly) honest** 100; **to go** (= remaining) 81; **to say the least** 28; **to some extent** 50

tolerate **C1** 59

tons (of sth) **B2** 89

tone (= general character/ attitude) **B2** 57

too *as in* **too good to be true** 84

top *n as in* **a silk top** 29; **off the top of my head** 83

torrential (rain) 28

torture *n, v* **C1** 94

tough (childhood) **B2** 19; tough (meat) **B2** 25; (= strong) **B2** 19, 64; (= strict) **B2** 19

toxic **C1** 46

trace *v* **B2**, *n* **C1** 94

trade union 67

traffic warden 26

tragedy **B2** 77

transaction **C1** 32

transfer *v* **B2** 65

transform **B2** 41, 45

transformation **C1** 41, 45

transition **B2** 21

transplant *v, n* 48

transport *n* **A2**, *v* **B1** 94

trap *v* **B2** 60

tray 25

treat *v as in* **treat sb like dirt** 4; **treat sb with respect** 4; **treat sb/ yourself (to sth)** 25

trek *n, v* 36

tremor 60

trial *as in* **trial and error** 85

trip (over) **B2** 10

tropical **B2** 39

true **A1** *as in* **it's true (that …)** 85; **too good to be true** 84

truly **B2** 16, 100

tumble dryer 46

tune *n* **B2** 42

tunnel *n* **B2** 98

turn out (to be sth) 73

turn up (= be found; arrive) 81

turnout **C1** 58

twist (your ankle) **C1** 15

two *as in* **two heads are better than one** 88; **two wrongs don't make a right** 88

typical (example) **A2** 4

tyre **B1** 26

ultimately **B2** 100

unacceptable **B2** 23

unanimous 43

unaware 32

unbiased 79

uncertainty **B2** 3

uncharacteristic 91

unconscious **B2** 15

unconventional 77, 99

uncooked 91

under

attack 98

construction 98

control 68

discussion 98

investigation 98

pressure 41

the weather 83

threat 47

undercooked 91

underemployed 91

underestimate *v* 41

undergo **B2** 36, 80

underpaid 91

undo 91

unemployed *adj* **B1** 65, 91

unfamiliar 91

unfavourable 99

unflattering 7

unforgettable 42, 74

unfortunate **B2** 73

unfurnished 38

unique (= special and unusual) **B2** 80; (= being the only one) 36

unit (= a single thing) **A2**, (= in a hospital) **B2**, (= a small machine) 79

unknown 91

unofficial 91

unpack 91

unpaid 91

unplug 40

unprecedented **C1** 91

unpredictable 43

unqualified 91

unsophisticated 23

unspoiled/unspoilt 36

unsuitable 1

untie 91

unwilling 19, 99

unwind (a bandage) 91; (= relax) 36

unwrap 91

up *as in* **be up to sb** **B2** 81; **up to** (= as far as) **B1** 81; **up to date** 73

update *v, n* **B1** 40

uphold **C1** 59

upper *adj* **B2** 63

upright *adv* 59

upsetting 99

upwards **B2** 40

urge *v* **B2** 56

urgent **B2** 72

utter (chaos/nonsense) 4

vacancy (= for a job) 64; (= in a hotel) 37

vacant (= of a job) 64

vaccinate 48

vaccine 48

vacuum *v* 30

vacuum cleaner 30

vague (= not clear in a person's mind) **C1** 74; (= not having enough information) **C1** 89

valid **B2** 53, 91

value *v* **B2** 66

vanish (into thin air) **C1** 11

variable *adj* **C1** 78

vary **B2** 78

vast (= extremely large) **B2** 55; vast (majority) **B2** 4

venue **B2** 78

verification 79

verify **C1** 79

vertical *adj* **B2** 7

via **B2** 27

vibrant **C1** 36

vice 74

vicious **C1** 99

victory **B2** 41

view *v* (= think about sth) **B1** 23

view *n as in* **in view of sth** 75

vigorously 13

villain 20

virtual **B2** 1

virtually 1, 100

virtue **C1** 74

virtuous 74

virus **A2** 15

visible **B2** 11

vision **B2** 11

visualize 93

vital **B2** 10

vitamin **B2** 48

vivid 74

V-neck(ed) 29

voluntary **B2** 51

volunteer **B1** 51

vow *v* **C1**, *n* 56

vulnerable **C1** 18

wage **B2** 67

waistcoat 29

wake *n as in* **in the wake of sth** **C1** 69

wander (a)round **B2** 10, 36

ward *n* **C1** 52

warm up/down 10

warm (welcome) **B1** 44

warrant *n* **C1** 53

watermelon 24

way *as in* **by the way** 87; **no way** **A2** 83

weaken **C1** 10, 93

wealth **B2** 50

wealthy **B2** 50

weapon **B1** 55

weather *as in* **under the weather** 83

weather forecast 28

weed *n* **C1**, *v* 39

weeding 39

weird **B2** 99

welcome *adj as in* **a welcome change** 45; **make sb feel welcome** 44

welcome *n as in* **a warm welcome** 44

well behaved 5

well-being **C1** 52

well done 25

well informed 17

what *as in* **what a pity/ shame** 34; **what for?** 83; **what if ...?** 52

wheel *n* **A2** 26

when *as in* **when it comes to sth ...** **B2** 83

whereas **B2** 75

whether (or not) **B1** 81

while (= although; whereas) **B2** 75

whisk *n, v* 24

whisper *v, n* **B2** 12; **in a whisper** 12

white *adj* **A1** *as in* **(as) white as a sheet** 86

whole *as in* **on the whole** 34, 87

wholesale (change) 45

wicked 99

wide *adv as in* **wide awake** 31

widen **C1** 10

widespread **B2** 28

widow *n* **C1** 22

widower 22

wig 29

wildlife **B2** 39

will *n* **B2** 58

willing **B2** 99

windscreen 26

windscreen wiper 26

wing mirror 26

wipe *v* **C1** 40

wipe sth out 47, 48

wisdom **B2** 21

wise **B2** 21

with *as in* **with hindsight** 74; **with regard to sb/ sth** **C1** 75; **with the exception of sth/sb** **C1** 97

withdraw **B2** 32

withstand 80

witness *n* **B2** 27

wonder *n as in* **no wonder** 84

wood(s) **A2** 39

work *n* **A1** *as in* **out of work** 65

work *v* **B1** *as in* **work like a dream** 86

workout (= exercise) **C1** 10

work out **A2** 10

work sth out **B1** 32

world **A1** *as in* **it's a small world** 88

worn out (= exhausted) 5, 31; (= no longer useful) 5

worse *adv* **B1** *as in* **be worse off** 66

worsen 18

wound *v, n* **B2** 15

wrap *v* **B2** 15

wreck *v, n* 56

wrinkle *n* 7

yawn *v* 31

yell *v* **C1** 12

you *as in* **you bet** 83; **you never know** 81, 84; **you're kidding** 83; **you're not gonna believe this** 2

your *as in* **your/the best bet** 83

youth **B2** 34

youth hostel 37

zebra crossing 26

Abbreviations used in the book

adj	adjective
adv	adverb
[C]	(of a noun) countable
conj	conjunction
inf	informal
n	noun
OPP	opposite
pl	plural
pp	past participle
prep	preposition
pt	past tense
sing	singular
sb	somebody
sth	something
SYN	synonym
[U]	(of a noun) uncountable
v	verb